LITERATURE OF THE

CW00376975

During and in the aftermath of the dark period of the Holocaust, writers across Europe and the United States sought to express their feelings and experiences through their writings. This book provides a comprehensive account of these writings through essays from expert scholars, covering a wide geographic, linguistic, thematic, and generic range of materials. Such an overview is particularly appropriate at a time when the corpus of Holocaust literature has grown to immense proportions and when guidance is needed in determining a canon of essential readings, a context to interpret them, and a paradigm for the evolution of writing on the Holocaust. The expert contributors to this volume, who negotiate the literature in the original languages, provide insight into the influence of national traditions and the importance of language, especially but not exclusively Yiddish and Hebrew, to the literary response arising from the Holocaust.

ALAN ROSEN is most recently the author of *The Wonder of Their Voices: The 1946 Holocaust Interviews of David Boder* (2010) and the *Sounds of Defiance: The Holocaust, Multilingualism, and the Problem of English* (2005), editor of *Approaches to Teaching Wiesel's* Night (2007), and co-editor of *Elie Wiesel: Jewish, Moral, and Literary Perspectives* (2013). He lectures regularly on Holocaust literature at Yad Vashem's International School for Holocaust Studies and other Holocaust study centers. His current book project is entitled "Killing Time, Saving Time: Calendars and the Holocaust." Born and raised in Los Angeles, educated in Boston under the direction of Elie Wiesel, he lives in Jerusalem with his wife and four children.

LITERATURE OF THE HOLOCAUST

EDITED BY

ALAN ROSEN

CAMBRIDGE
UNIVERSITY PRESS

CAMBRIDGE
UNIVERSITY PRESS

University Printing House, Cambridge CB2 8BS, United Kingdom

Published in the United States of America by Cambridge University Press, New York

Cambridge University Press is part of the University of Cambridge.

It furthers the University's mission by disseminating knowledge in the pursuit of education, learning, and research at the highest international levels of excellence.

www.cambridge.org
Information on this title: www.cambridge.org/9781107008656

© Cambridge University Press 2013

First published 2013

Printed in the United Kingdom by Clays, St Ives plc

A catalog record for this publication is available from the British Library

Library of Congress Cataloging in Publication data
Literature of the Holocaust / edited by Alan Rosen.
pages   cm
Includes bibliographical references.
ISBN 978-1-107-00865-6 – ISBN 978-1-107-40127-3 (pbk.)   1. Holocaust, Jewish (1939–1945), in literature.   I. Rosen, Alan, 1954– editor of compilation.
PN56.H55L59   2013
809′.93358405318–dc23
2013006195

ISBN 978-1-107-00865-6 Hardback
ISBN 978-1-107-40127-3 Paperback

Contents

Notes on contributors   *page* vii
Acknowledgments   xii

Introduction   1
Alan Rosen

PART I: WARTIME VICTIM WRITING   13

1   Wartime victim writing in Eastern Europe   15
    David G. Roskies

2   Wartime victim writing in Western Europe   33
    David Patterson

PART II: POSTWAR RESPONSES   49

3   The Holocaust and Italian literature   51
    Robert S. C. Gordon

4   German literature and the Holocaust   68
    Stuart Taberner

5   Hebrew literature of the Holocaust   84
    Sheila E. Jelen

6   The Holocaust and postwar Yiddish literature   102
    Jan Schwarz

7   The Holocaust in Russian literature   118
    Leona Toker

8   The Holocaust in English-language literatures   131
    S. Lillian Kremer

9   Polish literature on the Holocaust   150
    Monika Adamczyk-Garbowska

10 Hungarian Holocaust literature   164
    Rita Horváth

11 French literature and the Holocaust   174
    Jeffrey Mehlman

PART III: OTHER APPROACHES   191

12 Oral memoir and the *Shoah*   193
    Alessandro Portelli

13 Songs of the Holocaust   211
    Shirli Gilbert

14 Sephardic literary responses to the Holocaust   225
    Judith Roumani

15 Anthologizing the Holocaust   238
    Alan Rosen

16 The historian's anvil, the novelist's crucible   252
    Eric J. Sundquist

Guide to further reading   268
Index   301

Notes on contributors

MONIKA ADAMCZYK-GARBOWSKA is Professor of Comparative Literature at Maria Curie-Skłodowska University in Lublin, Poland. Her books include *Isaac Bashevis Singer's Poland: Exile and Return* (1994, in Polish), *Contemporary Jewish Writing in Poland: An Anthology* (2001, with Antony Polonsky), *Shades of Identity: Jewish Literature as a Multilingual Phenomenon* (2004, in Polish), *Kazimierz vel Kuzmir: A Shtetl of Various Dreams* (2006, in Polish), *My Home Used to Be There ... Memorial Books of Jewish Communities* (2009, co-editor, in Polish), *The Aftermath of the Holocaust: Poland 1944–2010* (2011, with Feliks Tych, in Polish, English edition forthcoming).

SHIRLI GILBERT is Ian Karten Senior Lecturer in Jewish/non-Jewish Relations at the University of Southampton, where she convenes the MA program in Jewish History and Culture and teaches courses on the Holocaust and music and resistance. Her book *Music in the Holocaust* (2005) was a finalist for the National Jewish Book Award and was the basis for a large-scale educational website (http://holocaustmusic.ort .org). Her current research is on Holocaust memory in apartheid and post-apartheid South Africa, and includes a book project based on the letters of a Jewish refugee from Nazi Germany who fled to South Africa in 1936.

ROBERT S. C. GORDON is Professor of Modern Italian Culture and a Fellow of Gonville and Caius College at Cambridge University. He has written widely on modern Italian literature, cinema, and cultural history. He is the author of *Primo Levi's Ordinary Virtues* (2001) and the editor of Leonardo de Benedetti and Primo Levi, *Auschwitz Report* (2006) and *The Cambridge Companion to Primo Levi* (2007). His most recent book is *The Holocaust in Italian Culture, 1944–2010* (2012).

vii

RITA HORVÁTH has authored books and articles in English and Hungarian on Holocaust literature and history. She was a 2009–2010 scholar-in-residence at the Hadassah-Brandeis Institute, and continues as an Institute research associate. Currently a research fellow at the Yad Vashem International Institute for Holocaust Research, her book project is entitled, "Escaping Traumatic Circularity: Testimonies and the Novel of Formation." She teaches courses on literature at the Eötvös Loránd University in Budapest and Bar-Ilan University in Israel.

SHEILA E. JELEN is Associate Professor of English and Jewish Studies at the University of Maryland, and is currently director of the Comparative Literature Program. She is the author of *Intimations of Difference: Dvora Baron in the Modern Hebrew Renaissance* (2007) and has co-edited several volumes, including *Modern Jewish Literatures: Intersections and Boundaries* (2011) and *Jewish History and Literature: An Interdisciplinary Conversation* (2008). She is an associate editor at *Prooftexts: A Journal of Jewish Literary History* and is currently working on a project titled "Salvage Poetics: Literature, Photography and the Popular Ethnography of Jewish Eastern Europe."

S. LILLIAN KREMER, University Distinguished Professor, Emerita, Kansas State University, has been a Fulbright Lecturer in Belgium, and a guest lecturer in several European countries and Israel, at the US Holocaust Memorial Museum, and numerous American universities. She is the author of *Witness Through the Imagination: The Holocaust in Jewish American Literature* (1989) and *Women's Holocaust Writing: Memory and Imagination* (1999), and editor and contributing author of *Holocaust Literature: An Encyclopedia of Writers and Their Work* (2003), a two-volume reference work honored by *CHOICE*, the American Library Association and the Association of Jewish Libraries. Fellowships from the National Endowment for the Humanities and the Memorial Foundation for Jewish Culture have supported her scholarship.

JEFFREY MEHLMAN is University Professor and Professor of French Literature at Boston University. His most recent books include *Walter Benjamin for Children: An Essay on His Radio Years* (1993), *Emigré New York: French Intellectuals in Wartime Manhattan, 1940–1944* (2000), and *Adventures in the French Trade: Fragments Toward a Life* (2010). His numerous translations include Jean-Denis Bredin's *The Affair* (1986) and Pierre Vidal-Naquet's *Assassins of Memory: Essays on the Denial of the Holocaust* (1992).

DAVID PATTERSON holds the Hillel Feinberg Chair in Holocaust Studies in the Ackerman Center for Holocaust Studies at the University of Texas at Dallas. A winner of the National Jewish Book Award and the Koret Jewish Book Award, he has published more than 30 books and 150 articles and book chapters. His books include *Sun Turned to Darkness* (1998), *Along the Edge of Annihilation* (1999), *Wrestling with the Angels* (2006), *Open Wounds: The Crisis of Jewish Thought in the Aftermath of Auschwitz* (2006), *Emil L. Fackenheim: A Jewish Philosopher's Response to the Holocaust* (2008), *A Genealogy of Evil: Anti-Semitism from Nazism to Islamic Jihad* (2011), *Genocide in Jewish Thought* (2012), and others. He is the editor and translator of *The Complete Black Book of Russian Jewry* (2002) and co-editor (with Alan L. Berger) of the *Encyclopedia of Holocaust Literature* (2002).

ALESSANDRO PORTELLI teaches American literature at the University of Roma "La Sapienza." He is the author of a number of books, including *The Text and the Voice: Writing, Speaking and Democracy in American Literature* (1994); among his works in oral history are *The Order Has Been Carried Out: Memory, History and Meaning of a Nazi Massacre in Rome* (2003) and *They Say in Harlan County: An Oral History* (2010). He has served as advisor to the Mayor of Rome on the city's historical memory and has done extensive fieldwork on folk music in both Italy and the United States.

ALAN ROSEN is most recently the author of *The Wonder of Their Voices: The 1946 Holocaust Interviews of David Boder* (2010) and the *Sounds of Defiance: The Holocaust, Multilingualism, and the Problem of English* (2005), editor of *Approaches to Teaching Wiesel's* Night (2007), and co-editor of *Elie Wiesel: Jewish, Moral, and Literary Perspectives* (2013). He lectures regularly on Holocaust literature at Yad Vashem's International School for Holocaust Studies and other Holocaust study centers. His current book project is entitled "Killing Time, Saving Time: Calendars and the Holocaust." Born and raised in Los Angeles, educated in Boston under the direction of Elie Wiesel, he lives in Jerusalem with his wife and four children.

DAVID G. ROSKIES is a cultural and literary historian of East European Jewry, and has published extensively on memory, catastrophe, and the return to folkore and fantasy. His major works are *Against the Apocalypse: Responses to Catastrophe in Modern Jewish Culture* (1984), the companion volume, *The Literature of Destruction* (1989), *A Bridge of Longing: The Lost*

Art of Yiddish Storytelling (1995), *The Jewish Search for a Usable Past* (1999), and *Yiddishlands: A Memoir* (2008). His *Holocaust Literature: A History and Guide*, co-authored with Naomi Diamant, appeared in 2013. Professor Roskies holds a joint appointment at the Jewish Theological Seminary, where he serves as the Sol and Evelyn Henkind Chair in Yiddish Literature and Culture, and at Ben-Gurion University of the Negev, where he is Visiting Professor of Jewish Literature.

JUDITH ROUMANI is an independent scholar of comparative literature, editor of the online journal *Sephardic Horizons*, and translator. She is the author of *Albert Memmi* (1985) and has published numerous essays on Sephardic literature. Her translation of Renzo De Felice's *Ebrei in un paese arabo* was published as *Jews in an Arab Land: Libya 1835–1970* (1985). She has recently authored a chapter on Francophone Sephardic literature in *Sephardism*, edited by Yael Halevy-Wise (2012), and is a 2013–2014 Sosland Research Fellow at the United States Holocaust Memorial Museum.

JAN SCHWARZ is an assistant professor in Yiddish Studies, Lund University, Sweden. He was previously Senior Lecturer, Department of Germanic Studies, University of Chicago (2003–2011). He has published *Imagining Lives: Autobiographical Fiction of Yiddish Writers* (2005), *Survivors and Exiles: Yiddish Culture after the Holocaust* (forthcoming), and articles on Holocaust literature, Yiddish culture and literature, and American Jewish literature. He was a special editor of *POLIN* 20 (2007), "Making Holocaust Memory," and of *Prooftexts: A Journal of Jewish Literary History* 30/1 (2010), "Multilingual Jewish Literature in America."

ERIC J. SUNDQUIST, the Andrew W. Mellon Professor of the Humanities at Johns Hopkins University, is the author or editor of twelve books, including *To Wake the Nations: Race in the Making of American Literature* (1993), which received the Christian Gauss Award from Phi Beta Kappa and the James Russell Lowell Award from the Modern Language Association; *Strangers in the Land: Blacks, Jews, Post-Holocaust America* (2005), which received the Weinberg Judaic Studies Institute Book Award; and *King's Dream* (2009).

STUART TABERNER is Professor of Contemporary German Literature, Thought and Society at the University of Leeds, and a research associate in the Department of Afrikaans & Dutch, German & French at the University of the Free State, South Africa. He has published widely on German literature and the Holocaust, German debates on coming to terms with the past, and on broader issues relating to contemporary

German culture and society. Recent books include *German Literature of the 1990s and Beyond* (2005), *German Culture, Politics and Literature into the Twenty-First Century* (ed. with Paul Cooke, 2006), *Contemporary German Fiction: Writing in the Berlin Republic* (ed., 2007), *The Cambridge Companion to Günter Grass* (ed., 2009), *Germans as Victims in the Literary Fiction of the Berlin Republic* (ed. with Karina Berger, 2009), *The Novel in German since 1990* (ed., 2011), and *German Writers of the 21st Century* (ed. with Lyn Marven, 2011).

LEONA TOKER is Professor in the English Department of the Hebrew University of Jerusalem. She is the author of *Nabokov: The Mystery of Literary Structures* (1989), *Eloquent Reticence: Withholding Information in Fictional Narrative* (1993), *Return from the Archipelago: Narratives of Gulag Survivors* (2000), *Towards the Ethics of Form in Fiction: Narratives of Cultural Remission* (2010), and articles on English, American, and Russian literature. She is the editor of *Commitment in Reflection: Essays in Literature and Moral Philosophy* (1994) and co-editor of *Rereading Texts/Rethinking Critical Presuppositions: Essays in Honour of H. M. Daleski* (1996) and *Knowledge and Pain* (2012). She has founded and is editing *Partial Answers: A Journal of Literature and the History of Ideas*, a semiannual periodical currently published by the Johns Hopkins University Press.

Acknowledgments

Friends and colleagues are crucial to all scholarship; at least for me, the subject of the Holocaust makes extra demands, intellectual and emotional. This collective endeavor has benefited from the advice and labor of many, including Robert Gordon, Yisrael Cohen, Sheila Jelen, Nehemia Polen, Martin Farren, Beate Müller, Simone Gigliotti, David Patterson, Florent Brayard, David Roskies, and Elie Wiesel. My wife, Ruth, again shared her exceptional scholarly and editorial skills.

My orientation toward Holocaust literature is indebted to many as well. A class with Maurice Natanson was revelatory; conversations with Raul Hilberg and Emil Fackenheim pivotal; with Terrence Des Pres inspiring; with Irving Halperin nurturing. My conversations over the years with important writers have been indispensable; I thank all, and mention especially Aharon Appelfeld, Ilona Karmel, Cynthia Ozick, and Elie Wiesel. In addition to the volume's contributors, I am similarly indebted to decades of conversations with literary scholars of the Holocaust, including Alvin Rosenfeld, Lawrence Langer, Geoffrey Hartman, and Sidra Ezrahi. My debts to students are equally great and ongoing: at Boston University, Bar-Ilan University, the International School for Holocaust Education, Yad Vashem, as well as at the sites of many guest lectures and seminars in Israel, Europe, and North America. All the volume's contributors have worked intensively and shared generously, and I am grateful to them for their efforts and for what I have learned from them.

I thank the staff of the Yad Vashem library, always essential companions to this my scholarship. The library's director, Dr. Rob Rozett, actively promotes a nurturing atmosphere. Linda Bree, Maartje Scheltens, and the other Cambridge University Press staff have been thoughtful, resourceful, and sensitive to the special demands of this subject.

ALAN ROSEN

TAMMUZ, 5772/JULY 2012

Introduction

Alan Rosen

As with most world literature, Holocaust literature has regularly invoked imagery of the heavenly bodies: the sun, the moon, and especially the stars. "Our eyes register the light of dead stars," begins André Schwarz-Bart's formidable 1959 Holocaust novel, *The Last of the Just*. Premised on the laws of light and optics, this opening sentence sets forth the novel's memorial mandate: to bring before the reader's (and narrator's?) eyes the light that continues to radiate from the Holocaust's no longer living victims.[1]

But stars have also held a special attraction for Holocaust literature because of the insignia, the Star of David, that Jews were forced to wear in order to set them apart from the general population. "Today two harsh decrees reached us. First, the Star of David decree," writes Warsaw diarist Chaim Kaplan on November 30, 1939. Like many, Kaplan turned the decree inside out: with the prospect of the 'Star of David' insignia soon to be affixed not only to clothing but to Jewish businesses, he conjectures that "everywhere we turn we shall feel as if we were in a Jewish kingdom." Strikingly, Kaplan concludes the star-burdened entry by pondering the role of the Jewish poet in a time of catastrophe: "A poet who clothes adversity in poetic form immortalizes it in an ever lasting monument."[2] The Cambridge *Literature of the Holocaust* aims to pick up where Kaplan's meditation left off, surveying how, during the war and in its aftermath, writers – some of whom were gifted poets, some journeyman diarists like Kaplan, and some merely children – clothed the ever-intensifying adversity in a stunning variety of literary forms.

The "adversity" – what we now call the Holocaust (or, in its Hebrew counterpart, the *Shoah*), the notorious attempt by Nazi Germany to destroy European Jewry – grew in its proportions as the months and years went on. Accelerated persecution of Jews began in Germany in 1933, encompassed Austria and Czechoslovakia in the late 1930s, and then, with the German invasion of Poland in September, 1939, expanded to Eastern Europe and, progressively, to all areas of Europe that came under German occupation.

The methods used differed from country to country. But they most always were accompanied by brutality and privation, and, in time, by exclusion (utilizing the Star of David insignia), plunder, deportation, and murder.

Arenas of terror invented to carry out this program came to dot the European landscape. First established in Germany in 1933, concentration camps dealt ruthlessly with many types of prisoners; Jews eventually came to form a major constituency. Once the war began in 1939, ghettos, which eventually numbered close to a thousand, soon were established to isolate the Jews of Eastern and Central Europe. Special work battalions and camps exploited the labor of the prisoners, whom Benjamin Ferencz called "less than slaves." When, in 1941, Germany broke its treaty with the Soviet Union and invaded its former ally, it accompanied its invasion with mass executions of Russian, Ukrainian, and Baltic Jewries. Finally, the death camps operating in German-occupied Poland from late 1941 until 1945 were designed to murder large transports of Jews upon arrival. The transports from ghettos or communities to these camps were carried out mainly in cattle-cars under crowded and primitive conditions. The decimation of European Jewry unfolded largely parallel to the events of World War II. But, in contrast to the ugly hostilities waged between that war's armed combatants, the Holocaust targeted civilians – Jewish men, women, and children – for enslavement, humiliation, and murder. This sad chronicle provides the setting, backdrop, and coordinates for much, if not all, of Holocaust literature.

History has played a dominant role in establishing the Holocaust's factual and interpretive coordinates. This volume chronicles not the history of the Holocaust, but rather the wartime and postwar response in literature to the victims' plight. Some of this literature was written by victims who eventually perished, some by the minority of victims who gratefully survived, and some either by contemporaries who, in Israel, England, the Americas, or elsewhere were not on the scene, or who were born after the events took place.

As this collection hopes to show, literature too has made its special contribution. A few words may be in order to suggest, even in a limited and foreshortened way, the specific vocation of literature in regard to the Holocaust. If history has sought objectivity, a dispassionate assemblage of the facts of when, where, and how the events unfolded, literature has been shamelessly subjective, offering ardently personal perspectives on what transpired. Emotion was not to be avoided, but rather intensified. In a related sense, if history has generally concerned itself with the macro level – the group, the institution, the movement – literature has focused on the individual. It is via the individual that empathy comes to the fore. The difference appears again in the approach to language. History is measured by the transparency of its language, the degree to which the reader follows the chronicle of events without noticing the language in which they are rendered. Historian Saul Friedlander's *The Years of Extermination*, for example, provides a window on the events of this era, at its best when the window itself goes unnoticed. In contrast, literature aims to make the language conspicuous, to thicken it, as it were, and by doing so to make the reader aware of the means used to create the effect. At times figurative language – image, symbol, metaphor ("dead stars," for example) – achieves this end. At other times, tone or voice, sarcasm or indignation, guide the reading: "A Jewish policeman? Oh, I can't believe my eyes!" writes Peretz Opoczynski from the Warsaw ghetto in late 1941, addressing his fellow ghetto residents with, as David Roskies reminds us, a distinctly blended intonation borrowed from Yiddish storytelling at its finest.[3] History would rarely choose such a register to chronicle the ghetto's immense deprivation. Or again, it is the prerogative of language to double back on itself. So Paul Celan's eerily famous lines, "Black milk at daybreak we drink it at evening / we drink it at midday and morning we drink it at night / we drink and we drink," pivot around a compulsive act of drinking, senseless except in the quiet violence of the reiterated act.

Prose does this as well, with its own capacity to meditate on language's tested powers in the midst of carnage. Hungarian survivor Elie Wiesel reports on a scene of selection at Auschwitz:

> Every few yards, there stood an SS man, his machine gun trained on us. Hand in hand we followed the throng.
> An SS came toward us wielding a club. He commanded:
> "Men to the left! Women to the right!"

Up until this point, the memoir, like many before and many after, depicts the anguished moment of arrival in which families were torn apart. But then the author brings to the fore the role language plays:

> Eight words spoken quietly, indifferently, without emotion. Eight simple, short words. Yet that was the moment when I left my mother.[4]

Guns, clubs, commands: the tools of the enemy may wreak death and destruction on the remnants of Hungarian Jewry, but in Wiesel's revisiting of this scene, an astonishingly few words cause the greatest damage. The enemy's unexceptional words do not fade away. They are retrieved out of the past and put on display, so that the reader may appreciate their explosive force. The window thus clouds over, the words take on a heavy substance of their own, and the reader engages with the events attentive to what Vilna ghetto poet Abraham Sutzkever called the "charred pearls," the wounded words with which he formed his resilient poems.[5]

In truth, the line between history and literature need not be so sharply drawn (Alessandro Portelli and Eric Sundquist's essays will delineate some of the fault lines). Indeed, the fruitful interplay between the two can be noted by the fact that the mission statement for the Warsaw ghetto chroniclers, including diarists and reportage, was set forth by a historian, Emanuel Ringelblum – who was himself guided by a previous generation's determination to have individual Jews record the facts. As Ringelblum recognized and advocated, for the victim to unflinchingly record the facts in the appalling flux of ghetto life and death took a rare form of literary resolve.

History enters here through another door as well, since the *history of Holocaust literature* figures prominently in this collection. The volume's first two essays, by David Roskies and David Patterson respectively, inaugurate this approach, making wartime writing a point of departure. Such a strategy might seem obvious. Yet it is not uncommon for surveys or critical studies of Holocaust literature to presume that the war years gave rise to little of any literary substance; from this vantage point, the real career of Holocaust literature took off in the postwar years, in the form of the memoirs written by former inmates of concentration camps. Indeed, a focus on the camps, the conditions of which allowed for little in the way of actual composition (though see Roskies on the Sonderkommandos and Gilbert on songs), posited the postwar years as a natural beginning for literary reflection and the memoir as the genre that set the standard.

But the war years actually yielded a bounty of writing in all genres, much of which was lost in the convulsive uprootings of wartime Europe. Yet a portion did survive. To be sure, literature authored in ghettos, in hiding, and under other circumstances of privation may demand its own herme-neutic, one that recognizes the fragmented, groping view of events that could not help but shape these productions. This recognition is stimulated by Roskies' and Patterson's inventories of these essential, and often essen-tially courageous, writings.

Most of the volume's other essays, even while working independently, follow their lead. In some cases, they start from what Leona Toker precisely formulates as "the first literary record of the shocked realization of the nature of atrocities." This realization did not always come directly, nor was the literary record necessarily straightforward. Indeed, oblique entry, what Sheila Jelen shrewdly refers to as "writing *around* the Holocaust," was often the order of the day. In other cases, the story of literary response to the Holocaust picks up in the early postwar period. Whether wartime or postwar, the starting point has been chosen in order to retrieve earlier responses, many of which have remained obscure. Decade by decade, the essays try to show the often devious route by which a Holocaust literature has unfolded (see, for instance, the contributions of Rita Horváth and Jeffrey Mehlman). This circuitous development obtained especially, but not only, in countries ruled for years by communist governments whose terms of engagement with the Holocaust were such that, as Monika Adamczyk-Garbowska notes, "the meanderings of state censorship created a situation in which certain topics appeared and disappeared."

More generally, Holocaust literature's terms of engagement have oscillated between two poles. On the one hand, it has angled for comparison, for something familiar, or familiar enough, for the reader who was not on the scene to latch onto, to enable, in Wiesel's formulation, one who was (fortunately) *not* there to feel "as if" they had been.[6] "I saw a flood once in the mountains," begins Rachel Auerbach, writing in the wake of the Great Deportation in Warsaw in the summer of 1942. The flood offers an analogy, a metaphor, a basis of comparison; it demonstrates the resolute search for terms. Yet even while stepping outside the actual sphere of the events, it delineates an approach to them: the "I saw" establishes a standard for chronicle, for description, for anguish, for assessment. The flood is not conjured; it is witnessed.[7]

But not every writer felt analogy even roughly suitable. The diary of the Polish physician Zygmunt Klukowski records a scene of plunder in the aftermath of an October 1942 roundup of Jews; the sense of scandal gathers momentum word by word, sentence by sentence:

> From the wide-open Jewish apartments people grab everything they can lay their hands on. Shamelessly they carry loads of poor Jewish belongings or merchandise from the shops ... Altogether the spectacle is unbelievable, hard to describe. Something equally terrifying, horrible, has never been seen or heard about, by anyone, anywhere.

To chronicle what is said to be without analogy, to be unprecedented and unparalleled – "never been seen or heard about, by anyone, anywhere" – has a riveting force of its own. In this case, the force is intensified because Dr. Klukowski is describing the violation not (or at least *not directly*) of people but of possessions. At the center of the debacle are the things that "people grab" and "carry" in a manner that dislodges them from the life of the Jews to whom they belonged.[8] If the spectacle of plundering "belongings or merchandise" solicits such a level of rhetoric – and the internal poise of his description convinces me that it is fitting – one is hard put to imagine what could be said when the violation, as we know that it did, moves to (or *back to*) people. Holocaust literature oscillates between these poles, seeking analogies in nature (floods or dead stars) or history (previous catastrophes), while (often at the same time) detailing the failure to find them.

The chapters that follow survey a variety of literary responses to the Holocaust, subsuming individual writers within the larger patterns of national literatures, language groups, or specific kinds of writing. Yet this approach is meant to expand the repertoire of names, carving out a larger space for authors who have little notoriety outside of their specific time and place, together with those whose accomplishments have reached further. Of wartime writers, the only one who remains widely known is Anne Frank, the Dutch teenage diarist who perished in the Bergen-Belsen concentration camp and whose stature as a writer has become greater in recent years. But other wartime diarists – the above-mentioned Chaim Kaplan, Abraham Lewin, Victor Klemperer, Moshe Flinker – have also had increased exposure, as scholarly and popular awareness of contemporary responses to the plight of wartime Jewry has circulated more widely.

Certain postwar writers, survivors all, have pondered the Holocaust for decades on end, experimenting with a range of genres or inventing others to meet their needs. Elie Wiesel's Yiddish memoir of his Hungarian family's deportation in 1944, first published in 1956, details the illusion of well-being that dogged his community even after most of European Jewry had been murdered. But it focuses on the nurturing relationship developed by father and son as they together try to endure the rigors of Auschwitz, a winter death march to Germany, and the radical privations of Buchenwald. Relocating to the United States, he chose French as his main literary language and produced over the next decades essays, novels, memoirs, and plays, most of which have dealt with the survivor's struggle in the aftermath of the Holocaust. Eventually, the struggle of the *children* of survivors has come to share center stage with that of the survivors. To foster an apt commemorative idiom, Wiesel has also invented a skeletal form that he refers to as "dialogues." His writing shares features with the austere universe of the French existentialist writers, but it also draws deeply from the well of Jewish history and tradition, joining the angst of ethical dilemma with the world of Jewish learning, law, and mysticism.

Like Wiesel, Primo Levi, an Italian Jewish survivor who wrote about the Holocaust from multiple vantage points over a forty-year period, moved from a devastating memoir of deportation to Auschwitz to the more flexible realms of fiction, poetry, and essay, often relying, in Robert Gordon's words, on "oblique or metaphorical" entry, but ultimately choosing the essay form as a hybrid venue for testimonial ethics. Indeed, both Wiesel and Levi have been drawn to the essay as a supple means to fuse storytelling with ethical inquiry. Abraham Sutzkever penned his own memoir of the Vilna ghetto. But his particular achievement came in lyric poetry, first in the ghetto and then, after the war, continuing for some five decades in the very different surroundings of Tel Aviv. His hundreds of lyrics and prose poems have cultivated an unsentimental imagery and idiom of commemoration. As editor of the journal *The Golden Chain*, he also played a consummate mentoring role, creating a post-catastrophe venue for sophisticated Yiddish literature, a portion of which was dedicated to the Holocaust. His counterpart on the continent was Paul Celan, who, based from 1948 on in Paris, fashioned German lyric poetry into a rigorous, if elliptical, Holocaust vocabulary. His short prose meditations on the poetic vocation after the Holocaust revealed the deliberation that shaped his dark aesthetic and the Jewish Eastern European sensibility that underlies the verse steeped in contentious allusion to European letters. The demons of clinical depression drove him to suicide at the age of fifty, the merciless complement to a life lived in service to versifying the Holocaust.

Jorge Semprun and Charlotte Delbo, non-Jewish resistance fighters deported to Buchenwald and Auschwitz (then Ravensbrück) respectively, crafted innovative memoirs in French and continued in later writings to explore the nature of time, memory, and literature. Born and bred in Spain, Semprun's multiple postwar recountings of his Buchenwald internment not only stretch literary form but double back on themselves, challenging their perspective and the version of truth it implies. Delbo, for her part, angled between reportage, lyrical prose, and austere drama to commemorate the women with whom she was deported and to search for the pristine words to do so.

Rachel Auerbach, Vasily Grossman, Aharon Appelfeld, and Imre Kertész, writers who shaped the Holocaust's literary idiom in their respective countries and languages, receive attention in the essays that follow; other writers, such as the novelists Margo Minco from Holland and Danilo Kiš from Serbia, do not, which speaks not to their accomplishments but rather to the organizational constraints of a volume such as this.

"Blessed is [God]," writes Rabbi Baruch Rabinowitz, a religious leader of the Munkacs community in prewar Hungary, "Who sent His angels to accompany me every single day. Even when little separated me from death, I was saved – and not by natural means."[9] Religious writing constitutes an

underrepresented domain of Holocaust literature. Most literary study of the
Holocaust has favored the secular genres, presuming that only when traditional religious belief is absent or aborted can artistry flourish. But just as
one would not think of early modern England without the martyrology of
John Foxe, the sermons of John Donne, or the lyrics of the metaphysical
poets, so did the response of many Jews come via traditional forms of
religious writing. Like the English examples, they are no less literary for
being so. Some emerged almost straight from the killing fields. Rabbi
Shimon Huberband's chronicle of the war's first year, written in Warsaw
shortly after the events unfolded, serves not only as an elegy to the Jews lost
but also as a tribute to the indefatigable effort of Poland's religious Jews to
persevere in their observance of tradition; the somewhat later incantatory
report from the pen of Rabbi Moshe Rothenberg takes both elegy and
tribute to another level of desperation. The Warsaw ghetto sermons of
Rabbi Kalonymous Kalman Shapira, or the crisis-pitched Torah commentary of Rabbi Elchonon Wasserman and Rabbi Shlomo Zalman Ehrenreich,
display the disciplined vehicle of religious preaching up against unfathomable cruelty.

   Postwar religious responses – memoirs, poems, letters, essays, tales, and
stories – have been equally dedicated to finding an idiom steeped in faith
while sufficiently able to inventory the often inexhaustible list of losses.
These traditional responses do not shy away from extracting from the welter
of destruction meaningful lessons and from viewing the victims through the
prism of sacrifice, martyrdom, and a call for divine vengeance. Indeed,
the most basic unit of all Holocaust literary commemoration may be
the synagogue memorial plaques formulaically listing the names of
murdered family members, each of which is followed by the Hebrew
abbreviation הי"ד, "may God avenge his (or her) blood." Above all, this
literature, cataloging atrocity and defamation, nonetheless testifies to mirac-
ulous interventions at every fateful turn of the road. This rhetoric marches
to a different drummer than most of the better-known examples of
Holocaust literature. But to ignore it filters out the articulate sensibility of
the devout that has fashioned its response through an ensemble of its own
literary media.

   Yiddish, Hebrew, German, Ladino, Italian, Polish, Russian, Hungarian,
and of course, English: the languages in which the story of the Holocaust is
told shape the story that emerges. This multilingual premise regarding
Holocaust storytelling mirrors the social make-up of prewar Europe; the
choice of language among European Jews was never neutral. The lingua
franca of most of pre-World War II East and Central European Jewry was

Yiddish, a fusion language originating among the Jews of Central Europe in the medieval period, blending German, Hebrew, and eventually Slavic, and written in Hebrew characters. It was transported east when Jews were driven out of those Central European lands. Groomed as a vital literary language in the nineteenth century, Yiddish served interwar Jewry as a language of learning, letters, politics, culture, and daily affairs. Yet its primacy in all these realms was challenged (or complemented) by a surge in the popularity of vernacular tongues, and also by the Zionist's resurrected claims for Hebrew.

The story of Ladino runs along a parallel track. Spoken by the Jews of medieval Spain, peppered with Hebrew and Aramaic words, written in its own particular nuance of Hebrew characters, Ladino traveled with fifteenth-century Spain's expelled Jews to places of refuge in the Balkans, Turkey, Palestine, and North Africa. The language became a portable homeland in these lands of expulsion, binding descendants of refugees together centuries later. Ladino remained the lingua franca in some communities, such as Salonika, in the twentieth century, and, as Judith Roumani recounts, nurtured a legacy of its own literary forms.

During the Holocaust, contention over languages intensified: idealistic calls for a return to Jewish languages competed with realistic defections to the vernacular. Speaking a flawless German, Polish, or Ukrainian could help one escape the persecutor's net. In the main arenas of terror, Jews forged their own tongues: coded communication in the ghetto, a fabricated jargon in the camps. For some, the choice of a language to write in was a choice of a universe of meaning. So Moshe Flinker, hiding with his sizable religious family in Brussels and pining for a future as a diplomat in Israel, penned the bulk of his diary in Hebrew, occasionally turned to his native Dutch, and filled the back pages with Arabic grammar exercises. In Lodz, another youthful diarist – whose name and fate remain unknown – was less ideologically wed to any specific tongue but rather shuttled to and fro among four: Hebrew, Yiddish, Polish, and English.[10] Other writers chose a language of composition – and then felt called upon to choose again, the rapidly changing circumstances compelling them to switch from one language to another. When the Great Deportation of Warsaw Jewry to Treblinka began in summer 1942, diarist Abraham Lewin exchanged Yiddish for Hebrew; poet Yitzhak Katzenelson did the same when penning his elegy to this devastation; and chronicler Rachel Auerbach traded Polish for Yiddish. Such changes attest to facility and diglossia, the ability to maneuver in more than one tongue, and the changing need to do so in the tongue that mattered most. The shift to a different tongue at a decisive moment may also have sent a signal (to them? to us?), a pointed recognition of watershed events that demanded a new (or, in the case of Hebrew, an ancient) constellation of meaning.

In the war's aftermath, language continued to be marked by these wartime struggles. A certain swath of English-language Holocaust literature comprises, as Lillian Kremer reminds us, "a tapestry of autobiographical writing by refugees and survivors who have abandoned their birth languages." Some abandoned, yet others, as Jan Schwarz details persuasively, cleaved to what had been intimately owned since their earliest days. Chava Rosenfarb's weary assessment catches the postwar tone unnervingly well: "If writing is a lonely profession, the Yiddish writer's loneliness has an additional dimension. His readership has perished. His language has gone up with the smoke of the crematoria."[11] But not entirely. Rosenfarb, Sutzkever, and other Eastern European Jews refused to heed the writing on the wall and continued to ply their lonely trade in Yiddish, widening its tonality to try to accommodate even the Holocaust's vast losses. Others refused in a different fashion, as Stuart Taberner sketches in relation to postwar German literature, to let the enemy set the linguistic terms. So Paul Celan, carrying from his native Czernowitz a quiver of languages, chiseled his ever-diminishing poems in German, not granting the perpetrators the possibility of forcing him to abandon his mother tongue but rather crafting it to sing in a voice precisely counter to theirs. Still others opted for an adopted tongue, either to establish a buffer between the war's devastating events and their recollection of them, or to recruit a specific tongue to better probe the Holocaust's overwhelming legacy – or both. Thus, Elie Wiesel has said that French provided him with a "refuge" – but he also believed it offered the challenge of addressing the Holocaust, the most irrational event, in French, the most rational of languages, the heir of Cartesian philosophy. For Wiesel, the collision of the irrational with the rational sculpted an appropriate idiom of Holocaust witness.[12]

France itself was only a temporary refuge for Yiddish poet Yitzhak Katzenelson, who in 1944 sought the proper terms to gauge the disappearance of Eastern European Jewry. "Rising over Lithuanian or Polish towns," he wrote in the final canto of his epic poem, *The Song of the Murdered Jewish People*, "the sun will never find / A radiant old Jew at the window reciting Psalms."[13] The light of dead stars and the unrequited rays of an ever-seeking sun are necessarily the lamps by which we read Holocaust literature. The volume's essays endeavor to guide us both in what to read and how to go about doing it.

Notes

1. André Schwarz-Bart, *The Last of the Just* (*Le Dernier des justes*) (Paris: Éditions du Seuil, 1959).
2. Chaim Aron Kaplan, *Scroll of Agony: The Warsaw Diary of Chaim A. Kaplan*, 2nd rev. edn. (New York: Collier Books, 1973), pp. 78–79.
3. Peretz Opoczynski, "The Jewish Letter Carrier," trans. E. Chase, in Jacob Glatstein, Israel Knox, and Samuel Margoshes (eds.), *Anthology of Holocaust Literature* (New York: Atheneum, 1980), p. 57.
4. Elie Wiesel, *Night*, trans. Marion Wiesel (New York: Hill and Wang, 2006), p. 29.
5. Abraham Sutzkever, "Charred Pearls," in David G. Roskies (ed.), *The Literature of Destruction: Jewish Responses to Catastrophe* (Philadelphia: Jewish Publication Society, 1989), p. 500.
6. *A Passover Haggadah*, commentary by Elie Wiesel, illustrations by Mark Podwal (New York: Simon and Schuster, 1993), p. 69.
7. Rachel Auerbach, "Yizkhor 1943," in Roskies (ed.), *Literature of Destruction*, p. 459.
8. Zygmunt Klukowski, quoted in Jan Tomasz Gross, "Two Memoirs from the Edge of Destruction," in Robert M. Shapiro (ed.), intro. Ruth R. Wisse, *Holocaust Chronicles: Individualizing the Holocaust through Diaries and Other Contemporaneous Personal Accounts* (Hoboken, NJ: Ktav, 1999), p. 229.
9. Rabbi Baruch Rabinowitz, "Miracle upon Miracle," in Esther Farbstein (ed.), *The Forgotten Memoirs* (Brooklyn: Shaar, 2011), p. 322.
10. Anonymous Boy, in Alexandra Zapruder (ed.), *Salvaged Pages: Young Writers' Diaries of the Holocaust* (New Haven, CT: Yale University Press, 2002), pp. 361–94.
11. Chava Rosenfarb, "Feminism and Yiddish Literature: A Personal Approach," in Naomi B. Sokoloff, Anne Lapidus Lerner, and Anita Norich (eds.), *Gender and Text in Modern Hebrew and Yiddish Literature* (New York: Jewish Theological Seminary, 1992), p. 226.
12. Robert Franciosi, ed., *Elie Wiesel: Conversations* (Jackson: University Press of Mississippi, 2002), pp. 7–8, 21, 78.
13. Yitzhak Katzenelson, *The Song of the Murdered Jewish People* (XV:7), in Roskies (ed.), *Literature of Destruction*, p. 546.

PART I

Wartime victim writing

CHAPTER I

Wartime victim writing in Eastern Europe

David G. Roskies

Diaries

Certain genres come to the fore under certain historical circumstances, and diaries, we know, are especially prevalent in wartime. "Everyone" wrote diaries, historian Emanuel Ringelblum reported in 1943, "journalists, writers, teachers, community activists, young people, even children."[1] And although most of those written in the Warsaw ghetto were destroyed during the Great Deportation, a significant number did survive: diaries written on the run, in a safe house, a monastery, an underground bunker, a loft, a pit, a labor camp, a transit camp – diaries in every European language.

In the Jew-Zone, the ghetto often served as a buffer against the truth: ghetto diarists were preoccupied with themselves or their fellow Jews and barely able to account for the behavior of the Germans. Not so the Hebrew pedagogue Chaim Kaplan, who began keeping a diary in 1933 and renamed it *Megilat yisurin* (in English, *Scroll of Agony*) on July 29, 1940, to signal a shift in perspective from the individual to the sacerdotal. Kaplan consistently reports on German actions, and he consistently employs Scripture to underscore the desecration of God's covenant and the daily degradation of God's chosen. "How has Warsaw, the royal, beautiful, and beloved city become desolate!" he writes on the first day of the Jewish year 5700 (in the Western calendar, September 14, 1939). Biblical analogies eventually fail him, as death itself ceases to have meaning, especially after Kaplan introduces a sinister confidant in the person of Reb Hirsch. "My Hirsch cannot be budged from his opinion," Kaplan writes on June 16, 1942. "A catastrophe will befall us at the hands of the Nazis and they will wreak their vengeance on us for their final downfall,"[2] Whether Hirsch was a real person or a literary invention, we will never know. His role, however, is clear: he is Kaplan's alter ego, his naysayer, the speaker of unspeakable truths. Hirsch's prophecy of doom, which proves to be accurate (the Great Deportation is a month away), anticipates the diary's last, truly eschatological sentence, written in the diarist's own voice: "If my life ends, what will become of my diary?"

In the Vilna ghetto, the voice of Zelig Kalmanovitsh – as befitted a founder of the famed YIVO Institute – was that of a public intellectual. In Yiddish, he lectured on Peretz and Ahad Ha'am and delivered an occasional sermon. But Kalmanovitsh kept his diary in Hebrew, replete with scriptural and Talmudic passages to underscore his return to the fold. He believed that history would revere the memory of the people of the ghetto. "Your least utterance will be studied," he prophesied in 1942, "your struggle for man's dignity will inspire poems, your scum and moral degradation will summon and awaken morality."[3] Most stunning was the voice of Ringelblum, whose every waking hour was dedicated to preserving the inner Jewish dialogue: between past and present, the elite and the folk, Hebrew and Yiddish. Oblivious to the conditions outside his underground bunker, he completed his most sustained piece of historical research, *Polish-Jewish Relations During the Second World War*, after Polish Jewry was no more. The work was written in Polish for a Poland that no longer had any Jews.

The art of ghetto reportage

Diarists recorded what they experienced, heard, and dreamed. But the reporter's job was to cover every late-breaking development and draconian measure, on a beat where "images succeeded one another with cinematic speed."[4] The daily assignment was to write about a whole people *in extremis*, through the prism of the unique social organism that was the ghetto, as if for a deadline sometime in the future, when the war was over, and these writings would see the light of day.

In the ghettos in years 1–4, reportage was the bedrock of shared communication. Like song and epic poetry, reportage was not a stand-alone genre designed merely to transcribe or testify or record. It presupposed a collective audience, schooled in a very particular mental curriculum. No subject was too terrible for the reportorial pen, as long as there was room in the horrific present for some reference to a shared past. Reportage was a game of *déjà vécu*, even if the purpose of the analogy, or allusion, was to underscore the irreparable break between the familiar past and the unbearable present.

Peretz Opoczynski was a seasoned reporter before the war, becoming the scribe of urban poverty and neglect in Warsaw. Working as a letter carrier in the Warsaw ghetto by day – an unnerving and thankless job that he described in one of his finest reportorial fictions – he managed to produce carefully wrought vignettes of ghetto life in the early 1940s by describing a single ghetto courtyard or profession and tracing its changing fortunes and misfortunes over a specific period of time, ranging from one day in the life of ghetto smugglers to several years in the life of an apartment complex. Welcomed in 1941 by the ghetto population as the first in Poland's history, the Jewish letter carrier eventually must bear witness to the people's despair. Yet in the voices that greet and ridicule him at his debut on the ghetto streets, he picks up on something not heard since the days of the greatest of Jewish humorists, Sholem Aleichem: "A Jewish mailman? Oh, I can't believe my eyes! Tell me, who are you looking for? At what address? We'll show you, you won't have to waste time looking. Jews, will you get a load of this: we've got a Jewish mailman, just exactly as if we were in Palestine!"[5]

This ironic sense of living "in Palestine" pervades the writings of many ghetto chroniclers, for whom the analogy is always sardonic. Echoing the monologues of Sholem Aleichem allows Opoczynski to conjure up a *shtetl*-like environment where Jews are all on intimate terms with one another, and then to use this model of solidarity as a foil for unmasking the *shmendrikes*, the self-hating assimilationist Jews, the corruption, and the apathy that takes hold of the ghetto population. Thanks to the modern Yiddish classics, Opoczynski had a rich and adaptable model of the *shtetl* (a small town with a large Jewish population in Central and Eastern Europe) as collective hero – or antihero – especially in time of crisis.

Oskar Rosenfeld became a refugee for the second time when, in November 1941, he and five thousand other Jews were deported from Prague to the Polish industrial city of Lodz, which had been renamed Litzmannstadt after a Nazi general on April 11, 1940. Thanks to his credentials and impeccable German, Rosenfeld landed a secure job working on the official ghetto chronicle, but on February 17, 1942, he also began keeping a combination diary and literary journal, of which twenty out of twenty-two notebooks would survive. Three days into his writing – after describing the first public hanging in the ghetto, dutifully recorded by a German film crew – he described the ghetto landscape, a panorama in snow that turned subjective at the mention of the children:

> Bleak and barren roads, partly snowed in and partly covered with mud, stretch between houses dotting the landscape. Stunted trees and bushes extend their meager trembling branches toward the sky. Throngs of children in rags cross the streets, their yellow, weatherworn faces furrowed, weary. At times a fleeting smile appears on one of those faces, sometimes one [pair] of those bloodless lips begins to sing. At times these children throw snowballs like children everywhere in freedom. Nobody can tell what the morrow will bring. What will happen with all of us? . . . And yet, everybody wants to live, "to live it," to know that this life was not completely senseless after all.[6]

Life on this barren soil where nothing can grow has already turned adults into innocent children. No one knows what tomorrow will bring, or even if there will be a tomorrow. Only innocent children, "like children everywhere," think there will be a tomorrow. All roads leading out of the ghetto have been destroyed, so there remains only the slimmest hope of communicating with the people who live in freedom. The Jews in the ghetto write to sustain a future that they know will exist – if at all – without them.

Josef Zelkowicz from Lodz also led a double life. His day job, working alongside Rosenfeld, was to report on the productivity of the dizzying array of workshops and makeshift factories in which every able-bodied ghetto Jew was forced to work – and on the social assistance needed by the sick, the old, and the unemployed. Some of these reports are dry as dust, but many have the tone of an omniscient narrator, free to formulate broad, transcendent truths and generalizations and free to pass judgment on the sordid conditions of the ghetto.

When not reporting on the carpenter's strike in the winter of 1941, or the removal of forty-six patients from the psychiatric ward in the ghetto and their subsequent deportation, Zelkowicz penned the reportage "Twenty-Five Live Chickens and One Dead Document." It was the true story of a murderous guard at the ghetto fence known as "Red-haired Janek," a pure-blooded Christian Pole who passes himself as a *Volksdeutsch*, or ethnic German, a veritable VIP. This time, however, Janek's deal to smuggle twenty-five chickens into the ghetto had fallen through, so he plotted revenge against his Jewish partner by shooting and killing twenty-four innocent Jews in reprisal.

Schooled in Jewish historical memory, Zelkowicz understood the treacherous workings of memory through time. To signal that knowledge, he framed the story of the live chickens and the dead document within a double frame, the first an epigraph, in Aramaic: "Through a cock and a hen Tur Malka was destroyed ([Babylonian Talmud,] Tractate Gittin 57a)."

"Tur Malka" was another name for Jerusalem, and Zelkowicz expected his readers to remember the rabbinic legend that blamed the catastrophic Jewish rebellion against Rome on a banal incident with a cock and a hen. Roman soldiers had seized these animals from a Jewish wedding procession, the Jews beat the soldiers up, and the emperor thought a rebellion had broken out. Zelkowicz's point is that if such a trivial event could have had such disastrous consequences then, it could happen again. The Germans were no less cruel than the Romans. Wearing two hats – that of the criminal investigator and that of the keeper of Jewish historical memory – Zelkowicz raised the stakes, for if the Lodz ghetto were analogous to Jerusalem, then nothing less than the survival of the Jews as a people was hanging in the balance.

Another ghetto reporter was Leyb Goldin, who had worked as a professional translator of European literature before the war. His sole surviving work from the Warsaw ghetto is the masterful 1941 "Chronicle of a Single Day," in which he breaks himself up into two voices: Arke, the cynical superintellectual and one-time revolutionary, and his stomach. Arke knows about the malleability of time not only from reading *The Magic Mountain* but also from having done time before the war, in solitary confinement. But the war has been going on for two years, "and you've eaten nothing but soup for some four months, and those four months are thousands and thousands of times longer for you than the whole of the previous twenty months – no, longer than your whole life until now."[7] Starvation time is further broken down into three uneven segments: before the single bowl of soup handed out each afternoon at precisely the same hour, during the soup, and after the soup. Ghetto time defies all clockmakers, including those we call writers.

The search for historical meaning

To the Jews of Eastern Europe, schooled in collective memory, the search for ancient analogies always began with the Tanakh, the Hebrew Bible. Faced with a catastrophe of unprecedented scope, both ubiquitous and inescapable, Jewish writers and chroniclers reached into the fund of Jewish collective memory for historical archetypes. Yitzhak Katzenelson organized and presided over public readings of the Hebrew Bible in his own rhymed Yiddish translations, in which he sought to demonstrate that the Prophets had never been more alive, more relevant. The most ambitious publication of the underground press in the Warsaw ghetto was his *Job: A Biblical Tragedy in Three Acts*, of which Dror published about 150 copies on June 22, 1941, the day that Germany declared war on the Soviet Union. Gracing the cover was Shloyme Nusboym's illustration of Job crouched on the ground, nursing his wounds. While *Job* focused on the existential and erotic struggle of the individual Jew, *By the Waters of Babylon: A Biblical Folk Drama in Four Acts* described the plight of the nation and ended with a verse translation of Ezekiel's vision of the dry bones.

Working by analogy, trying things on for size, comparing and contrasting present and past – these practices did not always lead to an experience of déjà vu. "The tragedy is tremendous," Rosenfeld recorded in Notebook E, in midsummer 1942:

Those in the ghetto cannot comprehend it. For it does not bring out any greatness as in the Middle Ages. This tragedy is devoid of heroes. And why tragedy? Because the pain does not reach out to something human, to a strange heart, but is something incomprehensible, colliding with the cosmos, a natural phenomenon like the creation of the world. Creation would have to start anew, with *berajshit* [the first word of the Hebrew Bible]. In the beginning God created the ghetto.[8]

Ghetto chroniclers were the first to perceive the outlines of something new: the birth of a new archetype of destruction. Was the measure of this new catastrophe the distance, the unbridgeable gap, between the spiritual superiority of prior generations and the demoralization of their own?

Did everyday acts of heroism count as Kiddush Hashem or only as acts of extraordinary self-sacrifice? The ghetto poets were divided on this point, with one school of thought represented by Yitzhak Katzenelson in Warsaw and the other by Abraham Sutzkever in Vilna and Simkhe-Bunem Shayevitsh in Lodz. Polish Jewry, Katzenelson resolved in year 4 of the war, was heir to a model of heroism perfected over millennia of exile in which the supreme act of self-sacrifice was performed "with no weapons and no spurs." "And if this Jew spills any blood," he proclaimed, "it is only his own."[9] A supreme instance of this type of Jew was the Rebbe of Radzyn, the scion of an illustrious Hasidic dynasty. In order to bring a trainload of Jews to burial, the Radzyner spurned efforts to buy him safe passage. "The Song of the Radzyner" was the last and longest epic poem that Katzenelson wrote in the Warsaw ghetto. It was an epic of the old school, about a named figure who was larger than life and who, like Rabbi Akiva and the ten martyred rabbis, turned private defiance into a supremely public act. Katzenelson's hero, moreover, was as fearless of death as of the pathos of God – a diminished, powerless God. The Radzyner redefined the meaning of martyrdom as absolute devotion to the people of Israel.

In the Vilna ghetto, even schoolchildren got into the act. The ghetto's history club put Herod on trial in front of an invited audience, and fifteen-year-old Isaac Rudashevski argued the case against him as a criminal, a Roman collaborator, and an agent of assimilation. After heated debate, the court declared Herod guilty. Sutzkever, meanwhile, immortalized the everyday courage of the teacher, Mira Bernshteyn, who plied her trade before an ever-dwindling class. The curriculum they were studying, according to Sutzkever, was I. L. Peretz's tale of triple martyrdom, "Three Gifts," which extolled the moral imagination of every man and woman and their courage to go beyond the letter of the law.

Not long after completing this most popular of his epic poems, Sutzkever shifted from the epic to the lyric, with a six-line poem commemorating a unique act of sabotage carried out at the ghetto gate:

> *A bliml*
> Farn veln durkhtrogn a bliml durkhn toyer
> hot mayn shokhn zibn shmits batsolt.
> Vi tayer iz far im atsind der frilingl der bloyer, –
> Dos bliml mitn shvartsapl fun gold!
> Mayn shokhn trogt zayn ondenk on badoyer:
> Der friling otemt in zayn layb – er hot azoy gevolt . . .
> Vilner geto, 29stn may 1943
> (*Flower*
> For wanting to smuggle a flower through the gates
> my neighbor paid the price of seven lashes.
> Now these blue petals with their nucleus of gold
> are such a precious sign of spring returning.
> My neighbor bears his scars with no regrets:
> Spring breathes through his flesh, with so much yearning.
> Vilna ghetto, May 29, 1943)[10]

Resistance is first and foremost an act of volition: for *wanting* to smuggle a flower into the ghetto, a Jew receives seven lashes but is rewarded for "so much *yearning*" by having his pain transmuted into life-giving breath. Written in honor of spring, this poem ends with the spring coming alive within his neighbor's body, which bears its scars "with no regrets." Resistance is no less an act of the imagination – a spontaneous, creative response to cruelty and horror. Standing in for the precious flower, the standard of beauty that cannot be falsified, is this perfectly crafted poem built on two sets of rhymes: the feminine rhymes *toyer*, *bloyer*, and *badoyer* and the masculine rhymes *batsolt*, *gold*, and *gevolt*. One set is in ethereal, mystical blue and the other in earthly, material gold – two opposing realms yoked together through the mysterious power of rhyme. The "neighbor" remains anonymous because he is Every-Jew, Everypoet, everyone willing to risk all in order to uphold an absolute standard that cannot be breached. Faced with an enemy that defiles and destroys, "these blue petals with their nucleus of gold" represent that which is most precious on earth, as in heaven. Not a Jewish stance, to be sure, but like religious faith, it demands a supreme act of self-transcendence.

Simkhe-Bunem Shayevitsh completed the process of defining martyrdom broadly. The mass deportations from the Lodz ghetto resumed on February 22, 1942, and Shayevitsh began writing a 448-line epic poem called

"Lekh-lekho" (Go forth), in which God's command to Abraham in Genesis 12 is transformed into an intimate, remarkably muted conversation between a father and his beloved eight-year-old daughter, Blimele (meaning little flower). Shayevitsh was a first-generation secular poet in whose library "lie holy books, / worldly books, my manuscripts. / Isaiah hobnobs with Goethe, / Reb Jonathan Eybeschuetz with Tuwim . . . And Yesenin wants to get drunk / and urinate in public, / but suddenly he sees Abraham / leading Isaac to Mount Moriah."[11] The intrusion of that "but suddenly" on the home and hearth of one ghetto family awaiting the expulsion order is the theme of this great poem; the attempt of an otherwise powerless father to draw out a semblance of meaning by redefining the biblical covenant in a collapsing universe. As they ascend this new Moriah, where no angel will intercede to stay the knife, the father instructs his daughter to face death with a smile, to defy the enemy with the indomitable spirit of the Jews.

Time after

"Am I the last poet in Europe?" Sutzkever asked himself at the end of June 1943. "Do I sing for the dead, do I sing for the crows?" The answer he arrived at was a study in realms of opposition forcibly wrenched together: "I am drowning in fire, in swamps, in brine, / Entrapped by yellow badged hours."[12] There were only two ways to escape from the yellow-badged hours: one was through the coming of spring, the regenerative cycle of nature, which for Sutzkever was always linked to the process of artistic creation; the other was through armed revolt. In his wartime poetry, Sutzkever tracks a paradigm shift that occurred in modern Jewish times. The new Jew, machine gun in hand, fighting as a Jew – the longed-for Jewish army finally fighting under its ancient banner – was born in 1943. From Sutzkever we learn that the labor pains attending that birth were terrible.

    "Abrasha" Sutzkever joined the United Partisans' Organization (known as the FPO from its name in Yiddish), under the command of Itsik Vittenberg, soon after its founding. In midwinter 1943, Liza Magun, the FPO's main courier and liaison to the Jewish underground in other ghettos, was caught and executed by the Gestapo. (Magun was to the resistance movement in Vilna what Tosia Altman and Zivia Lubetkin were to it in Warsaw.) More than a tragic loss and strategic setback, Magun's death made clear to Sutzkever that the FPO was fated to fight alone, because the ghetto population was utterly indifferent. Standing before his fellow partisans, who were gathered legally at a memorial ceremony for Magun, Sutzkever declaimed a thunderous poem of rage, written in the oracular mode of Hayyim Nahman Bialik.

Nowhere is the distance between poet and audience, between the one and the many, more pronounced than here, in "Lid tsu di letste" ("Song for the Last"). The farther apart the prophet is from the people, the greater the tension inside him between rage and sorrow, loathing and lamentation:

> I beat my skull on stones to find consolation
> for you in the fragments, you, the last,
> for I, too, am a letter in your book,
> my sun, too, is spring's leprous outcast.[13]

Deeper than the divide between the prophet and the people that refuses to hearken to his word is the gap between the different time zones that the two inhabit. The poetic prophet, alive to the cycles of nature, sees the first signs of spring. Yet just as the natural world is about to be reborn, the ancient cycle of a great and sorely tested people is about to be closed forever. Time has run out on this people, thunders the prophet, because so much of it has been squandered: "Millions at a time you were no one's, / but believed in your individuality." Even "when a thousand years of enmity / has walled the light out completely," it produced no palpable response, no protest, no vision for the future.[14]

By the end of 1943, year 4 of the war, metonymy became myth for the Jews who remained alive inside the Jew-Zone, most of whom were now alone: hiding alone, dying alone, fighting alone. For the young who took up arms, there were only three choices: go down fighting in a symbolic last stand against the Germans, turning the ghetto into a latter-day Masada; join a Soviet partisan brigade, where Jewish fighters were not always welcome; or forge whatever alliances were possible with the local underground in order to go on fighting as Jews. Mordecai Tenenbaum-Tamaroff belonged in the first group. The Sutzkevers belonged in the second. Szymek (Shimshon) and Gusta Draenger belonged in the third. Each group left behind a literary legacy in multiple voices and tonalities. The diary, last letters, and calls to arms issued by Tenebaum-Tamaroff in Warsaw and Białystok were lovingly collected, translated, and published by the surviving members of his Zionist movement. Sutzkever continued to date his poetry written in the Narocz forest, even as he edited and augmented his ghetto corpus for eventual publication. The return to the life-giving forest quickened his poetic spirit. "Stretch your hands out," he exulted in perfect rhyme:

> To that whiteness: In its cold and burning
> Veins

> You'll feel returning
> The redeeming life
> It contains.[15]

Yet surrounded at the same time by so much emptiness and enmity, he suddenly perceived the most terrifying of all metonymies:

> And if my people shall remain only a number,
> I adjure it: that from my memory it disappear.
> And may all the graves be buried deeper
> And may no dust remain of the years.[16]

The Great Deportation

Metonymy and myth are the two basic means of symbolic shorthand. One is punctual, bare-bones, a world in miniature, which draws on the acute observation of present reality. The other is the punctual rendered trans-temporal, a primal plot that recurs again and again, a foundational map of the future. Myth is rooted in collective memory; it is the alphabet used in the grammar of remembrance. What happened inside the Jew-Zone in year 4 of the war is that metonymy became myth. As one ghetto after another was liquidated – the smaller ones first, then the major ones – an entire people was reduced to bits and scraps, last letters, a few photographs, and piles of abandoned clothing. As the old, the infirm, the mothers and children were cast into the inferno, and all the strategies for survival failed, those few still left alive cast about for something – anything – that might represent the many, if only as a mnemonic. In the face of total destruction, every memento took on lasting significance.

For Rachel Auerbach, one of Ringelblum's closest associates, the part that stood for the whole had been the soup kitchen at 40 Leszno Street, where writers and intellectuals like Goldin received their daily ration – the kitchen Auerbach ran with selfless devotion and described with scholarly rigor for the Oyneg Shabes. But of what use was memorializing the social service network in Europe's largest ghetto after its liquidation? In the course of six weeks, 235,741 people were rounded up in one spot, the notorious assembly point called Umschlagplatz, and shipped off in cattle-cars to die in a place called Treblinka. A whole city of Jews, a city within a city, masses on masses of people – men, women, and children – were gone. The work of the Oyneg Shabes was temporarily suspended. The only task that remained for the surviving members of the staff was to chronicle the Great Deportation.

But where should they begin from: the perspective of the dead or that of the living? Each demanded a different lens. Yehoshue Perle renamed his ferocious contemporary chronicle of the Great Deportation "The Destruction of Warsaw" the moment he understood it to be a literal reenactment of the original *hurban* (the destruction of the Jerusalem temple). No less fearful was the fate of those still alive, as brilliantly captured by the metonymy of Perle's dog tag, number 4580, issued to the "Chosen-Peoplish" Jews, those thirty thousand who survived the Great Deportation just long enough to work as slave-labor. An empty number with no history was all that remained of a lifetime of collective dreams and personal ambitions. Perle's number was, he saw, a sign of the Apocalypse.

The Polish-language poet Władysław Szlengel likewise adopted multiple perspectives. A popular cabaret poet in the ghetto and a one-time member of the Jewish police, Szlengel decided at the beginning of year 4 that it was time to sort through his papers and compose a last will and testament with the sardonic title of "Co czytałem umarłym" ("What I Read to the Dead"). To set the antisentimental tone, Szlengel began by recalling a prewar Soviet film about trapped sailors on a sunken submarine. The last survivor, about to suffocate, had scrawled a final message that affirmed his faith that he was dying for a higher cause. But speaking for the Warsaw Jews, Szlengel could take no such comfort:

> With all my being I feel that I am suffocating as the air in my sunken boat slowly gives out. [Unlike the Soviet sailor] the reasons I am in this boat have nothing to do with heroism. I am here against my will, and without any reason or guilt.
>
> But here I am, in the boat. And although I am no captain, I still think that I should at least write the chronicle of those who have sunk to the bottom. I don't want to leave behind only statistics. Through my poems, sketches and writings I want to enrich (a bad word, I know) the historical record that will be written in the future.
>
> On the wall of my submarine I scrawl my poem-documents. To my companions I, a poet of AD 1943, am reading my scribblings.[17]

Among these "poem-documents" is one that recapitulates the methodical murder of Polish Jewry with absolute metonymic precision. "Things" tracks the six stages of the cross – not of one exemplary martyr or of the entire Jewish people, but of their "furniture, tables and chairs, / suitcases and bundles," as the owners are dispossessed and moved to ever more desolate and restricted quarters; forced, by station 4, to move "along a Jewish road / with no big bundles or little bundles, / no furniture or chairs"; reduced to carrying "a small suitcase and a knapsack, / no need for anything else," as they are marched off in even rows of five to the blockhouses reserved for slave-labor and finally, to their deaths, leaving behind their "abandoned apartments, / abandoned bundles, / suits and down covers, / and plates and chairs."[18] Aryans will then inherit the spoils in the first of two endings. In their Second Coming, however, the "Jewish things" return in a grand and vengeful procession of *materia mnemonica*, retracing the Via Dolorosa of a martyred people.

Like Szlengel casting about for some disastrous analog, Auerbach begins her own requiem for the dead in 1943 by recalling a flood she once saw in the mountains. Facing the raging waters from afar, she was close enough to see the gaping mouths of the helpless victims, but not to hear their cries. Just so, standing on the far side of the river of time, she is close enough to recall the catastrophe in every detail, but far enough away to conduct a search for meaning: "And that's how the Jewish masses flowed to their destruction in the time of the deportations. Sinking as helplessly into the deluge of destruction."[19] To make this leap from a natural to a historical disaster, Auerbach substitutes a "deluge of destruction" for a flood in the mountains to signify the primeval flood. Likening the Great Deportation to a flood in no way implies that she accepts the biblical belief that an act of God is a sign of divine retribution. On the contrary: the flood analogy means for Auerbach that the evil descended on the Jews from on high like a force of nature, fatally inevitable. The dead were blameless!

Auerbach proceeds to put flesh on the dialectic of destruction by drawing a composite portrait of her people, recalling them group by group: the children and the youth; the women and the men; the idealists and assimilationists; even the underworld, a distinct and especially vital branch of Polish Jewry; the grandmothers and grandfathers; and finally the pietists and the beggars.

Exhausted by the effort to recall each group of Jews individually, despairing of the possibility of ever completing the litany of losses, Auerbach makes her account of the flood more personal – and more gendered. She turns to an incident that happened to her while riding the Warsaw streetcar, the jarring moment that birthed this very work. Sitting opposite her was a Polish Catholic woman, her head thrown back, talking to herself. Seeing and hearing that bereaved mother crying, like one mad or drunk, reminded Auerbach of another woman who seemed drunk or mad with personal grief: Hannah in Shiloh, crying her heart out before God, because she is childless (1 Sam. 1). But as a Jew living on Aryan papers, Auerbach cannot cry in public. What can she do? She can sit down and write her chronicle. She can return to the ancient rite of Jewish mourning, to the recitation of *yizkor*:

I may neither groan nor weep. I may not draw attention to myself in the street.

And I need to groan. I need to weep. Not four times a year. I feel the need to say Yizkor four times a day.[20]

Auerbach's composite portrait of the living folk underwrites her personal covenant with a people that now lives only in memory.

The confessional diary

A Jew still alive in the Jew-Zone was a statistical error by the fall of 1943. For such a person to take pen in hand at that time was an act of profound self-awareness. At that precise moment, a unique form of confessional diary was born. Time in this diary flows forward and backward; events are both recorded as they happen and reflected on after the fact. The diarists have a terrible secret to confess, forcing them to backtrack to the time of the slaughter. However irrational, they blame themselves for being absent when the roundup occurred, for believing the false promises, for failing to secure a hiding place. They confess to having abdicated their role as father, mother, husband, wife, son, daughter, brother, or sister, their own survival predicated on the death of their loved ones. "Everywhere [I turn]," wrote Grete Holländer on October 31, 1943, "I encounter only dead people. Am I really still alive?"[21] Never far from Holländer's thoughts were her young daughter, Sonja, entrusted to a gentile couple, and "the terrible day" her husband, Marek, was taken from her, not to mention the four hundred women from the Czortków Lager who were taken away before her very eyes. Giving voice to her "unspeakable anger" at their murder, she began keeping a diary in pencil in notebooks typically used by schoolchildren.[22] To write, from that moment on, was for her to work through overwhelming loss and a crushing burden of guilt. In diaries such as hers, time was split in two: time before and time after.

The moment of truth in these confessional diaries was the moment of moral complicity, of radical self-confrontation, which each diarist reached by a different route. In the first days of the Great Deportation, Abraham Lewin abruptly switched the language in which he kept his ghetto diary from Yiddish to Hebrew. Then, on the day his wife, Luba, was rounded up in Umschlagplatz and shipped off to her death, Lewin began a new calendrical and moral reckoning. Interspersed with the terrible news that reached him hour after hour, which he labored to put into chronological sequence for the sake of future generations, were flashes of self-blame. "The

Świeca family has perished," he reported at the end of a lengthy entry dated the eve of Rosh Hashana in 1942:

> He [Mr. Świeca] gave himself up after seeing how his wife and two children were taken. Initially he went with us to Gęsia Street, later he went back, gave himself up and was sent away. I feel a great compassion and admiration for this straightforward person. Strong in mind as well as strong in body. I think that Luba would have done the same, but I didn't have enough strength to die together with her, with the one that I loved so much.[23]

"Where shall I start?" asks Stanisław Adler, hiding on the Aryan side of Warsaw. "There is an overpowering desire burning in me to put in writing as speedily as possible all that has happened to us in these years of war, especially that which I, myself, have been witness to in the last six months. Even now I am terrified that the dangers which threaten me from all sides might prevent me from finishing this manuscript."[24] Feeding Adler's panic is the knowledge that all his writing thus far "has turned out to be a Penelope's web": the border police burned his diary from the first months of the war; his reconstructed notes were also destroyed when he was interned in the Warsaw ghetto, and everything he wrote inside the ghetto he "had to leave for the wolves to devour" when he escaped to the Aryan side. "Against a logic which I cannot satisfy," he goes on to explain,

> and against a literary tradition which I consciously ignore, I feel almost impelled to start from the end of my story. This is not because it is my intention to begin with the impact of my personal experiences, but because I feel the need to vindicate myself. Instead of an axe or a club I am now holding a pen in my hand. I am alive and living here, and not lying in trenches in an unequal battle or in one of the collective graves of Warsaw Jewry.[25]

The specter of one's loved ones points to an essential feature of these confessional diaries: they labor to recreate what no longer exists. Their point of departure is when "my real life began to end." On the very day – May 22, 1943 – that Yitzhak Katzenelson arrived from Warsaw at the transit camp in Vittel, France, accompanied by his surviving son, seventeen-year-old Zvi, the poet and playwright began to keep a diary. Instead of bringing him and his son closer together, he recorded, the catastrophe had driven them further apart; both were going mad, in different ways. That distance, in turn, intensified Katzenelson's bereavement for three of the murdered millions, whose names – Hannah, his wife, and Bentsikl and Binyomin, their sons – he repeated like an incantation. Two weeks passed before he wrote another word in the diary. On July 21, the dam burst, with the following day marking the first anniversary, the *yortsayt*, of the start of the Great Deportation. From then on, Katzenelson backtracked to the slaughter, as if reliving it in real time, back to the liquidation of the Little Ghetto with all its orphans, who had performed the plays he had written for their benefit; back to the discovery that his loved ones had been taken to Treblinka; back to the cellar at Karmelicka 9, on the eve of the first armed resistance; back to finding his works strewn about the abandoned ghetto streets. Each diarist inhabited a private hell. Each labored to reconstruct a paradise lost.

Everything about these diaries was fraught with tension – especially the question of what language to write them in. "Ikh mit mayn zun Tsvi," Katzenelson began his diary in Yiddish. "Ani im Tsvi beni," he translated the words and continued in Hebrew. As simple a phrase as "I and my son Zvi" was for the diarist a statement of faith, because in all the surrounding rooms and apartments, Polish Jews, the last of the last, were making a point of speaking . . . in Polish. What was it that moved both Katzenelson and Lewin to switch from one Jewish language to another? Did writing in Hebrew automatically elevate one's private testimony to a metahistorical plane? Ensure the document's eternality? Render it more conspiratorial? Insert a psychological buffer zone? Or all four? Whatever the reasons, the confusion of languages signaled an attendant confusion of addressee. Who was this document intended to reach? Who was still left to decipher its contents? When the outside horror penetrates the inner defenses and refuses to let go is when the confessional diary is born.

The last to die: the Sonderkommando

In the end the Germans created Auschwitz-Birkenau – the last stop, the final destination. The transport from Luna, which included Zalmen Gradowski and his family, arrived on December 8, 1942. At the beginning of each of his chronicles, he lists his loved ones who had perished in the gas chambers:

My mother – Sarah	My wife – Sonia
My sister – Libe	My brother-in-law – Raphael
My sister – Esther Rokhl	My brother-in-law – Wolf[26]

Also included was the address of one of his five uncles living in the United States – "J. Joffe, 27 East Broadway, N.Y." – who could supply the details of his biography and a photograph of himself and his wife. Of powerful build, Gradowski had been handpicked for the thousand-member Sonderkommando: men who oversaw the murder of their own people, gave them instructions about where to undress and where to leave their belongings, shaved their heads, and led them to the baths; men whose job it was to pull the dead from the gas chambers, pry open their mouths to extract their gold teeth, and feed the bodies into the ovens; men whose own days were numbered, as he was to number the twenty-two months spent in their company and to mourn their liquidation, counting himself among the last 191 survivors. They were quartered in a special block, ate what no one else was allowed to eat, and saw what no one else was allowed to see.

Gradowski was not content merely to chronicle events. He wished also to contextualize them and anticipate the reader's response. Possessed of literary ambitions, with an iterative style and apostrophes to nature that betrayed his debt to Polish romanticism, Gradowski kept circling back to the question of Jewish passivity. To the postwar reader who sat out the war in the Free Zone, Gradowski addressed his "notes" from the underground, whose purpose was to explain how the people of Israel could have vanished so quickly from the soil of Europe. Were they merely casualties of the war? Were they destroyed by some natural disaster? And why did they, each individual and the millions in the aggregate, allow this to happen? As he labored to reconstruct the tortuous journey from ghetto to concentration and death camp, Gradowski dwelt on the myriad ways a person condemned to death could misread the signs. Of everything he witnessed in those twenty-two months, what stood out in his memory above all else was not the "courageous young man from a Białystok transport [who] had attacked some guards with knives, wounded several of them severely and was shot trying to flee" or the incident of the "Warsaw Transport" before which he bowed his head in deep respect, singling out "the splendid young woman, a dancer from Warsaw, . . . who snatched a revolver from [Walter] Quackernack, the Oberscharführer of the 'Political Section' in Auschwitz and shot the Referat-führer, the notorious Unterscharführer [Josef] Schillinger."[27] Rather, it was the fate of the Czech family transport: such intelligent and resourceful Jews, who had been allowed to live together, were duped together, and were gassed together on Purim, March 7, 1944.

To "The Czech Transport" Gradowski dedicated his most sustained work, in which he tried to understand not only the psychology of the murdered, but also the psychology of the mass murderers. His literary means were limited, but his insights were not. The Germans were engaged in a mythic, life-and-death struggle with the demonic *Juden*. The one myth that they were able to make real was the fires of hell – that is, the crematoria ovens – where the members of the Sonderkommando learned which body parts burned more quickly than others. All these crimes would be avenged – of this, Gradowski had no doubt whatsoever. After securing different hiding places for his writings, he led the one-day revolt of the Sonderkommando on October 7, 1944. He was caught, tortured, and publicly hanged. Gradowski believed that through his buried chronicles, future historians would understand the psychology of the murderers, the delusionary hope of the victims, and the uniquely tragic fate of the Sonderkommando.

Notes

1. Emanuel Ringelblum, "Oyneg Shabbes," trans. Elinor Robinson, in David G. Roskies (ed.), *The Literature of Destruction: Jewish Responses to Catastrophe* (Philadelphia: Jewish Publication Society of America, 1989), p. 386.
2. Chaim Aron Kaplan, *Scroll of Agony: The Warsaw Diary of Chaim A. Kaplan.* 2nd rev. edn., trans. Abraham I. Katsh (New York: Collier Books, 1973), p. 351.
3. Zelig Kalmanovitsh, "Three Sermons," trans. Shlomo Noble, in Roskies (ed.), *Literature of Destruction*, p. 511.
4. Ringelblum, "Oyneg Shabbes," p. 391.
5. Peretz Opoczynski, "The Jewish Letter Carrier," trans. E. Chase (modified by D. G. Roskies), in Jacob Glatstein, Israel Knox, and Samuel Margoshes (eds.), *Anthology of Holocaust Literature* (Philadelphia: Jewish Publication Society of America, 1969), p. 57.
6. Oskar Rosenfeld, *In the Beginning Was the Ghetto*, ed. and intro. Hanno Loewy, trans. Brigitte M. Goldstein (Evanston, IL: Northwestern University Press, 2002), pp. 29–30.
7. Leyb Goldin, "Chronicle of a Single Day," trans. Elinor Robinson, in Roskies (ed.), *Literature of Destruction*, p. 427.
8. Rosenfeld, *In the Beginning*, pp. 105–106.
9. Samuel D. Kassow, *Who Will Write Our History? Emanuel Ringelblum, the Warsaw Ghetto and the Oyneg Shabes Archive* (Bloomington: Indiana University Press, 2007), p. 328.
10. Trans. Anna Miransky. Abraham Sutzkever, *Lider fun yam-hamoves: fun vilner geto, vald, un vander* (Tel Aviv and New York: Remembrance Award Library, Bergen-Belsen Memorial Press, 1968), p. 75.
11. Simkhe-Bunem Shayevitsh, "Lekh-lekho," trans. Leah Robinson, in Roskies (ed.), *Literature of Destruction*, pp. 520–30.
12. Sutzkever, *Lider fun yam-hamoves*, p. 79.
13. Abraham Sutzkever, "Song for the Last," trans. C. K. Williams, in Roskies (ed.), *Literature of Destruction*, p. 498.
14. Ibid.
15. Abraham Sutzkever, "No Sad Songs Please," trans. C. K. Williams, in Roskies (ed.), *Literature of Destruction*, p. 501.

16. Sutzkever, *Lider fun yam-hamoves*, p. 108.
17. Kassow, *Who Will Write?*, p. 317.
18. Władysław Szlengel, "Things," trans. John R. Carpenter, *Chicago Review* 52 (Autumn 2006): 283–85.
19. Rachel Auerbach, "Yizkor, 1943," trans. Leonard Wolf, in Roskies (ed.), *Literature of Destruction*, p. 460.
20. Ibid., p. 464.
21. Alexandra Garbarini, *Numbered Days: Diaries and the Holocaust* (New Haven: Yale University Press, 2006), p. 147.
22. Ibid., pp. 145–48.
23. Abraham Lewin, *A Cup of Tears: A Diary of the Warsaw Ghetto*, ed. Antony Polonsky, trans. Christopher Hutton (Oxford: Basil Blackwell, 1988), p. 179.
24. Stanisław Adler, *In the Warsaw Ghetto 1940–1943: An Account of a Witness*, trans. Sara Chmielewska Philip (Jerusalem: Yad Vashem, 1982), p. 3.
25. Ibid.
26. Zalmen Gradowski, "The Czech Transport: A Chronicle of the Auschwitz Sonderkommando," trans. Robert Wolf, in Roskies (ed.), *Literature of Destruction*, p. 548.
27. Ibid., p. 549.

CHAPTER 2

Wartime victim writing in Western Europe

David Patterson

The victim wartime writers to be considered here are Jews for whom, although they were often unaware of it, wartime was to be a time of mass extermination. Despite their many differences in background, age, and upbringing, they had one thing in common: they put their words to the page along the edge of annihilation. This defining feature of their existential condition shaped the nature of their writing, the motives for their writing, and the stake in their writing. Pressed for time and in lands under German occupation, they had no time for rewriting. Regardless of genre, this victim wartime writing is characterized by an air of urgency, a sense of responsibility, and an impetus to testimony. And yet they had no real expectation that their words would see the light of day. Putting their pen to paper required both courage and faith on the part of these authors, as they took up their task in the midst of fear and foreboding.

As one might expect, much of the victim writing during the Holocaust took the form of diaries; they make up most of the writing that found its way into print. The Jews who kept their diaries did so in secrecy and at the risk of their own lives. Their entries measured not only the remains of the day but also the spilling of blood, charged as they were with a testimony not only to personal experience but also to communal ordeal. In contrast to the diaries of Eastern Europe, those that came from the West were not written in ghettos but in hiding places, camps, and sites where Jews awaited deportation. The fiction written during this time has similar characteristics, although there were far fewer works of fiction written under the shadow of Nazism; unlike the diaries, they were written by accomplished authors. Some are highly allegorical; others chronicle confrontations with the Nazi evil that had befallen the world. Letters make up yet another genre, and they have their distinctive features. Undoubtedly, given the dispersion of Jews throughout Europe, more people were writing letters than diaries or fiction; yet the number of published volumes of letters is comparable to published volumes of fiction, and there are far fewer than published volumes of diaries.

Whereas the authors of diaries and novels did not know whether anyone would ever read their work, the letter writers addressed their lines to a recipient, knowing all the while that a Nazi would also read them. The language of the letters, therefore, was at times oblique and coded. The Western European countries from which this victim wartime writing issues are Germany, the Netherlands, Belgium, and France.

Germany

One of the most famous diaries to emerge from wartime Germany is the diary of Victor Klemperer (1881–1960), who until 1935 had been a professor of literature at the Technical University of Dresden. A convert to Christianity, he survived the war largely because he was married to a Christian, Eva Schlemmer. On February 13, 1945, the day before the Allies bombed Dresden, Klemperer escaped to American-controlled territory. Originally published in 1995 as *Tagebücher*, his diary appears in English translation in three volumes, divided into the years 1933 to 1941, 1942 to 1945, and 1945 to 1959.

Several features of Klemperer's journal distinguish it from many other Holocaust diaries, beginning with his desperate attempts to deny that he was a Jew. On May 11, 1942, for example, he declared, "I am German, the others [Jews] are un-German."[1] As late as January 14, 1945, he lamented his plight by saying that no one experiences the "Jewish War" more "acutely and tragically" than "the star-wearing Jew" who "is truly German" (p. 391). He went so far as to compare Judaism to the Gestapo, noting on August 20, 1942 that its laws have "existed since the time of Ezra. The Gestapo is like Ezra" (p. 127). One can only imagine his consternation when a year later a Gestapo agent told him that he must identify himself loudly and clearly by saying, "I am the Jew Victor Israel Klemperer" (p. 251).

Other features of Klemperer's entries are more characteristic of the Holocaust diary. Much of his diary, for example, attests to the atrocities perpetrated by the Nazis and to Hitler's stated intention to exterminate the Jews (p. 21). Another notable aspect of Klemperer's diary is his acute awareness of the Nazis' assault on the word. Throughout his journal he refers to a book he was planning to write called "Lingua Tertii Imperii," or LTI, in which he would examine how the Nazis perverted the language to suit their totalitarian ends. In the entry of May 3, 1944, for example, he notes the frequent use of the word *total* in Nazi discourse (total victory, total commitment, total destruction, and so on), something that underscores the totalitarian nature of the ideology and the regime (p. 312).

The reach of the Nazi totalitarian regime extended into the personal letters written by German Jews. A case in point is Gertrud Käthe Chodziesner (1894–1943), who as a poet and fiction writer took the pen name Gertrud Kolmar. During the war she worked in an armaments factory in Berlin until her deportation to Auschwitz on March 2, 1943. Prior to her deportation she wrote letters to her sister Hilde Wenzel and her niece Sabine Wenzel, who had fled to Switzerland in 1938; in 2004 her letters appeared in English in a volume titled *My Gaze Is Turned Inward: Letters, 1934–1943*. Although she wrote little if any poetry during the war years, between December 1939 and February 1940 she wrote a novella called *Susanna*.

With her letters passing under the censor's eye, Kolmar never made any direct mention of the Nazis' persecution of the Jews but often expressed her longing for the child she never had, for romance, and for Palestine. Reading her missives today, when one knows what she could not know, can be maddening. On December 15, 1942, for example, she wrote, "All the suffering I had to bear and still will have to bear, I shall accept as punishment, and it will be just."[2] Such courage is rare; it can give meaning to a life that is otherwise unbearable, as Kolmar herself affirms in a letter dated November 25, 1941 (p. 85). In the anti-world, however, where the Jews were exterminated not for something they did but for being alive, it is drained of its meaning. Perhaps Kolmar had an intimation of the anti-world that was slowly swallowing her up when on June 2, 1941 she wrote, "That which is happening now is for me unreal, remote . . . It is as if I'm wandering in a world of in-between, a world that has no part of me and in which I have no part" (p. 71).

Kolmar's radical isolation is reflected in her novella *Susanna*, a first-person tale told by the governess of the slightly deranged Susanna, a girl of twenty-one, who can never marry but who longs for a lover. Although Susanna refers to herself as an animal,[3] she insists that, as a Jew, she is "the daughter of King David or of King Saul," whereupon the governess comments, "I was not proud, carried no mark of the royal house; I carried a stain," the stain of being a Jew (p. 172). What wisdom Susanna has comes from her nursemaid Seraphina, whose name invokes the Seraphim, angels of fire who ceaselessly proclaim the holiness of God. Seraphina tells Susanna that "all creation comes from God. For the Evil One cannot create anything, he can only destroy" (p. 177). With no connection to the outside world, Susanna is left to languish in her longing for her beloved, a Mr. Ruby, with whom she actually had no relation. In the end, when she discovers that Mr. Ruby has left for Berlin,

she cries out, "Oh, why are people not good?" (p. 199) and commits
suicide (p. 201). One can see in Susanna's story an allegory of the exile
that the Jewish people – and with them, perhaps, the *Shekhinah* or
Divine Presence – experienced under the Nazis. Indeed, the novel's
title brings to mind the apocryphal story of Susanna (included in the
Catholic Bible as Chapter 13 in the Book of Daniel), which is about a
righteous woman who was wrongfully accused of adultery. The implication, perhaps, is that the Jewish people suffer the Nazi persecution
through no fault of their own. In the novella, then, there is the frustrated
longing for goodness, as well as a profound fear of the Evil One, who can
only destroy. The mental disturbance that Susanna experiences is the
madness that sets in when goodness has fled the world, and, like the Jew,
one no longer has a place in it.

A mad desperation came over another letter writer from Berlin, a woman
named Hertha Feiner (1896–1943). Divorced from her non-Jewish husband
since 1933, Feiner addressed her letters to her two teenage daughters, Inge
and Marion, whom she had sent to a boarding school in Gland,
Switzerland, after the horrors of *Kristallnacht*, which took place on
November 9, 1938. Her letters date from January 1939 to December 17,
1942. Beginning in March 1940 she made repeated attempts to obtain
permission to emigrate to the United States. By the spring of 1942 she
was convinced that her one chance of avoiding deportation and death was to
have her children, whose father was not Jewish, return to live with her in
Berlin; on May 15 she wrote to them and asked that one or both of them
rejoin her. Their father, however, would not allow it.

Like other wartime letter writers, Feiner knew very well that her daughters were not the only ones who would read her letters. She therefore used
coded phrases, such as this one from a letter dated August 30, 1939: "We
must be careful to make sure that nothing happens, especially when going
swimming,"[4] where "going swimming" is a reference to the Nazis' actions
against the Jews. On June 2, 1942, to take another example, she used the
word *illness* to refer to her impending deportation, saying, "My illness has
gotten much worse . . . So you have to come now, and I know that you will
come gladly" (pp. 71–72). When neither Inge nor Marion offered to go to
Berlin and perhaps save her life, she wrote with some disappointment on
December 6, 1942, "I am firmly convinced that you would behave quite
differently toward me if you knew exactly what the situation here is" (p. 81).
As Hertha Feiner saw it, her daughters chose to abandon her, despite her
pleas and premonitions. On March 14, 1943 she was placed on Berlin's 36th
transport to Auschwitz, where she was murdered.

The Netherlands

Unlike Feiner, some Jews managed to get out of Germany, but they remained trapped in Europe; among them were Anne Frank (1929–1945) and her family, who fled to the Netherlands in 1933. After repeated attempts to get to the United States, Otto Frank (1899–1980) took his wife Edith (1900–1945) and his daughters Margot (1926–1945) and Anne into hiding on July 6, 1942, just after Anne's thirteenth birthday on June 12, 1942; that was the day she began her diary. Her last entry is dated August 1, 1944, three days before the Gestapo arrested the Franks – along with Hermann, Auguste, and Peter van Pels and Fritz Pfeffer. Hermann van Pels had begun working for Otto Frank in 1938, and the Franks befriended him and his family. Fritz Pfeffer was a German Jew who fled Berlin after *Kristallnacht* to set up practice as a dentist in Amsterdam; Miep Gies, who had made the arrangements for the Frank family to go into hiding, also came to his aid. They were sent to the transit camp at Westerbork, and on September 3 they were on a transport for Auschwitz. At the end of October, Anne and her older sister Margot were transferred to Bergen-Belsen, where both of them perished in March 1945. Otto Frank was the family's sole survivor. When he returned to Amsterdam, Miep Gies gave him the diary that she had gathered from the floor of the *Achterhuis* or "Secret Annex" on Prinsengracht Street. Anne's famous diary was first published in 1947; the first English edition (from which the citations that follow are taken) came out in 1952 as *Anne Frank: The Diary of a Young Girl*.

The stage and film adaptations of the diary made in the 1950s are most widely remembered for the line lifted from the July 15, 1944 entry: "I still believe, in spite of everything, that people are truly good at heart,"[5] a line that has served to divert people from the horror of the systematic murder of the Jews. Many other entries, however, confront the reader with the Holocaust. Living in constant terror, on May 26, 1944 Anne wrote, "All the fear I've already been through seems to face me again in all its frightfulness" (p. 256). That fear derives from a fear she expressed as early as November 20, 1942: "I have begun to feel deserted. I am surrounded by too great a void. I never used to feel like this" (p. 66). It derives from the evil that led to the extermination of the Jews.

Anne and her family are often portrayed as completely secular Jews, a move that might be used to de-Judaize the Holocaust. Yet, on April 11, 1944 she wrote, "It is God who has made us as we are, but it will be God, too, who will raise us up again . . . Who knows, it might even be our religion from which the world and people learn good, and for that reason and that reason only do we have to suffer now" (p. 221). What is perhaps most Jewish is her concern for other Jews, as when on March 27, 1943, she cried out her anguish over their suffering: "These wretched people are sent to filthy slaughterhouses like a herd of sick, neglected cattle" (p. 87). Such moments of torment over the fate of her people eclipse her moment of naïve, innocent hope that all people are truly good at heart.

In stark contrast to the concern for other Jews that Anne expressed in her diary is the diary of Etty Hillesum (1914–1943). She began her diary on March 9, 1941 and continued it until her deportation to Westerbork on July 5, 1943. Before leaving, she placed the diary in the care of Maria Tuinzing. Etty was murdered in Auschwitz on November 30 of that year. Portions of her diary were initially published in English under the title *An Interrupted Life* in 1983 (the Dutch edition did not come out until 1986). A more complete version of the diary, as well as letters from Westerbork, was published under the title *Etty: The Letters and Diaries of Etty Hillesum, 1941–1943* in 2002. Portions of Hillesum's diary are devoted to her sexual exploits with her psycho-chirologist and mentor Julius Spier, yet it contains no discussion of the assault on the soul or the absence of God that one finds in most Holocaust diaries. In her entry of June 15, 1942, she noted that there were rumors of people being tortured in Amersfoort, but she dismissed them.[6] Indeed, her entries are all but empty of the internal torment that pervades other wartime victim writings. On October 3, 1942 she conceded that "it is our complete destruction they want," but she demanded, "Let us bear it with grace" (p. 542). Nor did her confinement in Westerbork draw Hillesum out of her egocentrism, as on October 3, 1942 she declared, "I want to be . . . the thinking heart of a whole concentration camp" (p. 543). Not until the end was upon her, in a letter dated August 24, 1943, did she raise the cry that one finds in so many Holocaust diaries: "God Almighty, what are You doing to us?" (p. 647). That cry is a defining feature of much of the wartime victim writing. It underscores the tragic tale of a young Jewish woman whose naïve goodness blinded her to the radical evil that in the end swallowed her up.

One of Hillesum's fellow inmates at Westerbork also kept a diary; his name was Philip Mechanicus (1889–1944). The Dutch edition of his diary came out in 1964, the same year that it was published in English under the title *Year of Fear: A Jewish Prisoner Waits for Auschwitz*. In contrast to younger victim writers like Anne Frank or Etty Hillesum, Mechanicus was fifty-three years old when he was arrested on September 27, 1942; on October 25 he was sent to Amersfoort, and on July 29, 1943 he was transferred to Westerbork. The Nazis put him on a train to Bergen-Belsen on

March 8, 1944; the following October 9 they dispatched him to Auschwitz, where he was murdered.

With entries running from May 28, 1943 to February 28, 1944, Mechanicus' diary reflects the maturity and the skill of the journalist that he was. He was especially sensitive to the fate of the Jewish children. He noted on June 7, 1943, for example, that in Westerbork a day did not go by without the death of a Jewish child.[7] Attempting to speak for those who could no longer speak, Mechanicus attested to the Nazi assault not just on mothers, fathers, and children but on the very idea of a mother, a father, and a child. Mothers, he observed, would try to smile at babies "who would not grow or thrive" (p. 132). Conscious, moreover, of an inescapable responsibility, he bore witness to both the physical suffering and its metaphysical implications, relating as he did discussions among the Jews of Westerbork who tried to fathom the meaning of what was happening to them. "Jews may perish," said one rabbi, "but Israel is eternal" (p. 94). Mechanicus, however, despaired over the eternity of Israel in the face of the slaughter of so many of its children.

Another important camp diary is that kept in Bergen-Belsen by Abel J. Herzberg (1893–1989). The author of numerous stories, novels, and dramas, Herzberg was an accomplished writer at the time of his deportation. The Dutch edition was published in 1950; the English edition came out in 1997 under the title *Between Two Streams: A Diary from Bergen-Belsen*. He and his family were arrested and sent to the concentration camp in Barneveld in March 1943. In September 1943 Herzberg was transferred to Westerbork, and in January 1944 he and his wife were among the 172 prisoners taken to Bergen-Belsen to await an exchange for captured Germans. "Enjoying" such a status, Herzberg was awarded privileges that other inmates of Bergen-Belsen did not have. Thus, he was able to keep a diary; the entries begin on August 11, 1944 and end on April 26, 1945.

The title *Between Two Streams* comes from Herzberg himself. He gave his diary this title because in the concentrationary universe "two irreconcilable principles of life fought" against each other, "National Socialism and Judaism."[8] Thus, he perceived at the heart of the Holocaust a fundamental question concerning the value of the life of a human being: whereas the Nazis had no regard for human life, the Jews insisted upon the dearness of and a responsibility for the other person. One of Herzberg's more startling entries came in September 1944, when he offered his explanation of Christian hatred of Jews: it was not because Jews killed Christ – it was because they gave birth to him. "The guilt that the Christian feels because his heathen soul rebels against Christ," he maintained, "seeks to avenge itself on the one who placed him in the torment of ambivalence. That person is the Jew" (p. 68). To the Christian Jew haters, the Jews, who bore Jesus into the world, are the unpleasant reminders of an absolute account-ability. The opposition between the two streams of National Socialism and Judaism, as he wrote on September 5, 1944, comes to this: God is One, which means "creating and justifying a moral standard" (p. 68).

Another Dutch writer from the time of the Holocaust was murdered on March 22, 1945 in the camp where Herzberg wrote his diary; his name was Benjamin Wessels (1926–1945). Prior to his deportation to Bergen-Belsen, Ben wrote letters from Amsterdam and Westerbork to his friend Johan Schipper, who lived in his hometown of Oostvoorne. The English edition was published in 2001 under the title *Ben's Story: Holocaust Letters with Selections from the Dutch Underground Press*. The letters date from October 13, 1942 to November 17, 1943. Like other young Jews, Ben was separated from his parents, who were sent to Westerbork on August 24, 1943; from there they were soon deported to Auschwitz, where they were murdered. Ben's brother Nan had been sent to Auschwitz a year earlier and never heard from again. His longing to be reunited with his brother is an ongoing theme in his letters.

Like Hertha Feiner, Ben made use of coded phrases in his letters. On January 23, 1943, for example, he wrote that "running matches are now held everywhere," with "running matches" being a reference to roundups of Jews;[9] he was, however, more explicit on the following February 2, when he wrote, "Constantly, day and night, the chosen people are pursued" (p. 63). In the same letter he indicated that he knew that the "Promised Land" was Poland, but he had no idea what that meant: "If we have to go there, things can only turn out better. Worse is hardly possible anymore" (p. 64). Also like other letter writers, Ben expressed feelings of foreboding, saying, for example, on December 12, 1942, "We don't have the vaguest idea today whether we'll still be here tomorrow" (p. 55). As his fears intensified, so did his longing for his home; on July 30, 1943 he pleaded with his friend to send him a photograph of the house where he and his family had lived in Oostvoorne (p. 88). In less than a month he was in Westerbork, where conditions were especially grim, as suggested in his last letter from the transit camp, dated November 17, 1943: "If you send packages, by all means, register them! If possible, also send bread. That is very welcome" (p. 107). Written by a simple, innocent soul, Ben's letters reveal the assault on the Jewish soul that takes the form of an assault on home and family. Indeed, the Nazis rendered the Jews homeless before slaughtering them: living in hiding, in a ghetto, or in a camp, *every Jew* in Nazi Europe was homeless.

Belgium

The same age as Benjamin Wessels was another Dutch teenager named Moshe Flinker (1926–1944); however, he wrote his diary, with entries from November 1942 to September 1943, in Brussels, where he and his family had fled in 1942. The Flinkers remained relatively safe until April 7, 1944, the Eve of Passover, when the Germans began their roundup of Belgian Jews. The next day Moshe and his family were sent to Auschwitz. Although his six sisters and younger brother managed to survive, Moshe and his parents perished.

Originally written in Hebrew, Moshe's diary was first published under the title of *Hanaar Moshe* in 1958; the English translation *Young Moshe's Diary* appeared that same year. The entries reveal traces of greatness in a young soul struggling between hope and despair. His ordeal is rooted not only in his insight into history but also in his compassion for his fellow Jews. Painfully aware of what the unfolding events meant for his people, he saw more than ever the urgency of the Zionist cause; he saw, too, that the return of the Jewish people to their ancestral land was becoming increasingly impossible. A devoutly religious Jew, Moshe understood the Holocaust in terms of sacred history. "It seems to me," he affirmed on November 26, 1942, "that the time has come for our redemption."[10] Whereas many diary writers saw the absence of God in this catastrophe, Moshe saw the hand of God. Thus he incorporated his prayers into his diary, making the diary itself into a kind of prayer, even when praying itself became a struggle. In Moshe's movement from prayer to emptiness, from holy word to empty void, one perceives a defining feature of this victim's wartime writing: the diary begins with reverberations of a divine utterance and ends with lamentations over a deadly silence. Young Moshe's diary is a "reflection of [his] spiritual life," as he described it in one of his last entries, dated September 3, 1943 (p. 109). If that spiritual life revolved around God's presence and absence, then perhaps in Moshe's outcry over the silence of God one may hear an echo of God's own outcry.

France

Only slightly older than Moshe Flinker was a talented French wartime diarist named Hélène Berr (1921–1945). Deemed the "French Anne Frank," she began her diary on April 7, 1942; after leaving the diary on November 28, 1942, she returned to her journal on August 23, 1943. Hélène and her family were arrested on March 8, 1944 and sent to Drancy; less than three weeks later they were on a sealed train to Auschwitz. The following November she was sent to Bergen-Belsen, where she died on April 10, 1945, five days before the British arrived. Prior to being sent to Drancy, Hélène gave her diary to her friend Andrée Bardiau; it was published in January 2008. Her last recorded words, in an entry dated February 15, 1944, are from Shakespeare's play *Macbeth*: "*Horror! Horror! Horror!*"[11]

Much of Hélène's diary is focused on the darkness of the Holocaust as it gradually fell over France. Indeed, she felt an obligation "to write all the reality and the tragic things we are living through, giving them all their naked gravity without letting words distort them" (p. 156). Perhaps the first moment to bring her face to face with the history unfolding around her was on June 4, 1942, when she met a woman at the Sorbonne who "said without so much as a quiver that her father had died in the Pithiviers concentration camp . . . It seemed to me that I was suddenly in the presence of inconsolable, unavoidable, and immense pain" (p. 51). On June 9, 1942 she commented on having to wear the Jewish star, saying, "I suddenly felt I was no longer myself, that everything had changed, that I had become a foreigner, as if I were in the grip of a nightmare" (p. 56). One aspect of the Holocaust to which Hélène bore witness was the silence of the Church; on October 11, 1943 she cried out, "Is the pope worthy of God's mandate on earth if he is an impotent bystander to the most flagrant violations of Christ's laws? Do Catholics deserve the name of Christians . . . ? They crucify Christ every day . . . I sometimes used to think I was nearer to Christ than many Christians were, but now I can prove it" (pp. 160–61). On October 25, 1943, more than a year after the roundup of the Jews gathered into the Vélodrome d'Hiver on July 16, 1942, she wrote, "The feeling I had at the time of the mass arrest has lost none of its sharpness: why not me?" (p. 169). In the end she penetrated the depths of the evil engulfing her and the rest of the Jews, saying, "The monstrous incomprehensibility and illogical horror of the whole thing boggles the mind . . . They have one aim, which is extermination" (p. 258). The diary of Hélène Berr is among the most powerful, most penetrating of Jewish wartime victim writings during the Holocaust.

In sharp contrast to Hélène Berr, who was not a professional writer, is the established novelist Irène Némirovsky (1903–1942). Born in Kiev in 1903, she emigrated with her family to Finland in 1917; in 1919 they settled in Paris, where she married Mikhail Epstein in 1926. On February 2, 1939 they converted to Catholicism; when the Germans occupied Paris in June 1940, they fled to the village of Issy-l'Evêque. Prior to her flight from Paris, Némirovsky was a contributor to the anti-Semitic periodicals *Candide* and *Gringoire*. In 1941 she began work on a five-novel series known as *Suite française*, of which she completed two, *Storm in June* and *Dolce*, before she was arrested on July 13, 1942; neither her Catholic conversion nor her anti-Semitic sympathies could save her. Four days later she was on a transport from Pithiviers to Auschwitz, where she was murdered onAugust 17, 1942.

Although Némirovsky completed *Storm in June* and *Dolce* during the war, they were not published until 2004, after her daughter Denise had held the manuscripts for fifty years. *Storm in June* consists of a series of portraits of various families who run away from Paris upon the Nazi invasion in June 1940. Among them are the Péricand and Michaud families, a famous author named Gabriel Corte, and the portly aesthete Charles Langelet. In her novel Némirovsky shows how, almost without exception, the humanity of human beings ebbs away as the mounting chaos of war sweeps over them. "Panic obliterated everything that wasn't animal instinct," she writes.[12] As for Langelet, the man of great aesthetic sensibility, there was no humanity within him to be lost: "*He* was thinking about the cathedral in Rouen, the châteaux of the Loire, the Louvre. A single one of these venerable stones was worth more than a thousand human lives" (p. 105). Only the Michaud family retains some trace of its moral stature, yet even they see the war not as a series of man-made catastrophes but rather as a "storm like in nature" (p. 165), as if there were no human responsibility. The most tragic of the characters is Philippe Péricand, a young Catholic priest entrusted with the care of a group of orphaned boys. As they prepare to leave Paris, he pleads with them, "What I would like to have from each of you is a gesture of faith in God" (p. 23). During their flight, however, they stop in a village, where Philippe longs to "shower" the boys "with Grace," and "inundate their barren hearts with love and faith ... He, Philippe Péricand, had been chosen by God to soften them" (p. 127). Within minutes of experiencing this Christ-like aspiration the boys attack him and beat him to death (pp. 133–34).

The second novel in Némirovsky's *Suite française* is *Dolce*, a title that suggests a certain tranquility in the midst of the catastrophe that is consuming Europe. It takes place in the idyllic village of Bussy, where the French people and the German occupiers get along all too well. Indeed, the main story line concerns the love that arises between Lucille Angelliers and Bruno von Falk, a German who is living in the Angelliers' farm house. A secondary story line revolves around Benoît Sabarie, an escaped prisoner of war who returned to Bussy to marry his fiancée Madeleine. Quartered in the Sabarie house is a German named Bonnet, "a cultured man, gifted in all the arts" (p. 215), who is fond of quoting Nietzsche to Madeleine (p. 216).

Jealous of Bonnet, Benoît kills the German and seeks refuge in the Angelliers' home. Hiding the fugitive leads Lucille to break off her love affair with Bruno, who leaves for the Eastern Front with the other Germans in July 1941 to join the invasion of Soviet territory. The novel, then, has little connection with the Holocaust. Still, Némirovsky takes a hard look at the disgrace of French collaboration with the Nazis, saying, "The mothers of prisoners or soldiers killed in the war looked at them and begged God to curse them, but the young women just looked at them" (p. 221). In the end, when the Germans leave Bussy, almost all the townspeople feel more heartache than relief (p. 330).

In stark contrast to Némirovsky's tale of collaboration is the tale of resistance related in the novel *Army of Shadows* by Joseph Kessel (1898–1979). Born in Argentina, Kessel and his family settled in France when he was just a year old. He was a pilot in World War I, after which he became a journalist and a novelist. He wrote *Army of Shadows* while serving in de Gaulle's Free French Forces in 1943; in 1969 Jean-Pierre Melville made it into a film.

Kessel's tale is replete with the high drama of capture and escape, of dealing with informers and collaborators, and of wrestling with moral compromise. Philippe Gerbier, one of the main characters, for example, writes in his notebook, "The French were not prepared, not disposed to kill ... No question of any such repugnance now ... The Frenchman ... kills every day. He kills the German, the German's accomplice, the traitor, the informer."[13] Confronting French complicity in the actions against Jews and resistance fighters, Gerbier makes an observation about his friend Leroux, who left the police force to join the resistance: "One thought that gives Leroux no rest is the fact that there should exist members of the French police whose ferocity is equal to that of the Germans" (p. 133). As for hating the Germans, Luc Jardie, one of the leaders of the resistance, declares to Gerbier, "Everything that we have undertaken has been done in order to remain men of free thought. Hatred is a shackle to free thought. I do not accept hatred" (p. 160). For Luc Jardie, hatred, too, is one of the enemies that must be overcome.

In addition to being a tale of resistance, *Army of Shadows* is a testimony to the atrocities perpetrated against the Jews. Gerbier notes, for example, that "when a man of the resistance movement is caught on simple suspicion he nevertheless has a chance to survive. But if this man is a Jew he is sure to die the most horrible death. In spite of this there are many Jews in our organization" (p. 129). Most of the Jews who appear in the novel, however, are in prison. One of Gerbier's fellow prisoners relates, "Because I am a rabbi, the Germans assigned me to the committee charged with identifying the Israelites who were unwilling to declare themselves . . . Every week they brought before us men and women whom the occupation authorities suspected of being Israelites, and we had to say whether they were or not . . . The trouble was that if I said yes the people were deported to Poland only to die there . . . I always said no . . . So here I am . . ." (pp. 145–46). Thus, Kessel's novel contains one of the earliest accounts of what happened to Jews imprisoned in France.

In these examples of wartime victim writing, one discovers a wide range of viewpoints and passions, of artistry and insights, of devotion and desperation – from the devout Jew Moshe Flinker to the anti-Semitic convert Irène Némirovsky, from the innocent Anne Frank to the French resistance fighter Joseph Kessel. If there is a single thread, a single outcry, that binds together such diverse texts, the wartime writing of the renowned Jewish philosopher Emmanuel Lévinas (1906–1995) may help to identify it. He studied philosophy at the universities of Strasbourg and Freiburg, where in 1928 he studied under Edmund Husserl. While at Freiburg he met Martin Heidegger, the Nazi Party member who would become his chief philosophical opponent. A soldier in the French army, he was captured in 1940 and spent the war years in a prisoner of war camp. During his internment he kept a notebook in which he developed the notion of the *there is* which forms the basis for his book *Existence and Existents*. That he came to this concept during the Holocaust is no coincidence, for during the Holocaust the *there is* most concretely came to bear.

In *Existence and Existents* Lévinas describes the *there is* as "the impersonal, anonymous, yet inextinguishable 'consummation' of being, which surmounts in the depths of nothingness itself . . . It is not the dialectical counterpart of absence, and we do not grasp it through a thought. It is immediately there. There is no discourse. Nothing responds to us, but this silence."[14] The silence of the *there is* is akin to the silence that surrounds the examples of wartime victim writing examined here. One sees it in the "dark sky looming" silently over Hélène Berr[15] and in Victor Klemperer's inability to rid himself of fear,[16] in the nameless malaise that drains Gertrud Kolmar of her "mental fortitude,"[17] and in Moshe Flinker's cry of "I am completely in the grip of this nothingness."[18] It is the onset of what Elie Wiesel called *Night*. These authors penned their texts in the depths of a silence that refused meaning, in the silence of an indifferent world that was succumbing to a deadly darkness. It is a silence that threatened the very identity, the very being, of those who were marked for death simply for being Jewish.

There lies the horror that Lévinas associated with the "there is": horror "is a participation in the *there is*, in the *there is* which returns in the heart of every negation, in the *there is* that has 'no exits.' It is, if we may say so, the impossibility of death, the universality of existence even in annihilation."[19] And annihilation was never more universal than in the existence of these authors. Charged with the crime of being there, these authors had no exit. For them, death was not the last but continually the last. If they had an exit, it lay in their writing, through which they sought a voice, a link between word and meaning in a time when word and meaning came under a radical assault. Only through such a voice could the anonymous rumbling of the "there is" be overcome. Hence, theirs was no ordinary wartime writing: the enemy whom these authors faced was not only the one who bore arms but also the silence and the horror of the *there is*, of the darkening sky and the ineradicable fear, of the collapse of mental fortitude and the grip of nothingness. The generation that is now the heir to their writing has an obligation to resist that silence and that horror, lest the silent shadows of Auschwitz consume humanity.

Notes

1. Victor Klemperer, *I Will Bear Witness: A Diary of the Nazi Years, 1942–1945*, trans. Martin Chalmers (New York: Random House, 1999), p. 51. The page numbers of subsequent quotations are given in the text.
2. Gertrude Kolmar, *My Gaze Is Turned Inward: Letters, 1934–1943*, ed. Johanna Woltmann, trans. Brigitte M. Goldstein (Evanston, IL: Northwestern University Press, 2004), pp. 135–36. The page numbers of subsequent quotations are given in the text.
3. Gertrude Kolmar, *A Jewish Mother from Berlin and Susanna*, trans. Brigitte M. Goldstein (New York: Holmes and Meier, 1997), p. 171. The page numbers of subsequent quotations are given in the text.
4. Hertha Feiner, *Before Deportation: Letters from a Mother to Her Daughters, January 1939–December 1942*, ed. Karl Heins Jahke, trans. Margot Bettaure Dembo (Evanston, IL: Northwestern University Press, 1999), p. 11. The page numbers of subsequent quotations are given in the text.
5. Anne Frank, *The Diary of a Young Girl*, trans. B. M. Mooyart-Doubleday (New York: Modern Library, 1952), p. 278. The page numbers of subsequent quotations are given in the text.
6. Etty Hillesum, *Etty: The Letters and Diaries of Etty Hillesum, 1941–1943*, trans. Eva Hoffman (Grand Rapids, MI: Eerdmans, 2002), p. 416. The page numbers of subsequent quotations are given in the text.
7. Philip Mechanicus, *Year of Fear: A Jewish Prisoner Waits for Auschwitz*, trans. Irene S. Gibbons (New York: Hawthorne, 1964), p. 37. The page numbers of subsequent quotations are given in the text.

8. Abel J. Herzberg, *Between Two Streams: A Diary from Bergen-Belsen*, trans. Jack Santcross (London: I. B. Tauris, 1997), p. 4. The page numbers of subsequent quotations are given in the text.
9. Benjamin Leo Wessels, *Ben's Story: Holocaust Letters with Selections from the Dutch Underground Press*, ed. Kees W. Bolle (Carbondale: Southern Illinois University Press, 2001), p. 62. The page numbers of subsequent quotations are given in the text.
10. Moshe Flinker, *Young Moshe's Diary: The Spiritual Torment of a Jewish Boy in Nazi Europe*, trans. Shaul Esh and Geoffrey Wigoder (Jerusalem: Yad Vashem, 1971), p. 26.
11. Hélène Berr, *The Journal of Hélène Berr*, trans. David Bellos (New York: Weinstein Books, 2008), p. 262. The page numbers of subsequent quotations are given in the text.
12. Irène Némirovsky, *Suite française*, trans. Sandra Smith (New York: Alfred A. Knopf, 2006), p. 29. The page numbers of subsequent quotations are given in the text.
13. Joseph Kessel, *Army of Shadows*, trans. Haakon Chevalier (London: Cresset Press, 1944), p. 89. The page numbers of subsequent quotations are given in the text.
14. Emmanuel Lévinas, *Existence and Existents*, trans. Alphonso Lingis (The Hague: Martinus Nijhoff, 1978), pp. 57–58.
15. Berr, *Journal*, p. 61.
16. Klemperer, *I Will Bear Witness*, p. 218.
17. Kolmar, *My Gaze Is Turned Inward*, p. 118.
18. Flinker, *Young Moshe's Diary*, p. 81.
19. Lévinas, *Existence and Existents*, p. 61.

PART II

Postwar responses

CHAPTER 3

The Holocaust and Italian literature

Robert S. C. Gordon

Any "national" literature of the Holocaust must necessarily confront not only intensely challenging universal questions to do with the darkest sides of human nature and human history, not only the millennial history of racial difference and the persecution of the Jews, but also a panoply of "local" questions, of circumstance and immediate cause, of politics and individual choice, of family, community, town, and nation. The Italian case is no exception to this rule.

Fascist Italy was the model and prime ally for Nazi Germany. Even if its racial politics were less predominant than Germany's, its anti-Semitic Racial Laws of 1938, its colonial and anti-Slav violence, its aid with roundups and deportations after 1943 all point to a profound degree of complicity with genocide.[1] And yet there is also a powerful counternarrative to Italy's Holocaust, an array of delays, blockages, and obstacles Italians put in the way of the Final Solution, of heroic attempts by decent Italians to protect Jews and other victims. Furthermore, Italy – like Austria, France, and others – also has a narrative of "occupation" to set alongside its complicity, since during 1943–1945, when all deportations of Jews from Italy took place, large parts of the country were under de facto Nazi occupation. Something close to civil war ensued, during which the Nazis carried out deportations and dozens of civilian massacres, leaving devastating legacies of mourning and conflicted memory.

Millions of Italians suffered imprisonment in the network of Nazi holding, labor, concentration, and extermination camps: approximately eight thousand Italian Jews deported to Auschwitz, most of them murdered; tens of thousands of anti-Fascists sent to Mauthausen and the like; hundreds of thousands of Italian army conscripts, and forced and "voluntary" laborers, interned after Italy's armistice with the Allies in late 1943. And this is to exclude several hundred thousand Italian prisoners of war or enemy aliens in Allied war camps.

After the war, with little to distinguish one emaciated survivor or "retur-
nee" (*reduce* in Italian) from another, there was little opportunity for specific
or universal reflection on the genocide of the Jews. Where there was
contemplation of deportation, it was filtered through national lenses, linked
to Fascism, the civil war and Resistance, bombings and the dual occupation
of 1943–1945, difficult memories of the Axis wars in Russia, Europe, and
Africa, and the memory of imprisonment. Over the following decades, these
"national" dimensions to what was commonly labeled simply the *lager* (the
German term for concentration camp) in Italy continued to intersect with
local cultural and political flashpoints, from the Cold War struggles
between communism and the Catholic Church or Christian Democracy,
to convulsions such as the terrorism of the 1970s. Each moment reshaped
for local eyes the history and memory of the Holocaust.

Italian Holocaust literature, then, was inexorably immersed in these local
confusions, even if on occasion – and signally in the case of its most famous
figure, Primo Levi – it also rose above local issues to contribute compelling
reflections on larger historical and moral quandaries. This chapter offers one
possible path through that literature.[2] It follows a loosely chronological
structure, selecting eight emblematic moments and clusters of works from
the 1940s to the new millennium. The selection is neither comprehensive
nor intended to be canonizing: it includes a varied mix of survivor testimony, Holocaust "fiction" by survivors, but also other writers, and literature that draws more loosely or incidentally on Holocaust themes. The
chapter gives regular prominence to Primo Levi, not only for the quite
exceptional power and importance of his work, but also for its inventively
probing variety, a model for the diverse possibilities of telling stories about
the Holocaust in postwar Italy.

1945–1946: Debenedetti, Malaparte, Saba

The first significant narratives of the genocide in Italian came not from
survivors, but from the wildly contrasting pens of two literary intellectuals,
Giacomo Debenedetti and Curzio Malaparte.

Debenedetti's *October 16, 1943* was first published in book form in Rome
in 1945.[3] It is a short, restrained, vividly human, and at times trenchant, "on-
the-ground" chronicle of the night of October 16, when, in the former
ghetto area of Rome, over a thousand Jews were rounded up by the Nazis
and deported to Auschwitz. Interlaced with his diary of that night,
Debenedetti digresses back to September 1943 and the appalling, tragicomic

episode of the "tribute" of 50 kg of gold demanded from the Jewish community in Rome by the newly arrived Nazi authorities. A companion piece to *October 16, 1943*, *Eight Jews*[4] contemplates the Jewish victims of the massacre in the Fosse Ardeatine in March 1944, when 335 Italians including 75 Jews were murdered in the catacombs in reprisal for a Resistance attack. This cluster of events in Rome and its Jewish community were to become central motifs of Italian narratives of the Holocaust, returning in novels, films, and historiography throughout the postwar era, amounting to a distinct "Roman question" in the field of Holocaust memory in Italy (distinct from, if intersecting with, the Roman Catholic Church's "Holocaust question"). *October 16, 1943* is the Urtext of this tradition. In writerly terms, it stands as an influential model for the bystander-writer (between the survivor and the disinterested observer): sober and respectful, but with elements of narrative invention, "second-hand" listening and transmission, and tentative moral and psychological inquiry.

Debenedetti was in Rome during 1943–1944 and he spoke to victims and protagonists of the events he relates. His work was, in other words, also one of reportage. In this (but in little else), *October 16, 1943* resembles Curzio Malaparte's *Kaputt* (1945), a vast work of high literary performance and artifice, based on Malaparte's extensive traveling and reportage as a war journalist across Axis and occupied Europe.[5] In his account of his travels around the military postings and dining tables of the aristocracies of the Nazi imperium, Malaparte dwells on several occasions on the "Final Solution" taking place just a short distance from his bibulous diners. He witnesses the massacre at Iasi in Romania, and he strolls through a hideous scene of the Warsaw ghetto. His tone is of weary sorrow, of cynical detachment from his Nazi hosts, much as it will be when he wittily relates dining with Otto Frank, waiting for Ante Pavelić, or meeting Himmler in an elevator. For all its narcissism, *Kaputt* deploys considerable literary resource in capturing the physical degradation, the grotesque scenery of Nazi Europe, and the visceral horrors of war and genocide as they happened.

Debenedetti and Malaparte – writing before the end of the war, before the return of most camp survivors, and before the establishment of models for "witness" writing – represent a "pre-historic" model and anti-model for the field of Holocaust literature in Italy: neutral, compassionate, ironic, on the one hand, or melodramatic and narcissistic, on the other; Italian-centered or European-centered; from below or from above; from within the Jewish community or from within the Axis elite. Debenedetti and Malaparte are model and anti-model also at the level of influence: the former stands as a more or less declared reference point for many later

chronicles; the latter struggled to produce epigones, although any of the
riskier later fictionalizations of the Holocaust could, perhaps, be linked to
the power and dangers of this "performative" literary reportage. Both,
however, were knowingly literary, as is also the case with a third early
work worth mentioning for its eccentric form and incisive feel: the
Triestine-Jewish poet Umberto Saba's 1946 collection of fragments,
Shortcuts.[6] Saba's epigrams, annotations, and stories circle around and
return repeatedly to Majdanek and other camps, to Hitler and Mussolini
as grotesques. They offer shards of sense and nonsense from the maelstrom
of this early moment, torn between relief at the end of a nightmare and an
intuition of a profound caesura "after Majdanek."

1947: Levi, Millu, Bizzarri

Between 1945 and 1947, over fifty, mostly small, locally published and little-
read first-person survivor accounts of the camps appeared.[7] The authors
were mostly anti-Fascist partisans, alongside some ex-military and Jewish
survivors. Most were deliberately unliterary – even anti-literary, anti-
rhetorical – but they nevertheless shaped their language and pitch to
probe what remained of selfhood, memory, and suffering, deploying often
sophisticated resources to capture the trauma.

   Three texts give an indication of how these early works combined on
occasion raw testimony and something approaching a literary voice. The
first is the text that would come to define and condition the entire field of
writing on the Holocaust in Italy (and beyond): Primo Levi's *If This Is a
Man*.[8] Published in 1947 by a small publisher, having been turned down by
several larger houses, the first edition of this extraordinary work already
displayed the immensely subtle ethical and ethological features that would
make Levi's work so influential: its modest aspiration to offer "documents
for the calm study of some aspects of the human mind"; a sequencing by
stages of the destruction of man as both self and social animal; an acute
sensitivity to the problems of language and communication; a scientific
"lab-report" style.[9] It tethered its ethical energy to a sensitive human
dimension, through a strong sense of character, through pen portraits of
individuals who come alive as types and emblems of moral difficulty as well
as of human contact among victims, good or bad (Alberto, Lorenzo, Elias,
Henri, etc.). This is all transmitted in a style of low-key formality, with
rhetorical flourishes and erudite allusions accompanying the scientific analysis. *If This Is a Man* is a hybrid, then, of old and new, rather than a "degree
zero" of new writing about the "evil tidings" of Auschwitz.

Alongside Levi, among the early Jewish survivor memoirs was a surprising cluster of works by women, such as Liana Millu and Giuliana Tedeschi,[10] rich in literary resource and carefully attentive to the specifics of women's experience of the camps. Millu's *Smoke over Birkenau* is perhaps the most intense and elaborately developed. Its six stories, a mix of memoir and fiction, each center on a female protagonist thrust into the appalling dilemmas of suffering in the women's camp. Explorations of maternity, desire, family relations, and sexuality are built into compelling and stylistically elegant narrative shape, overshadowed by degradation and death.

Smoke over Birkenau, like *If This Is a Man*, was relatively neglected in 1947, but eventually (like Levi again) republished and lauded in the 1980s. The vagaries of publishing history were not so kind to a third, equally extraordinary, work of narrative from 1947, Aldo Bizzarri's *Proibito vivere* (Living is forbidden), set in an unspecified *lager* based on the author's experience as an anti-Fascist deportee to Mauthausen.[11] Bizzarri's novel makes use of the trope of the frame narrative, echoing the *Decameron* or the *Thousand and One Nights*. A group of prisoners gather every Sunday, in a moment's break in their slave-labor, to tell stories; but each week, they are fewer in number. Unlike Scheherazade's trick, the pleasures of storytelling cannot hold off death here. The stories start out as diversions from the hideous surrounding, but they constantly rub up against the *lager*, through motifs of solitude, fear, violence, love, loss, and death. Only the maverick of the group, Costantino, finds himself unable to tell diverting stories, reciting instead his mournful poetry. Levi, too, in a famous passage of *If This Is a Man*, evoked the stories told by prisoners to each other, in snatched moments of reprieve, as "stories of a new Bible." And he, too, on rare but poignant occasions – "at an uncertain hour," as he put it – moved from prose to poetry, as in his epigraph to the same book, to contemplate the deeper violence of the *lager* universe ("Consider if this is a man . . ."). For all three of these writers – Levi, Millu, and Bizzarri – the fate of the storyteller and the shape of his or her language already seem essential quandaries in these early, first-hand narratives of the Holocaust.

1953–1956: Meneghello, Piazza, Bassani

Conventional accounts of Holocaust literature suggest a period of silence from the late 1940s to the late 1950s. In Italy as elsewhere, however, there were voices in the silence. Three examples from 1953 to 1956 show how writing about the Holocaust was fomenting, if not always loudly apparent at this time.

A moment of oblique intersection between the literary sphere and early historiography came via an Italian ex-partisan living in England, later to become a feted novelist. Luigi Meneghello read the first serious history of the Holocaust to appear in English, Gerald Reitlinger's *The Final Solution*, in 1953 and, in a series of powerful articles for the Olivetti journal *Comunità* in 1953–1954, he summarized, adapted, and distilled the book, researching and adding his own vivid photographic images, under the title "The Extermination of the Jews of Europe."[12] Although there is little "literary" narrative to these articles, they belong in a literary history for three reasons: they tie incipient knowledge of the Holocaust to a Resistance figure, an important future writer and intellectual; they are symptomatic of a crucial symbiosis between Italy and a wider European culture in disseminating Holocaust knowledge; and they belong to a key trend toward "hybrid-ization" in writing on the Holocaust between narrative, first-person testi-mony, collaborative memory, oral history, and historiography. Aspects of this literary-historiographical hybrid, already present in Debenedetti, sub-tend Meneghello's "scribal" work of synthesis, and will come to further fruition in the oral history work of Alessandro Portelli or the memory-history hybrids of Rosetta Loy and others in the 1990s (see below).

A second example from this period, Bruno Piazza's *Perché gli altri dimenticano* (Because others forget), is a somber work of first-person testi-mony and is telling not so much for its literary qualities as for the moment and means of its publication.[13] Piazza, a Triestine Jew born in 1899, was deported from the Risiera di San Sabba camp to Auschwitz in 1944. He returned to Italy in 1945, but died in 1946. The publication of his book in 1956 flags up a complex, and often neglected, history of delay and cycle in the dissemination of Holocaust writing, as works are published or repub-lished at distances of decades from their writing or first publication. For Piazza, a new publisher kickstarted this excavation: the independent com-munist publishing house Feltrinelli, who would also bring Pasternak's *Doctor Zhivago* to Western fame, took up *Because Others Forget*, just as leftist Turin house Einaudi would publish the second and definitive edition of Levi's *If This Is a Man* in 1958. The genocide was beginning its move to the center stage of *engagé* literary culture in Italy.

If Meneghello and Piazza show history and testimony working at the edges of the literary sphere, a final example – Giorgio Bassani – suggests that a mainstream literature of the Holocaust was also taking shape. Bassani was embarking on the first stories of what would become his seven-volume *Novel of Ferrara* cycle. *Five Stories of Ferrara* (1956) taps into the intricate history and social mores of Jewish, middle-class Ferrara.[14] One story in particular, "A Plaque in Via Mazzini" (1952), represents a moment of emblematic importance in the history of Italian Holocaust literature. The protagonist Geo Josz, sole survivor of Ferrara's Jewish deportees to Buchenwald, presents for the first time in literary guise the uncomfortable, unassimilable problem of the witness-survivor. Josz forces the inhabitants of Ferrara to see their own amnesia, their rewriting of history to fit the present, and the faulty mechanisms of their memory and stone memorials. Josz and the motifs of Jewish history and narrative of the Holocaust are meshed in an inextricable web, with the memories and disavowed Italian histories of Fascism, the Resistance, and local Ferrarese politics.

1958–1963: Bruck, Levi, Bassani

The late 1950s and early 1960s saw a step-change in the profile of the Holocaust in Italy, as elsewhere. Following the international successes of Anne Frank's *Diary* and, in a different vein, the capture and trial of one of the most notorious of the Nazi leaders still at large, Adolf Eichmann, the emergence of a discrete and widely acknowledged historical "event" labeled the Holocaust is most often dated to this time. In Italy, furthermore, the period coincided with a so-called "economic miracle," including a rapid expansion in publishing and other culture industries, reflected in the sheer quantity and variety of material appearing in these years.

Within Holocaust literature, these years were marked not only by quantitative leaps but also by qualitative shifts, by an extension – even in the oeuvres of single authors – from testimony to other forms of fictional narrative or literature. Two key examples are Edith Bruck and, once again, Primo Levi. Bruck was born in Hungary in 1932 and deported to Auschwitz in 1944. She survived and moved to Israel, before eventually reaching Italy in 1954. Her first work, *Who Loves You Like This*, a strikingly intense testimonial account of this remarkable journey capturing the sharp voice and distorted horror of a young girl's experiences, appeared in 1959.[15] And it signaled a relatively new thread for Italy, one quite characteristic of the larger field of Holocaust writing, that of transnational and translingual migration, here from Hungarian to Hebrew to Italian, a product of the peregrinations of deportation and survival. (Elie Wiesel was living through comparable geographical and linguistic wanderings in the same period.)

The marked literary sophistication of *Who Loves You Like This* paved the way for Bruck's striking move (like Wiesel, again) into Holocaust fiction, in her second work, *Andremo in città* (We will go to the city, 1962), including a powerful story of a child's-eye fantasy of salvation.[16] Levi's trajectory over this period was comparable: after the republication of *If This Is a Man* in 1958, Levi set about writing *The Truce* (1963), which, although not a work of fiction per se, is permeated by the resources of the literary stylist, the comic storyteller, the picaresque travel writer, and the historical novelist. This is another hybrid project, part memoir and part literary elaboration. And it is striking to note that Levi's wider success in Italy, including winning prizes and the use of his work in schools, began with *The Truce*.

As if to confirm this newly enhanced role of Holocaust fiction, 1962 saw the publication of by far the most popular and internationally acclaimed work of Holocaust fiction in Italian. Bassani's *The Garden of the Finzi-Continis* offered a masterly conjoining of the traditional genres of adolescent love story, *Bildungsroman*, historical novel, and Proustian memory narrative, immersed in a careful evocation of 1930s Fascist anti-Semitism in Ferrara, and a framing pall of deportation and death. Besides the extraordinary literary achievement of the work and its publishing success, the book and its framing are significant for at least two reasons: first, because it continues Bassani's work of integrating histories of Fascism, the Jewish community, and the European Holocaust; and second, because the frame marks a key moment in readerly awareness of the Holocaust when a mere allusion to the camps touches the narrative with an appalling and moving horror, coloring and transforming the whole. The Holocaust, in other words, was now part of the culture's received vocabulary.

1966–1967: Pasolini, Artom, Limentani

From the mid-1960s, we find a further dispersal in the kinds of writing and literature surrounding the Holocaust. Levi, in an interview in 1963, claimed to have said all he had to say on the *lager*.[17] True to his word, over the following decade he published science-fiction, chemistry, or industry stories, poems about animals: apparently anything but the Holocaust. In fact, and symptomatically, this eclectic period in Levi's work does not so much reject the *lager*, as confront it in oblique or metaphorical ways. In the wider culture, the metaphorical "energy" surrounding the Holocaust grew markedly, often in distinctly loose form. A tool of the radical politics of the time, the Holocaust often appeared as a metaphor for power, ideology, and violence, for oppression, Fascism, capitalism (and more); and with it emerged a new vision of the "Jew" as emblematic victim and figure of modernity.

No figure embraced with more metaphysical intensity this new role for the Jews and the camps than writer and filmmaker Pier Paolo Pasolini.

Pasolini's allegorical poetry, drama, and film – his collection *Poetry in the Form of a Rose*, his play *Calderòn*, his film *Pigsty* (1969)[18] – are filled, among many other things, with images of Israel, of the *lager*, of modernity, and "The Jew." He drew on an eclectic, half-assimilated mix of Frankfurt School, Dante, St. Paul and the Gospels, on journeys to Israel, on his own experience of scandal and sexual-political persecution. He rarely addressed anything in the specific, concrete history of the Holocaust, but the topos now had its own autonomous vocabulary and power. Before his death in 1975, Pasolini waged a frenetic intellectual campaign against what he called the "genocide" [*sic*] of consumerism; and his final allegorical *lager* appeared in the hideous degradation and torture scenes of his last film, *Salò o 120 Days of Sodom* (1975).

If Pasolini provides startling evidence of how motifs of the Holocaust were now widely available for intellectual and aesthetic manipulation, less frenetic work from the late 1960s shows the terrain shifting in other directions. The Holocaust was also being acknowledged concertedly as a specifically Jewish history – one urgently connected to the contemporary State of Israel and the Six Day War – and at times a specifically Jewish-Italian history, even if only loosely connected to the core of the genocide. A good example is Natalia Ginzburg's memoir *Family Sayings* (1963), the story of her Jewish anti-Fascist family in Turin, including the murder by torture – only briefly evoked – of the narrator's first husband, Leone.[19] The book belongs, even for what it does *not* say, within the growing field of Holocaust literature, as *also* a story about the Holocaust. And something similar could be said of the publication and striking *succès d'estime* of the extraordinary Resistance *Diari* (Diaries) of Emanuele Artom.[20] Artom, a brilliant young Jewish intellectual, died fighting for the Resistance: as with Levi's brief moment as a partisan, and as in the thread of narratives about the Fosse Ardeatine massacre (where Jews were victims alongside many other Italians), in this web of stories, a national narrative is shown to include a Jewish element and, conversely, the Holocaust is shown to be – also – part of Italian history.

Meanwhile, a more conventional body of Holocaust novels, often written by those close to the experiences themselves, continued to grow. Once again, women writers were prominent. The first novel by Giacoma Limentani, *In contumacia* (In absentia, 1967),[21] is set in Rome, where the author was born in 1927 and where she lived through the Racial Laws and the Nazi occupation. Told from the point of view of a young girl, the story revolves around her traumatic experiences of a Fascist raid and of rape. Using the legalistic terminology of the title as its governing image,

Limentani probes the psychological trauma of the victim, her feelings of guilt and defilement, of failure or absence, that threaten to contaminate her innocence.

1974–1978: Morante, Millu, Bruck

During the turbulent years of the 1970s, mainstream writers and intellectuals continued to appropriate the Holocaust for varied purposes, and survivor-writers broadened their palate, often now dwelling on the problems of retrospection, history, and memory. Indeed, perhaps the dominant paradigm of all Holocaust literature was now that of memory.

By far the most important instance of the Italian Holocaust fiction of the 1970s was the controversial 1974 novel, *History*, by Elsa Morante.[22] This vast novel of World War II, set in Rome, places the Jewish experience and echoes of the Holocaust at its core. The protagonist, Ida, is half-Jewish. She is raped by a German (a citizen of Dachau) and later she and her son Useppe (a figure not unlike Grass's Oskar Matzerath) will witness the roundup and deportations of October 16, 1943, drawn in one convulsive sequence to the wailing voices from inside a cattle-truck at the Tiburtina station, and later the camp liberation photos of 1945. *History* is the most notable example of how the motifs of Rome and the Holocaust, in particular of Debenedetti's Rome of *October 16, 1943* and the events he chronicles, find their way in modulated form into the mainstream of Italian Holocaust-related narrative (indeed, some have claimed Morante came close to plagiarism in her calques from Debenedetti). On a larger scale, however, Morante's vision of what she calls the "scandal" of history uses the figure of the Jews, the aura of the Holocaust, and an allegorical analogy of the humble, the "wretched," children such as Useppe, and the victims of genocide.

Among the survivor-writers, two figures we have encountered before – Liana Millu and Edith Bruck – produce compelling works of fiction in the 1970s. Bruck's *Due stanze vuote* (Two empty rooms [with a preface by Levi]) also appeared in 1974.[23] Its three stories are set in a Hungarian village like the one Bruck grew up in, a suburb of New York, and a boat traveling to Israel. All three are stories of return and identity, centered on a loosely autobiographical protagonist, and her doubts over what remains of earlier places and earlier selves, over contacts with former victims, protagonists, and bystanders. They are stories of the residues of the trauma after twenty years. Interestingly, Italy is not one of the locations of *Two Empty Rooms*, but it hovers in the background, an image of home, a perspective from which the complex questions of post-Holocaust trauma and memory can be explored.

Bruck also published a collection of poetry in the 1970s, *Il tatuaggio* (The tattoo), which integrates stark reflections on Auschwitz with evocations of childhood, family, and love.[24] Levi too published his spare, but important corpus of poetry for the first time in the 1970s,[25] becoming part of a minor thread of Holocaust poetry in Italian, stretching back to Salvatore Quasimodo's eloquent poem "Auschwitz."[26]

Millu, over thirty years after *Smoke over Birkenau*, published a second book in 1978, *I ponti di Schwerin* (The bridges of Schwerin).[27] The novel tells two consecutive stories about the protagonist Elmina: her return from the camps, in the vein of *The Truce*; followed by her difficult reintegration and the emergence of her gender consciousness. Like *Two Empty Rooms*, and Levi's *Periodic Table*, which also appeared in this period, Millu's autobiographical narrative stretches the terms and purposes of the writer's first testimonies, embedding them in deeper historical and personal contexts. Millu had always brought a gendered perspective to her writing, but the powerful insistence on Elmina's gender as victim, resister, and survivor in *The Bridges of Schwerin* chimes also with 1970s feminist activism, in turn reflected in oral history work on the Holocaust which was published in the 1970s also.[28]

1981–1987: Pressburger, Bufalino, Levi

The 1980s saw a growing number of first-person testimonial texts being published for the first time or republished. A strikingly important example was Giuliana Tedeschi's *There Is a Place on Earth*, which reworked her 1946 *This Poor Body*.[29] Also emerging in the 1980s was a sub-genre of Jewish family narratives, within which the persecutions of the years 1938–1945 took their place as part of a longer genealogy of local, national, and Jewish identity. The family sub-genre perhaps finds its origin in "Argon," the remarkable first chapter of Levi's *Periodic Table*, or in Ginzburg's *Family Sayings*, and is developed in works such as Paolo Levi's *Il filo della memoria* (The thread of memory, 1984) or Vittorio Dan Segre's *Memoirs of a Fortunate Jew* (1985).[30] Indeed, it persisted into the twenty-first century: one of the most powerful works of recovered, posthumous testimony to appear since 2000 was Piera Sonnino's *This Has Happened*, also in its way a work of family history since Sonnino was the sole survivor of a family of eight deported to Auschwitz.[31]

The intensified exploration of Jewishness in these family excavations feels a long way from earlier attempts to "nationalize" the Jewish experience of the Holocaust by retelling it as a form of Resistance or patriotic anti-Fascism. In the wider literary sphere, we can see evidence of something comparable in the growing fascination in 1980s Italy for the literary culture of Jewish Mitteleuropa. The most direct link from Italian culture to central Europe comes via Trieste, and Triestine critic Claudio Magris' *Danube* (1986) captured this terrain to extraordinary effect, in a hybrid of travelog, literary fragment, and textual-memorial bricolage.[32] The Holocaust hangs like a shadow over works such as these, figuring a lost culture recovered in memory and literary history.

Bringing together both the family autobiography and the cross-fertilization with Eastern Europe were the ethnographic, magical stories of the Jewish ghetto in Budapest by two immigrant brothers (like Bruck, native Hungarians writing in adopted Italian): Giorgio and Nicola Pressburger's *Homage to the Eighth District* (1986).[33] The synthesis of a folklore of Ashkenazi wisdom and comedy with flashes of suffering and violence is a characteristic combination, hinted at also in some of Levi's *lager* stories of *Moments of Reprieve*, published in Italy in 1981.[34] Following Nicola Pressburger's early death, Giorgio would continue to write inventive, playful, and visionary work haunted by the Holocaust, in both his theater and novels, including his 2008 reworking of Dante, *Nel regno oscuro* (In the dark kingdom).[35]

Within the mainstream of Italian literary fiction, also, the figuring of the Holocaust as an incidental source of character, mystery, and heightened intensity continued. The most sophisticated example was undoubtedly Gesualdo Bufalino's baroque first novel *The Plague-Spreader's Tale* (1981).[36] Self-consciously drawing on Mann's *Magic Mountain*, Bufalino's Sicilian story of desire, memory, sickness, and suicide in a postwar sanatorium revolved around the figure of Marta, revealed over the course of the novel as a Jewish *lager* survivor, who had also been a Kapo (one of those camp inmates who were given positions of power over their fellow prisoners).

Family stories, Mitteleuropean tales, Jewish literary lovers languidly dying: these sub-genres and motifs circulating in the 1980s pale in comparison with the overwhelming profile and the immense national and international fame now enjoyed by Primo Levi (a fame only morbidly redoubled by his death in 1987). Between 1981 and 1986, Levi was widely translated and lionized abroad, and published no fewer than seven books of stories, essays, poetry, and fiction, including *If Not Now, When?* and *The Drowned and the*

Saved.[37] The former was Levi's only fully fledged attempt at Holocaust fiction, as well as at (Jewish) Resistance fiction. It, too, was steeped in the Eastern European Jewish tradition, whose somewhat alien feel for Levi was underlined in the appending of a bibliography to the book (although, as we will see below, in this pseudo-scholarly apparatus, Levi was once again anticipating new trends). *The Drowned and the Saved* took Levi beyond narrative into the realm of the essayist and moralist, attentive to problems of memory and distance, in dialogue with other works of testimony and history, and aware of contemporary problems of war, violence, and genocide. This was to become his most influential of books into the 1990s and 2000s, picked up by thinkers such as Giorgio Agamben and widely cited for its acute discussion of the problems of witnessing, shame and memory, the "grey zone" of moral responsibility, and more. In these essays, and in all of his late works, we can see Levi experimenting with form and formulae, with the problematic of what happens to a literature of the Holocaust "after" the work of testimony, in the strict sense, is done.

1997–1999: Loy, Affinati, Janeczek

As in the United States and the rest of Europe, Italy in the 1990s saw a genuine explosion of interest in the Holocaust. After the collapse of Cold War ideologies, as the anti-Fascist consensus in Italy frayed, as new genocidal violence erupted in ex-Yugoslavia and in Rwanda, the *lager* became ever more a moral and cultural pivot, and cultural production flourished. Signs of this were to be found in literature of the most varied kind. In mainstream novel publishing, motifs of the Holocaust were frequent presences: two bestsellers were Susanna Tamaro's *For Solo Voice*, whose title story is a moving monologue by an aging Holocaust survivor, and Paolo Maurensig's Mitteleuropean story of chess and the Holocaust, *The Lüneberg Variation.*[38]

The year 1997 alone (perhaps not coincidentally ten years after Levi's death) saw a remarkable concentration of Holocaust narrative. These included Lia Levi's fourth novel, *Tutti i giorni di tua vita* (All the days of your life), a saga of Jewish family life under Fascism;[39] *Canone inverso*, a second bestseller by Maurensig;[40] Rosetta Loy's *First Words*, a reflection on the author's childhood memories around 1938;[41] Eraldo Affinati's *Campo del sangue* (Field of blood), a chronicle of the young author's walk from Venice to Auschwitz;[42] and Helena Janeczek's *Lezioni di tenebra* (Lessons of darkness), in which the phenomenon of second-generation memory and trauma – a recurrent feature of late-twentieth-century Holocaust literature – is filtered through a highly problematic relationship between mother and daughter, as well as through another case of language transmission between Polish, German, and Italian.[43]

From this cluster of work, a series of recurrent tropes and motifs emerges, several of which are best described as postmodern. Loy is most striking as an instance of moral-historical inquiry carried out through a combination of intimate childhood autobiography and scholarly research. Loy splices together syntheses of historiography, in particular around the controversial issue of Roman Catholic Church neglect of Nazi anti-Semitism, with guilt-laden memories of her own childish betrayal or indifference toward her Jewish neighbors. Affinati's *Field of Blood* shares both elements in Loy's work, although it deploys them in very different ways: it is also "self-centered" and therefore testimonial, but in a second-hand way (his walk to Auschwitz echoes millions of train deportations to Auschwitz, including his mother's narrow escape by leaping from a cattle-truck). And it, too, is heavily intertextual, recording the journey as much through Affinati's readings about the Holocaust as through the walk itself. Finally, both Loy and Affinati invest strongly in a sense of place, in the "geography" of memory, whether that be Rome or the road to the *lager*. For Janeczek, too, the physical site of memory at Auschwitz is an essential testing-ground for the novel's explorations. And the literal and cultural geography of Affinati and Janeczek remind us that, increasingly, interrogation of the Holocaust is also an interrogation of a European identity, born out of the dissolution of the Nazi pan-European project. All these three elements – vicarious testimony, mediating textuality, and transnational sites of memory – fit a certain ethical late-postmodernism, as do contemporary hybrid works of narrative historiography of this period, influenced by microhistory and oral history, such as Alessandro Portelli's *The Order Has Been Carried Out*, an account of the history and memory of the Fosse Ardeatine massacre.[44]

Unsurprisingly, given the outpouring of material on Holocaust and memory in the late 1990s and early 2000s, the same period saw signs of a contrarian tiring with the obsession, a frustration with the commercialization or exploitation of the Holocaust, as well as increasingly difficult intersections with the contemporary politics of Israel.[45] A signal of something similar in Italy was the highly tendentious, in some respects anti-Semitic, polemic by respected historian and columnist Sergio Romano, *Lettera a un amico ebreo* (Letter to a Jewish friend), with its gentle suggestion to his "friend" to stop talking so much about the Holocaust.[46] Cultural flashpoints such as these are symptomatic of the difficulties and risks that accompanied the stretching of the cultural forms, shapes, and profile of the Holocaust at the turn of the century.

Far more affectingly, and from the heart of the literary sphere we have been mapping out here, Edith Bruck, by now author of an extraordinarily rich body of Holocaust literature and testimony, published in 1999 a contemporary reflection on her public role as a Holocaust survivor. Entitled *Signora Auschwitz* (as a schoolchild mistakenly names Bruck in one of her many school visits), the book evokes the devastating psychological lacerations of playing the part of the witness for a lifetime, forced to relive her trauma daily in front of uncomprehending schoolchildren, but aware that the choice not to bear witness, to forget, is impossible.[47] Something of this bind had been there in the problem of language intuited by Primo Levi and others back in the 1940s, in the impossibility of finding the words to pass on an inkling of the experience of the camps; but now Bruck is as if stuck in another world, with an audience who has not the slightest cultural or historical bond to what it is she has to say, and what it is that tortures her every time she says it. The demand for Holocaust talk risks becoming inversely proportionate to understanding of it; but as Bruck and all the others struggling to write the Holocaust into literature in the twenty-first century know, the risks of staying silent, even after sixty years or more, are greater still.

Notes

1. Joshua Zimmerman, ed., *Jews in Italy under Fascist and Nazi Rule, 1922–1945* (Cambridge University Press, 2005).
2. See also Risa Sodi, *Narrative and Imperative: The First Fifty Years of Italian Holocaust Writing (1944–1994)* (New York: Peter Lang, 2007).
3. Giacomo Debenedetti, *16 ottobre 1943* (Rome: OET, 1945); *October 16, 1943/ Eight Jews*, trans. Estelle Gilson (Notre Dame: University of Notre Dame Press, 2001).
4. Giacomo Debenedetti, *Otto ebrei* (Rome: Atlantica, 1944). *Eight Jews* (see note 3).
5. Curzio Malaparte, *Kaputt* (Naples: Casella, 1944); *Kaputt* (New York Review of Books Classics, 2005).
6. Umberto Saba's *Scorciatoie e raccontini* (Milan: Mondadori, 1946); "From Shortcuts and Very Short Stories, 1934–1948," see *The Stories and Recollections of Umberto Saba*, trans. Estelle Gilson (Riverdale-on-Hudson, NY: Sheep Meadow Press, 1993).
7. Anna Bravo and Daniele Jalla, eds., *Una misura onesta: Gli scritti di memoria della deportazione dall'Italia 1944–1993* (Milan: FrancoAngeli, 1994).
8. Primo Levi, *Se questo è un uomo* (Turin: De Silva, 1947; 2nd edn. Turin: Einaudi, 1958); *If This Is a Man* (New York: Orion, 1959).

9. Levi co-authored a medical report on the camp in 1946: Leonardo De Benedetti and Primo Levi, *Auschwitz Report* (New York: Verso, 2006).

10. Liana Millu, *Il fumo di Birkenau* (Milan: La Prora, 1947); *Smoke over Birkenau*, trans. Lynne Sharon Schwartz (Philadelphia: Jewish Publication Society, 1991); Giuliana Tedeschi, *Questo povero corpo* (This poor body) (Milan: EdIt, 1946) (but see note 29).

11. Aldo Bizzarri, *Proibito vivere* (Milan: Mondadori, 1947).

12. Ugo Varnai (pseud. Luigi Meneghello), "Lo sterminio degli ebrei d'Europa, I–III," *Comunità*, December 22–24, 1953–April 1954; later in Luigi Meneghello, *Promemoria* (Bologna: Il Mulino, 1994). Cf. Gerald Reitlinger, *The Final Solution: The Attempt to Exterminate the Jews of Europe, 1939–1945* (London: Vallentine Mitchell, 1953).

13. Bruno Piazza, *Perché gli altri dimenticano* (Milan: Feltrinelli, 1956).

14. Giorgio Bassani, *Cinque storie Ferraresi* (Turin: Einaudi, 1956); *Five Stories of Ferrara*, trans. William Weaver (New York, Harcourt Brace Jovanovich, 1971).

15. Edith Bruck, *Chi ti ama così* (Milan: Lerici, 1959); *Who Loves You Like This*, trans. Thomas Kelso (Philadelphia: Paul Dry Books, 2001).

16. Edith Bruck, *Andremo in città* (Milan: Lerici, 1962).

17. Primo Levi, *The Voice of Memory: Interviews 1961–1987* (New York: New Press, 2001), p. 81.

18. Pier Paolo Pasolini, *Poesia in forma di rosa* (Milan: Garzanti, 1964); *Poems*, trans. Norman MacAfee with Luciano Martinengo (New York: Vintage Books, 1982); *Calderòn* in *Teatro* (Milan: Garzanti, 1988).

19. Natalia Ginzburg, *Lessico famigliare* (Turin: Einaudi, 1963); *Family Sayings*, trans. D. M. Low (New York: Arcade, 1987).

20. Emanuele Artom, *Diari: gennaio 1940–febbraio 1944* (Milan: CDEC, 1966).

21. Giacoma Limentani, *In contumacia* (Milan: Adelphi, 1967).

22. Elsa Morante, *La storia* (Turin: Einaudi, 1974); *History*, trans. William Weaver (New York: Knopf, 1977).

23. Edith Bruck *Due stanze vuote* (Venice: Marsilio, 1974).

24. Edith Bruck, *Il tatuaggio* (Parma: Guanda, 1975).

25. Primo Levi, *L'osteria di Brema* (Milan: Scheiwiller, 1975); *Shema*, trans. Ruth Feldman and Brian Swann (London: Menard Press, 1976).

26. Salvatore Quasimodo, "Auschwitz," in *Il falso e vero verde* (Milan: Mondadori, 1956); *Complete Poems*, trans. Jack Bevan (New York: Schocken Books, 1984).

27. Liana Millu, *I ponti di Schwerin* (Poggibonsi: Lalli, 1978).

28. See especially Lidia Beccaria Rolfi and Anna Maria Bruzzone, eds., *Le donne di Ravensbrück: Testimonianze di deportate politiche italiane* (Turin: Einaudi, 1978).

29. Giuliana Tedeschi, *C'è un punto della terra* (Florence: La Giuntina, 1988); *There Is a Place on Earth: A Woman in Birkenau*, trans. Tim Parks (New York: Pantheon Books, 1992).

30. Paolo Levi, *Il filo della memoria* (Milan: Rizzoli, 1984); Vittorio Dan Segre, *Storia di un ebreo fortunato* (Milan: Bompiani, 1985); *Memoirs of a Fortunate Jew* (University of Chicago Press, 2008).

31. Piera Sonnino, *Questo è stato* (Milan: Il Saggiatore, 2004); *This Has Happened*, trans. Ann Goldstein (New York: Palgrave Macmillan, 2006).
32. Claudio Magris, *Danubio* (Milan: Garzanti, 1986); *Danube*, trans. Patrick Creagh (New York: Farrar, Straus and Giroux, 1989).
33. Giorgio and Nicola Pressburger, *Storie dell'ottavo distretto* (Casale Monferrato: Marietti, 1986); *Homage to the Eighth District*, trans. Gerald Moore (London: Readers International, 1990).
34. Primo Levi, *Lilít e altri racconti* (Turin: Einaudi, 1981); *Moments of Reprieve*, trans. Ruth Feldman (New York: Summit, 1986).
35. Giorgio Pressburger, *Nel regno oscuro* (Milan: Bompiani, 2008).
36. Gesualdo Bufalino, *Diceria dell'untore* (Palermo: Sellerio, 1981); *The Plague-Spreader's Tale*, trans. Patrick Creagh (London: Harvill, 1999).
37. Primo Levi, *I sommersi e i salvati* (Turin: Einaudi, 1986); *The Drowned and the Saved*, trans. Raymond Rosenthal (New York: Summit, 1988).
38. Susanna Tamaro, *Per voce sola* (Venice: Marsilio, 1991); *For Solo Voice*, trans. Sharon Wood (Manchester: Carcanet, 1995); Paolo Maurensig, *La variante di Lüneberg* (Milan: Adelphi, 1993); *The Lüneberg Variation*, trans. Jon Rothschild (New York: Farrar, Straus and Giroux, 1997).
39. Lia Levi, *Tutti i giorni di tua vita* (Milan: Mondadori, 1997).
40. Paolo Maurensig, *Canone inverso* (Milan: Mondadori, 1997); *Canone inverso*, trans. Jenny McPhee (New York: Holt, 1998).
41. Rosetta Loy, *La parola ebreo* (Turin: Einaudi, 1997); *First Words*, trans. Gregory Conti (New York: Metropolitan, 2000).
42. Eraldo Affinati, *Campo del sangue* (Milan: Mondadori, 1997).
43. Helena Janeczek, *Lezioni di tenebra* (Milan: Mondadori, 1997).
44. Alessandro Portelli, *The Order Has Been Carried Out: History, Memory and Meaning of a Nazi Massacre in Rome* (New York: Palgrave, 2003).
45. See, e.g., Norman Finkelstein, *The Holocaust Industry* (New York: Verso, 2000).
46. Sergio Romano, *Lettera a un amico ebreo* (Milan: Longanesi, 1997).
47. Edith Bruck, *Signora Auschwitz* (Venice: Marsilio, 1999).

CHAPTER 4

German literature and the Holocaust

Stuart Taberner

What is most striking in relation to German literature and the Holocaust – if we take this to mean writing in German ranging from first-hand accounts to fictional works – is the absence of a single defining text such as Anne Frank's *Het Achterhuis: Dagboekbrieven/ The Diary of a Young Girl* (1947/ 1952), Primo Levi's *Se questo è un uomo/If This Is a Man* (1947/1958), or Elie Wiesel's *La Nuit/Night* (1958/1960) which transcends its linguistic (e.g. Dutch, Italian, French) context to become part of the transnational corpus of books about the Nazi ghettos and concentration camps. Edgar Hilsenrath's *Nacht* (1964), a harrowing account of life and death in the Prokow ghetto, certainly achieved some limited global impact after its 1966 release as *Night*, and Paul Celan's poem "Todesfuge" ("Deathfugue," 1948) is widely taught, but neither resonate with a wider audience in quite the same way. And the East German writer Jurek Becker's novel *Jakob der Lügner/Jacob the Liar* (1969/1975, with a new translation in 1996), although turned into an Oscar-nominated foreign-language film in the mid-1970s, only became truly well known outside Germany after its 1999 adaptation as a Hollywood movie starring Robin Williams.

Hilsenrath's brutally realistic ghetto reportage, Celan's haunting death camp poem – "Your ashen hair Shulamith we dig a grave in the breezes there one lies unconfined"[1] – and Becker's story of a young boy who concocts clandestine radio and news bulletins suggesting imminent liberation (with sometimes fateful consequences) nevertheless display key features of Holocaust literature in general. Similar to *If This Is a Man*, *Nacht* was initially considered by its publisher to be too distressing for a broad readership. The first edition of 1964, then, had a short print-run and was only reissued following the success of *Der Nazi und der Friseur*, which appeared in 1977, six years *after* its English translation as *The Nazi and the Barber* – German publishers were now concerned by the second book's satirical depiction of both the SS camp guard who "becomes" a Jew after 1945 *and* the Jews he encounters when he fights for Israel in May 1948. The issue here was not only (West) Germany's awkward philo-Semitism but also a broader anxiety, from the early 1960s, relating to an emerging body of Holocaust *fiction*. Philosopher Theodor Adorno's 1949 dictum that to write poetry after Auschwitz would be "barbaric" had been often ignored, of course.[2] (Adorno has been interpreted to mean that after the Holocaust, art, and especially poetry, is impossible because art's imperative is to beautify the world, and nothing can be beautiful after Auschwitz, or more specifically to mean that any attempt to write literature about the camps would inevitably transform the Holocaust into an *aesthetic* experience.) But the appearance of texts employing a wider range of aesthetic strategies than, say, Celan's instinctively appropriate lachrymose mix of poetic abstraction and cruel reality or Nelly Sachs's melancholic expansiveness – "O the Chimneys / On the ingeniously devised habitations of death / When Israel's body drifted as smoke" (1947, trans. Michael Hamburger)[3] – shaped perhaps the most crucial debate of Holocaust literature. Is it right to go beyond the (appa-rently) "authentic lived experience" of Frank, Levi, and Wiesel and *fabulate* the ghettos and death camps?

This chapter will proceed chronologically and will reference specific conditions of a work's publication and reception. To begin with, however, some issues relating to the complexities of texts written in the language of the perpetrators, that is, *German*, merit attention.

First and foremost, the question of *who* writes appears more urgent in relation to German-language works. There is an obvious distinction to be made between writing by Jews, whether those who evaded deportation in hiding or in exile or those who were more directly victims or survivors of the ghettos, mass killings, and death factories, or later generations, and writing by Germans (or Austrians) as contemporaries and descendants of perpetra-tors, fellow-travelers or bystanders or, less often, resisters and rescuers. Of course, large numbers of Jews were *also* Germans. Many of these vigorously identified with German culture even during their persecution. Thus Victor Klemperer, spared deportation only by the "timely" bombing of Dresden, exclaimed in his posthumously published wartime diaries: "I am a German, the others are un-German" (1995).[4] Others, however, struggled with a heritage, and a language, in which they had grown up but which had subsequently treated them so cruelly. The little-known but impressive exile poet Stella Rotenberg puts it as follows:

> ON WRITING VERSE
> My mother had a treasure stored.
> A rich and precious store of words.

> ...
> Now, onto the wound
> her murderers inflicted,
> I pour her balm, her words drop
> by drop.
> ...[5]

For non-Jews, too, the question of their identity as Germans is similarly pressing but here, not surprisingly, it is differently focused. From Heinrich Böll's fabulation of an encounter between an SS captain and a Jewish girl in *Wo warst du, Adam?/Where Were You, Adam?* (1951/1954), to Martin Walser's 1998 *Ein springender Brunnen* (*A Gushing Fountain*), in which the author's alter ego turns away, in May 1945, from his Jewish classmate Wolfgang, non-Jewish authors have obsessively explored what it means to be German after the Holocaust.

Non-Jewish German and Jewish German writers have different experiences of the Holocaust, and thus different memories and different immediate concerns.[6] In the first postwar years, German suffering was thus often juxtaposed *with* Jewish suffering in an undifferentiated adumbration of war as a catastrophe overwhelming all equally. From the early 1960s, the emphasis was on German guilt *for* Jewish suffering. And more recently, German suffering is thematized as coming *after* Jewish suffering, implying – for the most part – a recognition of the causal (and ethical) precedence of Germans as perpetrators over Germans as victims. Indeed, to do any differently, that is, to write as if from the perspective of Jews, might risk appropriating their stories, and their anguish too. That non-Jewish writers have been sensitive to this danger is evidenced by Hans Magnus Enzensberger's insistence in 1959, in the first significant response to Adorno's "no poetry after Auschwitz" dictum, that Sachs was able to write of the camps because she had been a victim, unlike "Germans." When German authors *have* told Jewish stories, indeed, some readers have wondered whether this might amount to wrongfully expropriating the victim's story. This concern was expressed, for example, in relation to Wolfgang Koeppen's "writing-up" of survivor Jakob Littner's story in *Aufzeichnungen aus einem Erdloch* (*Notes from a Hole in the Ground*, 1948, republished in 1985, and again in 1992 along with an explanatory foreword by Koeppen).

Exploring further the question of *who* writes, matters are complicated still more by the fact that a good number of the victims and survivors composed their responses in German but had, before their flight or deportation, been members of Jewish populations outside of Germany. These included Paul

Celan, from Czernowitz, H. G. Adler, from Prague, and Elias Canetti, who was born in Bulgaria but who was raised in German in Vienna from age seven. First and foremost, the use of German testifies to the prestige German culture had enjoyed before Hitler's coming-to-power among well-educated Jews living as members of an often despised minority in regions within the German sphere of influence or in the states that had emerged from the collapse of the Austro-Hungarian empire in 1918. Works by Celan, Adler, and Canetti are steeped in references to German culture and pervaded by a profound sense of hurt at an unexpected rejection (worse: an unprecedented barbarity).

> Black milk of daybreak we drink it at sundown
> we drink it at noon in the morning we drink it at night
> we drink and drink it.[7]

– thus read the first lines of Celan's "Deathfugue," suggesting, perhaps, the death camp inmates' realization that the German culture they had imbibed as children has only now revealed itself as poisonous. "Der Tod ist ein Meister aus Deutschland" ("Death is a master from Germany") is the refrain that accompanies this realization, as the golden-haired (German) Margareta and the ashen-haired (Jewish) Shulamite are simultaneously united and divided by their shared, but quite contrary proximity to genocide. Celan, Adler, and Canetti, moreover, lived much of their lives in exile. Celan fled the communist regime in Romania in 1947, first to Vienna and then Paris. Adler moved to England after surviving Theresienstadt, Auschwitz, and other camps. And Canetti quit Austria in 1938 following the Nazi takeover. Indeed, a sense of uprooting suffuses the work of many who escaped the Nazis before or even after 1939 for Palestine, the United States, Britain, Scandinavia, Central America, Argentina, Australia, and other destinations, or who left after 1945, as displaced persons, refugees from communism, or homeless migrants. And here an additional complication arises too. Thus some, such as the poet and translator Michael Hamburger, who left Germany as a child in 1933, wrote in English, the language in which he was subsequently schooled. Others rejected German, for example Aharon Appelfeld, an Israeli writer born, like Celan, in Chernivtsi who grew up speaking German but chooses to write in Hebrew. And still others are so much better known in translation that it is often assumed that they originally wrote key texts in English, for instance Viktor Frankl's *Man's Search for Meaning* (*Trotzdem ja zum Leben sagen*, 1946), a psychiatrist's account of everyday life in the camps framed as a search for meaning even in despair and a key text for the development of logotherapy.

1933–1950s

These are some of the issues that must be borne in mind: *who* writes, the significance of *when* an author writes, and in which social and political context, and the problems of identifying precisely *what* "German Holocaust literature" – to use a term we have shied away from thus far – encompasses. Do we mean texts by victims *and* perpetrators? Texts by Germans *and* non-German Jews? Texts by exiles living outside of German-speaking countries? Should we also include writers who were brought up in German but now write in another language?

Moreover, many of the earliest texts scarcely seem to focus on the persecution of Jews *as* Jews but are rather much more concerned with the wider political struggle against German Fascism. Anna Seghers's *Das siebte Kreuz* (*The Seventh Cross*, 1939), for example, takes place in 1937 and describes the recapture, killing, or surrender of six of seven escaped anti-Fascists from the fictitious Westhofen Concentration Camp (the seventh escapes to Holland). In *Transit* (*Transit Visa*, 1943), similarly, Seghers interweaves the stories of a group of refugees (many of whom are Jewish, although this is not very important within the text) struggling to acquire travel documents to flee the German invasion of France. Here, as in Seghers's *Der Ausflug der toten Mädchen* (*The Outing of the Dead Girls*, 1943), the tone is often existential, implying the randomness of individual fates and the enormous consequences of trivial choices. Unlike *Das siebte Kreuz* and *Transit*, however, in *Der Ausflug der toten Mädchen* the persecution of Jews *as* Jews is central: Netty describes the deportation of her Jewish mother (Seghers was born Netty Reiling).

The existential mood that characterizes much of the literature of persecution and exile of the 1930s and 1940s – the naturalistic style of Lion Feuchtwanger's exile novel *Die Geschwister Oppermann* (*The Oppermanns*, 1933) and his internment memoir *Der Teufel in Frankreich* (*The Devil in France*, 1940) is unusual – also suffuses Gertrud Kolmar's novella *Susanna*, written just before her deportation to Auschwitz in February 1943, and her poems in *Das lyrische Werk* (*Dark Soliloquy*, posthumously published in 1975). Here, there are few direct references to anti-Semitism but a pervasive anxiety of outsiderdom: "The murderers are loose! / They search the world / All through the night / oh God, all through the night!"[8] The same applies to texts by writers such as Grete Weil (*Ans Ende der Welt* [At the world's end], 1949) and Stephan Hermlin, for example *Die Zeit der Gemeinsamkeit* (*The Time of Togetherness*, 1949), a depiction of the Warsaw Ghetto Uprising as the ultimate expression of the individual's essential humanity. Some are more "political," mostly by authors, such as Brecht, Seghers, and Hermlin, who later declared allegiance to the GDR. Others, usually by writers who emigrated to Israel or took up residence in West Germany (or the United States), mobilize more abstract imagery to define "metaphysical" causes for Jewish suffering: an eruption of evil, or destiny. We might think here of Else Lasker-Schüler, with her poetry indebted to Jewish mysticism, or her play *IchundIch* (*IandI*, written 1940/1941, published in 1970), which explores the absence/presence of God during the Holocaust. Or, we might think of Rose Ausländer: "Phoenix / my people/the burned / arisen" ("Phoenix," my trans.).[9]

Even *Die größere Hoffnung* (*The Greater Hope*, 1948) by Ilse Aichinger, which depicts the interminable fear and violent death of a young girl with two "wrong" (i.e. Jewish) grandparents, remains largely allegorical rather than concrete. (Aichinger herself had two "wrong" grandparents – her mother was Jewish.) In non-Jewish writers of the period, such abstraction may appear at best naïve, at worst exculpatory. Hans-Werner Richter's *Sie fielen aus Gottes Hand* (*They Fell from God's Hand*, 1951) at least avoids the excessive sentimentality of Ernst Wiechert's *Missa sine nomine* (1950), in which a Jewish survivor dispenses forgiveness to those "good" Germans unwittingly caught up in Nazism. Yet Richter's portrayal of an encounter between "representative" individuals in a displaced persons camp, including a former SS guard and a Jewish boy whose parents were killed in the Warsaw Ghetto Uprising, still blurs the distinctions between victims and perpetrators. A rather improbable reconciliation is also implied in Alfred Andersch's *Sansibar oder der letzte Grund* (*Flight to Afar*, 1957), in which Judith is helped to flee to Sweden by an anti-Nazi trio of communist, "ordinary" worker, and pastor. Andersch's *Efraim*, from 1967, is likewise problematic on account of its gauche philo-Semitism.

Such black/white characterizations are typical of a wave of early postwar texts attempting to make sense of the Holocaust within contemporary, broadly Christian categories. Albrecht Goes's *Brandopfer* (*The Fire Victim*, 1954) thus has a German woman "purifying herself" by fire during an Allied air raid – she is rescued by a Jew from the righteous punishment rained down from the heavens. Similarly, *Das unauslöschliche Siegel* (*The Indelible Seal*, 1946) by Elisabeth Langgässer, whose father was of Jewish descent, includes both Christian motifs and a startling abstraction: her baroque extravaganza pictures Nazism as a contest between God and the devil.

Thomas Mann's *Doktor Faustus* (*Doctor Faustus*, 1947) stands out in German literature of this period. From as early as 1940, in fact, the Nobel Prizewinning author had been confronting German audiences from his Californian exile with details of atrocities against Jews (and others) in radio broadcasts on the BBC. Yet even as Mann's depiction of Adrian Leverkühn's Faustian pact with the devil, narrated by his friend Serenus Zeitblom, works well as an allegory for the clash between Apollonian and Dionysian chacteristics that (for Mann) define the German soul – enlightened humanism on the one hand (Zeitblom) and a hubristic attraction for the irrational on the other (Leverkühn) – the novel remains far removed from the realities of the camps. (In Goethe's *Faust*, to which Mann refers, Faust makes a deal with the devil to exchange his soul for unlimited knowledge and worldly pleasures.) Indeed, almost no details of Nazi cruelty are given. An allusion to the way the population of Weimar was forced to march past Buchenwald by the US army in April 1945 is about as concrete as Mann's philosophical reflection on the dualisms of self-realization/self-destruction, genius/madness, and culture/barbarity gets.

1960s–1980s

It was only from the early 1960s that German *fiction* became less abstract and more "documentary," for reasons that we shall explore shortly. However, already from the mid to late 1940s, we find examples of a more graphic form of *reportage*. In relation to "work camps" set up after 1933 (rather than the wartime death camps where Jews in particular were murdered on an industrial scale), key examples are Wiechert's *Der Totenwald: Ein Bericht* (*The Forest of the Dead*, 1945) and Eugen Kogon's *Der SS-Staat* (*The SS-State*, 1946). Wiechert's text provides an account of his internment in Buchenwald, whereas Kogon's is a sociological examination based on the author's seven years in the same camp. (Erich Maria Remarque's *Der Funke Leben* [*Spark of Life*, 1952] draws on Kogon's *SS-Staat* to produce a novel in a more documentary style *avant la lettre* – Remarque wrote the text in memory of his sister, Elfriede Scholz, who was beheaded by the Nazis "in his stead"). In relation to the "Holocaust proper" (if such a term be acceptable), H. G. Adler's *Theresienstadt 1941–1945*, written in 1948 but published in 1955, clearly stands out.

Reportage, documentary, sociological and psychological analysis, and fiction come together in the wake of the trial of Adolf Eichmann in Jerusalem in 1961 and the first trials of Auschwitz guards in West Germany from 1963 to 1965. Most important are two dramas, Rolf Hochhuth's *Der Stellvertreter* (*The Deputy*, 1963), which caused much controversy with its depiction of Pope Pius XII cynically sanctioning the Church's silence in relation to the murder of European Jews, and Peter Weiss's *Die Ermittlung* (*The Investigation*, 1965). In *Die Ermittlung* we see how the punctilious detailing of the *systemic* perpetration of the Holocaust in the Eichmann and Auschwitz trials – what Hannah Arendt called the "banality of evil" – refocuses literary fiction away from the abstract, the existential, and the metaphysical toward the concrete, the sociological, and the real. The play was based on a visit undertaken by Weiss, whose father was a Hungarian Jew, to the site of the Auschwitz concentration camp, as reported in his *Meine Ortschaft* (*My Place*, 1964). In this short narrative, Weiss reflects on its personal meaning for him as the "place" to which he was "supposed" to be delivered. In *Die Ermittlung*, however, the focus remains on the everyday cruelty of Nazi bureaucracy, rendered in quasi-documentary style as actors recite portions of trial evidence in highly estranged, depersonalized fashion:

> DEFENDANT 14:
> Your Honour
> I want to bring this to your attention
> I was only the jailer in Block Eleven
> I received my orders from my superiors
> and I had to obey them
> I am not the one
> who was responsible
> for what happened in the bunker
> it was the Criminal Officer
> . . .
> WITNESS 6:
> On the 3rd of September 1941
> the first experiments
> in mass slaughter
> using Cyclone B gas
> were carried out
> in the Bunkerblock.[10]

Weiss's play continues to be performed today, and not only in Germany. In late 2007, an English-language version was performed at London's Young Vic theater by Rwandan actors reflecting on the mass killing of some 800,000 Tutsis in their own country in 1994.

Before the mid-1960s, traces of the Holocaust were present for the most part in broadbrush allusions or metaphorical abstractions. Or, they were concealed within the self-dissolving formal density of a literary modernism no longer able to believe in progress or redemption, for example the poetry of Ingeborg Bachmann, or the absurdist theater and prose of Wolfgang Hildesheimer. Günter Grass's *Die Blechtrommel* (*The Tin Drum*, 1959), with its jarring portrayal of Sigismund Markus, murdered on *Kristallnacht*, and Mariusz Fajngold, a traumatized survivor of Treblinka, or his *Hundejahre* (*Dog Years*, 1963), with its depiction of a huge pile of bones in Stutthof concentration camp, were thus unusual in their time. From the mid-1960s, however, the lasting effect of the documentary theater is evident in works as different as Christa Wolf's (semi-autobiographical) *Kindheitsmuster* (*Patterns of Childhood*, 1976), which features a childhood encounter with a Jewish boy, or Erich Fried's "Vietnam War" poems (*And Vietnam and*, 1966), which draw parallels between the gas chambers and napalm. It is also evident in the wave of "father novels" that appeared especially after the student protests of the late 1960s. For example, Bernhard Vesper's *Die Reise* (*The Journey*, 1977), Christoph Meckel's *Suchbild* (*Picture Puzzle: On My Father*, 1980), or Elisabeth Reichart's *Februarschatten* (*February's Shadow*, 1984) each examine the complicity of the author's father in Nazism. More recently, Hanns-Josef Ortheil's *Abschied von den Kriegsteilnehmern* (*Farewell to the Wartime Generation*, 1992) and Stephan Wackwitz's *Ein unsichtbares Land* (*An Invisible Country*, 2003) use documentary sources to reconstruct, in fiction, the extent to which their families were caught up in the enthusiasm for Hitler.

Günter Grass's *Aus dem Tagebuch einer Schnecke* (*From The Diary of a Snail*, 1972) is the most prominent example from the early 1970s of the hybridity that has become characteristic of German literature relating to the Holocaust. Here, Grass mixes fact and fiction in his juxtaposition of an account of his political campaigning with a highly inventive reconstruction of literary critic Marcel Reich-Ranicki's "submerging" during the Nazi period, with information on the deportation of Danzig's Jews. Peter Schneider's *Vati* (*Daddy*, 1987) also mixes in documentary material in its portrayal of the "Angel of Death," Josef Mengele.

The German Democratic Republic (GDR)

Of the texts from the 1970s and 1980s mentioned in this chapter so far only one – Wolf's *Kindheitsmuster* (1976) – is by an *East* German writer. The small number can be accounted for by the fact that the communist authorities tended to play down the complicity of "ordinary" Germans and to assert instead the principal responsibility of advanced capitalism for the rise of Hitler: Weiss's *Die Ermittlung*, with its focus on the entanglement of big business and power politics, was enthusiastically staged in East Germany. Until relatively late in the GDR's forty-year existence, moreover, the state focused on the "martyrdom" of communists in the camps set up inside Germany (especially if these had been liberated by the Red Army in

1944–1945) rather than on the death factories in the east where the vast majority of Jewish victims were murdered. This marginalization of Jewish victimhood is apparent in the work of Brecht, Seghers, and Hermlin from the 1930s to the late 1940s, and indeed into the late 1950s with the publication of (German-Jewish writer) Bruno Apitz's *Nackt unter Wölfen* (*Naked among Wolves*, 1958). Apitz's novel, which tells of the real-life rescue of a four-year-old Jewish child by inmates of Buchenwald, became a key element in the GDR's foundational narrative of anti-fascism. In Peter Edel's *Bilder des Zeugen Schattmann* (*Impressions of the Witness Schattmann*, 1969), alternatively, Jews are less important *as* Jews than as members of a communist resistance group.

There are exceptions, of course. In Franz Fühmann's short story *Das Judenauto* (*The Jewish Car*, 1962), for example, a young boy internalizes the prevailing anti-Semitism of the early 1930s and distracts his classmates' attention from an embarrassing display of sexual excitement (he gets an erection in public) by raging against Jews. Johannes Bobrowski's *Levins Mühle* (*Levin's Mill*, 1964) traces German anti-Semitism back even further to the 1870s with a story of a Jewish mill owner whose business is sabotaged by a German competitor. Jurek Becker's *Jacob der Lügner* (*Jacob the Liar*, 1969), on the other hand, originally written in 1962 as a film script that could not be filmed for fear of upsetting the GDR's Russian allies (in the more plausible of the novel's two endings, the Red Army does not arrive in time to stop the deportation of the inmates), is set in the Lodz ghetto. Becker later moved to West Berlin, where he wrote *Bronsteins Kinder* (*Bronstein's Children*, 1986). In this book, a Jewish boy discovers after the war that his father is keeping his former camp guard in an outhouse, a find that initiates painful conversations between father and son. In Franz Wander's *Der siebente Brunnen* (*The Seventh Well*, 1971), in contrast, the brutality of the camps is made palpable via the stories of a number of individual Jews, orthodox and secular, from different countries and different backgrounds. Wander's book, remarkable for its frankness, was reissued in 2005 and appeared in English translation in 2007.

1990s onwards

That Wander's *Der siebente Brunnen*, quickly forgotten in its time, was republished, in German and English, more than thirty years later tells us much about the focus in recent years on the Holocaust as *trauma*, that is, as a physical and mental wound inflicted on individuals. Just as in Britain, France, the United States, Israel, and elsewhere, therefore, we encounter in the German-speaking countries a wave of memoirs, such as *weiter leben* (*To Continue to Live: A Childhood*, 1992), an account of a childhood endured in Theresienstadt and Auschwitz by Ruth Klüger, who also wrote the after-word to the 2005 edition of Wander's book. These memoirs testify to a contemporary interest in the (intergenerational, crosscultural) transmission of individual *experience* and *memory* and the possibility of *empathy* or even *witnessing* in relation to events of which we have no direct knowledge. And in German literature, as in other literatures, these issues feature in a surge of "family novels." These include Uwe Timm's *Am Beispiel meines Bruders* (*In My Brother's Shadow*, 2003), in which the author juxtaposes his older brother's letters from the Eastern Front with his present-day knowledge of German atrocities, and Ulla Hahn's *Unscharfe Bilder* (*Blurred Images*, 2003), in which the author confronts her father in order to attempt to understand his possible involvement in atrocities. It also includes Arno Geiger's *Es geht uns gut* (*We're Doing Well*, 2005) and Eva Menasse's *Vienna* (2005), the first of which tells of a "perpetrator family," whereas the second explores the author's Jewish roots and the loss of Jewish family members in the Holocaust.

German unification in 1990 is often held to have initiated a "normal-ization" of the German-speaking countries' relationship to their Nazi past. Indeed, the imminent passing of the wartime generation appeared to coincide with a broad acknowledgment that Germans (and Austrians) had come to "own" their history and take responsibility for it. In a changed global context in which other nations were beginning to accept their complicity not only in the Holocaust but also in historical injustices ranging from slavery to (de)colonization, to "ethnic-cleansing," and in which *all* memory (the perpetrators' as much as the victims') is seen as valid, might we not now expect German literature to appear less "burdened"?

Jewish writers have been instrumental in drawing attention to the risk that the acceptance of responsibility might all too easily become fetishized as a self-congratulatory display of "normality," even national identity. In Maxim Biller's *Harlem Holocaust* (1990), the American-Jewish writer Warszawski is adulated by his German readers for his satirical attacks upon their Nazi past that ultimately confirm their tolerance. In Vladmir Vertlib's *Das besondere Gedächtnis der Rosa Masur* (*The Remarkable Memory of Rosa Masur*, 2003), similarly, the extended memoir commissioned by the town of Gingrich from a newly arrived (from the former Soviet Union) "Jewish fellow-citizen," Rosa Masur, is eagerly digested by the cloyingly philo-Semitic town council, not least because it barely mentions the Holocaust but instead offers a titillating tale of another (non-German) dictator, Stalin. More broadly, Biller and Vertlib are two of a highly visible "third generation" (after Auschwitz) of Jewish authors who, from the mid-1980s, have begun to write about the possibility (better: reality) of Jewish life in present-day Germany and Austria.

The contemporary emphasis on (the possibility of) "normality," in respect of non-Jewish Germans, Jews themselves, or their relationship to one another, can be traced in two developments in recent German literature. First, we now see a greater focus on the perpetrator, and particularly on the perpetrator's circumstances, motives, and choices, and on the question of whether to understand is to forgive. Second, we now see a greater emphasis on "affect," that is, on the attempt to create an empathetic connection to the victims via an imaginative reconstruction of their lives.

Alfred Andersch's 1980 story *Der Vater eines Mörders* (*The Father of a Murderer*) had already explored the biography of one prominent perpetrator, Heinrich Himmler, and was followed seven years later by Peter Schneider's fictionalization in *Vati* (*Daddy*, 1987) of an attempt by Josef Mengele's son to understand his father's horrific crimes. A decade later, Turkish-German writer's Zafer Şenocak's *Gefährliche Verwandtschaft* (*Perilous Kinship*, 1998) likewise attempts to understand a perpetrator-figure. Here, however, there is a twist, in that the perpetrator in question is the protagonist's Turkish grandfather, a man who may have been partially responsible for the slaughter of the Armenians in 1915. Via the presence of the protagonist's Jewish mother, the Holocaust and the Armenian massacre are placed in parallel, a mode of comparison between state-sponsored exterminations that had long been controversial, even taboo. (Edgar Hilsenrath, in fact, had intimated a similar parallel in his 1989 novel *Das Märchen vom letzten Gedanken* [*The Story of the Last Thought*].)

Bernhard Schlink's 1995 *Der Vorleser* (*The Reader*, 1995), which was phenomenally successful in English (before it was a success in German, in fact) and was turned into a film by Stephen Daldry in 2008, focuses not on the "big" perpetrators but on (the fictional) Hanna Schmitz, an unexceptional woman who became a concentration guard in Auschwitz. To this extent, it reflects the pronounced interest in recent years in "ordinary" people and the Holocaust. At the same time, Schlink's novel stands out for its very direct — and widely criticized — proposition that it might be possible to *understand* the perpetrator's motives. Thus, the story is told in flashbacks by Hanna's much-younger lover Michael, who offers a defense that might, initially at least, appear plausible and which was not presented at her trial in the early 1960s. This is that Hanna was illiterate and "allowed" herself to be recruited into the SS in order to avoid a promotion at work that would have exposed her. For the novel's critics, the concerns were twofold. First, that a lack of learning might "excuse" the perpetrator (many of the most senior Nazis were highly educated, in any case). Second, that the reader is encouraged not only to understand but also to forgive the perpetrator.

Robert Schindel's *Gebürtig* (*Born-where*, 1992) and Elfriede Jelinek's *Die Kinder der Toten* (*The Children of the Dead*, 1995) offer a distinct contrast with the conventional storytelling mode of *Der Vorleser*. Indeed, both present non-linear narratives in which multiple strands interconnect and diverge. Both novels also thereby reflect on storytelling, Jewish existence after the Holocaust (Schindel is Jewish, Jelinek's father was a Czech Jew), and the inadequacies of German (or, more accurately in these texts, Austrian) "coming-to-terms with the past." In *Gebürtig*, some two dozen figures, mostly Viennese Jews of the second generation, embark on erotic yet always burdened relationships with non-Jews. These relationships occur within framing narratives that feature, for example, the trial of a former guard at the Ebensee concentration camp or the son of the Nazi governor general of Poland, who is haunted by memories of playing as a five-year-old boy in sight of Auschwitz. In *Die Kinder der Toten*, a multitude of zombies, including some who died in the camps but also more recent victims of the systemic racism and sexism that the controversial Nobel Prizewinning author sees as typifying modern-day Austria, disturb, even brutalize the guests at a pension. The "undead" of Austria's Nazi past thus return to dispose of the Alpine Republic's idyllic (self-)delusion. In fact, Schindel's *Gebürtig* and Jelinek's *Die Kinder der Toten* are prime examples of the contemporary focus on the epistemological challenge of the Holocaust – what can we *know*, of ourselves, of our drives and motives, after the "break with civilization" (*Zivilisationsbruch*) that was Auschwitz? – in which the undermining of narrative authority and a proliferation of competing perspectives destabilize all certainties, whether historical, moral, or ethical.

Better known outside the German-speaking world, however, are two books by W. G. Sebald: *Die Ausgewanderten* (*The Emigrants*, 1992), in which three of the four stories feature Jews confronting the disruptions of modernity culminating in the Holocaust, including the painter Max Aurach (the real-life artist Frank Auerbach) who fled to England in 1939; and his final work *Austerlitz* (2001). The novel *Austerlitz* in particular tests the limits of any *affective* reconstruction of a Jewish biography by a German writer. That is, it questions whether it is possible, or even ethical, to piece back together a life shattered by the Holocaust via an empathetic re-imagining of its former wholeness. The frequent intrusion of documentary – including a sixteen-page quotation from Adler's *Theresienstadt* – thus establishes a contrast between the numbing overload of available facts about the Holocaust as a *system* for disposing of "unwanted" Jews, and the heartbreaking inadequacy of what we can reassemble of the fates of the *individuals* whose lives were destroyed. (In the wake of *Austerlitz*, Adler's own Holocaust novel, *Die Reise* [*The Journey*, 1962], a complex work of literary modernism shot through with a similar sense of dislocation, was belatedly translated.) Sebald's German narrator sets out to reconstruct the life of Jacques Austerlitz, a Jewish émigré who as an adult had been driven by unsettling flashbacks to endeavor, in vain, to establish a "full" account of his childhood in Prague before he had been taken to England on a *Kindertransport* (shiploads of European Jewish children sent to and taken in by Britain in the months preceding the outbreak of World War II). However, the narrator's reconstruction of Austerlitz's reconstruction is necessarily deficient. His desire to close the distance between the German descendant of the perpetrators and Austerlitz, the Jewish survivor, is always frustrated by his awareness that his empathy, even identification, with his Jewish subject will always be ethically burdened by the quite different nature of each man's relationship to the Holocaust.

German-language Holocaust literature provokes many of the same questions that apply to Holocaust literature in other languages. Is it permissible to attempt to represent the unrepresentable, that is, the true horror of the camps? Does such an attempt not already trivialize the suffering of those who were there, by turning it into something that is to be consumed by readers? Is it not the case that any fictionalization of the Holocaust necessarily turns it into an object of our aesthetic pleasure, or makes it appear less bad than it actually was (because it would be impossible to describe the real extent of the suffering)? At the same time, however, there are specific issues that apply only to literature written in the language of the perpetrators. Who is writing, victim or perpetrator, or the descendants of either victims of perpetrators? What does it mean to write in German in any case, especially for Jewish victims, but also for the descendants of the perpetrators? And to what extent is it possible, or even desirable, for the descendants of perpetrators to write the stories of the victims, or to identify with their suffering? Finally, in what ways has the peculiar historical context in which German-language Holocaust literature has been written – particularly Germany's division into two competing countries, each with its own ideological perspective on the Nazi past – shaped not only its aesthetic strategies but also its presentation of issues of victimhood and perpetration?

Notwithstanding the particular complexities of writing about the Holocaust in German, there nonetheless exists an abundance of reportage, documentary work, and fiction by German-language authors that addresses, whether directly or indirectly, its horror and lasting impact. From even before the death camps were operational, these writers depicted the rise of anti-Semitism in Germany, and its institutionalization, and the flight of Jewish refugees. Later, they wrote about the utter inhumanity of conditions in the camps – Adler's *Theresienstadt* is unsurpassed – and began, even in the immediate aftermath of mass murder, to produce the first attempts to engage in fiction with the horrors and dilemmas of Nazi brutality and the struggle for survival. For many decades, two German-language Holocaust literatures existed in parallel: that written by Jewish survivors, detailing their awful experience of persecution, and that written by the descendants of the perpetrators, which attempted to address questions of historical and national responsibility for the crime. More recently, as the generations most directly affected fade away, and as the Holocaust begins to take on a universal significance beyond German or even Jewish history, these two strands are less distinct. Today, an emphasis on "ordinary" people, whether Jews or not, whether victims or perpetrators, has begun to emerge, not only in German-language Holocaust literature but also in literature written in other languages. "What would you have done?"[11] – the question posed by Hanna in Schlink's *Der Vorleser* – challenges each of us, regardless of nationality and ethnicity, to consider our own conscience, our own courage, and our own values. The question may be unfair, or even suspect (it might imply that perpetrators had no other choice), but it is one that – in an age in which racism, ethnic cleansing, and mass killings are once again all too common – is hard to ignore.

Notes

1. Paul Celan, *Poems of Paul Celan*, trans. Michael Hamburger (New York: Persea Books, 1988), p. 60.
2. Theodor W. Adorno, *Prisms* (Cambridge, MA: MIT Press, 1983), p. 34.
3. Nelly Sachs, *O the Chimneys: Selected Poems*, trans. Michael Hamburger, Ruth and Matthew Mead, and Michael Roloff (New York: Farrar, Straus and Giroux, 1967), p. 7.
4. Victor Klemperer, *Tagebücher 1933–1945*, ed. Walter Nowojski with Hadwig Klemperer, vol. 1 (Berlin: Aufbau Verlag, 1995), p. 210.
5. Stella Rotenberg, *SHARDS*, trans. Donal McLaughlin and Stephen Richardson (Edinburgh Review, 2003), p. 10.
6. See Stephan Braese, *Die andere Erinnerung – Jüdische Autoren in der westdeutschen Nachkriegsliteratur* (Berlin: PHILO, 2001).

7. Celan, *Poems*, trans. Michael Hamburger, p. 60.

8. Gertrud Kolmar, "Dark Soliloquy," trans. Henry Smith: http://voicesinwar time.org/content/gertrude-kolmar-german, accessed December 5, 2012.

9. Rose Ausländer, "Phönix," in Klaus Hammer, "Die 'schwarze Sappho unserer östlichen Landschaft.' Heute jährt sich zum hundertsten Male der Geburtstag der deutsch-jüdischen Lyrikerin Rose Ausländer," *Allgemeine deutsche Zeitung für Rumänien [Kultur]* (11.05.01), p. 5.

10. Peter Weiss, *The Investigation*, trans. Alexander Gross (London and New York: Marion Boyars, 2010), p. 169.

11. Bernhard Schlink, *The Reader*, trans. Carol Brown Janeway (London: Random House, 1997), p. 110.

CHAPTER 5

Hebrew literature of the Holocaust

Sheila E. Jelen

Introduction

Hebrew literary responses to the Holocaust are frequently characterized by a complex engagement with the Hebrew language itself. The liturgical and scholarly language of the Jews, Hebrew was transformed in the modern era into the lingua franca of the State of Israel. In light of the fact that the literature under investigation documents responses to the destruction of a population that often lived between Hebrew and Yiddish, with Hebrew being the language of prayer and sacred study and Yiddish being the vernacular tongue, the separation of Hebrew responses to the Holocaust from Yiddish ones is a product of the reinvention of Hebrew, since the inception of Modern Zionism, as a Jewish secular language existing independent of its Yiddish peer. This chapter will focus on literary responses to the Holocaust in Israeli Hebrew-language literature. I will also have an eye toward assessing the cost of excising Yiddish, both as a language and as a symbol of Jewish life in the Diaspora. Hebrew Holocaust literature has been produced in non-Israeli contexts as well, most notably in the American Hebrew poetry of Avigdor ha-Meiri, Reuven Wallenrod, Israel Efros, and Gabriel Preil, among others. This chapter, however, will trace Hebrew responses to the Holocaust, primarily in Palestine and Israel, from 1945 to the present.

Our survey begins with discussion of a "bridge generation" – mostly multilingual, Eastern European-born writers who immigrated to Palestine before the war and chose not to write explicitly about the Holocaust in its aftermath, but alluded to it obliquely and subtly in their Hebrew works. This is followed by an exploration of "the seventh million" or trends in Israeli literary responses to the Holocaust, beginning with an interrogation of the theme of collaboration and resistance in Israeli drama and continuing with the poetry and fiction of Holocaust survivors who made their careers in Israel and their literary reputations in Hebrew. We conclude with a discussion of the work of the second and third generations – the population that inherited the trauma of their forebears, both individually and collectively, and who wrote in Hebrew after the war because that was their native tongue and they no longer lived in a multilingual, or diglossic Jewish diaspora environment.

The bridge generation

Those writers who left Eastern Europe before World War I, or during the interwar period, had the good fortune of avoiding the war which swept their communities and families of origin off the map between 1939 and 1945. At the same time, their misfortune was felt in the pain of their losses, and in their guilt over having, in many cases, quite deliberately turned their backs on the homes which they viewed, in their youth, as backwaters. Among the poets whose careers began before the Holocaust, and who wrote about the war in selected poems, were Yaakov Fichman (1881–1958), David Shimoni (1891–1956), Yaakov Shteinberg (1887–1947), and Avraham Shlonski (1900–1973).

Notable in his having authored a sustained epic on the Holocaust in Hebrew in the years immediately following the war was Uri Tzvi Greenberg (1894–1980). A Yiddish and Hebrew modernist poet, Greenberg escaped to Palestine two weeks after the Nazis marched into Warsaw. He had been living in Palestine since 1923 but had returned to Europe in the 1930s to work for the Jewish press. His entire family perished during the war, and he stopped writing during those years. Throughout the late 1940s, however, he struggled with the immensity of his loss in a poetry which frequently figured the poetic "I" as the prodigal son. His most notable expression of the struggle with his own sense of guilt can be found in his *Rehovot ha-Nahar* (*Streets of the River*, 1950), a collection of poems written in a wide range of styles.[1] In this collection, Greenberg grapples with the Holocaust on both a personal and a national level, considering his own pivotal role as a first-generation Israeli hammering out a new sovereign state not after, but in the course of, the destruction of his family and community of origin. Greenberg's intensely emotional rhetoric, his wide range of styles, all point to his grappling with the personal sacrifices he made, knowingly or unknowingly:

> Yes I saved this body of mine when I fled the house of
> Father and mother . . .
> But I did not save my soul . . .

A soul faint and rank and embittered by tears,
Plucked of its feathered glory, its wings cropped.[2]

Two critical writers of the Modern Hebrew Renaissance who, in their early
twenties, left their families in order to settle in Palestine during the early
decades of the twentieth century found themselves in the unique position,
after the Holocaust, of literary spokespeople not of the experience of the
Holocaust, but of the Eastern European Jewish world that had been
destroyed. Dvora Baron (1887–1956) and S. Y. Agnon (1888–1970) each
earned a reputation in the first half of the twentieth century as Hebrew
writers living in Palestine, and subsequently, in the newly established state,
who wrote consistently, and against the general literary grain of their milieu,
about the Eastern European world they had left behind. Their depictions
were not sentimental. Nor were they tinged by any sense of the impending
or immediate past destruction of the worlds they depicted. Rather, the sense
of the Holocaust in their fiction is largely a function of their reception in the
post-Holocaust period. Neither Agnon nor Baron explicitly discuss the
Holocaust in their work, but their later stories, their post-Holocaust stories,
represent, to a large extent, a greater affective relationship and a broader, less
ideological, and more ethnographically charged panorama of engagement
with their native towns. Baron's contribution to the idea of a literature of
the Holocaust in Hebrew, which does not directly address the Holocaust, is
in her loving depiction of the world of Eastern European Jewish society "in
its transition from an object of social critique and scrutiny to a mythical
construct."[3] As Baron's later works become more leisurely in pace, more
panoramic in scope, and more philosophically charged in their engagement
with issues of representation, she acknowledges, obliquely, the role of the
writer as a vehicle of memory.

   Much critical discussion has focused on the seemingly surprising fact that
Agnon, the quintessential modern Hebrew writer of Eastern European
Jewish experience, never explicitly responded to the Holocaust in his
fiction.[4] Like Baron, however, it is through his lyrical depictions of his
shtetl of origin, Buczacz, figured in his fiction as Szibusz, and in the subtle
changes that he imposes on his stylization of his *shtetl* stories in the post-
Holocaust period, that his engagement with the Holocaust becomes
apparent. Just as Baron's fiction becomes far more ethnographically self-
conscious in the post-Holocaust period, so too does Agnon's positioning of
his narrator as "chief chronicler" and "primary witness" of his hometown in
his prewar *A Guest for the Night* (1938–1939) become more fully developed
and beautifully articulated in later works on his hometown during the

post-Holocaust period.[5] Agnon's posthumous *Ir Umeloah* (1973), a fiction-alized mythic history of Buczacz, serves as another manifestation of Agnon's subtle engagement with the Holocaust, not through any explicit reflection on it, but through his sharpening of a poetics of witnessing and chronicling, established in his fiction in the pre-Holocaust period and foregrounded in later works.[6]

The important Hebrew European-born modernist Leah Goldberg (1911–1970) famously resisted assuming any obligation to represent the Holocaust in her poetry or other literary work. In the immediate postwar years, she published a statement refusing any attempt to use literary expression as a venue for discussing the ravages of the war.[7] Even so, Goldberg does in fact write several important literary works on the Holocaust, the first being a poem "For the Four Sons" (1950), in which she casts "the Wise Son" of the Passover Haggadah in the role of a victim of the Holocaust. She also authored a play, "Lady of the Castle" (1955), in which she depicts a young woman who is still in hiding in a Polish castle years after the end of the war, because her savior, a Polish nobleman, has imprisoned her, purportedly out of love for her and the need to keep her with him. The young woman is liberated by an Israeli social worker and a librarian who are in Europe scouting out surviving children (and books) a few years after the end of the war. "Lady of the Castle" presents Israel's youth as a needed antidote to the fustiness and sinister overtones of the world of European nobility and wealth.[8]

The seventh million

Contemporary Israeli society has been forged in the psychic crucible of the Holocaust, or the *Shoah*. This is due, in large part, to the presence of about seventy thousand survivor immigrants who made Israel their home in the late 1940s and early 1950s, and also to the widespread perception, in Israel and beyond, of a causal link between rising international awareness of the plight of the Jews of Europe during World War II and the political birth of the State of Israel in 1948. In the 1994 film *Don't Touch My Holocaust*, there is one scene which depicts Tel Aviv apartment blocks in the 1950s as a series of concentration camp barracks in which every family harbors its own nightmares and secrets, its own post-traumatic manifestations. These images, of the Israeli population as "the seventh million" and of the city of Tel Aviv as an improvised madhouse, will both serve as starting points for this discussion of Israeli Holocaust literature. The relationship between nation-building and individual trauma, between an ideology of power and the repudiation of victimhood have all contributed to the Israeli Holocaust literary canon.

During the first years after the establishment of the State of Israel, "the Holocaust seemed to offer, more than any other event in Jewish history, proof of the central Zionist thesis, according to which Jewish history in the Diaspora was apocalyptic and the survivors of the Holocaust were victims of their own political shortsightedness."[9] The Israeli government elected to call Holocaust Remembrance Day, established in 1952, "Yom ha-Zikaron la-Shoah vela-Gevurah" (Day of Remembrance for Holocaust and Heroism). The original date chosen for this remembrance holiday was the 14th of Nisan in the Jewish calendar, the first day of the Warsaw Ghetto Uprising, in keeping with the Israeli valorization of the ghetto fighters. Ultimately, this date was rejected because of its proximity to Passover (which falls the next day, the 15th of Nisan). Notable, however, was the way in which the selection of the 14th of Nisan as the preferred date for national Holocaust remembrance reflects the fact that during those early years of the state, survivors were largely viewed, in public discourse, either as heroes or collaborators, with very little nuancing of those two extremes. Hanna Yablonka explains that, "Israel was going through a political and military trial during this period, fighting for its survival, and it was not sufficiently mature to absorb successfully any myth other than that of heroism in the face of the enemy."[10]

During the 1950s, two public debates surrounding the Holocaust raged in Israel. The first was the enactment of the "Law for the Punishment of Nazis and Their Collaborators." The second was the debate over the acceptance of reparations from Germany. The "Law For the Punishment of Nazis and Their Collaborators" was largely geared toward Jews viewed as "collaborators." Because the law was not internationally recognized, Nazis could not be legally extradited to Israel in order to be punished. Thus, there were several instances of survivors being publically tried as stand-ins for the Nazis whom the Israelis could not prosecute. Yablonka points out that, "complaints and accusation were lodged daily – from survivors against other survivors – claiming that they had served in the Jewish police, in the Judenrat, or as kapos, in the concentration camps during the war."[11] Needless to say, this environment did not serve survivors well, because they were viewed as automatically suspect if they did not qualify as "heroes" in the strictest sense of the term.

Several plays produced in Israel from the 1950s through the 1980s embody the dialectic between heroism and collaboration that characterized Israeli discourse on the Holocaust during those years. The first, *Hannah*

Senesh (1958) by Aharon Megged, tells the heroic story of a young Hungarian woman, Hannah Senesh, who emigrated to Palestine before the Holocaust and parachuted back into Europe for the British army, purportedly to rescue Hungarian Jews and bring them back to Palestine. She was caught, tortured, and summarily executed, but her story became, alongside the stories of ghetto uprisings, one of the key tropes of heroism in the fledgling state. Ben Zion Tomer, in *Children of the Shadows* (1962), tells of a young man, Yoram (Yossele), transplanted from Europe just before the war, who is integrated into Israeli society, while the rest of his family gets caught in Europe during the Holocaust. Miraculously, most of Yoram's family members survive, with the exception of his sister, Esther, and they arrive en masse in Israel just after Yoram's marriage to Nurit, a native Israeli. Yoram's brother-in-law Sigmund (his late sister Esther's husband) materializes separately as a homeless street bard in Tel Aviv, and is identified by Yoram and his newly arrived brother. Sigmund is somehow implicated in his wife's death, as well as in the deaths, apparently, of many others. Described as an "erstwhile doctor of philosophy, authority on Renaissance art, fervid believer in humanism," the nature of Sigmund's crime is unclear, although he presumably collaborated with the Nazis in some way.[12] Yoram, as a result, must decide whether to alert Israeli authorities about Sigmund's presence in the country. The assumption that Sigmund is essentially guilty provides a sense of the dominant thematic in survivor communities of the period; one was considered guilty, it seems, until he or she could be proven innocent.

Natan Shaham's *Heshbon Hadash* (A new reckoning) (1954) similarly betrays a preoccupation with "collaborators," sketching a complex portrait of Rezso Kastner, an important member of the Hungarian Jewish community and a leader of the Budapest Judenrat. Written during the Kastner trial in Israel, Shaham explores the moral complexities of declaring Jewish collaborators "guilty."[13] Motti Lerner's *Kastner* (1985) treats the same character, depicting how Kastner negotiates with the Germans, in order to forestall the mass deportation of the Jews of Hungary, which would ultimately lead to the death of nearly a half a million Hungarian Jews in a matter of months. While engaging in negotiations and incurring enormous debts, he unwittingly bankrolls the mass deportation of Hungarian Jewry to the death camps. Although he is reassured that the Jews will be kept alive until his negotiations are completed, they are in fact gassed upon arrival at Auschwitz. Portraying the protagonist as dangerously naïve but unmistakably human, *Kastner* challenges fixed notions of collaboration and heroism. By the play's end, he is to be pitied rather than denigrated.

Alongside a fascination with "collaboration," the theme of resistance plays a large role in Israeli drama of the Holocaust, most notably in Joshua Sobol's internationally recognized triptych: *Ghetto* (1984), *Adam* (1989), and *Underground* (1991). Of *Ghetto*, which traces a series of events in the Vilna ghetto as documented in the diary of Hermann Kruk, the former director of the Grosser Library of Warsaw from June 1941 until July 1943, Sobol says,

> What I tried to show in *Ghetto* was that the Jews in Vilna tried to resist the Nazis, not by using force against them but by resisting spiritually and morally, by trying to survive not only as living creatures but mainly as human creatures ... For years this was not mentioned here in Israel. The consensus was that most of the people went as sheep to the slaughter whilst there was a minority of heroes who stood up and resisted the Nazis, gun in hand.[14]

While Sobol presents an alternative to the notion of armed resistance in his plays, he is still committed to the idea of resistance as a form of spiritual and emotional resilience.

The valorization of resistance and vilification of collaboration that was evident in Israel throughout the early years of the state were called into question long before Lerner or Sobol wrote their qualifications and critiques of these tendencies in the 1980s. The years of the Eichmann trial, 1961–1962, marked a turning point in popular Israeli conceptions of survivors and, by most accounts, the beginning of a watershed of literary expression on the Holocaust.[15] An important member of the Nazi party and one of the engineers of the Holocaust, Adolf Eichmann was captured in Argentina in 1960 by Mossad agents and put on trial in Israel. Hannah Arendt was famously (or infamously) critical of this trial, arguing that it was, in essence, staged to further the Zionist ideology which posited that Jewish suffering could be avenged only through active demonstration of Jewish military prowess and political power. Hanna Yablonka expresses a more positive outlook on the trial: "Two of the remarkable effects of the Eichmann trial were to change perceptions of the Holocaust as a national catastrophe into personalized stories of individuals with faces and names and to give a crucial momentum to Holocaust research."[16]

During the Eichmann trial, Israeli survivors stood up in public for the first time and testified about their experiences, most notably Yehiel Dinur (Yehiel Feiner 1909–2001), a Polish survivor who had been writing novels since the end of the war under the name Ka-Tzetnik. Ka-Tzetnik is derived from the German acronym for concentration camp (*Konzentrationslager*) and was a commonly used term among the inmates. On the stand, Ka-Tzetnik identified himself for the first time, and in describing his experiences, he fainted, creating national sympathy and an outpouring of public grief. Dinur's fainting on the stand marked a transition in Israeli consciousness of the Holocaust, particularly from a literary perspective. In pre-1967 Israel two types of Holocaust literature were primarily in circulation. The first was a pedagogical literature of heroism and resistance, used in the schools. The second was a pornographic literature called "Stalags," replete with Holocaust-themed perverse sex and sadism. "Throughout his oeuvre Ka-Tzetnik may be said to maintain an ambivalent position between these two categories."[17] Ka-Tzetnik's writing is best known for presenting the point of view of the Muselmann, the drowned, the victim in the course of his or her victimization, and for being unafraid to render, in language, depths of violence and perversity. When asked by the judge in the Eichmann trial why he used the pen name Ka-Tzetnik, he replied,

> This is not a pen name. I do not see myself as an author who writes literature. This is a chronicle from the planet of Auschwitz, whose inhabitants had no names ... they were neither born nor bore any children; they were neither alive nor dead. They breathed according to different laws of nature. They were called Ka-Tzetnik. They were skeletons with numbers.[18]

Central to Ka-Tzetnik's oeuvre is the sextet, *Salamandra: A Chronicle of a Jewish Family in the Twentieth Century*, written between the late 1940s and the late 1980s. Because of the explicit and psychologically disturbing nature of much of these works, and despite their wide translation, Ka-Tzetnik is not well known outside of Israel.

An important group of writers, primarily known in Israeli literary historiography as members of the "Palmah generation" (writers who were born in Israel or were brought to Israel as very young children and came of age during the War of Independence in 1948), wrote novels about the Holocaust during the 1960s, in the aftermath of the Eichmann trial. These writers include Haim Gouri (b. 1923), Yoram Kaniuk (1930–2013), and Hanokh Bartov (b. 1926).[19] Haim Gouri, most notably, wrote a daily report during the Eichmann trial on the proceedings for the Hebrew newspaper *Lamerhav*. His columns were later collected in *The Glass Booth* (1962, English 2004). This was followed by a novel called *The Chocolate Deal* (1965) in which two survivors come together after the war in the European landscape to cope with their losses, one seeking out material success through shady business negotiations and the second struggling to make sense, existentially, of his experiences. Gouri's sustained engagement with the Holocaust is remarkable because in his other fictional and journalistic work, he is known to be an icon of the Palmah generation, "with their secular humanist values, their indictment of the Diaspora, and their vision of Israel as a radical departure from Jewish history."[20] Gouri's engagement with the Holocaust in several genres at once, therefore, reflected the intense need in Israel in the 1960s, created in large part by the Eichmann trial, to confront Jewish life in the Diaspora.

Unlike Yehiel Dinur, Aharon Appelfeld (b. 1932) is well known not only in Israel but around the world for his suggestive fiction about Holocaust survivors. And unlike the writers of the Palmah generation, his work has been characterized as being "of" the Holocaust and not simply, selectively, "about" it. Indeed, Appelfeld has been charged with having taken the Holocaust as his "whole literary vocation."[21] In his work, Appelfeld rarely touches on the subject of the Holocaust directly. Rather, he depicts the survivor's psychological scars and delicate social and familial networks. Born in Czernowitz Bukovina, he was deported as a child of eight to a Ukranian concentration camp with his father. He escaped and joined the Russian army as a cook for several years before immigrating to Palestine in 1946 and being reunited with his father there. Part of Appelfeld's mythology in Israel revolves around his relatively late introduction to the Hebrew language, and his explicit desire to write in that language because of what he considers its unusual brevity, as based on biblical and rabbinic diction and lexicon. Indeed, his poetic is a poetics of brevity in which allusion plays a greater role than does exposition, and the Holocaust, in most cases, is insinuated instead of visualized or spelled out. His most internationally recognized work is *Badenheim Ir Nofesh* (*Badenheim 1939*) (1979, English 1980), an allegory of European Jewry's impassive acceptance of its own progressive incarceration and extermination.[22] In *Badenheim 1939* the middle-class Jewish resort vacationers willingly embark on a cattle-car journey at the end of a long process of ghettoization and dehumanization, even as they find ways to justify and embrace their destiny without any instinct what-soever toward resistance. Appelfeld's novel has been harshly criticized for espousing the rhetoric and ideology of the Zionist "negation of Diaspora," in which the Holocaust was viewed as the inevitable result of de-territorialization, materialism, and historical short-sightedness. Appelfeld's approach has been characterized as "backshadowing," or expecting the Jews in his fiction to have the same gift of hindsight that Jews in the post-Holocaust period have.[23]

Despite criticism levied against his best-known novel, as opposed to simply being a mouthpiece for post-Holocaust Israeli ideologues who espoused the negation of the Diaspora and the valorization of resistance at the expense of any careful consideration of the moral and emotional stakes of survival, Appelfeld has publically voiced his ambivalence about his experience as a young survivor in Palestine in the immediate postwar years:

> From the moment I arrived in Israel, I hated the people who forced me to speak Hebrew, and with the death of my mother tongue, my hostility toward them only increased. This hostility did not, of course, change the situation, but it did clarify it. Quite obviously, I was neither here nor there. What had been mine – my parents, my home, and my mother tongue – was now lost to me forever, and this language, which promised to be my mother tongue, was nothing more than a stepmother.[24]

Appelfeld has been called Israeli literature's "insider/outsider" in that most treatments of his work do not acknowledge his contribution to a modern Hebrew literary tradition stylistically or thematically.[25] Rather, his work is most frequently read as a literature of the Holocaust written in dialogue with European literary models. Appelfeld himself resists the notion that he is strictly a writer of the Holocaust and considers himself a writer of modern Jewish experience in which the Holocaust figures prominently as an oblique rupture in the lives of communities and individuals, but not as the sum total of their experience. Appelfeld is best known for writing around the Holocaust, for locating the traumatic events of the Holocaust elsewhere, but allowing them to permeate the drama of the unfolding narrative in unmistakable ways. In *The Immortal Bartfuss*, for example, we read of a man who is, in the same breath, "immortal" and mired in the mundane:

> Bartfuss is immortal. In the Second World War he was in one of the smaller of those notorious camps. Now he's fifty, married to a woman he used to call Rosa, with two daughters, one married, He has a ground-floor apartment, not very large, with two trees growing at the entrance. Every day he rises at the same time, a quarter to five. At that hour he still manages to take in the half-light of the morning, the fog, and the quiet before everyone gets up . . . He drinks a cup of coffee and lights a cigarette right away.[26]

This is a portrait of a man trapped in a sense of his own immortality in relation to the profound mortality of all those who died all around him during the war. And this sense of his super-human properties translates itself into a psychological unwillingness to inhabit the domestic spaces he has so carefully crafted in the years after the war. As in much of Appelfeld's work, the Holocaust punctuates the psychological reality of his protagonists, even if it does not play a significant dramatic part in the unfolding story.

Appelfeld's oeuvre can be divided into three main periods, ranging from the publication of his first collection of short stories in 1962 to his most recent work, published in English in 2011.[27] The first period was dominated by surrealistic short fiction, the second is the period in which he made his reputation through the publication of books such as *Badenheim 1939* (1979) and the *Age of Wonders* (1978), novels in which realism is tempered by a kind of scattered consciousness and a sense of psychological disjuncture among his protagonists. Finally, during the third period, Appelfeld began depicting the actual event of the Holocaust more explicitly, and a sense of continuity between his literary and autobiographical universe began to emerge.

Dan Pagis (1930–1986), like Aharon Appelfeld, survived the war as a child. He emigrated to Palestine in 1946 to be reunited with his father who had gone to Palestine in 1934, when his son was only four years old. Unlike Appelfeld who managed to escape the camps, Pagis was incarcerated for three years in Transistria. Closely mentored by Leah Goldberg, Pagis began his poetic career as a kibbutz schoolteacher but soon distinguished himself as the leading scholar of Medieval Hebrew poetry and became one of Israel's most celebrated poets.[28] Pagis's poetry, unlike Appelfeld's prose, does not display any conventional Zionist sentiments. His greatest strength as a poet of the Holocaust lies in his absolute rejection of the possibility of resolution. The Holocaust, to him, is an open wound that resists closure or redemption. His concise trademark poem, "Written in a Sealed Railway Car," invoking the voice of the biblical Eve as she and her son Abel are transported to their death, concludes:

> if you see my other son
> cain son of man
> tell him that i

The open-ended nature of Eve's fundamental faith in her family and the naïveté with which she fails to recognize her sons' animosity yield a stark indictment of humanity. Pagis's poem has served for many years and in many classrooms as what has been called "a textual touchstone" for discussions of Hebrew poetry on the Holocaust.[29] This poem is one of a series of poems by Pagis published in the wake of the Eichmann trial of 1961–1962 that uses the first human family's strife as a parable of the Holocaust. Pagis's work, like that of Appelfeld, has been identified as possessing a "submerged freight of horror." However, because the latter's medium is poetry, this sense of the submerged is even more abstract.[30] Pagis frequently utilizes biblical figures and liturgical allusions as well as collective and unnamed voices in order to call upon the familiar repertoire of Holocaust images. At the end of a poem entitled "Testimony," in an allusion to the thirteen attributes of faith written by Moses Maimonides which states that God "has no body nor the image of a body," Pagis writes:

> And he in his mercy left nothing of me that would die.
> And I fled to him, floated up weightless, blue,
> Forgiving – I would even say: apologizing –
> Smoke to omnipotent smoke
> That has no face or image.[31]

As in Paul Celan's renowned "Todesfuge" ("Deathfugue"), the image of the victims' bodies turned to smoke in the crematoria is immediately recognizable as not only a trope of the Holocaust, but as a trope of the struggle for poetic form and formal beauty in a world filled with the stench of singed human flesh.

In sharp contrast to Pagis's minimalistic, existentially oriented engagement with the Holocaust, Abba Kovner's (1918–1987) work is highly ideologically and politically marked. A founder and leader of the Vilna ghetto underground and, subsequent to the ghetto's liquidation, a commander of a Jewish partisan unit within the Soviet partisan organization, the Ukrainian-born Hebrew poet also fought in Givati, an elite unit in the Israeli army during Israel's War of Independence. The two events – the Holocaust and the establishment of the State of Israel – work in tandem in his poetry, creating a forceful, prophetic rhetoric. It was Kovner who popularized the phrase "like sheep to the slaughter" to describe the experience of Eastern European Jewry in the Holocaust, employing it in a 1942 manifesto and call to arms which galvanized the Vilna ghetto:[32]

Jewish youth, do not be led astray. Of the 80,000 Jews of the "Jerusalem of Lithuania" [Vilna], only 20,000 have remained. Before our eyes, they tore from us our parents, our brothers and sisters . . .
All the roads of the Gestapo lead to Ponary.
And Ponary is death!
Doubters! Cast off all illusions. Your children, your husbands and your wives are no longer alive . . .
Hitler aims to destroy all of the Jews of Europe. The Jews of Lithuania are fated to be the first in line.
Let us not go like sheep to the slaughter!
It is true that we are weak and defenseless, but resistance is the only reply to the enemy!
Brothers! It is better to fall as free fighters than to live by the grace of the murderers.
Resist! To the last breath.[33]

Best known for his presence in Israel as a public figure, he spent the years after the war testifying about his experiences and grappling with the difficult task of enjoining others to remember the Holocaust. Kovner did not view his poetry as a representation of history. In fact, he explicitly acknowledged that historical reality eluded him, being, as he was, in the thick of the horrors: "I am not sure if I have a conception . . . a clear idea about what happened during that period. If I had . . . I would have written the history of those times or described my experiences then."[34] Kovner was instrumental in founding a museum dedicated to Mordechai Anielewicz, the leader of the Warsaw ghetto, at Kibbutz Yad Mordechai in the Negev, as well as the Diaspora Museum at the University of Tel Aviv. His "Scrolls of Fire," modeled after the Hebrew national poet Chaim Nachman Bialik's poem of the same name, attempts to tell of the suffering of the Jewish people through the story of a "child with sad eyes" who saw the high priest throw a key from the top of the burning temple. Only the child saw the "shining key fall from the sky and sink under the waters of the lake behind the shtetl." Kovner, presumably figured in this poem as "the sad-eyed child" whose witnessing of the destruction of the temple bestowed upon him knowledge of the key to Jewish history, considered his poetry autobiographical and never left any explicitly autobiographical prose. While a controversial figure in Israel in the last few decades because of his role as a mastermind and exemplar of the ideology of the valorization of resistance, his life and poetry were dedicated to creating a sense of the continuities of Jewish history for better or for worse, in Diaspora and in the land of Israel:[35]

> The murdered Jewish people
> Whether silently or aloud, speaks to the living Jewish people thus:
>
> "You who could not help us, listen with your ears and hearts to our
> Testimony, the last vestige of life;
> Try to understand what it means to cease to exist, and
> What things strengthened our spirits at moments of parting . . ."[36]

The second generation

Several Israeli writers are notable for continuing the work of the "bridge generation," those writers, mentioned earlier, who were established European-born Hebrew writers before the Holocaust, emigrated to Palestine in the pre-Holocaust period, and continued their literary work in the post-Holocaust period with only oblique, if any, reference to the Holocaust. These "bridge" writers' reaction to the Holocaust, as argued above, was to acknowledge it through a deepening of their engagement with the landscape left behind, to adopt a more ethnographic stance vis-à-vis their

European subject matter, without ever addressing its destruction explicitly. A younger generation of writers, who escaped the fate of European Jewry as children and established themselves in Israeli letters several decades after the war, grapples far more explicitly with the presence of war in the worlds they left behind. Their near-escape from the ravages of the war, and their sense of having lived, in effect, a parallel life "over there" finds expression in their imagining themselves back in the landscape of their childhood, experiencing the war, as if they had not escaped in time. Yehudah Amichai's novel *Not of This Time, Not of This Place* (1963) and Shulamit Hareven's short story "Twilight" (1980) both imagine their protagonists simultaneously in Israel and in Europe.[37] Born in 1924 in Germany, Amichai's family emigrated to Palestine in 1935. Hareven, born in 1931 in Poland, emigrated in 1940. In their respective stories, they shift continuously back and forth in time between their lives as they could have been and their lives as they were, between the people they knew as children and those they could have known as adults had immigration and war not intervened. Each author poses the question of where subjectivity is more "real" – in their Israeli adopted homeland, or in the world that gave them birth?[38] The opening passage of "Twilight" reflects on the possibility of living in two places simultaneously, and on the vehicle, through language, of return to lost worlds:

> Last night I spent a year in the city where I was born. I had long known the password for getting there: Dante's line. "I am the way to the city of sorrow." In a clear voice I said: *"Per me si va nella città dolente,"* and time split open and I was there.[39]

In the case of this generation of writers who could have been killed in the Holocaust had their families not immigrated to Palestine when they were young children, the sense of belonging in two worlds simultaneously – a world which could have been theirs had they not left it behind, and had it not been subsequently destroyed, and the world of the modern State of Israel – serves as something of a psychic and narrative rupture. The literary effect of juxtaposing and weaving the two worlds together is distinctly postmodern, in contrast to the allusions to the world of Eastern Europe in the work of Dvora Baron and S. Y. Agnon, which were largely rendered in a realist or modernist retrospective vein.

Beginning in the late 1970s, children of Israeli survivors began to struggle, across the aesthetic spectrum, with the silence imposed on survivors who did not fit, as described above, into the categories of hero or collaborator, those who were not worthy either of valorization or of vilification. In film, the visual arts, as well as in music and literature, children of survivors began building new bridges to their parents, as well as to their own, unspoken pasts. By the mid-1990s Israeli reactions to the Holocaust had been "transformed" into a national obsession, with artists from all walks of life working to reverse the repression of Holocaust memory. Children of survivors Savyon Liebricht and Nava Semel are among the better-known authors of their generation, not only telling the story of survivors and the "intergenerational transmission" of their stories to their children, but also differentiating, in significant ways, between male and female survivor experiences, acknowledging the sexual traumas endured, and transmitted, from grandmother to mother, from mother to daughter. This aspect of the Holocaust has rarely been told, and particularly in Israel, as earlier discussed, it surfaced only as a form of underground pornography for years after the war.

A contemporary Hebrew poetry on the Holocaust has been populated by writers such as Ronny Someck, Rivka Miriam, and Leah Aini writing about the experience of living in the "second generation."[40] Dorit Peleg, Itamar Levi, and Yaakov Buchan have also, recently, written novels representing the experiences of children of survivors in a magical realist style, inspired, in part, by David Grossman's monumental novel of the second generation, *See Under: Love* (1986). Although David Grossman is not a child of survivors, his novel set the stage for a national discussion of the trauma of the second generation, as an experience not simply of individuals, but of a whole culture. At the heart of *See Under: Love* is a writer of the Modern Hebrew Renaissance, Anshel Wasserman, who acts as a Jewish Scheherazade, telling installments of a sensational Hebrew children's tale night after night to the commandant of a mythical concentration camp in the hope that he will be rewarded for his efforts with death. He desires death because his wife and child were killed upon arrival at the camp, and because he longs to share their destiny, as well as the destiny of his co-religionists dying by the thousands every day, all around him.

In *See Under: Love* Grossman uses the literary legacy of the Modern Hebrew Renaissance in order to map out the dilemmas of Holocaust representation. The experience of finding a voice to express the inexpressible makes its way into Grossman's novel through the experience of a Hebrew Renaissance writer struggling to script a vernacular Hebrew culture from literary materials. He brings his project of the revival of Hebrew as a vernacular language to the camps, weaving together the two discussions of "the representation of reality": the challenges of Holocaust representation, and the challenges of Hebrew representation in the period of the Modern Hebrew Renaissance.

The struggle for the Hebrew language in Grossman's novel of the second generation is, in part, a struggle to resuscitate Holocaust memory from the dialectics of Zionist ideology. Grossman's novel brings our discussion full circle, back to the Hebrew language as the language of choice for many modern Jews in a hostile world at the end of the nineteenth century. By removing the late-nineteenth-century European-born Hebrew writer from a Zionist trajectory and keeping him in Europe, Grossman leaves us with a strong sense of the fundamental tragedy of modern Jewish experience. That tragedy is largely the one of Jewish genocide imposed on the Jews from without, but also the coercive forgetting imposed upon Jews from within as they attempted to reinvent themselves as Israelis. The story of the Holocaust, told in Hebrew in the past few decades is, again and again, an expression of the struggle to remember, despite the ideology of the negation of the Diaspora which reared its head most unabashedly at the moment when Jewish survivors were in greatest need of recognition and compassion. The efforts of the second and, most recently, the third generation (in the important 2000 novel of Amir Gutfreund entitled *Our Holocaust*)[41] to reclaim the story that could not have been told in Hebrew in the years immediately following the war have flowered into a sophisticated and compelling commentary both on the events of the Holocaust and on the role of the Hebrew language in the telling of stories about the Holocaust.

Notes

1. Alan Mintz, *Hurban: Responses to Catastrophe in Hebrew Literature* (New York: Columbia University Press, 1984), pp. 165–202.
2. Uri Tzvi Greenberg, *Streets of the River* (Jerusalem and Tel Aviv, 1954), p. 63. Trans. Mintz, *Hurban*, p. 183.
3. Sheila E. Jelen, *Intimations of Difference: Dvora Baron in the Modern Hebrew Renaissance* (Syracuse University Press, 2007), p. 40.
4. Dan Laor, "Did Agnon Write about the Holocaust?" *Yad Vashem Studies* 22 (1992): 17–63, and Sidra Dekoven Ezrahi, "Agnon Before and After," *Prooftexts: A Journal of Jewish Literary History* 2/1 (1982): 78–94.
5. S. Y. Agnon, *A Guest for the Night* (New York: Schocken Books, 1968); S. Y. Agnon, *Ir Umeloah* (Jerusalem: Schocken Books, 1973).
6. Mintz, *Hurban*, p. 159.
7. Wendy Zierler, "Four Sons of the Holocaust: Leah Goldberg's 'Keneged Arba'ah Banim,'" *Shofar* 23/2 (2005): 34–46.
8. Leah Goldberg, "Lady of the Castle," trans. T. Carmi, in Michael Taub (ed.), *Israeli Holocaust Drama* (Syracuse University Press, 1996), pp. 21–78.
9. Hanna Yablonka, "The Formation of Holocaust Consciousness in the State of Israel: The Early Days," in Efraim Sicher (ed.), *Breaking Crystal: Writing and Memory after Auschwitz* (Urbana: University of Illinois, 1998), p. 122.
10. Yablonka, "Formation," pp. 123–29.

11. Ibid., p. 123.
12. Ben Zion Tomer, *Children of the Shadows*, trans. Hillel Halkin, in Taub (ed.), *Israeli Holocaust Drama*, pp. 127–85.
13. Glenda Abramson, *Drama and Ideology in Modern Israel* (Cambridge University Press, 1998).
14. Ibid., p. 174.
15. Hanna Yablonka, *The State of Israel vs. Adolph Eichmann* (New York: Schocken Books, 2004).
16. Hannah Arendt, *Eichmann in Jerusalem: A Report on the Banality of Evil* (New York: Viking Press, 1963); Yablonka, "Formation," p. 133.
17. Omer Bartov, "Kitsch and Sadism in Ka-Tzetnik's Other Planet: Israeli Youth Imagine the Holocaust," *Jewish Social Studies* 3/2 (1997): 42–76.
18. Quoted in Bartov, "Ka-Tzetnik's Other Planet," p. 54.
19. Haim Gouri, *The Chocolate Deal* (New York: Holt, 1968); Yoram Kaniuk, *Adam Resurrected* (New York: Harper, 1978); Hanokh Bartov, *The Brigade* (New York: Holt, 1968).
20. Mintz, *Hurban*, p. 240.
21. Mintz, *Hurban*, p. 259.
22. Aharon Appelfeld, *Badenheim 1939* (Boston: Godine, 1980). See also *Tzili: The Story of a Life* (New York: E. P. Dutton, 1983).
23. Michael Andre Bernstein, *Foregone Conclusions: Against Apocalyptic History* (Berkeley: University of California Press, 1994).
24. Aharon Appelfeld, "The Story of a Life," *World Literature Today*, trans. Aloma Halter (January–April, 2005): 32.
25. Lincoln Shlensky, "Lost and Found: Aharon Appelfeld's Literary Affiliations and the Quest for Home in Israeli Letters," *Prooftexts: A Journal of Jewish Literary History* 26 (2006): 406.
26. Aharon Appelfeld, *The Immortal Bartfuss*, trans. Jeffrey Green (New York: Weidenfeld and Nicolson, 1988).
27. Aharon Appelfeld, *Ashan* (Yerushalayim: Akhshav, 1962) and Aharon Appelfeld, *Mayim Adirim* (Or Yehudah: Zemora Bitan, 2011).
28. Ranen Omer-Sherman, "Responding to the Burden of Witness in Dan Pagis's 'Written in Pencil in the Sealed Railway-Car,'" in Marianne Hirsch and Irence Kacandes (eds.), *Teaching the Representation of the Holocaust* (New York: MLA, 2004), p. 304.
29. Omer-Sherman, "Responding to the Burden," p. 306.
30. See Robert Alter, Introduction to Dan Pagis, *Points of Departure* (Philadelphia: Jewish Publication Society of America, 1981), p. xii.
31. Dan Pagis, "Testimony," trans. Stephen Mitchell, in *Points of Departure*, p. 25. On the allusion to Maimonides see Robert Alter's Introduction to Pagis's volume, p. xiii.
32. Yitzhak Arad, Yisrael Gutman, and Avraham Margaliyot, eds., *Documents on the Holocaust* (Jerusalem: Yad Vashem, 1981), p. 434.
33. Dina Porat, *The Fall of a Sparrow: The Life and Times of Abba Kovner*, trans. and ed. Elizabeth Yuval (Stanford University Press, 2010), p. 71.

34. Ibid., p. xviii.
35. See Abba Kovner, *Kol Shire Abba Kovner*, ed. Dan Miron (Jerusalem: Mosad Bialik, 1996–2003). In English, see Abba Kovner, *Selected Poems of Abba Kovner*, ed. Stephen Spender (Harmondsworth: Penguin, 1971).
36. Porat, *The Fall*, p. 39.
37. Yehuda Amichai, *Not of This Time, Not of This Place*, trans. Shlomo Katz (New York: Harper and Row, 1968); Shulamit Hareven, *Twilight and Other Stories*, trans. Miriam Arad (San Francisco: Mercury House, 1992).
38. Efraim Sicher, "The Return of the Past: The Intergenerational Transmission of Holocaust Memory in Israeli Fiction," *Shofar* 19/2 (Winter 2001): 26–52.
39. Shulamit Hareven, "Twilight," in *Twilight and Other Stories*, p. 1.
40. Leah Aini's work can be found in English translation in *Dreaming the Actual: Contemporary Fiction and Poetry by Israeli Women Writers*, ed. Miriam Glazer (Albany: State University of New York, 2000).
41. Amir Gutfreund, *Shoah Shelanu* (Tel Aviv: Zemorah Bitan, 2000).

CHAPTER 6

The Holocaust and postwar Yiddish literature
Jan Schwarz

Postwar Yiddish Holocaust literature

"What affects me the most," laments Chava Rosenfarb, "is the continual sense of isolation that I feel as a survivor – an isolation enhanced by my being a Yiddish writer. I feel myself to be like an anachronism wandering about a page of history on which I don't belong." The fate of the Yiddish language is at the crux of this isolation: "If writing is a lonely profession," continues Rosenfarb, "the Yiddish writer's loneliness has an additional dimension. His readership has perished. His language has gone up with the smoke of the crematoria. He or she creates in a vacuum, almost without a readership, out of fidelity to a vanished language – as if to prove that Nazism did not succeed in extinguishing that language's last breath, and that it is still alive."[1]

Post-1945 Jewish writers, whatever their individual biographies and languages, wrote in the shadow of the Holocaust. Yiddish writers in particular were compelled to bear witness, and to commemorate the destruction of Central and Eastern European Jewry (Ashkenaz), where the majority of Jewish victims had been Yiddish speakers. Yiddish writers' identification with the *kedoyshim* (holy martyrs), as the victims of the Holocaust were called, resulted in works of great artistic and emotional power. As a result, testimonies, life writing, chronicles, historical novels, and poetic lamentation (*klog lider*) came to define the generic map of Yiddish writing after 1945.

This emphasis on testimonies and historical documentation was prominently displayed in two monumental book projects: the over one thousand *Yizker* books (books of remembrance), and the book series *Dos poylishe yidntum* (Polish Jewry), which included 175 volumes, published between 1946–1966 in Buenos Aires. These collectively conceived book projects drew on several models: on the *pinkes*, the Jewish community record books, on historical and anthropological documentation, and on social realism. These two book projects encapsulate the fundamental tenor of post-1945 Yiddish culture by affirming a fundamental humanist belief in progress and justice. They chronicle the religious and cultural history of Jewish communities, document Jewish spiritual and physical resistance to the Final Solution, and highlight the *Sheyres-ha-pleyte*'s (the surviving remnants, the Yiddish phrase for "Holocaust survivors") tenacity and heroism.

Written primarily in Hebrew and Yiddish, the *Yizker* books created a virtual encyclopedia of hundreds of Jewish communities in Central and Eastern Europe, from the smallest towns and villages to the provincial and governmental centers. Originally composed, edited, and published by a collective of writers associated with the town or city's *landsmanshaft* (the organization of Jews who originally came from a particular town or city in Central and Eastern Europe), the *Yizker* books transcended their initial internal Jewish context and have become important source material in a larger public and academic setting.[2] *Dos poylishe yidntum*, on the other hand, indicated the existence of a transcontinental Yiddish cadre of writers and mass readership; they became a cultural matrix for Yiddish readers' continued engagement with Ashkenazi history, culture, and the promulgation of young Yiddish literary talents.

Yiddish poets such as Jacob Glatstein, Chaim Grade, and Abraham Sutzkever turned to collective forms of commemoration. Eschewing their prewar modernist experiments, they infused their postwar poetry with religious imagery, conventional rhymes, and neoclassical forms. Characteristically, Glatstein expressed the desire that his poetic lamentations be included anonymously in a future *sider*, Jewish prayer book. Without returning to the Jewish faith, Glatstein returned to Jewish religious archetypes and myths in his powerful Holocaust poetry collected in *Ikh tu dermonen* (*I Keep Recalling: The Holocaust Poems of Jacob Glatstein*, 1993), one of the finest examples of Yiddish poetic lamentations. In this collection, Glatstein used traditional religious imagery as in the poems "On yidn" ("Without Jews," 1946) and "Nisht di meysim loybn got" ("The Dead Don't Praise God," 1946) based on Psalms:

> Di toyre hobn mir mekabl geven baym sinay
> Un in Lublin hobn mir zi opgegebn.
> Nisht di meysim loybn got,
> Di toyre iz gegebn gevorn tsum lebn.
> (We accepted the Torah on Sinai
> And in Lublin we gave it back.
> The dead don't praise God –
> The Torah was given for life.)[3]

In the postwar poetry of the Hebrew and Yiddish poet Aaron Zeitlin, the guilt and shame of survival is a central theme. The survivor feels condemned to live a shadowy afterlife following the extinction of his people. This sense of being the last surviving remnant of a great tradition imbues Zeitlin's Holocaust poetry with a note of hopelessness and despair. The poet is left only with words "Gornisht oyser verter" ("Nothing Remains but Words," 1947), the title of one of his poems. This theme is highlighted in the poet Kadya Molodovsky's introduction *Eykha betsibur* (Lamentation in a communal voice) to *Lider fun khurbn: antologye* (Poems of the Holocaust: anthology):

> Yiddish poetry in the twenty years after the Holocaust is lamentations in a communal voice. No nation and language are able to comprehend such poems. We move in a world of shadows – shadows of our dear ones, parents, brothers, sisters, and whole communities. They appear in front of our eyes in the horror of their death. It is the valley of death. We sink into it in our dreams at night, and it doesn't disappear in the light of day. Shadows are now our constant companions from which the Yiddish poem cries out. Ash and desolation are the words of the Yiddish poem.[4]

God figures prominently even in secular Yiddish Holocaust poetry, providing a metaphorical presence that serves to channel a voice for the Jewish collective by using a traditional mode. This enables these mainly staunchly secular writers to identify fully with the suffering and destruction of their people. One of the most iconic examples of Yiddish Holocaust poetry in this vein is Molodovsky's 1945 poem "El khonen" ("God of Mercy"):

> El khonen,
> klayb oys an ander folk,
> derveyl.
> Mir zenen mid fun shtarbn un geshtorbn,
> mir hobn nit keyn tfiles mer,
> klayb oys an ander folk,
> dervayl,
> mir hobn nit keyn blut mer
> oyf tsu zayn a korbn.
> A midber iz gevorn undzer shtub.
> Di erd iz karg far undz af kvurim,
> nishto keyn kines mer far undz,
> nisht keyn klog-lid
> in di alte sforim.
> (O God of Mercy
> For the time being
> Choose another people.
> We are tired of death, tired of corpses,

We have no more prayers.
For the time being
Choose another people.
We have run out of blood
For victims,
Our houses have been turned into desert,
The earth lacks space for tombstones,
There are no more lamentations
Nor songs of woe
In the ancient texts.)[5]

Abraham Sutzkever's incarceration in the Vilna ghetto from 1941 through 1943 set him on a Zionist course toward the Land of Israel, where he settled in 1947. In the poem "Di froy fun mirml afn Per-lashez" ("The Women of Marble in Pere Lachaise," 1947) about the cemetery Pere Lachaise in Paris, Sutzkever contemplates what homeland and exile means for the Yiddish poet after the destruction of his hometown Vilna. Chopin, his world-renowned Polish compatriot who lived most of his life in Parisian exile, decided that his heart should be removed and buried in Warsaw while his tombstone in Pere Lachaise would remain a site of pilgrimage for music lovers. In contrast, the Yiddish poet has lost his Jewish homeland forever and the thought of erecting a memorial to him in Poland is ridiculously misplaced:

I was left in Pere Lachaise
Numb, no words:
Was it worth collecting
Thirty years,
Losing all my loved ones,
Hanging by a thread,
Emerging from the oven
With unburned tears,
That I should now,
At Pere Lachaise,
Hear
That my almighty heart
Is worth a farthing.
And if I write a will that says
My heart should be brought home –
The entire, sad, eternal world-people
Will laugh.[6]

New York City's Yiddish world after 1945 is vividly portrayed in the philosopher Abraham Joshua Heschel's review "After Maydanek" of the Yiddish poet Aaron Zeitlin's *Gezamlte lider* (Collected poems, 1947):

We still feel the blow to our head. It feels like the heavens above us have
fallen in chunks. We have not yet grasped the disaster that has befallen us.
We are still before the funeral – still prepared to sit *shiva*, confounded,
confused and petrified.

   How do we endure this? How do we bear the pain? Are we idiots? Are we
base? When I think of my people, burned and cremated in Poland, a shudder
courses through my veins. I feel the nails of insanity.

   I choke on pain and drive away from myself the picture, the sound, the
woe. No, one cannot drive away an ocean, one can bury oneself in a hole, in a
pit of forgetfulness.

   How worthless is such a life in hiding. The sound of the ocean roars in the
distance, there is nowhere to run away. Our misfortune is [as] large as God.
We mask the sound of the shudder with cheap noisemakers. Talk is a waste
of time, we won't experience any good fortune (and even saying these words
is foolish). We have Tisha B'Av all year and yet – we put on Purim plays.

Heschel, a refugee from Warsaw and Vilna via the Lehrhaus in Frankfurt,
used his review of Zeitlin's poetry to sharpen his criticism of secular Jewish
culture, and its worship of European art and literature. The demand of the
day, according to Heschel, was for Jews to return to the sources of religious
Jewish tradition. Heschel had commemorated these in his lecture at the
YIVO Institute of Jewish Research in January 1945, "Di mezrekh eyrope-
isher tkufe in der yidisher geshikhte" (The Eastern European period in
Jewish history) and published in an English version as *The Earth Is the Lord's*
in 1950. Heschel views Zeitlin's poetry as an authentic expression of
religious tradition (*yidishkeyt*), quoting from the poem, "Nokh a kleyne
poeme, geshribn 1946" ("Yet Another Small Poem," written in 1946) in
which the poet rejects his former glorification of Goethe, the icon of the
German Enlightenment:

   As for me, I was a man of letters in Warsaw,
   who believed like all the others
   in the same Goethe and in other such brilliant egoists.
   I did not know how short the distance is between Faust and fist,
   From Goethe's "uebermensch" to the "untermensch" and to the Hitlerites.
   What would privy councillor Goethe have done in Hitler's time?
   He would have sat in Weimar and looked from a distance
   how his Germans gassed my millions.
   He who spoke of literature with Napoleon,
   would probably have spoken to Hitler
   with a polished profound epigram.
   Not even an eyebrow would have twitched –
   Can then a Goethe sanctify the Name of God?
   Can he sacrifice himself? Such people can only create poetry,

while the Hitlerites annihilate.
Oh, the big egoists, who make the words!
Esau, how I now see the connection
Between your wordsmiths and your murderers![7]

Instead of being blinded by the light of the Enlightenment, it was time, in Heschel's words, to "appreciate the value of the small fire of our eternal light." This echoes Glatstein's famous poem, "A gute nakht, velt" ("Good Night, World," 1938), where the poet returns to Jewish sources, leaving behind "Wagner's pagan music" and choosing instead "the humming of Hasidic melodies." The Jewish enlightenment, the Haskala, of the past 150 years had created spiritual confusion among Jews by alienating them from their religious sources.

A similar theme is addressed in Chaim Grade's novella *Mayn krig mit Hersh Raseyner* (*My Quarrel with Hersh Rasseyner*, published in English translation in *Commentary* in 1953). Set in Paris in the spring of 1948, Grade's novella depicts a day-long argument about secularism vs. traditionalism between the Yiddish writer Chaim Vilner and his opponent Hersh Rasseyner, an ultra-orthodox follower of the Musar movement. Although they discuss the implication of the Holocaust for Jewish life in the Diaspora, neither Zionism and Israel nor the United States is mentioned in the story. The two protagonists take up a two-decade-long argument originating in their hometown of Vilna, the Jerusalem of Lithuania. The debate is about their commitment to ultra-orthodox faith, secularism, and the fate of *klal-yisroel*, the Jewish people, conducted by displaced *ost-Juden* in the cultural capital of the West.

A recurrent trope in post-Holocaust Yiddish literature presents the Yiddish writer as belonging to the last survivors of the Ashkenazi civilization. Each of his or her words bears the stamp of Ashkenaz as a synecdoche of a civilization that has ceased to exist. Isaac Bashevis Singer's last demon in the story "Mayse Tishevitz" ("The Last Demon," 1959) has survived the cataclysm in a small town in Poland, where it spends the time counting letters and creating children's rhymes. As long as the Hebrew alphabet can be mined for Yiddish rhymes, the last demon keeps busy in his isolation on a hayloft in a *Judenrein* town in Poland. His power to lure people to do evil has vanished, for not a single Jew remains to be tempted. What does last is the formulaic scheme of good and evil, as performed by the demon storyteller with a Yeshiva education. The demon's storytelling is suffused with elegiac melancholy. The Hebrew alphabet in an old Yiddish storybook is the only thing that keeps it alive:

On a yidish os –
iz a shed a yid – oys . . .
(When the last letter is gone
The last of the demons is done.)[8]

Like Singer's demon hiding in the attic, Yiddish survivor-writers such as
Grade, Sutzkever, and Zeitlin became portable archives and encyclopedias
of Eastern European Jewish culture, spending the most productive years of
their artistic careers in exile in New York and Tel Aviv. They made the
Yiddish language their lifeline to the 600-year-old Jewish civilization, after
the complete destruction of its material and social infrastructure. The
Yiddish writers remained in exile in perpetuity, with no illusion of ever
returning to their homelands. As the last representatives of their culture,
Yiddish writers continued to create works premised on the existence of
Ashkenaz as an exilic culture (*goles kultur*).

   During the war, Jews wrote in the desperate moments they seized while
in ghettos, concentration camps, or in hiding, not knowing the full scope of
the destruction of Jewish life. After the war, a more complete account of
what had happened to Jews on the sites of thousands of ground zeros –
camps, ghettos, mass graves – was made public in the form of trials of
perpetrators, collaborators (including Jewish ones), survivor testimonies,
and media coverage. The first years after the war saw an outpouring of
Jewish testimonial writing.[9] Although Jews bore witness in most European
languages during and after the war, the primary languages of Jewish testimonies were Polish and Yiddish, due to the vast size of the Jewish community in Poland prior to 1939. Yiddish and Hebrew, in particular, enabled
the murdered witnesses and survivors to speak directly to other Jews. They
also afforded the writers access to journalistic outlets and readerships
anxious to learn about what had happened during the war. The Yiddish
and Hebrew cultural world welcomed and supported the Jewish testimonies
that were published in the press, book series, and individual book
publications.

   Historical and literary issues related to the publication of original Jewish
documents written during the war were hotly debated in the Yiddish press.
This public discourse anticipated the discussions that would take place
decades later in the field of Holocaust studies on issues such as the "limits
of representation" and what it meant to write "poetry after *der khurbn*" (the
Yiddish word for the Holocaust). Materials rescued from the ghettos, such
as the Ringelblum archive, diaries of cultural and political figures, as well as
ordinary people were edited for publication in *Dos poylishe yidntum*. The

diary, in particular, became a template that authenticated the testimonial account of a specific time and place. For Yiddish writers, the acts of addressing a specific readership and shaping public memory determined how they transformed their wartime writing into testimonial literature.

In Yiddish "communal memory" after 1945, the basic distinction was between survivors (*Sheyres-hapleyte* or *lebensgeblibene*) and non-survivors; between those who had lived through the war in Europe, and the Jews who were kept safe in the Soviet Union and overseas.[10] The small group of Yiddish writers with first-hand knowledge of the *khurbn* based on their experiences in concentration camps, ghettos, or in hiding included Mordechai Shtrigler, Isaiah Shpiegl, Leib Rochman, Abraham Sutzkever, and Chava Rosenfarb. What sustained their creative work as writers during the war was their deep sense of connection to a global Yiddish cultural network. They wrote and published prolifically in the period following the war, even as they meticulously honed their artistic craft. After six years of war, they were free to build Yiddish literature and culture anew, a mission they fully embraced.

Sutzkever and the short-story writer Isaiah Shpiegl, who survived the Lodz ghetto and Auschwitz, rewrote their wartime writing as part of an ongoing artistic process. Similarly, Leib Rochman based his rewriting of his war diary on the journal that he had written in hiding during 1943–1944, protected by Polish farmers in his hometown Minsk Mazowieck, 35 kilometers from Warsaw. The original title of the manuscript "Dos tog-bukh fun tsvantikstn yorhundert 1942–1944" (The diary of the twentieth century 1942–1944) indicates that Rochman originally conceived the book in universal terms. When the Minsk Mazowieck *landsmanshaft* decided to underwrite its publication, the war diary was framed as a memorial book and the original title was replaced by the scriptural quote *And in Your Blood Shall You Live* (Ezekiel 16:6–7). I. B. Singer praised the work's excellent language and that it reads "like good belletristic."[11] Shmuel Niger characterized the book as being "not only a chronicle, not a collection of 'episodes'. . . . it is, if you will, a novel."[12] Rochman's wartime diary is one of the most artistically accomplished testimonial works about the experience of surviving the relentless "Jew hunt" by Polish farmers and Germans in the heart of Poland in 1943–1944.

In contrast to Rochman's diary, Mordechai Shtrigler's extensive manuscripts written during the war were lost and later reconstituted from memory by the author from his new perch as a Yiddish journalist in postwar Paris. Thus, Shtrigler's Yiddish documentary writing of approximately 1,500 pages, entitled *Oysgebrente likht* (Extinguished lights), was published in six volumes between 1946 and 1953 in *Dos poylishe yidntum.*[13] They depicted his experiences in Maydanek and in a labor camp, the Hasag factory in Skarzysko-Kaminenna, near Radom. Shtrigler's introduction to the first volume *Maydanek* (1947) combines its various generic features of historical document, eyewitness accounts, personal reminiscences, and imaginative sections about the inner life of the camp inmates.

Shtrigler utilized a variety of literary styles and genres to reach a readership with the full force of his chronicles of survival. As long as the author anchored the narrative in a specific locale and at a specific point in the German extermination process, the Yiddish readership was willing to accept a great deal of poetic license. Yiddish testimonies were typically less concerned with who had done what to whom than with employing the full range of literary techniques to recreate the inner experience of Jewish life under Nazi rule. Yiddish critic Shmuel Niger pointed out that Shtrigler "is not concerned with telling us exactly what happened to Hitler's victims." He rather "touches the deep dimension" of their tragic experiences.[14]

Sutzkever and Glatstein would abandon their sense of objectivity when presented with a compelling account of the last hours of Gerer Hasid's monologue, ostensibly written in the Warsaw ghetto on April 28, 1943. The story, "Yosl Rakover redt tsu got" (Yosl Rakover speaks to God), was published by Sutzkever in his literary journal in 1954 as an authentic historical narrative. The Polish-born Jewish writer Michal Borwitz documented in an article in a French Yiddish journal the following year that the text was authored by the writer Zvi Kolitz (1918–2002), who had never set foot in the Warsaw ghetto, and published in a Buenos Aires Yiddish newspaper, *Di yidishe tsaytung*, on September 25, 1946. As a result, Sutzkever and Glatstein retracted their initial enthusiastic support of the account's historical authenticity.[15] As the Wilkomirsky affair in the 1990s revealed, the temptation to claim the authenticity of fictional texts as authored by "real" Holocaust victims in the throes of resistance and suffering was not always easy to overcome. Frequently, mythology and historical documentation was pitted against each other in the Yiddish writers' response to how the Jews had confronted their destruction. The temptation to glorify the Jewish victims remained strong among Yiddish writers.

Some Yiddish writers watched the destruction of their communities from a safe vantage point as exiled writers living in the United States, Cuba, Argentina, and the Soviet Union. I. B. Singer, Aaron Zeitlin, Melekh Ravitsh, and Kadya Molodovsky had already made a name for themselves as young writers in Warsaw during the 1920s and 1930s, prior to their emigration to North America (in some cases via Cuba) in the 1930s. This group's recent migration to the Americas informed their writing of exile, which remained steeped in Polish Yiddish culture prior to the destruction. The old guard of Yiddish writers had arrived in New York in their teens prior to World War I. They had embraced American urbanity, modernism, and Anglophone culture, while pursuing careers as Yiddish cultural workers, poets, and novelists. Jacob Glatstein, Aaron Leyeles, H. Leivick, and Mani-Leib devoted their artistic careers to building Yiddish culture in the United States. In the aftermath of the war, these modernist iconoclasts changed into guardians of the flock, espousing a commitment to Holocaust commemoration in their poetic lamentations. The old guard became an important cultural liaison to the newly arrived Yiddish survivor-writers, whose urgent messages from a world of total destruction and genocide they helped introduce to the American world. The poet H. Leivick, for example, wrote introductions to Shtrigler's literary testimonies and the Vilna poet-partisan Shmerke Katsherginski's collection of Yiddish songs of the Holocaust. He also published his own eyewitness account from a visit to the displaced persons camps in Germany in 1946.[16]

Initially few in numbers, Anglo-Jewish writers such as Cynthia Ozick, Irving Howe, Bernard Malamud, and Saul Bellow became crucial conduits of Yiddish culture to the larger American world, while also contributing to the renaissance of post-1945 Jewish American literature. They published anthologies, translations, and criticism of Yiddish literature that introduced the mostly unknown European world of their parents to an American readership.[17] Most Yiddish writers did not participate in the Anglo-Jewish world until the early 1960s that, significantly, first saw English translations of Glatstein and Grade's work. Glatstein took the initiative to break "the walls of invisibility" which had surrounded Yiddish culture in the 1940s and 1950s by organizing the Yiddish poetry series at the famed 92 Street Y in New York, 1963–1969. Although the exposure of these events was relatively limited, the Yiddish poetry series at the Y marked an important step toward making contemporary Yiddish poetry and its pervasive response to the Holocaust visible to an American readership.[18]

In Israel, Sutzkever, Yosl Birstein, Leib Rochman, and others involved in the writer group "Yung yisroel" (Young Israel) created Yiddish cultural institutions, journals, and artistic works which responded to the particular conditions of the newly founded Jewish state. As the editor of *Di goldene keyt*, the premier Yiddish literary journal after 1945, Sutzkever created an island of high-brow Yiddish literary and critical discourse in an otherwise unfriendly Israeli society which viewed Yiddish as a remnant of the Diaspora destined to die out, or as nostalgic entertainment exemplified by the stand-up comedy of the popular Dzigan and Schumacher and Itsik Manger's *Lider fun gan-eydn* (Songs of paradise) staged as a play in Tel Aviv in the 1960s. Israeli Yiddish writers continued to bear witness to the *khurbn*, while also expanding their artistic reach to include portrayals of Israel's landscapes, immigrants, and survivor population as in the poignant short fiction of Yosl Birstein.[19]

A few Yiddish writers such as Melekh Ravitsh, Rokhl Korn, Yehuda Elberg, and Chava Rosenfarb settled in Montreal, where they continued the vibrant Yiddish culture that had thrived in the city since the early part of the century. After the decade of silence in the 1950s, Soviet Yiddish culture was resurrected in 1961 when the communist regime allowed the creation of a new journal *Sovetish Heymland* published in Moscow. In its pages, a new cadre of Yiddish literary talents such as Eli Schekhtman and Josef Kerler made their debut. Most of these writers would emigrate to Israel in the 1970s and 1980s, where they continued their Yiddish literary careers. For brief periods in the 1940s and 1950s, small Yiddish cultural centers in Paris and Warsaw were created by surviving writers such as Shmerke Katsherginski, Chaim Grade, and Shtrigler (in Paris), and by Berl Mark and Mikhl Mirsky (in Warsaw). Most of these writers moved on to permanent settlement in the United States, South America, and Israel. The short-lived Yiddish cultural life under communist rule in Poland came to an abrupt end with the anti-Semitic campaign and expulsion of the last remnant of Polish Jewry in 1968.

Following the public recounting of survivor testimonies that took place at the Eichmann trial in 1961, Yiddish writers were encouraged increasingly to address the traumatic war experiences characterized by the emotional composite of vengeance, guilt, and suicidal despair. This new phase of Yiddish writing was initiated by Singer's *Shadows on the Hudson* (serialized in *Forverts*, 1957–1958 but first published in book form in English translation, 1998); Rochman's modernist novel *Mit blinde shrit iber der erd* (With blind steps over the Earth, 1966) and *Der mabl un andere dertseylungen* (The flood and other stories, 1976); Sutzkever's *Di ershte nakht in geto* (The first night in the ghetto, 1979); and Chava Rosenfarb's short stories from the 1980s and 1990s translated into English as *Survivors* in 2004.

Hertz Dovid Grein, like most of the other characters in Singer's *Shadows on the Hudson*, arrived in the United States one or two decades before the Holocaust; others, such as the character Anna, have escaped war-torn Europe under dramatic circumstances. Like Singer's other novel about Holocaust survivors, *Enemies: A Love Story* (1972), which is a more artistically successful variation on the same theme, Grein finds himself entangled with three women at the same time: his loyal wife, his long time lover, and his most recent infatuation, Boris Makover's daughter, Anna. Its main characters drift aimlessly, sexually and professionally, outwardly successful in the United States but inwardly suffering desperately over their loss of family, career, and home in Europe. Their pursuit of happiness in the USA remains unfulfilled, trapping them in serial relationships and get-rich schemes. In a few cases, they seek out the certainty of clear-cut solutions to their predicament in orthodox Judaism (Boris Makover and, eventually, Grein himself) and spiritualism (Dr. Margolin). The novel succeeds in depicting the plight of the *sheyres hapleyte*, the traumatized survivors of the Holocaust, exiled from their Ashkenazi Jewish homelands in a crassly materialistic and intellectually superficial USA. Singer's survivor guilt of not having had "the privilege of going through the Hitler Holocaust" sharpened his deliberate exposition of nihilism and self-destructive tendencies.[20] Like other post-1945 Yiddish writers, his enormous output on the staff of a Yiddish newspaper, continued productivity and embrace of new genres into old age, poignantly reflected his work's life-affirming character.

Chava Rosenfarb (1923–2011) wrote poetry during her four-year incarceration in the Lodz ghetto. Deported to Auschwitz with her family in August 1944, Rosenfarb survived with her mother and sister, was liberated from Bergen-Belsen, and began to publish Yiddish poetry in 1947. It took her thirteen years to write her magnum opus *Der boym fun lebn* (*The Tree of Life*, 1972), a three-volume depiction of life in the Lodz ghetto, 1939–1944. This monumental work was translated into English in 1985 (and reprinted in 2004) by the author and her daughter Goldie Morgenthaler, and received the prestigious Manger Prize in 1977. The work is a novelistic chronicle that portrays ten main characters from different social and cultural strata of the Lodz ghetto population. These include one character based on the Yiddish poet Simcha Bunim Shayevitsh (1907–1944), Rosenfarb's poetic mentor in the ghetto, and Mordechai Chaim Rumkowski, the "eldest" of the Jews in the Lodz ghetto, portrayed under his own name, which lends a documentary dimension to the work. The novel is terminated before the deportation of the surviving remnant of the Lodz ghetto to Auschwitz; the last pages are left blank in order to express the insufficiency of words to articulate the unspeakable nature of the concentration camp experience. In her last novel, *Briv tsu Abrashn* (Letters to Abrasha, 1992), however, Rosenfarb tells harrowingly about the character Miriam's incarceration in the Auschwitz, Sasel, and Bergen-Belsen camps.

Rosenfarb's short-story collection *Survivors*, originally published in *Di goldene keyt* in the 1980s and 1990s, depicts Holocaust survivors in

Canada. The stories focus on rootless refugees who, despite their outward success, are plagued by survivor guilt, and live a shadow existence. The novella *Ednia's Revenge* is a confession narrated by the Jewish Kapo, Rella. The relationship between Rella and Ednia as it develops over decades in Montreal is the main focus of the story. Rella's one and only act of human empathy as a Jewish Kapo was to save Ednia from a selection for the gas chamber. During the decades of upward social mobility and business success as a designer in Montreal, Rella is haunted by the fear that Ednia will reveal her past as a Kapo. Both of them belong to a small circle of Holocaust survivors who participate in the cultural riches of the Canadian metropolis. It turns out that their survival has been bought at a high price. Rella's sexual favors to a German overseer in the camp secured her a privileged status. Another member of this community, Lolek, a survivor character from Lithuania, who claims to be a Jewish partisan, actually survived in hiding.

Unlike Singer's characters, who are rooted in Judaism and/or Jewish culture, Rosenfarb's circle of survivors have made a deliberate effort to distance themselves from their Jewish roots. They speak Polish or English among themselves, and Ednia is drawn to the Christian cross as a symbol of suffering and redemption in Jesus. Rella's only reason to live is her friendship with Ednia, the only witness to Rella's humanity in the camps. When Ednia terminates their friendship, Rella decides to take her own life. The sleeping pills she has been hoarding from the day of liberation serve as replacement for family, history, and identity by offering the alluring promise of death:

> These pills were the only possessions that I brought with me to Canada from the European continent. They took the place of my parents, my grand-parents, my sixteen-year-old brother and my ten-year-old sister; my darling Maniusha. They took the place of all my aunts, uncles, and cousins, of my hometown, my childhood, early adolescence, and my first and only love. Sleeping pills became my life – and my death. And now they have become my only road back to innocence.[21]

Chaim Grade's last novel *Fun unter der erd* (From under the ground) was serialized in the *Forverts* (1979–1982), but was left unfinished with his sudden death. The novel's main theme is embodied by the character of Shayke Tshemerinski, a stand-in for the Yiddish poet and partisan Shmerke Katcherginski (1908–1954), upon his return to Vilna after liberation in 1944.[22] Tshemeriski becomes the director of the Jewish museum, the main repository of Jewish culture in Vilna in the aftermath of the war. He heroically resists the Soviet attempt to eliminate Jewish cultural treasures, books, and archives. Grade's last novel is a historical *roman-à-clef* about an almost *judenrein* Vilna that provides the setting for Tshemerinski's enactment of the moral imperative of saving the Jewish cultural heritage. In depicting the destroyed Jewish Vilna from the perspective of the partisan-poet Tshemerinski, Grade's work came full circle from his autobiographical lamentations, *Di zibn geselekh* (*The Seven Little Lanes*, 1955) set in Vilna in 1944. A Jewish doctor who has returned from the Soviet Union to Vilna in the novel's first chapter expresses the painful futility of Tshemerinski's endeavor:

> And if it were a palace instead of this ghetto-prison that was officially designated as a museum; and even if the Soviet state should employ a whole staff to sort out and catalogue the books, the Torah scrolls and other holy texts, the overflowing bags and boxes with cards by scholarly *nudniks* [bores] who for decades prepared to write important works – would the slaughtered Vilna be resurrected? Can mountains of moldy books replace a city of living and breathing Jews?[23]

Postwar Yiddish Holocaust literature is characterized by a strong sense of continuity as indicated by the proliferation of the historical novel and life writing depicting *A velt vos iz nishto mer* (*Of a World That Is No More*, 1946), the title of Singer's posthumous childhood memoir. In the novels of Grade, Singer, and Rosenfarb, taking place, respectively, in prewar Vilna, Warsaw, and Lodz, these major Jewish urban centers were resurrected on a grand novelistic canvas derived from nineteenth-century epic works by Tolstoy and Dostoyevsky.[24] These works parallel the *Yizker* book and *Dos poylishe yidntum*'s emphasis on the collective body of the Ashkenazi Jews' history and anthropology, governed by the drive to create a usable past for the surviving remnant of Jews.

Sutzkever's surrealist prose poems *Griner akvarium* (*Green Aquarium*, 1953–1954), *Dortn vu es nekhtikn di shtern* (*Where the Stars Spend the Night*), and *Di nevue fun shvarts-apln* (The prophecy of the pupils), (1975–1989) stand as the apotheosis of modernism in Yiddish postwar literature. Like Sutzkever's turn to a classical form, the sonnet, in his series of poems *Lider fun togbukh* (*Poems from a Diary*, 1974–1989), Aaron Zeitlin's "Zeks shures" ("Six Lines") encapsulates in haiku-like fashion an unredeemable duality (just short of the seventh line of completion, the messianic *oylem hobe*, the world to come) through which the poet articulates his sense of futility, sorrow, and defiance:

> Kh'veys: keyner darf mikh nisht af ot dem oylem,
> mikh, verter-betler oyf dem yidishn beys-oylem

ver darf a lid – un nokh dertsu af yidish?
(I know that in this world no one needs me,
me, a word-beggar in the Jewish graveyard.
Who needs a poem, especially in Yiddish?)[25]

The rhyme "*yidish/meridish*" (Yiddish/rebellion) in the poem's third and sixth lines crystallizes subtly the poet's vision of "*mer idish*" (more Yiddish) as a comfort and revolt in the Jewish graveyard after 1945. The Yiddish artistic word not only survives but continues, like Singer's demons, to act out of spite and against all odds, turning hopelessness into rebellion against the decline of the Yiddish speech community.

Notes

1. "Feminism and Yiddish Literature: A Personal Approach," in Naomi B. Sokoloff, Anne Lapidus Lerner, and Anita Norich (eds.), *Gender and Text in Modern Hebrew and Yiddish Literature* (New York: Jewish Theological Seminary, 1992), p. 226.
2. Almost the entire run of *Yizker* books and a large portion of modern Yiddish literature are available online in full text versions. Thanks to the National Yiddish Book Center, the New York Public Library, and other institutions, anyone with a computer can access a significant part of Yiddish print culture.
3. *I Keep Recalling: The Holocaust Poems of Jacob Glatstein*, trans. Barnett Zumoff (Hoboken, NJ: KTAV Publishing House 1993), p. 92.
4. Kadya Molodovsky, ed., *Lider fun khurbn: antologye* (New York, 1962), p. 10. My trans.
5. Trans. Irving Howe, in *The Penguin Book of Modern Yiddish Verse*, ed. Irving Howe, Ruth R. Wisse, and Khone Shmeruk (New York: Viking 1986), pp. 330–33.
6. *Abraham Sutzkever, Selected Poems*, ed. and trans. Benjamin Harshav (Berkeley: University of California Press 1991), p. 205.
7. Aaron Zeitlin, *Gezamlte lider* (New York: Matones, 1947), vol. II, pp. 472–73. Trans. Morris M. Faierstein in Abraham Joshua Hescheli, "After Majdanek: On Aaron Zeitlin's New Poems," *Modern Judaism* 19/3 (1999): 264–271, Appendix 1. The Heschel quote above is also from this article, which was originally published in *Yidisher kemfer* 29/771 (Oct. 1, 1948).
8. I. B. Singer, "The Last Demon," in *The Collected Stories of Isaac Bashevis Singer* (New York: Farrar, Straus and Giroux, 1996), p. 187.
9. The Polish Jewish Historical Commission and David Boder's interviews of Jewish survivors in multiple languages including a significant part in Yiddish are the most important projects to collect Jewish testimonies in the aftermath of the war (1944–1946).
10. The term "communal memory" used in connection with Yiddish Holocaust literature was introduced by David G. Roskies, "What Is Holocaust Literature?" *Studies in Contemporary Jewry*, 21 (2005): 172–73.

11. Yitskhok Varshavski, Review of *Un in dayn blut zolstu lebn*, "*Tsvey vikhtike bikher fun yunge yidishe shraybers.*"

12. Shmuel Niger, "Farbrekhn un shtrof," *Der tog*, Dec. 30, 1951. Repr. in *Yehuda Elberg: Eseyen vegn zayn literarishn shafn*, ed. Gershon Viner (Bar Ilan University, 1990), p. 68.

13. The volumes are: *Maydanek* (vol. 20, 1947), *In di fabrikn fun toyt* (In the factories of death, vol. 32, 1948), *Verk 'Tse'* (WORK 'C', vols. 64–65, 1950), *Goyroles* (Destinies, vols. 85–86, 1952) in *Dos poylishe yidntum* series (Buenos Aires: Central Union of Polish Jewry).

14. Niger, "Farbrekhn," p. 68.

15. First published in English, ref. Yosl Rakover, "Yosl Rakover redt tsu got," *Di goldene keyt* 18 (1954): 102–10. Zvi Kolitz, "Yossel Rakover's Appeal to God" (a new translation with afterword by Jeffrey V. Mallow and Franz Jozef van Beeck), *Cross Currents* (Fall 1994): 362–77. Micha Borwicz, "Der apokrif unter nomen 'Yosl Rakover redt tsu got,'"*Almanakh* (Paris) (1955): 193–203.

16. H. Leivick, "*Oysgeloshene likht tindn zikh vayter on*," in Mordkhe Shtrigler, *Maydanek* (Buenos Aires, 1947); Introduction to Arn Tverski, *Ikh bin der korbn un der eydes* (I am the victim and the witness) (New York, 1947); H. Leivick, "Dos folk zingt eybik," in Shmerke Katsherginski and H. Leivick (eds.), *Lider fun di Getos un Lagern* (New York: Altveltlekher Yidisher Kultur-Kongres, 1948). xxvii–xxxix. H. Leivick, *Mit der sheyres-hapleyte: tog-bukh fartseykhenungen fun mayn rayze iber di yidishe lagern fun der amerikaner zone in Daytshland* (New York, 1947).

17. Irving Howe, in particular, was a crucial proponent of Yiddish culture in the United States after 1945 in works such as *World of Our Fathers* (1976) and anthologies of Yiddish literature beginning with *The Treasury of Yiddish Stories* (1954).

18. The 92nd Street Y's Poetry Center's Yiddish and Hebrew Poetry Series featured more than thirty Yiddish poets, and a handful who wrote in Hebrew. These poetic performances are described in my article "Glatshteyn, Singer, Howe, and Ozick: Performing Yiddish Poetry at the 92 Street Y, 1963–1969," *Prooftexts: A Journal of Jewish Literary History* 30 (2010): 61–96.

19. *A mantl fun a prints* (1970) and *Dayne geselekh, yerushalayim* (1989).

20. The quote is from Singer's author's note in *Enemies: A Love Story* (New York: Farrar, Straus and Giroux, 1972).

21. Chava Rosenfarb, *Survivors: Seven Short Stories* (Toronto: Comorant Books, 2004), p. 86.

22. The novel was serialized in weekly installments in *Forverts*, March 25, 1979 to June 27, 1982. Chaim Grade died suddenly of a heart attack on June 8, 1982.

23. *Forverts*, March 25, 1979.

24. I. B. Singer, *Di familye moskhat* (*The Family Moskat*, 1950); Chaim Grade, *Der mames shabosim* (*My Mother's Sabbath Days*, 1955), and *Di agune* (*The Agunah*, 1961); Chava Rosenfarb, *Botshani* (Bochiany, 1983)

25. Trans. Robert Friend, in *The Penguin Book of Modern Yiddish Verse*, p. 538.

CHAPTER 7

The Holocaust in Russian literature

Leona Toker

The Soviet Jewish mortality toll during World War II was over 2 million, including over 200,000 soldiers killed at the front. Yet the total number of Soviet citizens who perished during the war was over 20 million. This proportion made it possible for Soviet literature to downplay the specificity of the Holocaust, representing the slaughter of the Jews mainly in terms of the Nazi murder of civilian populations in occupied areas. The subject of the Holocaust was taboo for long stretches of Soviet history; the trans-literated word itself came into use only after *perestroika*.

In fact, the Soviet blocking of information about the Nazi persecution of the Jews following the Molotov–Ribbentrop Pact of August 1939 was one of the reasons for the insufficiently strenuous efforts of Jewish civilians to evacuate eastwards during the first days of the war. As if by inertia, news of the massacres of Jews on the Soviet territories in late summer of 1941 likewise received little or no media coverage.

Whereas Holocaust survivors in the West could, if they wished, testify about their experience after the war, the ideological climate in the Soviet Union was not conducive to publication of survivor memoirs. Unless they had a record of fighting the Nazis along with the Soviet partisans, the survivors of ghettos and Nazi camps were suspect in the eyes of the author-ities and of a part of the population. The Soviet ideal of heroic resistance and self-sacrificial death blocked the possibility of publishing memoirs of sheer survival up until the beginning of the twenty-first century. By then most of the survivors had emigrated or died, some having left manuscripts in private archives.

In contrast to West European literatures, major works of Russian liter-ature of the Holocaust came from the writers who learned about the mass slaughter of Jews *ex post facto*. The earliest works were written by military journalists, such as Ilya Selvinsky, Vasily Grossman (1905–1964), Ilya Ehrenburg, and Lev Ozerov (Gol'dberg). Selvinsky's poem "Ya eto videl!" (I saw this!), written after the Soviet army regained the Crimean city of

Kerch' (that had been briefly occupied by the Germans) where a ravine with the bodies of seven thousand Jews was discovered, was the first literary record of the shocked realization of the nature of atrocities;[1] Grossman's essay "Ukraina bez evreev" ("Ukraine Without Jews"), published in *Einikeit*, the Yiddish periodical of the Jewish Anti-Fascist Committee, and his short story "Staryi uchitel'" ("The Old Teacher"), published in the journal *Znamia* (7–8, 1943), move also toward an understanding of their scale. Grossman's reportage about the fate of Jews in his native Berdichev (where his mother perished in 1941) and other Soviet territories was eventually suppressed, but his long essay "Treblinskii ad" ("The Hell of Treblinka") appeared in the journal *Znamia* in 1944 and, reprinted as a pamphlet, was used at the Nuremberg trials. Grossman had come to the site with the Soviet army and participated in the study of its topography and documentation as well as in interviewing witnesses. Though not all of his data were precise, his powerfully written account, complete with interpretive comments, has not lost its relevance to this day. It is, of course, punctuated by praise of the Soviet army as the liberating force and by references to the victims' expectations that Stalin would avenge their death. The former was genuine; and the latter was not entirely lip service either: revenge was, indeed, among Stalin's special talents. Grossman shows that the advance of the Soviet army was too slow to stop the murders but that it did prevent a total destruction of the evidence.

Whereas "The Hell of Treblinka" makes it clear that the overwhelming majority of the victims were Jews, Ilya Ehrenburg's 1944 poem "Babi yar"[2] does not mention nationality, though the reference to the victims as "my innumerable kin" is sufficiently suggestive. Over 33,000 Jews were killed in the ravine of Babi Yar, near Kiev, on September 29–30, 1941 (and more than double that number by the end of the occupation, with the total number of victims, of all nationalities, estimated at over 200,000). Lev Ozerov's poem, of the same title,[3] suggests the Jewishness of the procession of victims toward Babi Yar mainly by a reference to the Jewish cemetery that they pass. All of these early works are characterized by heart-rending moves of self-projection into the recent past, attempts to imagine the experience of the victims.

During the war the hostility of Soviet discourse-control to the singling out of the place of the Jews among the victims of the Germans (except for purposes of foreign relations, including appeal to American Jewish organizations) was partly explicable by the unwillingness to give non-Jewish soldiers the impression that they were fighting to protect the Jews. But the attitude prevailed in the postwar years as well: the truth about the

Holocaust might have raised too many unwelcome questions and analogies (e.g. with the organized Ukrainian terror famine of 1929–1932). The hypocritical ideological principle of nationality being irrelevant to the communist view of the world was translated into the injunction "not to divide the dead" in print or in memorial sites. Insistence on statistical facts was condemned as promoting Jewish nationalism. An additional problem was presented by the participation of the Ukrainians, Latvians, Lithuanians, and others in the slaughter of the Jews: though many collaborationists were tried and punished, literary references to their role in the killing of Jews were often attacked as attempts to stir up national conflicts. Part of the problem was associated with the peculiarly Soviet aesthetics: narrative details in Soviet literary works were usually treated as assessments of the "characteristic": in a work of fiction, a Ukrainian character in the role of a Nazi henchman would have been considered as widely representative unless underplayed or vastly compensated for by stories of the salvage of individual Jews by heroic non-Jewish families.

Together with Ilya Ehrenburg, Grossman had put together a collection of materials on the slaughter of the Jews on the Soviet territories during the German occupation; it was presented to the Jewish Anti-Fascist Committee of the USSR in 1945; parts were soon published in English abroad and parts printed by the Soviet Yiddish publishing house Der Emes. Yet the full Russian publication of *Chernaia kniga* (*The Black Book*), as the collection came to be known, was delayed by the censors' demands to reduce the visibility of the Jews among the victims and of the local population among the perpetrators (even though, in references to the latter, Ehrenburg insisted on the term *polizei* instead of ethnic terms). In 1946, under A. A. Zhdanov's ideological controls, the wartime liberalization of the Soviet discourse came to an end. The publication of *The Black Book* was forbidden in October 1947. The volume would come out abroad, in languages other than Russian; in 1980 it would be published in Russian in Jerusalem, and only in 1991 and 1993 in Kiev and Vilnius respectively.

In 1947, on the wings of his wartime popularity as a military reporter, Ehrenburg published the multiplot novel *Buria* (*The Storm*), which may have helped to implant the subject of Babi Yar most firmly in the collective memory. Its cross section of characters and paradigm of ideas were precisely modulated in terms of Stalinist political correctness at the beginning of the Cold War. Ehrenburg also implemented the lessons of his failed struggle for the publication of *The Black Book*: fine calculations of balance and the sifting of data allowed him to get away with a laconic episode of Jews being slaughtered in Babi Yar: old Hannah obeys the fake deportation order and, on arriving at the killing ravine with her granddaughter, attempts to beg for the little girl's life, naïvely offering her own instead, in a secular version, as it were, of Jewish martyrdom. Foreshadowed by the Germans' killing of a saintly Ukrainian and the emergence of another Ukrainian as a closet anti-Semite and anti-communist, the episode is complete with gestures of dignified resistance among the doomed and with a German officer's brutality. The theme of the victims' delusions about their destination effects a delay in the use of the toponym Babi Yar, until, on the very scene, it is named by a victim, gaining emphasis from its direct-speech sound-bite format. The hold of the toponym on the reader's memory is then reinforced by its becoming a recurrent signal of pain in a Soviet Jewish officer's inside views.

The novel represents practically all Nazi collaborators as, among other things, Jew-hunters; to emphasize that Babi Yar was not an isolated event, *The Storm* includes an episode of an old Jewish couple's public execution; moreover, Hannah's émigré elder son is shown perishing in an Auschwitz gas chamber, its horror distanced by the detached lyricism of his inner life.

Much of Ehrenburg's immediate audience, its war memories still fresh, tended to read *The Storm* for the love story between a Russian hero and a Frenchwoman. In retrospect, however, the love story seems to be part of the politically correct packaging of what, judging by his 1944 poem, Ehrenburg urgently wished to tell. The reference to the God of Hannah's young days not helping her may have been read as conventionally atheistic; in retrospect, however, it may also remind the initiated reader of the rabbinical notion of God hiding his face (*hastarat panim*).

The text of the novel consistently includes Jewish names in lists of warriors at the front or resistance fighters in the German rear; though, in tune with the specifically Soviet decorum, it places Jewish names last in all positive contexts.

The year 1947 still saw the publication of accounts of Jewish armed resistance to the Nazis in the ghettos of Minsk, Kaunas, and Vilnius, and among the Soviet partisans in the forests. The book of the Minsk ghetto and partisan fighter Hirsh (Girsh) Smoliar, *Mstiteli getto* (*Ghetto Avengers*), was published in Moscow that year, as was a collection of records about Jewish partisans, *Partizanskaia druzhba*. The Yiddish publications of the period, such as Peretz Markish's epic poem *Milkhome* (*War*) and several stories by David Bergelson could still engage in mourning the Jewish victims.

Except for a trickle in Yiddish, the first wave of publishing on the Holocaust ended in 1948. A radical change of policy was signaled by the closing of the Jewish Anti-Fascist Committee, followed by the arrests of its members, and a high rate of mortality among them, starting with the murder of the actor Mikhoels. Preparations seemed to be under way for Stalin's own "final solution" of the Jewish question – the deportation of the Jews to Siberia under conditions which would lead to massive loss of life on the transports and in places of resettlement. This was only prevented by the dictator's death in March 1953.

Ehrenburg's 1954 novella *Ottepel'* (*The Thaw*), celebrated less for its content than for its title, gave the name to the period of liberalization under Khrushchev. At the outset of this period Vasily Grossman worked on what would become his greatest achievement, the novel *Zhizn' i sud'ba* (*Life and Fate*), a largely self-sufficient sequel to his war novel *Za pravoe delo* (*For the Just Cause*). Whereas much of the careful if somewhat transparent balances in Ehrenburg's *The Storm* meant lessons learned from the official attacks on *For the Just Cause*, Grossman himself rejected such lessons. *Life and Fate* is, like *The Storm*, a multiplot novel, with scenes of intellectuals' work and private lives, of the battle for Stalingrad, and of Holocaust episodes that are more developed than in all the previous Russian-language works. The episodes are placed together for an in-depth probing of themes rather than for a sense of balance.

What kept *Life and Fate* from the press in the 1960s was not only the frankness of its fictional refraction of Holocaust materials but also, and perhaps mainly, its themes of the Soviet double-think, of the parallels between Hitler's and Stalin's regimes, of the grass-roots anti-Semitism, and of the incipient turn to official anti-Semitic policies in the Soviet Union even before the war is over. The typescripts of the novel were confiscated by the KGB – an event that added to the impetus of the rise of the *Samizdat*, the less easily controllable dissemination of manuscripts by manifold retypings by supportive readers.

The Soviet policy of obscuring the place of the Jews among the victims of Nazi atrocities continued during the "Thaw," with the partial understated exceptions of the media reports on the trials of Nazi criminals and their local collaborators. Whereas Stalin, apparently apprehensive of memories of his own problematic role at the beginning of the war, tended to discourage literary discourse on that part of recent history, in the years of the "Thaw" Soviet victory over Nazi Germany was successfully competing with the October Revolution as the "legitimating myth"[4] of the Soviet regime; not surprisingly, this entailed further reduction of the place of the Jews among the victims as well as the heroes of World War II.

Against such a background, the publication of Evgeny Evtushenko's poem "Babi yar" in the influential newspaper *Literaturnaia gazeta* (September 19, 1961) produced a shock comparable to that of the publication of Solzhenitsyn's

Odin den' iz zhizni Ivana Denisovicha (*One Day in the Life of Ivan Denisovich*) in *Novyi mir* a year later. Testimony to the poem's effect is provided by, among other things, its inclusion in Dmitri Shostakovich's Thirteenth Symphony. The poem does not visualize the slaughter at Babi Yar but protests against the absence of a monument at the site, as well as against anti-Semitism throughout history. Here the topos of imaginative self-projections takes the shape of the speaker identifying himself with an ancient Hebrew in Egypt, with a Jew dying on the cross, with Dreyfus, with Anna Frank, with victims of Russian pogroms and the Nazi extermination drive. The poem ends with the claim that though the speaker has no Jewish blood in his veins, by anti-Semites he is hated like a Jew and is therefore "a real Russian."

As in the case of many other caprices of the "Thaw," the publication of the poem was followed by official and unofficial attacks on the author and the editor. On September 24, the newspaper *Literatura i zhizn'* published a poem by Aleksei Markov that starts with the line "What kind of a Russian are you . . .?" and goes on to accuse Evtushenko of neglecting the heroism of the millions of Russians who had lost their lives fighting fascism. The vocabulary of this poem tellingly includes the word "cosmopolite," which, during Stalin's anti-Semitic operations, was used as a euphemism for Jew. The famous poet and translator Samuil Marshak wrote a verse rejoinder, in which he placed Markov in the line of notorious anti-Semites. Another verse rejoinder came from Konstantin Simonov (who, however, had managed to avoid references to the Jewishness of the victims in his wartime report on the liberation of Majdanek). Ehrenburg and others likewise attempted to defend Evtushenko. Two years later, at a meeting with the literary community, Khrushchev reiterated the official condemnation of the poem for failing to present the Nazi crimes "truthfully" in making it seem as if Jews were their *only* victims.

Evtushenko had difficulties getting published for over twenty years, which, however, only enhanced his fame, turning his poetry into a much sought fruit, not forbidden but severely rationed. More than twenty years later, already at the beginning of the *glasnost'* period, the impact of his "Babi yar" was partly replicated by Andrei Voznesensky's 1986 poem "Rov" ("The Ditch"),[5] written after the poet learned about the population digging for valuables in the mass grave of slaughtered Jews near Simferopol. It is less well remembered that back in 1965 Voznesensky also wrote the poem "Zov ozera" ("The Call of the Lake"),[6] on finding out that a lake popular with fishermen had been created by the Germans over the mass grave of slaughtered Jews.

Evtushenko's next contribution to the memory of the Holocaust came in his 1964 poem "Bratskaia GES," a pean to post-Stalinist monumental socialist construction. Among the monologues of the builders of this power plant is that of Izia Kramer, a ghetto survivor, who tells about his love for the seventeen-year-old Riva and about her being driven to death by a female guard. When the poem was published in 1965, most of its readers shared its optimism; some considered its Bolshevik enthusiasm a small price to pay for the haunting lines of Izia Kramer's monologue.

Another literary event associated with the Kiev massacre came in 1966, at the end of the "Thaw." This was the publication, in the journal *Yunost'*, of *Babi Yar: A Documentary in the Form of a Novel* by Anatoly Kuznetsov (1929–1979). A half-Russian half-Ukrainian survivor of the Nazi occupation, Kuznetsov had seen much and eventually collected a great deal of second-hand information about the killings in the ravine; it was he who had first shown the site to Evtushenko. His narrative produced a sensation in the Soviet Union, was reissued as a book, gained immediate fame abroad, and was translated into several languages, in its heavily censored form. After the Soviet suppression of the Prague Spring in 1968, having lost all hope of publishing his works undistorted and unable to develop as a writer in the stifling atmosphere of "stagnation," Kuznetsov defected to England. He then published the uncensored version of *Babi Yar* in Russian and in English: it contains the material that came out in *Yunost'* in regular typeface; bold type is used for the passages and expressions that, the author claimed, had been deleted from that version; and later additions, some restoring passages that had been self-censored before submission to *Yunost'*, appear in square brackets. Though the accuracy of the typographical distinctions is at times doubtful, the interweaving tripartite structure adds considerable cultural-history value to the work, along with its value as Holocaust testimony.

Kuznetsov had not so much chosen the subject of his major work: the subject had chosen him. The Kiev suburb where he had lived with his mother and grandparents during the war was in close vicinity to Babi Yar. His direct memories are supplemented by "documents," namely, Soviet media reports, and the announcements, proclamations, and edicts issued by the German occupiers of Kiev. The book also includes the materials of the interviews Kuznetsov conducted with two survivors: one of them is Dina Pronicheva, who had managed to creep away from under corpses at night (this account of the events was made use of in D. M. Thomas's *The White Hotel* [1981] and, from the perspective of a fictional perpetrator, apparently also in Jonathan Littell's *The Kindly Ones* [2006]). The would-be novelistic form of the narrative points to the possibility of elisions and transformations in the boy observer's experience, yet the speaker clearly makes a valiant effort to establish the historical truth about matters of public interest.

Kuznetsov's narrative stages tensions between the struggle for existence and the workings of a humanistic conscience. Both collide with the pervasive sense of the absurd: feats of ingenuity and endurance are repeatedly thwarted by unforeseen contingencies; survival is a matter of chance loopholes in a general fatality; conscience is helpless in the face of violent outer forces and insistent inner drives. The largely chronological arrangement of the narrative partly diverts the reader's attention from the thematic juxtapositions of episodes that repeatedly suggest this darkly sober view of the human condition.

Like Grossman in "The Hell of Treblinka," Kuznetsov traces the stages of the mass slaughter operation in a way that helps to explain the reasons for the apparent passivity of the masses of Holocaust victims. He mentions, among other things, that when the Jews were made to report to the assigned location on September 29, rumors had been circulated that they would be deported to Palestine. Like Grossman, he registers the transition to the burning of the corpses after the decision had been taken to remove the evidence of their crimes. As in Grossman's essay, the details of the construction of the furnaces and the arrangement of the piles of corpses are presented with an industrial worker's attention to detail. The tone of the narrative is more restrained than Grossman's: inset stories of Pronicheva and Vladimir Davydov exempt the authorial speaker from the need for self-projection into the midst of the victims. Grossman deals with the eleventh-hour insurrection and break-out from Treblinka; Kuznetsov's narrative likewise records that when the job of burning corpses was all but completed and the execution of the work team clearly scheduled (two years after the events of September 1941), 330 prisoners broke out of the camp; most perished during the escape attempt. Another shared topos is the memory of an unnamed prisoner who chooses a martyr's death over betraying his comrade's escape plans.

However, it is another concern of Kuznetsov's narrative that helped it through the nets of the censorship in the Soviet Union of 1966: large consignments of non-Jews were also eventually executed at Babi Yar – Gypsies, hostages, Soviet prisoners of war, chance victims of punitive roundups, and the citizens who had infringed the sundry draconian rulings of the occupiers. This issue is introduced on the opening page by the words of a passerby, who counters the question whether it was there that the Jews were killed by saying "and what about all the Russians who were killed here, and the Ukrainians and other kinds of people?" This episode helps to adduce the mandatory Soviet bias, but the narrative also shows that, having started with Jews, slaughter develops its own momentum.

A third concern of the book, almost completely expunged from the 1966 *Yunost'* publication, is the parallels between the murderous Nazi regime and the Stalinist regime which had also exacted many millions of victims. Kuznetsov would die of a heart attack in 1979; in the early nineties his uncensored *Babi Yar* would return to the Moscow presses.

Meantime, the climate of the "Thaw" also allowed for the publication of some translated Holocaust materials. The *Diary of Anna Frank* came out in 1960, with Ehrenburg's preface mentioning "the six millions." Three years later the reconstructed diary of Maria Rolnikaitė, a young survivor of the Vilnius ghetto, came out in Yiddish; under the title *Ya dolzhna rasskazat'* (*I Have to Tell You*), a censored Russian translation came out two years later, to be greeted by some readers (unfairly) as the work of the Soviet Anna Frank. Another child survivor, who had been sheltered during the war by a heroic Lithuanian family and rose to literary fame in the 1960s, was Icchokas Meras. His 1960 autobiographically based *Geltonas Lopas* (*The Yellow Patch*) came out in Russian in 1963. The same year, in Vilnius, Meras published a collection of short stories whose symbolic title story "Žemė visada gyva" ("The Earth Is Always Alive") deals with the mass shooting of Jews, adults and children. His 1963 novel *Lygiosios trūksta akimirka* (translated into Russian as *Vechnyi shah*, 1965, and into English as *Stalemate*, 2005), a stylized tale of spiritual resistance in the ghetto, eventually came out in many languages, including German and French. Meras's 1965 novel *Ant ko laikosi pasaulis* (*What the World Rests On*; Russian *Na chem derzhitsia mir*, 1966) traces the life of a Lithuanian peasant woman who shelters a Jewish boy during the German occupation. Innovative in structure and style, Meras's works were part of the Lithuanian national literary process as well as part of the conversation about the Holocaust in which the emphasis lay on heroism and self-sacrifice rather than on victimhood and struggle for survival.[7]

Since the early sixties, literary works that touched on the Holocaust had better chances of making it into the press if they seemed to have some other agenda, especially one useful for the period needs of the Soviet public relations. Thus Ilya Konstantinovsky's *Srok davnosti* (*The Statute of Limitations*, 1966), whose plot is riveted around a young Jewish girl betrayed to the Gestapo by a Polish-German couple in order to take possession of her baby, outwardly targets West Berlin, and, by imputation, West Germany in general, for sheltering the guilty, rejecting guilt, and raising the postwar generation in ignorance of the recent past. The repertoire of the novella's ideas, however, seems to be geared up to preempting a similar ignorance on the part of the Soviet reader.

Indeed, limited as references to the Holocaust were in Soviet literature, they could suffice to create a private chamber of horrors in the minds of the reading public and map approaches to it. Near the middle of his novella, for instance, Konstantinovsky's narrator offers an explanation of postwar anti-Semitism, without calling it by name: people were so tormented by the sight of those brought en masse to the gas chambers, and so tormented by their own inability to rescue or help them, that in the end they started hating those who were being gassed. By contrast, one of the inmates of the Pawiak prison in Warsaw, a traditionally anti-Semitic Catholic peasant by the name of Tselina (possibly an allusion to the French writer Celine), ends by fervently praying for the Jewish heroine led away to the execution.

During the period of the "Thaw," Jewish literature was no longer taboo. Translations of the works of Yiddish writers such as Sholom Aleikhem were published, and even some translations from Hebrew, including Bialik's poems on the Kishinev pogroms. Some works on the Holocaust in Yiddish had been published in Moscow during the war, for example Der Nister's *Korbones* (*The Victims*), but the "Thaw" period also saw the publication of the Holocaust works of those Soviet Yiddish writers who had fallen victim of Stalin's 1948 anti-Semitic about-face: among those executed on "The Night of the Murdered Poets," August 12, 1952, was the prizewinning poet Peretz Markish (1895–1952), whose novel *Der Troyt von Doires* (*Footsteps of Generations*), dealing with the resistance of Polish Jews, came out, duly censored, in 1967.

The rupture of the relationship between the Soviet Union and Israel after the Six Day War of 1967 doubled as a signal to impede the trickle of Holocaust literature. Though the Yiddish newspaper *Sovietishe Heimland* continued to print poems and narratives about the Holocaust (because of its limited and dwindling readership it was not perceived as a threat) and though Der Nister's *Vidervuks* (*Regrowth*, 2011) came out in Yiddish in Moscow in 1969, much of the major Yiddish writers' work has not been translated into Russian to this very day, partly because it presents too radical a vision of the Jewish predicament to accommodate Soviet and even post-Soviet topoi. At this late date these works have little chance of making contact with the Russian literary process, even though some have much to say on Russian and Jewish-Russian cultural history.

The onset of the "stagnation period" in the USSR largely meant a gap in the history of Russian Holocaust literature. Yet the moratorium on the subject was not complete. A sprinkling of poems about the Holocaust could be found in collections of verse by such poets as Boris Slutsky, Yulia Neyman, and Semyon Lipkin.[8] The literary panorama of the "stagnation period" was, indeed, characterized by the presence of the so-called "intermediate literature" (*promezhutochnaia literatura*), whose slightly unofficial flavor allowed it to compete with the growing corpus of the *Samizdat* (literature disseminated by secret home retypings) and *Tamizdat* (works smuggled out and published abroad). Anatoly Rybakov's novel *Tiazhelyi pesok* (*Heavy Sand*), published in 1978, could be considered a part of this "intermediary" corpus: the engaging but sober tone of its Soviet Jewish industrial-engineer narrator purports to lay a realistic basis for an epic fantasy of a Jewish family in an unnamed small Southern Ukrainian town, its larger-than-life members (many of them versions of biblical types) counterbalancing every anti-Semitic stereotype, and its cast of characters multiplying over three decades sufficiently to accommodate a vast paradigm of heroic resistance or cruel death at the hands of the Nazis. The customary Soviet emphasis on the ethos of resistance and on the personal dignity of the victims is not an attendant but the central issue of this novel; the nationality of the *polizei* is tactfully downplayed; and the mandatory theme of internationalism takes the shape of close friendly relationships between neighbors belonging to different ethnic groups, their joint struggle against the Germans, the martyrdom of both Jewish and non-Jewish resistance fighters, as well as the tendency of assimilationism in the survivors' marriages.

The ethos of resistance is also prevalent in Mikhail Lev's Yiddish novels dealing with Sobibor and with Aleksandr Pechersky, the Jewish hero of its uprising. These novels were published in Russian as well.[9] By contrast, Aleksandr Borshchagovsky's 1980 play *Damskii portnoi* (The ladies' tailor) represents the night of a Kiev Jewish family just before Babi Yar; its repertoire of ideas includes normal and even moving human life before it was cut short, the self-delusion of the victims, and the various moral stands of non-Jewish neighbors. Without sweeping under the carpet the cruel treacherousness of a part of non-Jewish environment, the play, like Rybakov's *Heavy Sand*, maintains the Soviet topos of human brotherhood – the reciprocal help of Jews and non-Jews and their shared victimhood. This representational topos was in keeping with the Soviet opposition to the idea of the national links between Jewish people across state borders, which translated into militancy against the State of Israel, especially since 1967. It may well be that some literature about the Holocaust was allowed into the press in order to help the self-presentation of Brezhnev's policies as anti-Israel but not anti-Semitic. Soviet discourse also holds the copyright on the slanderous comparisons between Zionism and Nazism, which two decades later gained popularity among left-wing circles in the West.

Literary treatments of the Holocaust started coming out again during the period of *glasnost'* and *perestroika*, even though the dominant cultural agenda of the period was more receptive to reconceptualizations of Soviet history, its leaders, its victims, its prisons and camps. Grossman's *Life and Fate* was published in 1988; in 1990 a film was made on the basis of Borshchagovsky's *The Ladies' Tailor*, starring Innokenty Smoktunovsky (a guarantee of success). Boris Slutsky's posthumous *Zapiski o voine* (Notes about the war), edited by Pyotr Gorelik and including the chapter "The Jews," was published in 2000. Educational programs for teaching Russian Holocaust literature in high schools were developed by the newly formed research center, directed by I. Altman. Uncensored memoirs of Rolnikaite were reconstructed in 2012. Some Holocaust memoirs, newly written or extracted from old desk drawers, appeared also in Belarus' and Ukraine.

Since the bulk of the Russian literature of the Holocaust is part of the Soviet literary corpus, it is largely devoid of the theological dimension. Neither the idea of afterlife nor the concept of religious martyrdom were admissible in the framework of Soviet ideology; this was one of the reasons why the consolatory motifs frequently resorted to were the motif of revenge and the motif of moral victory either through resistance or through the preservation of human dignity of the victims. The literary corpus developed in the dynamic tension between ethically fueled creative energies and official ideological and administrative controls. This process was further complicated by the partial seepage of official ideology into the consciousness of the writers, and by the channeling of some constituents of the ethical repertoire (such as the ethos of sheer survival) into the companion corpus, the literature of the Gulag.

Notes

1. "Ya eto videl!" *Bol'shevik* (a Krasnodar newspaper), January 23, 1942. Repr. in *Krasnaia zvezda*, the main newspaper of the Soviet army.
2. *Novyi mir* (January 1945): 16.
3. "Babi yar," *Oktiabr'* 3–4 (1946): 160–63. Repr. in Ozerov's 1947 collection *Liven'*.
4. Zvi Gitelman, "Politics and the Historiography of the Holocaust in the Soviet Union," in Zvi Gitelman (ed.), *Bitter Legacy: Confronting the Holocaust in the USSR* (Bloomington: Indiana University Press, 1997), p. 28.

5. "Rov," *Yunost'* 7 (1986): 6–15.

6. "Zov ozera," in *Den' poezii – 1966* (Moscow: Sovetskii pisatel', 1966), pp. 57–61.

7. Another important event was the 1967 publication of *Ir be ginklo kariai* (*Unarmed Warriors*), a collection of materials about Lithuanians who sheltered Jews during the German occupation, put together by Sofija Binkienė. It may have been allowed into the press in order to balance the trials of Lithuanian collaborators with the Nazis, yet it is an important and moving document. In 1967 Binkienė herself was officially recognized by Yad Vashem as a "Righteous among the Nations."

8. See entries on these writers in Maxim D. Shrayer, ed., *An Anthology of Jewish-Russian Literature: Two Centuries of Dual Identity in Prose and Poetry*, vol. 11 (Armonk, NY: M. E. Sharpe, 2007).

9. Mikhail Lev eventually emigrated to Israel. Among Russian-language Jewish writers who emigrated, the subject of the Holocaust was explored in the stories of Efraim Sevela and in some of the works of Felix Kandel.

CHAPTER 8

The Holocaust in English-language literatures

S. Lillian Kremer

English-language Holocaust literature is a tapestry of autobiographical writing by refugees and survivors who have abandoned their birth languages, by contemporaries based on research and imagination, and by post-Holocaust generations. American writing, the most prolific of the English-language contributions, accelerated when fueled by the 1961 Jerusalem trial of Adolf Eichmann, the intellectual debate aroused by Hannah Arendt's analysis of the trial, and use of Nazi annihilation rhetoric by Arab nations during the 1967 Six Day War. While the *Shoah* was conspicuously absent from most Anglo-Jewish writing, those who found refuge in England as part of the *Kindertransport* and other émigré writers have incorporated Holocaust themes into British literature. Among the Commonwealth nations, Canadian Holocaust literature is most abundant, perhaps because of Canada's own substantial immigrant Jewish population and its cultural links to the United States.

Kindertransport narratives

Decades after their childhood emigration to Britain, American Lore Segal and British writers Karen Gershon, Lotte Kramer, and Gerda Mayer created the *Kindertransport* genre, addressing the initial stress of separation from parents and the later pain of parental and extended families' demise as well as the emotional stress of exile and assimilation to English society. Segal established the genre's subject matter and tone in *Other People's Houses* (1964). She conveys the loneliness of a child refugee, the discomforting adjustment to foreign culture, and the burden of presumed responsibility for her parents' survival. Narrating from the child's point of view, Segal relates the historic and personal: the annexation of Austria, the family home commandeered by the SS, parting with her distraught parents, initial feelings of alienation, and satiric accounts of English food and class prejudice. Holocaust witness, guilt for being absent when her parents perished, yearning for a lost home, and Zionist aspiration are recurrent themes in Gershon's fiction and poetry. Her fictionalized autobiography, *Bread of Exile* (1985), maps the isolation engendered by feeling unwelcome when England interned German-Jewish refugees as possible enemy aliens. In *A Lesser Child* (1994) she chronicles the impact of the rise of Nazism on the private life of an assimilated German-Jewish child. Following decades of silence, Kramer re-engaged long-repressed memories in poems of childhood trauma in Nazi Germany, meditations on the lives lost in Europe, and English safety juxtaposed with European peril. The range of her subjects and tone emerge in "Cocoon," depicting a middle-aged child survivor hiding behind voluntary amnesia; in "At Dover Harbour," contrasting refugees' views of continental Europe as "Hard and calloused with bitter blood" and England, "the heart's island" that calls the poet "to whispering benedictions"; and in the biting satire of "A New Subject," debunking racial "science" as a teacher touting Aryan superiority selects a perfect specimen, only to have a classmate reveal that the ideal is a Jew.

English playwright Diane Samuels takes further the child refugee themes, interweaving scenes from wartime Germany and contemporary London. *Kindertransport* centers on Eva/Evelyn, who survives wartime trauma by becoming English. The postwar reunion of *Kindertransport* refugee and survivor mother reveals the resentment of a child blaming parents for sending her abroad alone and the survivor parent's agonizing recognition that the beloved child prefers the surrogate parent, rejecting association with a threatened people. Having internalized the hatred of others, Eva Schlesinger becomes Evelyn Miller. Her reinvention as an English Christian to escape anti-Semitism not only cancels her Jewish identity, but erases her daughter's Jewish legacy as they share contemporary British life devoid of Jewish connection.

Christian anti-Semitism and the Holocaust

Many English-language writers acknowledge that racist theory shaped Nazi anti-Semitism. But they also weave in the history of Christian anti-Jewish persecution. Indeed, the Nazis drew on church protocol of persecuting Jews (imposing yellow badges, defiling Torah scrolls, burning synagogues, humiliating rabbis, establishing ghettos, expropriating property, expelling Jewish communities, and inciting mass murder), and followed church practice in coordinating acts of violence with the Jewish calendar. Many writers thus correlate events from past and contemporary Christian anti-Semitism and the Holocaust. English poet Jon Silkin, for example, connects the martyrdom of York Jewry in 1190 to the annihilation of European Jewry in the Holocaust, associating earlier indifference to the plight of England's Jews with later indifference to the annihilation of European Jewry in "The Coldness." "The Legend of the Last Jew," American novelist Arthur Cohen's internal narrative for *In the Days of Simon Stern* (1972), structurally foreshadows the Holocaust sequence and thematically reveals the similarities to, and distinctions between, church and Nazi anti-Semitism. Set in modern Spain at a time when the church has achieved universal conversion to Catholicism, the tale charts the trial and martyrdom of Don Rafael Acosta, a descendant of forced converts of Iberia and a secret Jew. The trial evokes persecutions of the Spanish Inquisition and anticipates the Holocaust.

American Leslie Epstein dramatically links Christian and Nazi anti-Semitism by staging a Nazi-sponsored street play derivative of medieval morality drama as Holocaust prologue in *King of the Jews* (1979). Adhering to medieval form, a wagon appears where actors perform an anti-Semitic diatribe characterized as an accurately portrayed historic event for an audience of soldiers, ethnic Germans, Poles, and reluctant Jews. The play's Elders of Zion conspire in Prague's Jewish cemetery against Europe. After the play's concluding scene depicting Nazi rescue of Christian Europe, the audience is urged to wreak vengeance on the Jews. Assaults begin as pageant cart bells and peeling church bells resound, metaphorically connecting medieval church-orchestrated pogroms with the Nazi orchestrated terror. Epstein ironically juxtaposes the drama's Elders of Zion canard with historic German establishment of the *Judenrat*, the Jewish Council of Elders forced to administer Nazi decrees in Europe's ghettos.

American Marge Piercy's exhaustively researched World War II novel *Gone to Soldiers* (1987) places traditional European anti-Semitism, rather than racist theory, at the center of active French collaboration with Nazi Germany. She conveys how this was expressed in the wartime French press, in an art exhibit supporting anti-Jewish legislation, and most vilely in the French police roundup and deportation of Jewish immigrants and French Jews. Similarly, the novel chronicles American anti-Semitism flourishing in State Department suppression of Holocaust reports, in Congressional anti-immigration legislation, in housing covenants, workplace discrimination, weekly anti-Semitic radio rants by Father Coughlin and Reverend J. Frank Norris, mainline press Holocaust silence, and postwar mistreatment of Jewish displaced persons by General Patton.

Holocaust universe

American literature chronicles the barbarism of the Nazi universe from its early manifestations in *Kristallnacht* and the fall of Warsaw, to *Einsatzgruppen* mass killings, to establishment of a huge complex of ghettos, concentration camps, and SS-operated death camps. Playwright Arthur Miller depicts an antechamber to the camp universe in *Incident at Vichy* (1964) set in 1942 at a French detention center where a group of non-Aryan-appearing men await checks of their documents and penises that will determine whether they are deported and killed. Their fate is in the hands of a German professor of "racial anthropology" and French Vichy police. In *Broken Glass* (1994) Miller dramatizes an American woman's obsession with *Kristallnacht*, the orchestrated 1938 Nazi attack on synagogues, Jewish shops and homes, accompanied by assault, murder, and massive arrest of Jews while German police observe passively.

Americans who treat the Holocaust terrain directly, more often set their works in major ghettos and labor camps rather than in concentration and death camps. Assisted by Polish and Yiddish translators, John Hersey chronicles the epic story of the Warsaw ghetto in *The Wall* (1950). In the guise of a recovered "Archive" of dated entries, Hersey charts events from the September 1939 fall of Warsaw to the month-long April 1943 Warsaw Ghetto Uprising. A small group of ghettoites under the direction of an archivist document ghetto hardships, clandestine educational and cultural programs, operations of the *Judenrat*, ghetto police, political and resistance organizations. Leon Uris, too, employs the journal form in *Mila 18* (1961) to tell the story of the Warsaw ghetto.

The family ordeal in Susan Fromberg Schaeffer's *Anya* (1974), based largely on the author's interviews with survivor Anya Savikin Brodman, reveals Jewish experience in Nazi-occupied Vilna: exclusion from public places, curfews, confiscation of personal property, dismissal from employment, mandatory wearing of yellow stars, subjection to state choreographed anti-Jewish street violence, forced separation from the non-Jewish population in sealed ghettos, followed by death or deportation to concentration camps. Survivor interviews, rather than historic research, was the source for Schaeffer's depiction of the Vilna ghetto situated in the worst section of the city, its rotting buildings and primitive plumbing inducing rampant disease, its food privations and increasingly frequent death selections of children, the aged, and the infirm.

The fictional Baluty Suburb of Leslie Epstein's novel is based on his research of Lodz ghetto and its flamboyant, enigmatic Jewish elder, Chaim Rumkowski. Much of the novel's authenticity stems from Epstein's representation of social and political factions, including the tenacious struggle of child smugglers, factory workers engaging in large-scale work stoppages, sabotage operations, a clandestine nursery defying the German ban on Jewish births, and the *Judenrat*'s management of work assignments, food and housing distribution, police operations, and, most tragically, compilation of deportation lists. The fictional elder, Trumpelman, embodies the conflict of men whose tragedy was compounded by forced complicity with Nazis in the hope of saving as many co-religionists as possible. True to the historic model, Trumpelman is a complex and contradictory figure: a sinner-savior, a charismatic healer, a persuasive speaker, a charlatan, a dictator, a gullible victim. Among others who have treated Rumkowski's character are Saul Bellow, in a brief vignette of Nazi evil and absurdity in *Mr. Sammler's Planet* (1970), and playwrights Harold and Edith Lieberman in *Throne of Straw* (1982) dramatizing Lodz Jews' response to Nazi oppression.

Survivor of the Cracow ghetto, Plaszów and Skarzysko labor camps, and Buchenwald concentration camp, Ilona Karmel writes as an eyewitness. *An Estate of Memory* (1969), mapping the ordeal of four women begins in *medias res*, forcing readers to navigate a bewildering environment without conventional literary connections – a strategy that suggests the disorientation experienced by ghetto and camp arrivals. Camp quarters consist of mud-splashed, ash- and straw-littered rotten plank floors, furnished with a double tier of lice-infested bunks and slop pails emanating suffocating chlorine and urine odors. Women ravaged by typhus and dysentery are denied access to latrines. Extending their vulnerability is labor in munitions factories triggering prolonged illness from toxic chemicals for some and rapid death for others. At roll calls, they endure rigorous calisthenics, flogging, lengthy periods of kneeling on gravel, and the dread of periodic death selections. Their lives focus on the acquisition, distribution, and supplementation of inadequate rations; their conversations, dreams, and relationships are food centered; and they measure their value to Germans according to a food calculus. The women who have created a surrogate family sustain each other by a moral code appropriate to their circumstances. To steal food from the Nazis is moral; to take a deceased inmate's portion is acceptable. However, to steal from a fellow prisoner is occasion for severe reprimand. Moral implications of *lager* existence are central as quandaries arise while victims struggle to survive in a universe designed for

their demise. Victims agonize over whether individual behavior might result
in collective retaliation; whether to protect themselves during a "selection"
or allow another to use their hiding place; how to cope with an informer, a
denouncer; how to decide whose suffering should be allayed and whose
should be ignored.

Concentration and death camps are rendered less frequently than ghettos
in English-language works. Thomas Keneally does depict the Plaszów
concentration camp, while Karmel and Piercy deal with the horrors of
Drancy and Auschwitz. The latter also references the munitions work of
Dora Nordhausen realistically and metaphorically in the fevered imagination of a child survivor whose mother and twin sister labor in this underground hell. Arthur Miller's teleplay *Playing for Time* (1985), an adaptation
of an Auschwitz memoir of the same title by Fania Fenelon, a French Jew
who played in the Auschwitz women's orchestra, faithfully delineates the
deprivation and degradation of the comparatively privileged women struggling to perform satisfactorily and survive.

Historic and imagined Nazis

While most Jewish writers focus on the victims of Nazism and give little
attention to historic Nazis or characters for whom they have provided
models, non-Jewish writers including Martin Amis, D. H. Thomas,
William Heyen, William Styron, and Keneally explore Nazi psychology
or culture, and Robert Harris fabricates a postmodernist counterfactual
novel of Nazi victory in *Fatherland* (1992). Aside from Keneally and
Heyen, the Holocaust is of minor interest to these writers who focus on
postmodernist experimentation with perception and form as in *The White
Hotel* and *Time's Arrow*. Styron's shallow portrait of Rudolf Hoess in
Sophie's Choice (1979) centers on his Auschwitz domestic life rather than
his role in the construction and operation of gas chambers and crematoria.
Although neither character's motivation is fully elucidated in Australian
Keneally's *Schindler's Ark* (1982), known in America as *Schindler's List*,
Amon Goeth, SS officer in charge of liquidating the Cracow ghetto and
commandant of Plaszów, is a crude, violent foil to suave, benevolent Oskar
Schindler, a Nazi opportunist who arrives in Poland to exploit Jewish
economic losses and metamorphoses into the rescuer of 1,100 of his factory's
Jewish slave-laborers. Heyen, American nephew of two German soldiers,
writes powerful confessional poetry preoccupied with expiation and
memory of his family's history and legacy in *The Swastika Poems* (1977),
My Holocaust Songs (1980), and *Erika, Poems of the Holocaust* (1984).

He identifies the crimes of the Third Reich and indicts Himmler, Mengele, Göring, and little-known members of his own family, the architects, enablers, and bystanders, while memorializing their victims. Attuned to the moral imperative of memory, he demands that contemporaries and future generations "hear," "see," and "remember."

Among Jewish writers, Leslie Epstein and Ilona Karmel depict camp commandants in sharply drawn sketches; George Steiner offers a protracted Hitler portrait; and poets Leonard Cohen, A. M. Klein, Michael Hamburger, and Charles Reznikoff indict the guilty in either solemn or satiric tone. Amon Goeth appears briefly and repeatedly in Karmel's autobiographical novel as a sadist diabolically denying camp inmates the meager rations allotted by German law, leading a dog trained to strike in response to the word *Jude*, and selecting old women to be flogged or shot. Reznikoff eschews poetic language and imagery, invoking courtroom testimony from the Nuremberg and Eichmann trials in his book-length poem, *Holocaust* (1975). British play-wright Peter Barnes adopts and then purges the comedic voice in the controversial *Auschwitz* (1987) to satirize Nazism's impersonal language and corruption and then to denounce Nazi bureaucrats who calmly discuss killing "undesirables" and competitive bidding for gas chambers. Hamburger, who began writing about the Holocaust thirty years after his childhood emigration, testifies to the unhealed wound inflicted by Nazism. "In a Cold Season" moves from the bureaucratic mind-set of Eichmann, to personalize his villainy by recalling the poet's murdered grandmother forced to write a reassuring postcard to her family. Similarly, in "Security" the poet juxtaposes his English children's safety with his youthful vulnerability and the atrocities he could have experienced had his family remained in Germany.

Canadian Mordecai Richler repeatedly casts Nazis as the subject of serious and satiric censure. Following brief Jewish confrontation of ex-Nazis in *The Acrobats* (1954), *A Choice of Enemies* (1957), and *Cocksure* (1968), his sustained treatment in *St. Urbain's Horseman* (1971) evolves on realistic and mythic levels. Protagonist Jake Hersh, obsessed with Josef Mengele, invents the Horseman, a postmodern golem, able to traverse time and distance to locate and denounce Mengele. Fellow Canadian, poet Leonard Cohen satirizes Hitler, Göring, Goebbels, and Eichmann and juxtaposes gardens with concentration camps to highlight the absurdity of the Nazi universe in *Flowers for Hitler* (1964).

Many of the ideas George Steiner explores in essays find fictional develop-ment in *Anno Domini* (1964) and *The Portage to San Cristobal of A. H.* (1981). Whether set in a French seaside village, a country mental asylum, or a South American jungle, Steiner's stage is the courtroom. Despite the magical realism indulgence of the novel, the monologues for Israeli

Nazi-hunters and A. H. embody thoughtful reflection on the Holocaust and language, specifically the impact of Nazism's rhetoric on civilization and the human psyche. The closing monologue of A. H., built on false analogies of Aryan and Judaic principles, highlights Nazi lies, distortions, misrepresentations, defiling Jews and Judaism. Leslie Epstein's ironic designation of the Nazis as "Brave Ones," "Warriors," "Others" alludes to Nazideutsch, echoing Steiner's connection of linguistic and political corruption, from designating people as vermin to genocidal extermination. Epstein's ghetto chief officer, F. X. Wohltat, is based on historian Gerald Reitlinger's account of Hans Biebow's ghetto role and is influenced by Hannah Arendt's assessment of Nazis as bourgeois businessmen, ordinary job-holders, and family men. Wohltat, like Biebow, exploits ghetto labor to enrich himself.

Resistance

Debunking the myth that Jews passively acquiesced to Nazism, English-language Holocaust literature chronicles resistance including concealed or open hiding in works by Louis Begley, Elżbieta Ettinger, Irena Klepfisz, Schaeffer, Dan Jacobson, and Art Spiegelman; "organizing" food, medicine, and clothing in the ghettos and camps, by Schaeffer, Karmel, Epstein, and Piercy; work sabotage in the ghettos by slowing production and manufacturing defective materials, by Epstein, Karmel, and Keneally; militant resistance in the form of courier services, sabotage of Nazi equipment, escapes from ghettos and camps, ghetto uprising, blowing up a crematoria oven, individual and team operatives in organized resistance and partisan units in fiction by Piercy, Ettinger, Hersey, and Uris; and celebration of a historic resistance fighter, Hanna Senesh, by poet Ruth Whitman in her "imagined diary," *The Testing of Hanna Senesh* (1986). Ordinary prisoners sought to sustain survival through the efforts of concentration camp old-timers or "old numbers" advising newcomers, fellow prisoners helping the ill stand through roll calls, picking lice from each other and nursing one another, and office and warehouse workers sharing life-sustaining information and supplies.

Ettinger's autobiographical novel, *Kindergarten* (1970), set in the Warsaw ghetto and Aryan Poland, effectively links themes of resistance and Holocaust-wrought character transformation. The active resistance theme is centered on a partisan representative of women relying on "Aryan" looks and forged identity documents to work as couriers. Her teenage daughters survive outside the law, "passing" as Catholics. They adopt Polish customs, habits, and mannerisms; guard every word, every gesture, lest they betray nervousness or unfamiliarity with the adopted routine. Drawing on her experience, Ettinger masterfully represents the anxiety engendered by open hiding – eluding blackmailers, the constant need to alter identity and relocate, fidelity to the assumed identity coupled with the incessant fear of discovery and denunciation.

While Michael Chabon invokes the tradition of the golem as a figure of Jewish resistance for themes of imaginary and real "escape" in *The Amazing Adventures of Kavalier and Clay* (2000), Piercy pays homage to men and women who fought fascism in the cafés of Paris, countryside hideouts, the Montaigne Noire, and the torture chambers of the Milice and Gestapo. Her resisters are members of Jewish and French resistance units. The fictional resistance, based on extensive historic research, centers on the Lévy-Monot patriarch's roles as maquisard leader and commander of the "Armand-Jules," the Jewish army; and on female couriers, supplying false Aryan documents and leading downed Allied pilots over heavily patrolled borders into Spain, finding safe housing for children who could pass as Gentiles, and guiding others across the Pyrenees for eventual emigration to Palestine. Her resistance figures, drawn from the ranks of the Jewish Scout Movement, Zionist organizations, and the Jewish immigrant communities, disrupt the Germans through sabotage, free captives from French collaborationists, and assist Allied preparation for the cross-Channel invasion.

Spiritual resistance, maintaining one's humanity in the face of intentionally dehumanizing conditions of captivity, appears in many works, including those by Karmel, Piercy, Cohen, and Epstein. In these writings, prisoners nurture each other intellectually, culturally, and spiritually through religious observance in individual or communal prayer, recitation of poetry and song, ghetto plays, concerts, and classes, narratives of prewar life and anticipation of postwar restoration, and the Zionist dream of rebirth in the ancestral homeland.

Survivor syndrome

Survivor syndrome is a persistently developed theme of English-language Holocaust fiction. American novels focusing on the subject generally begin and end in the post-Holocaust era and return through memory and nightmare to the Holocaust universe. In addition to briefly rendering the survivors' long-term Holocaust-inflicted physical ailments, writers address survivors' psychological struggles: depression stemming from guilt for outliving families and friends, dysfunctional postwar parent/child relationships, recurrent nightmares, voluntary and involuntary memories of

Holocaust indignities, betrayals, torture, impairment of the capacity to love and trust, failure to resume prewar ambitions and professions, identity and religious crises. Unlike the pre-Holocaust immigrants of Jewish-American fiction, these immigrants often avoid assimilation and acculturation. They grapple instead with the European past and labor to preserve Jewish particularity, history, and tradition. Many authors surround protagonists with survivor communities functioning like a Greek chorus commenting on the behavior and views of the principal dramatic figures and incorporating diverse national Holocaust histories.

Edward Lewis Wallant's *The Pawnbroker* (1961) introduces characteristic devices of American Holocaust fiction: dramatically juxtaposing survivors' pre- and post-*Shoah* lifestyles and counterpointing survivors with prewar immigrants and native-born Americans. Sol Nazerman's ironic occupational metamorphosis from cultured professor to pawnbroker is a grotesque adoption of the moneylender role long and ardently assigned the Jew in Christian art and politics. Bearing disfiguring scars from a Nazi medical experiment, Nazerman suffers Holocaust nightmares and involuntary recollections evoking the concentration camp universe. Dark images of filth, disease, and pollution of black Harlem stimulate recollection and objectify his weariness with life, his sense of impending collapse. Devastated by loss of his family, he maintains an emotional wall, distanced from contemporaries and engaging in meaningful dialogue only when an antagonist provokes him. Philosophically and psychologically estranged from his bourgeois suburban sister who emigrated before the Holocaust in search of economic advancement and assimilation, he also resists the efforts of the emblematically named social worker, Marilyn Birchfield, who offers him genuine, albeit naïve, friendship. These relationships reflect postwar Holocaust silence, potential auditors reluctant to hear, and survivors assuming the innocent cannot enter the Holocaust universe, even through empathetic imagination.

Nearly a decade after Wallant's introduction of a survivor protagonist, Saul Bellow evokes the Holocaust through the survivor's traumatic incremental memories of a mass killing in *Mr. Sammler's Planet*. At first, Bellow presents a brief synopsis of the massacre and Sammler's survival struggle. A more complete account near the novel's midpoint shifts from remembrance of physical detail to philosophic speculation and moral judgment. The entry in the final chapter focuses on anticipatory terror, memory based on heightened sensory perception of being buried alive. Through this pattern Bellow suggests permutations of Holocaust memory, recall of the event dependent on the contemporary context and the stimulus. Like Wallant,

Bellow depicts continued trauma decades after victimization by focusing on contemporary behavioral and emotional disorders. Convinced that he is marked forever and distinguished from the Holocaust uninitiated, the elderly one-eyed survivor wonders if he belongs among the living. Even his contemporary anxiety arising from an encounter with a petty thief manifests itself as "The breath of wartime Poland passing over . . . damaged tissues."[1] Descending into the subway to escape the pickpocket, Sammler relives his fall into the mass grave and his later imprisonment in a mausoleum. Like Nazerman, Sammler is surrounded by a community of survivors whose Holocaust-era abuse parallels his experiences, whose psychological suffering mirrors his own, and whose choral commentary corroborates his narrative.

Cynthia Ozick's 1983 survivor portraits in "Rosa" and *The Cannibal Galaxy* enhance understanding of survivor syndrome. Rosa Lublin of *The Shawl* (1989) collection, whose last name evokes the killing centers of Poland, lives a bitter survival, the hell of lost family, lost aspirations, lost language, failed communication with those who evade her Holocaust testimony and those who would exploit her history. Ozick repeatedly employs key images and tropes – shawl, fence, and electricity – to link the two narratives "The Shawl" (1980) and "Rosa" (1983) and to suggest the Holocaust's pervasive intrusion in the survivor's psyche. The introductory short story derives its power from metaphor, dramatic and poetic concentration, delineating a young mother's traumatic witness of a German soldier tossing her infant against the concentration camp's electrified fence. The discursive sequel portrays the title character at fifty-eight, recalls her prewar life and dramatizes her dysfunctional postwar existence. Antithetical survivors, Rosa and Stella, her niece and concentration camp fellow prisoner whom she blames for her infant's death, perceive each other as mentally ill. Rosa feigns acceptance of Magda's death to appease Stella, yet her invention of multiple adult lives for Magda and letters to her in elegant Polish epitomize the survivor's ongoing trauma. Emblematic of their polar attitudes is Stella's interest in establishing social relationships and embracing English contrasted with Rosa's isolation, faulty English, and stubborn attachment to Polish. Her linguistic syntactical mis-structuring and fragmentation evoke the Holocaust-wrought ruptures she endures. Increasingly tormented by the loss of her child and public indifference to her Holocaust witness, Rosa destroys her New York shop and is exiled to Florida for rest and recuperation. She lives in a seedy hotel and subsists on a diet evocative of *Shoah*-era starvation. Measuring time and life by the Holocaust, the survivor classifies three ages of experience: "The life before, the life during, the life after ... The life after is now. The life before is our *real* life, at home, where we was born." For Rosa, "Before is a dream. After is a joke. Only during stays and to call it a life is a lie."[2]

Although English novelist Anita Brookner does not advance survivor syndrome as expansively as do American writers and is a latecomer to the subject, she considers the long-term impact of Holocaust survival on two German-Jewish child refugees in *Latecomers* (1988), noting the effect of post-traumatic stress. Survivor syndrome looms large not only in literature of the 1960s–1980s by the first generation of Holocaust writers, but in second- and third-generation *Shoah* literature.

Second generation: inherited memory and trauma

Writing by children and grandchildren of survivors focuses not solely on survivor syndrome, but on the next generation's inherited memory and trauma, the impact of survivors' Holocaust silence or witness on their lives, their representation of the Holocaust legacy, and post-Holocaust Jewish identity and belief. American Art Spiegelman's critically acclaimed but controversial two-volume graphic novel *Maus* (1986, 1992) is a self-reflexive postmodernist work addressing the witnessing roles of survivors and their children. He juxtaposes European past and American present to convey his parents' prewar, Holocaust, and postwar lives and reveal how that history affected his psychological well-being and professional work. The Holocaust invades the American present in the form of survivors' perpetual mourning and remembrance and the psychological burden imposed on the son of being a replacement for, and in competition with, an unknown perished sibling. Spiegelman's multifaceted psychic trauma is manifest in anger accompanying the conviction that his problems are regarded as insignificant, frustration at the responsibility he bears for his father's welfare, and vacillation from alienation to ambivalence regarding Jewish identity.

The short stories of Thane Rosenbaum's *Elijah Visible* (1996) trace the angst-ridden life of the son of Holocaust survivors through multiple personas immersed in second-generation Holocaust trauma. The book's frame stories introduce Adam Posner's adult psychic trauma and conclude with its childhood manifestation. In "Cattle Car Complex" Posner, trapped in an elevator, suffers the claustrophobic terror of a Nazi cattle-car transport. Released, he awaits a concentration camp guard's command to step right or left. In "Little Blue Snowman of Washington Heights," the neighborhood becomes Nazi Germany where Adam, reliving his parents' memories as his present, is convinced that the Nazis have arrested his parents. *Second Hand*

Smoke (1999), whose title evokes crematoria smoke and inherited memory, examines contradictory responses of brothers to the absent or dominant influence of their survivor mother. Duncan, reared by his mother to be physically and emotionally strong, educated to avenge the shattered lives of Jewish victims of Nazism, is an aggressive, Holocaust-obsessed prosecutor of Nazi war criminals. Duncan's foil, his half-brother Isaac, whom the mother tattooed with her camp number and abandoned as an infant in Poland, is the caretaker of Warsaw's Jewish cemetery. Influenced by Isaac's spiritual approach, Duncan eventually sets a restorative course for himself.

Like the angry young men of Rosenbaum and Melvin Bukiet, rage is a dominant motif in J. J. Steinfeld's "Dancing at the Club Holocaust"(1993). Guilt and vengeance obsess his protagonist. Enraged by his parents' suffering, the son achieves catharsis, not on the psychiatrist's couch, but by burning a neo-Nazi meeting place where anti-Semitic films are screened.

Spiritual rupture, repair, and restoration: survivors and second generation

Questions regarding the nature of God, covenantal negation, and affirmation in the face of Holocaust atrocities engender recurrent alternate reflections in American Holocaust writing. Echoing the religious protestors in works by Elie Wiesel and I. B. Singer, Richard Elman's Holocaust victim in *Lilo's Diary* (1968) denounces God in a parody of sacred liturgy. Themes of post-*Shoah* crises of faith and the possibility of belief in a covenantal God are at the center of Hugh Nissenson's "The Pit" (1988) and "The Blessing" (1988). The protagonist of Thomas Friedman's *Damaged Goods* (1984) exercises religious rebellion by freeing himself from the constraints of his Orthodox community. Yet, he describes himself as "semi-observant, semi-religious," maintaining his connection to Jewish history and perpetuating the memory of Auschwitz. In *The Messiah Tarries* (1995) Melvin Bukiet ponders the nature of divinity in a post-Holocaust world that precludes redemption as he examines the place of Jewish law in the lives of American characters. He turns to black humor in *After* (1996) to follow the antics of a group of survivors dealing in the black market relying on lessons learned in a sub-camp of Buchenwald. These former yeshiva students are so overwhelmed by Nazi evil and its legacy that amorality has become the norm for their survival in the post-Holocaust world. The prewar pious have lost their traditional faith and find no reason to renew belief in a world that turns Jewish religious texts and literary treasures into pulp, that burns the books as it has their authors and readers. It is only with the birth of a child, with the next generation, that hope exists for something beyond mere survival, for the renewal of meaningful Jewish lives. Using the narrative conceit of a tennis match as a *beth din*, a religious court, Thane Rosenbaum's "The Rabbi Double-faults" (1996) presents a theological contest between rabbinic twin brothers whose antagonistic religious beliefs and practices are Holocaust-determined. Whereas the righteous and scholarly Israeli rabbi, who immigrated to Palestine in 1936, defends God's active, redemptive presence in the world, the "godless" American rabbi, an Auschwitz survivor, abandoned piety and judges God to have failed the covenantal role. In the last minutes of the game, God's advocate double-faults when his brother's arm brace falls, exposing his Auschwitz tattoo, proof of God's Holocaust-era silence.

Central to the agenda of religious survivors is regeneration of Judaism, and the preservation and transmission of Jewish history and civilization. In the fictional worlds of Cohen, Ozick, and Potok, the Jewish sacred legacy is an essential component of witness testimony. Potok's rabbis, yeshiva teachers and scholars build new centers of Jewish learning in the United States and Europe. For teachers and scholars of *The Chosen* (1967) and *The Promise* (1969), Hasidic community leaders of *My Name is Asher Lev* (1972) and *The Gift of Asher Lev* (1990), the way to derive meaning from the *Shoah* is to embrace a program of repair generating a religious renaissance. Similarly, Ozick's Joseph Brill of *The Cannibal Galaxy* develops a dual Hebrew/Western academic curriculum and her American Jews who become engaged in Holocaust commemoration, Enoch Vand of *Trust* (1966) and Bleilip of "Bloodshed" (1976), discover or return to Judaic studies or orthodoxy. Arthur Cohen's *In the Days of Simon Stern* (1973) employs religious thought, history, and sociology in modes ranging from an expository essay to tales within tales, dream-drama, sermon, letters, meditations, and commentaries narrated by a Torahic scribe, Nathan of Gaza, to foster the theme of survivor mission and post-Holocaust restoration. A descendant of rabbis, and a survivor of Auschwitz and Buchenwald, Nathan's authenticity springs from his Holocaust witness and prewar religious vocation. His post-Holocaust occupation is chronicling the life and times of Simon Stern, a messianic figure dedicated to healing Holocaust survivors. Stern builds a *Bene Brak*, modeled on that erected by the Hebrews after the destruction of the Holy Temple, where survivors will heal each other in body and spirit. Inverting Nazi death selections, Stern travels to the concentration camps to select restorers of diverse backgrounds united by their passion for renewal of Judaism and Jewry. Even the prewar secular Anglophile, Bellow's Sammler, manifests renewed interest in Jewish particularity and history. Although he indicts God for failure to uphold the covenant, and wants to reject God completely, an involuntary, unwelcome persistence of belief prevails. At the novel's end, he "was a man who had come back. He had rejoined life."[3] With acceptance of the judicial role his family imposes on him because of his Holocaust experience, Sammler contemplates typical Bellovian ethical questions aimed at "the true stature of a human being."[4] He rejects Hannah Arendt's "banality of evil" thesis arguing instead for an ethical code sanctifying life, leading to holiness, spiritual illumination, and social responsibility.

While some second-generation writers reiterate their parents' protest for God's lack of intervention, for others, as Alan and Naomi Berger explain in *Second Generation Voices*, the Holocaust witness leads to *tikkun atzmi* (self-healing), to *tikkun olam* (repair the world), and affirmation of Jewish identity. Protagonists in Lev Raphael's *Dancing on Tisha B'Av* (1990) struggle with societal marginalization as gay men and Jews. They experience strained relations with parents who either maintain Holocaust silence or indulge in persistent recollection and have deprived their sons of Jewish identity to protect them from the genocidal violence they encountered. In response to the spiritual void in his life and in opposition to his parents' estrangement from Judaism, the son of the titled story embraces Jewish practice and observance. Canadian-born Aryeh Lev Stollman's *The Far Euphrates* (1997), set in Ontario of the 1950s and 1960s, is an eloquent mystical coming-of-age narrative about the son of a rabbi who learns that the congregation's cantor and his twin were subjects of Mengele's medical experiments and internalizes their suffering. He retreats from the outside world in an act evocative of Divine withdrawal into self at the time of creation enabling him to rediscover God's mercy and loving kindness. Similarly, *The Illuminated Soul* (2000), a midrash on the mysteries of memory, includes the positive impact on a Canadian family of a refugee's wartime travels to save her family's fifteenth-century illuminated Hebrew manuscript.

Holocaust literary representation

Holocaust representation and reception have garnered the attention of critics and creative writers alike. In *Touching Evil* (1969) American novelist Norma Rosen examines two women's reception, the older having viewed early photojournalism of concentration camps and the younger the 1961 televised Eichmann trial. That there can be no return to pre-Holocaust normality is evident in each woman's Holocaust obsession and bearing "witness through the imagination" in their writing and lifestyle. Philip Roth's portrait of an artist as a young Jew in *The Ghost Writer* (1979) engages Holocaust representation and reception with a meditation on anti-Semitism and a critique of the Broadway revision and trivialization of *The Diary of Anne Frank*. Despairing of the de-Judaized play, Roth dislodges Anne from the mythic attic sentimentalist of that production to imagine an intellectually and morally astute Anne of the Westerbork transport, Anne of Auschwitz and Belsen. Through Nathan Zuckerman's voice, Roth reminds readers that although the fate of European Jewry is often met with indifference, Anne's story became popular because "the young girl of her diary was ... only dimly Jewish."[5] Just as he questions the clichés of Holocaust representation and response in *The Ghost Writer*, criticizing such sentimentality as metamorphosing tragedy into kitsch, so in *The Prague Orgy* (1985) Roth challenges Eastern European assault on Holocaust memory and Jewish identity.

Among English-language creative writers who have and continue to explore issues of reception and representation, Leonard Cohen portrays the Jewish artist coming to terms with the legacy of the Holocaust in *The Favorite Game* (1963); Frederic Raphael's fictional Jewish writer in *The Glittering Prize* (1976) realizes that *Shoah* remembrance will permanently affect his identity; Jerome Rothenberg adopts the legitimate voices of the perished in *Khurbn* (1989); Adrienne Rich renders the impact of Holocaust consciousness on the inner lives of contemporaries in "Eastern War Time" and juxtaposes widespread indifference to the Holocaust and poetry's role in keeping memory alive in "Then or Now" (1991); Harold Pinter argues for the need to attend to historic memory and moral engagement with the Holocaust in *Ashes to Ashes* (1996); Francine Prose critiques Holocaust envy, misappropriation, distortion, and consumerism in "Guided Tours of Hell" (1997); and Tova Reich and Howard Jacobson lend their satiric voices to explore the use and abuse of Holocaust memory in *My Holocaust* (2007) and *Kalooki Nights* (2007).

Representative of the younger generation's pains to write authentic Holocaust texts are Art Spiegelman's efforts to accurately render his father's Holocaust narrative in *Maus I* and *Maus II*. *Maus I* takes readers from prewar Poland to the gates of Auschwitz and the second volume deals with the challenge of representation of the concentration camp universe and its aftermath. Meticulously drawn details of hiding places, ghetto, Auschwitz barracks and work sites, gas chambers and crematoria mark Spiegelman's extraordinary ability to use "commix" to evoke historic authenticity. He scrupulously charts his efforts to recover the past through extensive research and interviews with his father, noting that his mother's story is mediated through Vladek. Agonizing over delineating Holocaust history in cartoon format, drawing people in animal forms, and avoiding the pitfalls of the medium, Spiegelman ponders whether reality is too complex for graphic representation and engages in harrowing self-rebuke for his literary and commercial success built upon genocide. Among the most powerful cartoon frames delineating both second-generation torment and creative angst are those revealing the cartoonist, mouse mask in place, sitting at his drawing table hovering over a mountain of mouse corpses, followed by frames of an aggressive interview with reporters and a series of the artist progressively miniaturized during an interview with his psychiatrist. Further exposition of Spiegelman's creative process is the subject of *Meta Maus* (2011), which includes the archive of audio interviews with his father, memories of his mother and interviews with people who knew her in the camps, historical documents, and an array of photos, drawings, and essays probing the questions that *Maus* provoked.

Growing up with Holocaust silence, Joseph Skibell, whose family lost eighteen members, gives voice to those who had been silenced through an imaginative recreation of his great-grandfather Chaim Skibelski and his fellow East European villagers in a novel of magical realism, *A Blessing on the Moon* (1997). Drawing on history, Talmudic fables, and Yiddish folktales, Skibell yokes the incredible and the true as his narrator/protagonist, the dead Skibelski, climbs out of a mass grave accompanied by his dead rabbi now metamorphosed into a talking crow. Together they survey victims, perpetrators, and bystanders of Jewish annihilation.

Bearing witness

So significant in North American Jewish literature are bearing witness to the Holocaust and consideration of post-Holocaust Jewish identity that many characters are identified as scribes, researchers, prosecutors, witnesses, moral mentors, teachers, and returned Jews. Cohen's Nathan of Gaza brings the dedication of a Torahic scribe to testimony of starvation, disease, and illness among the inmates of Auschwitz and also references Chaim Weizmann's Holocaust-era speech attesting to massive Jewish deaths. In an unremitting litany, Ozick's researcher for the Office of Strategic Services in *Trust* chants a roll call of the dead and the Nazi killing centers. Witness testimony appears as direct confrontation of a Jew and German in Ozick's "The Suitcase," and as oral history in "Levitation." By reciting a catalog of Nazi atrocities in their prosecution of A. H., Steiner's Nazi-hunters dramatize the process of bearing witness. Leiber, a survivor who crawled out from a mass grave, is a voice of historical memory and ethical imperative, never losing sight of the genocidal proportions, citing specific camps and the death tolls. Steiner commemorates the culture that nurtured the victims and condemns the culture that produced the perpetrators. Epstein introduces visual documentation, creating an artist and photographers who record ghetto life and death for posterity in the manner of the historic clandestine ghetto photographer, Mendel Grossman.

Philip Roth creates a survivor-mentor to successfully instruct a repentant lapsed Jew in "Eli, the Fanatic," as does Bernard Malamud in "The Last Mohican." Malamud's survivor leads an American painter through the Jewish ghetto, synagogue, and cemetery of Rome, exposing him to Holocaust history and a rediscovery of Jewish ethics. Similarly, in "Lady of the Lake," his Buchenwald survivor leads an apostate American Jew to recognition of the folly of his renunciation of Jewish identity. Canadian A. M. Klein's magisterial *The Second Scroll*, composed in five chapters named for the Pentateuch, blends poetry, fiction, and essay bracketing the Holocaust between European pogroms and the redemptive creation of the State of Israel, bearing both direct and indirect witness. Holocaust witness is the essential element of Henry Kreisel's poetry and fellow Canadian poet Irving Layton juxtaposes ex-Nazis and Jews in Canada, laments the victims, and condemns Holocaust indifference and amnesia.

Fealty to the imperative to remember and record – reflective of Arthur Cohen's conviction that post-*Shoah* generations are obligated "to describe a meaning and wrest instruction from the historical"[6] – is perpetuated in the work of many second-generation writers. Melvin Bukiet bears witness to Holocaust loss in *Stories of an Imaginary Childhood* (1992) by setting the work in a Polish *shtetl* of 1928, delineating the vibrant Jewish life soon to be extinguished and evoking the coming catastrophe allusively. He concludes with "Torquemada," recalling the long history of anti-Jewish persecutions heralding the Holocaust. Anne Karpf, the English daughter of Polish-Jewish survivors, alternates between Holocaust and post-Holocaust time in *The War After: Living with the Holocaust* (1996), a blended book of autobiography, biography, interview, and social history testifying to the continuing impact of the *Shoah* on survivors and their children. She maps the trajectory of her absorption and transformation of her parents' narratives, first to myth and morality fable and later to "edit" and "shape" taped documentary, distinguishing between what she was ready to hear and what her parents were ready to tell.

Canadian poet and novelist Anne Michael's *Fugitive Pieces* (1996) portrays a child survivor haunted throughout his life by his parents' murder and his sister's abduction. Rescued, adopted, and educated by a Greek man of letters, Jakob Beer grows up mourning the destruction of his family and striving to come to terms with his tortured memories in adopted languages foreign to his traumatic experience. His is a linguistic stance common to many Jewish survivors who abandoned their oppression-associated birth languages. Unlike Bernard Malamud's adult refugee in "The German Refugee" whose loss of language anticipates his suicide, Jakob Beer, and those he influences, discovers that language is the vehicle of witness and repair.

Thane Rosenbaum's *The Golems of Gotham* (2002) combines magical realism, Jewish legend, and mysticism to engage themes of inherited Holocaust suffering, the responsibility of the artist for preservation of memory, and ethics of Holocaust representation. In an effort to cure her father, the daughter of a second-generation blocked writer summons not only her survivor grandparents who committed suicide to return as golems but also Jerzy Kosinski, Paul Celan, Jean Amery, Piotr Rawicz, and Primo Levi, survivors who wrote compellingly about the atrocity and committed suicide. The literary golems eliminate vestiges of Nazism in the public sphere and inspire the writer to compose a Holocaust novel, thereby fulfilling his moral responsibility to art and history.

English-language literature of the *Shoah* contributes significantly to understanding the twentieth century's horrendous history, its psychological and theological aftermath, and the moral imperative to bear witness, thereby fulfilling an obligation inherent in the Jewish tradition of remembering and reiterating the historic narrative as inscribed in the Passover Haggadah.

Notes

1. Saul Bellow, *Mr. Sammler's Planet* (New York: Viking, 1970), p. 9.
2. Cynthia Ozick, "Rosa," in *The Shawl* (New York: Alfred A. Knopf, 1989), p. 58.
3. Bellow, *Mr. Sammler's Planet*, p. 264.
4. Ibid., p. 212.
5. Philip Roth, *The Ghost Writer* (New York: Farrar, Straus and Giroux, 1979), p. 144.
6. Arthur Cohen, *The Tremendum: A Theological Interpretation of the Holocaust* (New York: Crossroad, 1981), p. 2.

CHAPTER 9

Polish literature on the Holocaust

Monika Adamczyk-Garbowska

From the outset Polish literature on the Holocaust featured a clear division into victims/survivors (i.e. Polish-Jewish writers) and witnesses/observers (Polish non-Jewish writers). This fundamental division continues along successive generations, extending to those who were born toward the end of the war or even long after it. Such writers may be termed potential or vicarious victims and witnesses. While in other historical or cultural contexts such a division might provoke doubt, in this case it is justified, as the experiences and perspectives of these two main groups are diametrically different. Indeed, this division between victims and observers became apparent even before the end of the war in *Z otchłani* (From the abyss, 1944), a clandestinely published collection containing works by both Jewish and non-Jewish writers (including Michał Borwicz, Mieczysław Jastrun, Jan Kott, and Czesław Miłosz).

Each group contains generational sub-groups. Authors born before the war include adults and children. The best-known writers and poets in the "adult" generation are Adolf Rudnicki (1912–1990), Stanisław Wygodzki (1907–1992), and Artur Sandauer (1913–1989) on the Jewish side, and Tadeusz Borowski (1922–1951), Miłosz and Zofia Nałkowska (1884–1954) on the non-Jewish side. The second generation incorporates writers who were children during the war and came to see the Holocaust as fundamental in their formation as individuals and artists. Sometimes the Holocaust is present in their writing virtually from the beginning, as in the case of Henryk Grynberg (b. 1936), while in other instances it appears at a later stage, as in the case of Hanna Krall (b. 1935), for whom the decisive factor was her encounter with one of the leaders of the Warsaw Ghetto Uprising, Marek Edelman. The "children" group also includes Jewish authors who began to speak about their childhood experiences several decades after the war, such as Michał Głowiński (b. 1934) and Wilhelm Dichter (b. 1935). Their counterparts on the non-Jewish side include Andrzej Szczypiorski (1928–2000) and Jarosław Marek Rymkiewicz (b. 1935).

The third generation of writers did not experience the Holocaust directly. Among these are Piotr Matywiecki (b. 1943), conceived in the Warsaw ghetto, Anna Bikont (b. 1954), and Agata Tuszyńska (b. 1957), who were born in the 1950s and only discovered their Jewish roots as adults. Within this group there are also the "latecomers," such as Piotr Szewc (b. 1961) and Paweł Huelle (b. 1957), born into non-Jewish families after the war.

The position of victim dictates a different perspective from that of the observer. Jewish authors emphasize the destruction itself, various physical, religious, and cultural aspects of the tragedy. In contrast, non-Jewish writers are preoccupied by the question of Christian responsibility for what happened, and whether, and to what degree, they passed the humanitarian test. The victim's viewpoint, then, comes from inside the destroyed community; the observer's from outside it.

Again, Polish-Jewish writers have devoted little space to the suffering of non-Jewish Poles. Non-Jewish authors, for their part, developed a Polono-centric perspective. Madeline Levine, a translator of Polish literature on the Holocaust into English, is right when she says that "little attention is paid in Polish-Jewish literature on the Holocaust to the sufferings of the Polish population, the assumption being that the Poles were infinitely better off than the Jews because they were allowed the freedom to choose between resistance and compliance (an attitude which ignores the thousands of Poles who also died at the hands of the Nazis for no 'good' reason)."[1] But the Israeli scholar Sidra DeKoven Ezrahi is also right in saying that in Polish literature (by which she means that written by non-Jews) on the Holocaust, "the prevailing concern . . . is with the implications of the Holocaust for the Pole or for Poland, rather than for the victim, who often appears more as a mythical echo of the past than as a real, suffering Jew."[2] These attitudes are understandable. A full comprehension of the role of the "other" would require superhuman empathy.

For many Jewish writers the Holocaust is the most important or virtually the only theme. For instance, once Hanna Krall started writing about the destruction of the Jews she never really returned to previous subjects. Similarly, Henryk Grynberg considers the Holocaust fundamental, saying that "the Polish writer is not . . . performing his mission, unless he takes account of this vast theme, takes a stance, speaks out on this most important of the events that occurred within his memory or the memory of his loved ones."[3] And indeed, that is how many Polish-Jewish writers conceive of their mission.

For most non-Jewish writers, the Holocaust is a minor element of their oeuvre. To be sure, probably no major Polish poet has not at some stage of his or her career addressed the Holocaust. Władysław Broniewski (1897–1962) did so in the poems "To the Polish Jews" and "Ballads and Romances," Zbigniew Herbert (1924–1998) in "Mr Cogito Seeks Advice," Miłosz in "Campo dei Fiori" and "A Poor Christian Looks at the Ghetto," Anna Kamieńska (1920–1986) in "Mordekhay Gebirtig's Table," and Wisława Szymborska (1923–2012) in "Still." But for none of them is the Holocaust a central or recurring motif.

Polish-Jewish writers, moreover, often perceive the Holocaust in the context of previous tragedies, mourning the destruction of Eastern European Jewry and noting its effect for generations, including future ones. Non-Jewish writers highlight "reading the ashes,"[4] attempting to comprehend what happened, plumbing the Christian conscience, and expressing contrition over the destruction of Polish Jewry. Some see the Holocaust as an unprecedented event (Rymkiewicz refers to the *Shoah* simply as "that,"[5] reasoning that no word can reflect the terrible uniqueness of *that* tragedy), while others (such as Szczypiorski) place the annihilation of Europe's Jews in the context of twentieth-century totalitarianism.

The Holocaust affected not only subject matter but also the type and manner of writing by Polish authors. Rudnicki, a Jewish writer who before the war had aspired to enter the Polish mainstream and to that end had avoided Jewish themes, after the war expressed regret at not having written much about the Jews. Julian Tuwim (1894–1953), for his part, wrote his poetic manifesto *We, the Polish Jews* in April 1944 on the first anniversary of the Warsaw Ghetto Uprising, and emphasized his fraternity with his fellow Jews – a bond of which he became fully aware only as a consequence of the Holocaust.

For the first generation of Polish-Jewish survivors, an important theme is the *shtetl* (see Julian Stryjkowski [1905–1996], Arnold Słucki [1920–1972], Kalman Segal [1917–1980], Rudnicki, Zofia Grzesiak [1914–2004], and Stanisław Benski [1922–1988]). Particularly for those who were absent from Poland during the Holocaust, the focus on the *shtetl* is a form of surrogate testimony to that which was annihilated.

Polish-Jewish literature

The Holocaust changed the face of Polish-Jewish literature. It divided postwar Polish-Jewish writers into two groups: (1) those who, under the influence of their wartime experiences, resolved to devote their works to Jewish themes; and (2) those for whom the tragedy of the Jewish people was the impulse to take up writing. The leading representative of the former group is Rudnicki, and that of the latter Stryjkowski. Some writers became more conscious of their Jewish roots (e.g. Tuwim in his essay "The Monument and the Grave"), though they otherwise remained in the orbit of their previous subjects. Other writers, including Jastrun and Kazimierz Brandys (1916–2000), responded to the Holocaust, and the political situation in Poland after the war, by keeping silent about their Jewish background.

Most Jewish authors who began to write after the war would have become writers even without the experiences of the Holocaust. Yet the Holocaust dictated the themes of their work, The motif of survivor guilt present in Rudnicki's work, for example, also arises in many other Jewish authors. Leo Lipski (1917–1997), for instance, who writes out of direct experience about the Gulags, pays tribute to the victims of the Holocaust in "Roe Deer's Brother," in which he stated that with that story he wished to ease his guilt that he, too, was not on the other side of the ghetto wall.

Early postwar period

Until 1949 there was relative freedom of expression in Poland. Collections of poetry published shortly after the war included those by Jastrun (who had already in 1944 published the collection devoted to the Holocaust), Stanisław Jerzy Lec, Wygodzki, Brandys, Sandauer, Rudnicki, and Jerzy Andrzejewski. But the most important literary works of this period are Borowski's collections of short stories *We Were in Auschwitz* (1946), *World of Stone* (1948), and *Farewell to Maria* (also 1948, a selection published in English as *This Way for the Gas, Ladies and Gentlemen*), and Nałkowska's *Medallions* (1947). These works initiated a new type of literature about the war, which was in later years continued by other writers (including Grynberg). Borowski's short stories became world classics. An important collection published after the war is *The Song Will Survive Intact: An Anthology of Poems about Jews under the German Occupation* (1947), edited by Borwicz. It contains poems by Polish and Polish-Jewish poets from the 1944 underground volume *From the Abyss*, works by poets who spent the war outside Poland (Broniewski, Józef Wittlin [1896–1976], Antoni Słonimski [1895–1976], and Tuwim), poems by Polish-Jewish poets who perished in the Holocaust (Zuzanna Ginczanka [1917–1944], Henryka Łazowertówna [1910–1942], and Szlengel), by survivors (Izabela Gelbard [1893–1969], Stefania Ney-Grodzieńska [1914–2010]), and by poets who wrote in Yiddish, published in Polish translation.

Those of the older generation who most systematically addressed the Holocaust were Rudnicki and Wygodzki. In several of his best works Wygodzki expresses the survivor's sense of guilt. One such instance is a poem from the cycle *Pożegnanie* (Farewell), in which he asks why he did not share the fate of his loved ones. He specifically refers to the tragic episode when, deported to Auschwitz, he took cyanide, which he also gave to his wife and daughter. They both died, but he survived. The awareness that he had indirectly caused the death of those most dear to him only served to intensify his guilt.[6]

Stalinist period (1950–1955)

The foremost event in the Polish literature of this period was the publication in 1954 of Leopold Buczkowski's (1905–1989) *Black Torrent*, a work written shortly after the war that was innovative in its "broken" form, designed to reflect the disintegration of the world it was describing (his next Holocaust novel, *Pierwsza świetność* [The first glory], was to come out in 1966). Another important work was Tadeusz Różewicz's (b. 1921) volume of short stories, *Opadły liście z drzew* (The leaves fell off the trees, 1955). Różewicz, one of the most important Polish poets, writers, and playwrights of the postwar period, often returns to the topic of the war and the Holocaust in his later works.

1956–1968

After Stalin's death, cultural policy became more relaxed and there was a departure from the Socialist Realist method in literature and art. As a result, in 1956 a number of works were published that hailed the coming of a new era. One of these was *Głosy v ciemności* (Voices in the darkness) by Stryjkowski, written after the war in Moscow. For Stryjkowski, the breakthrough came on the day during the war when he heard of the failure of the uprising in the Warsaw ghetto and decided to save the world of Polish Jewry from oblivion. He compared his effort to "raising an Atlantis that seemed to have been lost and drowned forever."[7] It is thus unsurprising that *Voices in the Darkness* may be read in the context of the Holocaust, even though its action is set in the early twentieth century in Galicia. In most of the "voices" in this work, there are clear echoes of the Yiddish language: Yiddish lexical items, Yiddish syntax, Yiddish proverbs and emotive expressions, especially curses, but also words of endearment and diminutive forms, Yiddish forms of address and, above all, Ashkenazi pronunciation of Hebrew words.

This period was also a time of catching up, of publication of works that could not appear during the years of the Stalinist terror. Among these were wartime writings, such as Ludwik Hirszfeld's *Historia jednego życla* (Story of one life, 1957), Dawid Rubinowicz's *Diary* (1960), and Dawid Sierakowiak's *Diary* (1960). In 1962 Sandauer published his *Zapiski z martwego miasta* (Notes from a dead town).

This period also saw the initial publications of Henryk Grynberg, whose first work, the short story "The Antigone Team," about a crew of people exhuming bodies of Nazi victims in Poland, came out in 1959. The title of Grynberg's first novel, *The Jewish War* (published in English first as *Child of the Shadows* and then as *The Jewish War*, 1965), is an ironic reference to works by Joseph Flavius and Leon Feuchtwanger: The narrator is a little boy, in hiding with his family and friends, who observes the gradual disappearance of his loved ones. Grynberg's next work, *Victory* (1969), could not be published in Poland due to his refusal two years earlier to return to his homeland in view of the uncertain political situation and growing anti-Semitism. The novel covers the postwar period, and, like its predecessor, has an ironic dimension: the war is over, but who is really the "victor"?

1969–1989

This period can be divided into two distinct stages: (1) a muffled period caused by the intensification of censorship following the communist authorities' launch of the anti-Semitic campaign in the spring of 1968; and (2) a revival of interest in Jewish matters under the influence of Isaac Bashevis Singer being awarded the Nobel Prize in 1978, and the birth of the pro-democratic Solidarity movement in 1980. Nevertheless, in spite of censorship, the first of these decades still produced a few very important works by the generation of the children of the Holocaust.

One such is Bogdan Wojdowski's (1930–1994) novel on the life in the Warsaw ghetto, *Bread for the Departed* (1971). Born in Warsaw in 1930, Wojdowski spent more than two years in the Warsaw ghetto and was later taken into hiding "on the Aryan side." The novel covers the period from the establishment of the ghetto in 1940 until January 1943. It includes many key events, such as the "Grosse Aktion" (great action) of the summer of 1942, when thousands of Jews, including Janusz Korczak and children from his orphanage, were deported to Treblinka. The inexorable extermination of the ghetto is seen through the eyes of a young boy, who perceives the reality for what it is: the most abnormal of situations making up his daily life. The novel is set almost entirely inside the ghetto walls and concentrates on the isolation of its residents. This theme was taken up again later in Wojdowski's masterly short story "A Little Person, a Songless Bird, a Cage, and the World" (1975). Dedicated to a Polish-Jewish painter Izaak Celnikier, the story centers around a girl, Belcia, from the Warsaw ghetto, who while people are dying of hunger tries to save the life of a little bird. People perceive it as extravagant and laugh at her. Before dying, Belcia opens the cage and sets the bird free, although there is very little chance that the bird could survive in the wild. The narrator concludes that in the picture of the ghetto he is painting, there must be some small place for such unassuming creatures like Belcia and the bird.[8]

Another important publication of that time was Krall's book interview with Marek Edelman (1977), published in English first as *Shielding the Flame* and then as *To Outwit God*. Its main subject is the last days of the Warsaw ghetto. But by including prosaic and even shameful details, it shockingly punctures the heroic myths of that time. It nevertheless pays tribute to those who died in the uprising, reflecting their dedication and sacrifice. It has passed into the canon of Polish Holocaust literature alongside works by Borowski and Nałkowska.

Other book publications worthy of note during this period were *Gwiazda Dawida* (The star of David, 1975) by Maria Czapska (1894–1981) and *Conversations with an Executioner* (1977) by Kazimierz Moczarski (1907–1975). Some important works by non-Jewish authors came out abroad. These included *Jewish Themes* (London, 1977) by Stanisław Vincenz (1888–1971), which incorporated a chilling text about the Kolomyia Jews (a version of which, in Yiddish translation, had previously been published in the Kolomyia memorial book of 1957).

The single most significant event in the poetry of this period, though restricted to an underground audience, was the publication of Jerzy Ficowski's *A Reading of Ashes* in London in 1979. This volume contained poems which focus on both the Holocaust and the silence surrounding it in the postwar years. One of the poems, "Both Your Mothers" (dedicated to the poet's wife, Elżbieta, who survived the Holocaust as a baby adopted by Christians) talks about "two mothers," Jewish and Gentile, while the first poem in the volume "I Did Not Manage" deals with "rescue after the event," that is the attempt to preserve the memory of the victims of the Holocaust.[9] In a sense, the whole period from the turn of the 1970s and

1980s until today is about "reading the ashes," whether from the position of direct or indirect witness, or that of a survivor.

In the 1980s, on the tide of Solidarity under the leadership of Lech Wałęsa, and a relaxation of censorship surrounding Jewish topics (which continued even after the introduction of martial law on December 13, 1981), editions of important chronicles from the ghetto were published: those of Adam Czerniaków (1880–1942) and Emanuel Ringelblum (1900–1944), both in 1983, and that of Henryk Makower (1904–1964) in 1987. In 1982 another diary was published (Mary Berg's [b. 1924]), a translation from the English *Warsaw Ghetto: A Diary by Mary Berg*, first published in 1946 (though the original was written in Polish). But works of fiction also paved new ground. Krall's short novel *The Subtenant*, originally published in 1985 in Paris to circumvent censorship, offers an ironic juxtaposition of Polish and Jewish life under the Nazi occupation through a symbolic approach to "light" (a stereotypical view of the "heroic" deaths of Polish underground activists) and "black" (an equally stereotypical perception of the "passive" stance of Jews in the ghetto). This dichotomy is played out by the fictional characters Maria, a Pole, and Marta, a Jew, alongside the historical figures Krystyna Krahelska and Rywka Urman. Krahelska is killed by a bullet in the Warsaw Ghetto Uprising of August 1944, while Rywka Urman, crazed with despair and hunger, resorts to cannibalism in the Warsaw ghetto.

In Benski's first collection of short stories, *Ta najważniejsza cząsteczka* (That most important particle), the memory of the Holocaust is a constant companion to the handful of survivors who constitute most of his heroes. In the title story, the sense of guilt takes on a tragicomic dimension. A Jewish couple living in Warsaw after the war attempt to fit in with other Jewish survivors; fate has treated them kindly in comparison with what befell their relatives and friends. The narrator spent the war with his brother in New York, and his wife was deported to Uzbekistan. None of his family, most of whom are settled in the United States, were gassed, executed by firing squad in a forest, or starved to death. He recognizes how embarrassing this "exceptional" status is, but when he starts inventing a new biography for himself based on the experiences of others, his wife decides that they could not possibly have managed to survive it all.[10] From a different vantage point, Rymkiewicz's *The Final Station: Umschlagplatz* attempted to address the Holocaust from the position of a second-generation witness. And finally Grynberg, by now a resident of the United States, continued to write both poetry and prose. But his work, published in London and Paris, was available in Poland only through clandestine sources.

1989–2011

This period witnessed the return of writers previously known only in underground circles, and debuts by new authors. Indeed, Grynberg actually underscored the fact of his return in the title of his 1991 volume of poetry – *I Returned* – and since then his substantial presence on the publishing market and in public discourse has gained him the reputation of the "guardian of the graves."

Like Krall in *The Subtenant*, Grynberg compares ironically the so-called "heroic Polish" and the "passive Jewish" forms of wartime death. Other important motifs include the question of birthplace, and plumbing the mystery of his father's death: the narrator returning to the village of Radoszyna and attempting to talk to his former neighbors about his father, Abram. Most of the residents either do not remember him or have tried to forget about him, and are particularly unwilling to talk about the circumstances in which he died. Pursuing the truth becomes an obsession for the son. In *Dziedzictwo* (Heritage, 1993), Grynberg transcribes interviews conducted with residents of the village where his father was in hiding and where he was murdered.

In his later works Grynberg makes increasingly frequent references to the fates of others. In the docu-drama *Kronika* (Chronicle, 1984) he looks at the Lodz ghetto, in *Pamiętnik Marii Koper* (The diary of Maria Koper, 1993) he tells the story of a Jewish woman rescued by Polish farmers, and in *Children of Zion* (1994) he uses archival accounts of the fates of Jewish children from families deported to the eastern USSR during the war and ultimately taken to Palestine via Iran by Anders' Army. His collection of short stories *Drohobycz, Drohobycz* (1997) brings together the true stories of many survivors who settled in various countries after the war.

In the 1990s Krall's writing also blossomed. In book after book she blends true stories from the Holocaust with descriptions of Jewish life in Poland before the war, often drawing attention to seemingly insignificant details. This contrast adds expressiveness to her work. Many of her heroes are children of the Holocaust who, now in the prime of life, often do not know how they survived, who their parents or grandparents were, or what happened to them. Some of them have been seeking the truth for years; others have only just come to learn about their roots. Still others desire to escape from the past. Krall writes not only about survivors, but also about those who worked to save others, those who denounced others, those who stood by passively, and those who committed crimes. In addition to describing the life and nightmare of the war years, Krall makes frequent

references to the post-Holocaust landscape of Poland, blighted by efface-
ment of the memory of the Jews.

In 1994, on the fifty-first anniversary of the Warsaw Ghetto Uprising,
Wojdowski committed suicide, sharing the fate of other survivor-writers,
including Primo Levi, Jerzy Kosinski, and Jean Amery. His novel published
posthumously three years later bears the title *Tamta strona* (The other side),
and it is set near Warsaw, in a guest house visited by a last handful of Jewish
survivors. In this instance the words of the title, "the other side," are used
metaphorically to refer to death and not, as it usually does, to "Aryan"
Warsaw outside of the ghetto.

The 1990s also witnessed new Jewish authors who started to speak openly
about their roots, often in the context of their experiences during the
Holocaust. The best-known example is Michał Głowiński, an eminent
literary scholar who had never previously written about his childhood before
the 1998 publication of *The Black Seasons*, which tells of his experiences in
the Warsaw ghetto and of his hiding in a convent in the village of
Turkowice.

One feature of Holocaust literature generally is that it has forced writers
to seek new means of expression, a tendency also eminently visible in Polish
literature. A comparison of works of some Polish and Polish-Jewish writers
reveals striking differences. For instance, Rudnicki's prewar writing is
characterized by the egocentric stance of the narrator, while in his postwar
writing his tone becomes epic, and, in places, moralizing. Nałkowska,
known in her early period for modernist prose, uses a style in *Medallions*
that is laconic, even formally indifferent, and thus all the more wrenching.
Rymkiewicz, considered the main proponent of neoclassicism in Polish
poetry and a scholar of Romantic literature, wrote *Umschlagplatz* as an
autobiographical novel that was entirely unlike any of his other works. In
his prose based on his Holocaust experiences, Głowiński, a critic known for
his cool objectivity, gives vent to his emotions.

New names also came onto the scene at this time, authors who did not
decide to try their hand at writing until they had reached maturity. Among
these are Wilhelm Dichter, a 1968 émigré and retired scientist from
Massachusetts, author of the autobiographical novels *God's Horse* (1996)
and *School of the Godless* (1999); and Roma Ligocka (b. 1938), a painter and
scenographer who has spent over half her life in Germany and who wrote
The Girl in the Red Coat (2001) and *A Woman in Transit* (2002). Głowiński,
Ligocka, and Dichter belong to the generation of writers who experienced
the nightmare of the war as children. There is also, however, a still younger
group of Jewish writers born in the 1940s and 1950s. Most of them live

abroad: Viola Wein (b. 1946) and Eli Barbur (b. 1948) in Israel, Roman Gren (b. 1951) in France, and Ewa Kuryluk (b. 1946) and Anna Frajlich-Zając (b. 1942) in the United States; the Holocaust is not the main theme of this generation, but they do not ignore it entirely.

This phenomenon of mature writing debuts and unexpected re-orientations on Jewish themes, and indeed the emergence of writers of the younger generation, has the potential to continue in Poland for several reasons: significant interest exists in minority cultures and regional history; Jewish themes are still fairly fashionable; some writers have only recently discovered their roots, such as children of the Holocaust and their descendants. There remain, moreover, historical and political issues to be addressed, such as the Kielce pogrom of July 1946, and the postwar returns. These matters are touched on in poems now forgotten: Jastrun's "The Memory of Józef Oppenheimer" and "A Celebratory Poem," Adam Ważyk's (1905–1982) "Chronicle," Roman Bratny's (b. 1921) "A Stroll after the Pogrom," all included in the volume *The Song Will Survive Intact*; and Kalman Segal's short stories: "The Return of Józek Cytron" from *Stories from a Murdered Shtetl* (1956) and "Anopheles" from *People from Jama* (1957). The massacre in Jedwabne in July 1941 has also been addressed, in the extended reportage by Anna Bikont (*We of Jedwabne*, 2004), in which historical and sociological threads are interwoven with a quest for her own identity.

An unconventional approach appears in Matywiecki's book *Kamień graniczny* (*Boundary Stone*, 1994). It takes the form of short chapters comprising citations from letters and diaries from the Warsaw ghetto, furnished with comments by the author. In spite of its documentary nature, it is more a record of awareness about the Holocaust than of specific events that were part of it. Matywiecki's relationship with the ghetto is a special one: he was conceived there and was born "on the Aryan side" after its liquidation.

The children of Poles who witnessed the Holocaust also come of age as writers in this period. Among the works that speak of the Holocaust by underscoring the absence of the Jews are Huelle's *Weiser Dawidek* (1987), and Szewc's *Annihilation* (1987) and *Zmierzchy i poranki* (Dusks and dawns, 2000). Some Polish Jews long resident outside Poland but continuing to write in Polish also began to make a mark, including Irit Amiel (b. 1931), Janina Bauman (1926–2009), and Ida Fink (1921–2011), whose work came to be critically acclaimed in Poland only belatedly and who is probably better known in the United States. Books written much earlier, but forgotten or never published for political reasons, also began to live new lives. One notable example was Władysław Szpilman's (1911–2000) *The Pianist*, originally published in 1946 as *Death of a City*. Only in the wake of its success on the German market was a second Polish edition published in 2000.

Unusual conditions

Polish Holocaust literature, like all of Polish literature, developed in unusual conditions. The meanderings of state censorship created a situation in which certain topics appeared and disappeared; some works were published, but in censored form, or in very limited editions; some were considered politically correct, others not; some writers, like Fink or Miłosz (and, in the second half of the 1980s, some works by Krall and Rymkiewicz), were published first abroad either in Polish or in translation. This is why some works of value are still unavailable in wider circulation. For example, *Mice and Men*, Mina Tomkiewicz's autobiographical "bourgeois" novel about the Warsaw ghetto, was published first in a Hebrew translation in 1955, and appeared in Polish (by way of a London publishing house) only in 1966.

In terms of style, Polish Holocaust literature tends to be documentary in character and economical in its use of linguistic and artistic means; writers often avoid fictionalization, considering deliberate "enhancement" of events sacrilegious. The foremost works of Polish literature on the Holocaust – the narratives of Borowski and Nałkowska, Rudnicki's cycle from the "time of crematoria," Wojdowski's *Bread for the Departed*, Krall's *To Outwit God* and *Subtenant*, Grynberg's *Jewish War*, and Rymkiewicz's *Umschlagplatz* – exhibit an immense caution in the selection of words and means of expression. This type of prose was addressed to readers living in the shadow of war and capable of reading between the lines. It is no wonder that this is literature which is very hard for foreign readers to understand.

Polish literature is sometimes marked by didacticism, schematicism, and communist ideology (some writings by Rudnicki, Sandauer, and Wygodzki) or employs simplifications designed to convince the reader that in each group, whether Jews, Poles, or Germans, there were both "bad" and "good" people (e.g. Szczypiorski's *The Beginning* [1986 in Paris, first official Polish edition 1989], published in English as *Beautiful Mrs. Seidenman*). It also resorts to overuse of paradox (as in some works by Krall).

In contrast to Holocaust literature in general, there are few popular fictionalized works of Polish literature on the Holocaust. This may yet change, given that to the contemporary Polish reader the reality of the Holocaust is receding and becoming increasingly symbolic. This also raises the question of whether contemporary generations of writers are in fact dealing with the historical event that was the Holocaust, or whether their real theme is their own image of it. It is hard to say how the representation of the Holocaust in Polish literature will evolve in the future. But I assume that it will remain important, and that this dichotomy – Polish writers as observers, Jewish writers as victims – will be perpetuated.

Grynberg stated in one of his essays that "on the subject of the Holocaust, Polish literature has achieved more than the 'superpowers' – i.e. Russian and American literature, [more than] ambitious literatures such as Czechoslovak or Yugoslavian, [more than] the old masters such as English, French or Italian. Polish literature in this respect can compare with Jewish [literature in Hebrew and Yiddish]."[11] Grynberg did not issue this assessment simply to heap praise on his national literature, but rather in order to show that, in spite of its achievements, Polish literature still had much work to do. He wanted to point out that the Polish writer shoulders a great responsibility, arising from the fact that "he was at the epicentre of the greatest crime in history."[12] The plethora of works written since then is proof that the subject of the Holocaust remains an important obligation for Polish literature.

Notes

1. Madeline G. Levine, "Polish Literature and the Holocaust," *Holocaust Studies Annual* 3 (1985): 192.
2. Sidra DeKoven Ezrahi, *By Words Alone: The Holocaust in Literature* (Chicago and London: University of Chicago Press, 1980), p. 223.
3. Henryk Grynberg, "Holocaust w literaturze polskiej," in *Prawda nieartystyczna* (Berlin: Biblioteka Archipelagu), p. 91
4. Reference to Jerzy Ficowski's volume of poems *Reading of Ashes*; see note 9.
5. Jarosław Marek Rymkiewicz, *Umschlagplatz* (Paris: Institute Litteraire, 1988); *The Final Station: Umschlagplatz*, trans. Nina Taylor (New York: Farrar, Straus and Giroux, 1994).
6. Stanisław Wygodzki, "32" [selected poems from *Parting*], trans. Antony Polonsky, in Antony Polonsky and Monika Adamczyk-Garbowska (eds.), *Contemporary Jewish Writing in Poland: An Anthology* (Lincoln and London: University of Nebraska Press, 2001), pp. 82–83.
7. Julian Stryjkowski, Excerpt from *Judas Maccabeus: Afterword*, trans. Christopher Garbowski, in Polonsky and Adamczyk-Garbowska (eds.), *Contemporary Jewish Writing in Poland*, p. 55.
8. Bogdan Wojdowski, "A Little Person, a Songless Bird, a Cage, and the World," trans. Christopher Garbowski, in Polonsky and Adamczyk-Garbowska (eds.), *Contemporary Jewish Writing in Poland*, p. 244.

9. Jerzy Ficowski, "I Did Not Manage to Save," in *Odczytanie popiołów/A Reading of Ashes* (Warszawa: Wydawnictwo Browarna, 1993), p. 7.

10. Stanisław Benski, "Missing Pieces," in *Missing Pieces*, trans. Walter Arndt (San Diego: Harcourt Brace Jovanovich, 1990), pp. 142–43.

11. Grynberg, "Holocaust w literaturze polskiej," p. 91.

12. Ibid.

CHAPTER 10

Hungarian Holocaust literature

Rita Horváth

Numerous literary works, typically by survivors and their offspring and belonging to many genres, relate and try to understand the events of the Holocaust of the Jews of Hungary. The majority were written and published in the oppressive milieu of various phases of communist dictatorships as well as in the context of an ongoing and complex identity crisis concerning being Jewish. As a consequence, when we read these works together as they constitute one another's immediate environment, there emerges not a conventional literary history but a marked social-literary process through which, for the majority of the Jews in postwar Hungary, the trauma of the Holocaust – the gaping absence it creates and represents – has replaced all forms of Judaism (both as a religion and/or tradition) as their main, or, in most cases, sole identity-creating force.

The special identity crisis emerges forcefully in the most representative work on the Holocaust in Hungarian: Imre Kertész's tetralogy consisting of *Fatelessness* (1975), *Fiasco* (1988), *Kaddish for an Unborn Child* (1990), and *Liquidation* (2003). These four novels record the constant rethinking (and rewriting) of the story of the author's deportation to the concentration camp universe as a fourteen-year-old together with his becoming a witness and eventually a witness-artist in the completely unresponsive social-cultural milieu of Hungary. The novels, by recounting over and over the events of the Holocaust, as well as not finding a receptive audience, create an increasingly obsessive persona who, in Kertész's own words, becomes the "medium of Auschwitz."

Kertész's work also demonstrates that the identity crisis resulting from the fact that the Holocaust itself constitutes Jewishness for the overwhelming majority of Jews in Hungary is rooted not only in the trauma of the Holocaust itself but also in the earlier post-Monarchy identity crisis concerning Jewishness among the Jews of Hungary.

The Holocaust victimized less than 6 percent of Hungary's total population, as the Jewish inhabitants of Hungary, including the recently annexed territories, consisted of 725,000 Jews of the Jewish faith and 61,548 Jews who had converted to Christianity according to the last census taken before the German occupation of Hungary. The Holocaust in Hungary can be divided into two phases. The first phase, the phase of the Hungarian anti-Jewish policy, began in the spring of 1938 when the first (anti-)Jewish law was passed in the Hungarian Parliament.

During this phase, the Hungarian regime, by employing anti-Jewish legislation, systematically eliminated the Jews of the country from the economic and social spheres. In contrast to the Jews of much of Europe, however, the Jews of Hungary lived in relative safety during this phase, even though in the 1930s Hungary established increasingly close links with Nazi Germany and joined the Axis alliance in November 1940. Moreover, the Hungarian regime unequivocally demonstrated its murderous hatred toward the Jews by the 1941–1942 deportations to Galicia and the massacre at Délvidék (Novi Sad and in its vicinity, in the Bačka region), as well as by the institution of forced labor in the Hungarian army.

The second phase of the Holocaust, the phase of the German anti-Jewish policy, began abruptly on March 19, 1944, when the German army occupied Hungary in order to ensure Hungary's by then wavering alliance. The Hungarian administration remained intact and in force after the German occupation, and the new Hungarian prime minister, Döme Sztójay, his government, and the entire administrative apparatus quickly and efficiently implemented the anti-Jewish measures of Nazi Germany. The ghettoization and deportation of the majority of the Jews of Hungary happened within the short span of a few months, between April and July 1944. Almost all of the Jewish population of the Hungarian provinces were deported to Auschwitz. The more than 200,000 Jews of Budapest were eventually imprisoned in ghettos and numbers were marched into Germany. About 600,000 Jews from Hungary were murdered in the Holocaust. Budapest was liberated on February 13, 1945, and the whole of Hungary was liberated on April 4, 1945.

All the above enumerated crucial historical steps and arenas appear centrally in Hungarian Holocaust literature. Béla Zsolt's *Kilenc Koffer* (*Nine Suitcases*, 1946) narrates the author's experiences as a forced laborer on the Eastern Front, an inmate of the Nagyvárad (today Oradea Mare, Romania) ghetto, and a passenger of the Kasztner-train. Mária Ember's *Hajtűkanyar* (Hairpin bend, 1974) describes deportation to work camps in the vicinity of Vienna, and Imre Kertész's autobiographical novel,

Sorstalanság (*Fatelessness*, 1975), recounts the most representative story of the Hungarian Holocaust: deportation to Auschwitz. Iván Mándy's famous short story, "Egyérintő" ("One Touch," 1957), tells the story of young thugs beating to death an old Jewish man, whom they knew quite well, and captures the uncanny ease with which Jews could be killed in the Budapest of the 1930s. Mándy's short story is one of the few works that tries to understand how the Hungarian Fascist Arrow Cross reign of terror became possible. A second is István Örkény's psycho-realist short story, "Szédülés" ("Vertigo," 1980), which conveys not only the Arrow Cross era of terror but also its far-reaching and unforeseeable consequences for the future. Finally, György Moldova's *A Szent Imre-induló* (The Saint Imre-march, 1975) is about children in the large ghetto of Budapest, and Ernő Szép in his memoir-novel *Emberszag* (*The Smell of Humans*, 1945) relates the author's ordeal of being taken to forced labor after the seizure of power by Ferenc Szálasi, leader of the fanatical right-wing Arrow Cross party, toward the end of the war.

Hungarian Holocaust literature may signify artworks produced in Hungary in Hungarian by both Jewish, namely essentially affected, and non-Jewish authors, but it may also include literature about the Holocaust of the Jews of Hungary that was created by survivors all over the world. The unique features of Hungarian Holocaust literature are the consequences of the special characteristics of the Holocaust in Hungary – such as its belatedness, speed, and the relentless, well-organized, thorough nature of the deportation of the Jews of the provinces – as well as those of its aftermath, like the social and political treatment of the Holocaust trauma in postwar Hungary.

A number of mechanisms that fundamentally shaped Holocaust literature in general also shaped Holocaust literature in Hungary; many of the same concerns and issues surfaced. This was the case even though Hungarian culture operated under the conditions of various forms and phases of communist dictatorship from 1948 until the democratic transformation of Hungary in 1989. As in other countries, a large number of testimonies and memoirs were published both as separate volumes and in serialized form in journals in Hungary in the immediate aftermath of the Holocaust. Péter György in his *Apám helyett* (Instead of my father, 2011) sadly states that the authors of these early memoirs – such as Teri Gács and Vilma Sz. Palkó – were not forgotten, but went completely unnoticed.[1] The majority of the early memoirs have various degrees of literary merit but they all have unquestionable documentary value. Some of the early memoirs, such as Ernő Szép's *The Smell of Humans* and Béla Zsolt's *Nine*

Suitcases, however, are literary masterpieces, but they did not have any influence either. They became registered as masterpieces only in the 1980s when they were republished.

After the initial period of publishing memoirs, testimonies, and even diaries – such as the diary of a fourteen-year-old girl who was murdered in Auschwitz that was published by her mother Ágnes Zsolt (*Éva lányom*, 1948) – during the Stalinist-style communist dictatorship of the 1950s, the official silence engulfing the Holocaust in the public sphere was almost complete. However, films like Félix Máriássy's famous 1955 film, *Budapesti Tavasz* (Budapest Spring), demonstrated a trend that became more and more visible later as the dictatorship became less harsh: artworks concerning the Holocaust were usually published for and around the ten-year anniversaries of the liberation of Hungary by the Red Army.

Works of world Holocaust literature that were translated and published or produced as a play or film in Hungarian include Jorge Semprun's *The Long Voyage*, which was published in 1964 in Hungary in Pál Réz's translation, and Romain Gary's existentialist short story about Nazi concentration camp inmates that was adapted to a TV play entitled *Nő a barakban* (A woman in the barrack) by Hungarian artists in 1960. (The screenplay was written by Boris Palotai, it was directed by Éva Zsurzs, and it won the Golden Nymph Award in the Monte Carlo Television Festival.) Arthur Miller's *Incident at Vichy*, which was first performed in 1965 in Hungary, and the plays of Peter Weiss were also crucial Holocaust presences in the Hungarian literary scene and were produced very frequently in Hungarian theaters. Translated works thus constituted an integral part of Hungary's literary and cultural scene, since the published works of Holocaust world literature acted as fundamental reference points for Hungarian Jewish Holocaust writings. Nobel laureate and Holocaust survivor-writer Imre Kertész, for example, constantly and very critically refers to Semprun's *The Long Voyage*. One may also quote from Grácia Kerényi's autobiography, *Utazások könyve* (The book of voyages, 1977): "I call my experiences in 1944–45 a 'voyage,' based a little bit on [the title of] Semprun . . . everything that came in the aftermath of [our] 'long voyage' is of little significance. This is the basic frame of reference."[2]

From the 1970s on, the official attitude toward the topic of the Holocaust became more permissive, and child survivor-writers together with second-generation survivor-writers made their appearances on the literary scene. Crucial works, such as Kertész's *Fatelessness*, were published in 1975, even though they were not widely circulated. From the 1970s and 1980s on,

Holocaust literature permeated Hungarian literary life more and more overtly. Established artists such as István Vas, György Somlyó, and Piroska Szántó also started to publish their autobiographies and autobiographical novels as late as this. In addition, some early works, such as survivor-writer Imre Keszi's *Elysium* (1959), only now became part of Hungarian literary consciousness. In the case of *Elysium*, this happened because it was turned into a film by director Erika Szántó in 1986.

Elysium tells the story of a ten-year-old boy who was deported alone to Auschwitz from Budapest and was gassed after being a prisoner in a special part of a concentration camp in Germany that was used for conducting medical experiments on children. The other story line of the novel records the struggle for survival of the child's prominent family as well as their Hungarian rescuers in Budapest and their futile attempts to rescue the boy.

The story of the child is based on the real fate of the son of a well-known Hungarian Jewish musicologist, Bence Szabolcsi. What happened to Szabolcsi's child was typical, and learning about his fate through the novel demonstrates how the works of Holocaust literature, when they are read together, provide contexts for each other even at the level of historical events, creating a web of tradition that is dense enough to enable the construction of an identity based on the Holocaust for Jews who don't have an adequate number of personal/family stories. Ernő Szép, in his memoir *The Smell of Humans*, wrote about a child who was deported in exactly the same way:

> We were terribly saddened by the fate of a charming 12-year-old boy in our building, whose mother sent him out one morning to pick fruit in the garden of their villa on the outskirts of the town. The child was caught by the gendarmes who took him away. For days on end the desperate mother went running all over the place, but no trace of the child. (The father had been taken to the Russian front [as a forced laborer].) The poor woman cried night and day, blaming herself, suicidal. I couldn't bear to confront her; I did not know what to say to her.[3]

Szép, a successful poet, playwright, and novelist in his sixties, focuses on the utterly absurd experience of the forced labor of elderly intellectual men. The entire situation is so unbelievably tragic, grotesque, and humiliating that the narrator's "naïve" voice – mildly interested in the behavior and psychology of both the victims and the murderers – makes the reading almost unbearable. The book's last statement, however, calls attention to the effort demanded by this "naïve" voice: Szép announces that he cannot use it (or, in fact, any "voice" at all) to report the last period of chaotic terror filled with personal losses. Rather, he finishes his story by repeating the standard humanist statement according to which the events at the heart of the Holocaust cannot be recorded or even believed: "It was the 9th of November when we got home. I will not go on to narrate what happened starting on the 10th. That, I feel, is not to be described, not to be believed. And even what I have narrated here, even this, '*if you want, remember, if you want, forget.*'"[4]

It is oppressive in itself to have an enormous historical trauma as a dominant factor at the center of one's identity, but when a person's entire identity is based on an absence that is intensified by the lack of any discussion about it, then the devastation is overwhelming. Mihály Kornis's *Egy csecsemő emlékiratai* (A memoir of a baby, 2007) clearly demonstrates this phenomenon. One of the first things the autobiographical baby-protagonist, whose developing consciousness is the topic of the work, becomes aware of is his survivor mother's all-consuming grief. She is defined more by the absence of her murdered first husband, who perished as a forced laborer at the Eastern Front, than by the presence of her post-Holocaust family, even her baby son. This realization turns the absent first husband and his brother into central presences for the protagonist without his having any possibility of ever knowing them, that is, ever having a real/primary relationship with them.

Second-generation writings in world literature prove that the special burden of growing up in a survivor family and witnessing either the screaming silence or the stories of the survivors were an especially isolating experience anywhere. That is why finding as well as creating a community for and by second-generation survivors in the West was such a cathartic, liberating experience. However, for the Jews of Hungary, there existed the additional problem of the identity crisis concerning Jewishness itself. While for most second- and third-generation survivors outside of the Eastern bloc being Jewish had a certain traditional religious and/or national significance, for the overwhelming majority of the Jews who remained in Hungary after the 1956 uprising, being Jewish had little such meaning. Their identities as "others," an otherness that just happened to be called being Jewish, consisted mainly in the fact that they themselves and/or their family had been victimized in the Holocaust. Since the very identity of the majority of post-Holocaust Hungarian Jews is exclusively based on the trauma of the Holocaust, the almost complete silence shrouding that historical trauma resulted in an even more severe crisis of identity than in the West.

The family/generation novel genre, which is traditionally well equipped to deal with problems of continuity and discontinuity, has become one of the dominant genres of contemporary Jewish Hungarian literature precisely because works written within the genre from the 1970s onwards focus upon this special identity crisis. Post-Holocaust Hungarian Jewish family novels – such as Péter Nádas's *Egy családregény vége* (*The End of a Family Story*, 1993), Péter Lengyel's *Cseréptörés* (Pottery-breaking, 1978), Miklós Vámos's *Apák könyve* (*The Book of the Fathers*, 2000), Géza Bereményi's *Legendárium* (A collection of legends, 1977), Judit Fenákel's *A fénykép hátoldala* (The back of the photograph, 2002), and Gábor Schein's *Mordecháj könyve* (The book of Mordechai, 2002), or films shaped by the genre of family novel, such as István Szabó's *Sunshine* and Frigyes Gödrös's film *Glamour* – study the process during which the quest of survivors and their offspring to salvage any kind of meaningful tradition and continuity after the Holocaust in actual fact turn the Holocaust itself, along with the void it left, into their core tradition, their main heritage.

The title of one of Ágnes Gergely's elegies for her murdered forced laborer father, "You Are the Sign on My Door Jamb," demonstrates and symbolizes this process. By turning her murdered father into a *mezuzah*, a traditional Jewish parchment fixed to the doorpost, she identifies the Holocaust as the most important element of her Jewishness. The Holocaust replaces religion in defining Jewish identity.

Paradoxically, then, the break caused and represented by the Holocaust replaced the continuity of religion, tradition, and/or nationalist ideology as the main identity-constructing factor for Jews in Hungary. Therefore, post-Holocaust family novels all vibrate with the unbearable tension between notions of ending (they solemnly accept the Holocaust as an unequivocal end point) and a yearning for some kind of continuity while at the same time being informed by an inescapable awareness of the fact that the destruction of families and communities, together with their wealth of unique family traditions, legends, and stories embedded in the greater context of Jewish traditions, intensifies the problem of continuity – the mere possibility of any kind of continuity – to the extreme. László Márton's postmodern novel *Árnyas utca* (A shady high street, 1999) expresses visually as well as narratively how the entire Jewish community of a small town can disappear without being missed. It has a symbolic value that in Nádas's *The End of a Family Story*, the Holocaust survivor grandfather is the one who, most probably in vain, tries to perpetuate his family history, even at the cost of sacrificing the family's Jewishness.

Poet Miklós Radnóti's creation of a tradition for this Jewish identity crisis provides another reason why it permeates Hungarian Holocaust literature so deeply. Radnóti, who was murdered in the Holocaust and is one of the giants of Hungarian-language poetry, gave a simultaneous poetic expression to the Holocaust and to his self-fashioned all-embracing European, emphatically non-Jewish identity.

Radnóti's whole life was dominated by racial anti-Semitic ideologies in Hungary. He was born to Jakab Glatter and Ilona Grosz in Budapest on May 5, 1909. Radnóti was taken to forced labor camps three times from 1940 on, and the last time, in 1944, he was taken to the Bor camp-complex (Serbia). By the end of August 1944, the Germans had liquidated the *lagers* in the vicinity of Bor and many forced laborers were marched toward the West. On November 8 or 9, 1944, the exhausted poet was shot in the neck, along with twenty-one other men, into a mass grave near the village of Abda in northwestern Hungary. The mass grave was exhumed in 1946, and the poet was identified. On his body a notebook, the so-called "Bor notebook," was found containing his last poems.

Radnóti suffered a typical Jewish fate during the Holocaust, but he did not construct a Jewish identity. He repeatedly voiced his conviction that he did not feel himself to be a Jew, he had not had a religious upbringing, and historical forces – alien to his personality – transformed his Jewishness into his major "life problem." Instead of choosing a separate group identity such as being Jewish, Radnóti forged an identity as the heir and repository of the values of the entire European culture. Both communist and Christian ideals attracted him. He cared deeply for values such as humanism, human dignity, the power of reason, art, compassion, and sensitivity to social injustice, which were attacked and eradicated by fascism. He represented this view, widespread among highly assimilated Jews in Hungary, with exceptional consistency and took significant steps to make his chosen identity evident. As a poet he used the name Radnóti instead of Glatter, and in 1943, he converted to Christianity. He converted so late, because he did not want to do it in the hope that he would be treated differently from Jews. By the spring of 1943, it became obvious that conversion would not provide any escape.

Even though he did not identify himself as a Jew, he gave a truly exceptional poetic expression to the Jewish experience in the Holocaust. His last poems, found on his body in the mass grave, are generally read as the voice in which the collective fate of the Jews manifested itself. One of Radnóti's most famous poems, "Erőltetett menet" ("Forced March," 1944), was written in Bor following a forced march from one of its satellite camps, Lager Heidenau, to the main camp and, in the anticipation of a much longer march toward Hungary, captures in its rhythm and form the painfully achieved monotony of the march. The poem records how in these marches the person, who is reduced to "an errant mass of pain," has to decide anew at every moment whether to trudge on and whether to get up when fallen so as not to be killed instantly. The facts of a forced march, actual deaths of companions, anticipation of one's own death by a shot to the neck, and the terrible opposition between getting up and staying down, are also the topics of Radnóti's last poem, "Razglednica" ("Picture Postcards"), written just days before his own death.

Radnóti's poetry strongly echoes in post-Holocaust Hungarian literature. Artists such as Zsuzsa Beney, István Vas, and Piroska Szántó kept working to uphold Radnóti's belief system. His influence was so profound that the first Hungarian musical was based on his life story. *Egy szerelem három éjszakája* [Three nights of a love story] was first performed in the Petőfi Theater in 1960. Literary scholar Tamás Ungvári, who later wrote extensively about Hungarian Jewish and Holocaust literature, was involved in the production. Miklós Hubay wrote the play, and the words of the songs were written by survivor-poet István Vas, who personally knew Radnóti. It was turned into a film, directed by György Révész, in 1967.

Non-Jewish Hungarians also wrote important works of Holocaust literature in Hungary. The most famous examples are the poems of Catholic poet János Pilinszky. Distressingly, traditional literary anti-Semitism became reinvented and perpetuated in the high Hungarian literature of the 1970s, mainly as a consequence of viewing from the outside with an especially cold eye the above-described identity crisis concerning Jewishness and critiquing the petty bourgeoisie. Péter Hajnóczy's novel *A Halál kilovagolt Perzsiából* (Death rode out of Persia on horseback, 1979) employs a survivor family's Holocaust-based Jewishness as a symbol of inauthenticity. In this autobiographically inspired novel, the petty bourgeois members of the survivor family, who are shown to be inauthentic Jews and inauthentic sufferers, are contrasted to the existentially authentic, long-suffering alcoholic writer-protagonist.

Disturbingly, the deep identity crisis concerning Jewishness itself actively alienates most of Hungarian Jewish Holocaust literature from the rest of the Jewish world. Just think about the controversial and ambiguous reception of Imre Kertész's masterpieces by Jewish audiences, especially in the United States and Israel. Rejection is part of Kertész's experience with Western Jewish audiences, even though he is a steadfast supporter of Israel, and his views on Jewish identity are much more complex than they appear at first sight. The solely Holocaust-based Jewish identity that characterizes many Jews in Hungary who grew up before the 1989 democratic transformation of the country (and which Kertész exemplifies so uncompromisingly) is thus rejected by the general Jewish world. This phenomenon is all the more strange because an exclusively Holocaust-based Jewish identity permeating Hungarian Jewish literature of the second half of the twentieth century seems to be one of the extreme logical results of general trends in world Holocaust literature.

After the 1989 political changes, new trends emerged in Jewish Holocaust literature in Hungary in this respect. A new generation of authors, such as Gábor T. Szántó, Viktória Lugosi, and Géza Röhrig, made a point of rooting their identity not only in the void of the Holocaust but also in "positive" things such as tradition, religion, and nationalist ideologies. The Holocaust literature produced by them is different from what come before, but their work is also caught up in the literary and family tradition of the special identity crisis in which the discontinuity of the Holocaust replaces traditional continuity.

Notes

1. Péter György, *Apám helyett* (Budapest: Magvető, 2011), p. 20
2. Grácia Kerényi, Introduction to *Utazások könyve* (Budapest: Szépirodalmi, 1978).
3. Ernő Szép *The Smell of Humans: A Memoir of the Holocaust in Hungary*, trans. John Bátki (Budapest: Central European University Press, 1994), p. 45.
4. Ibid., p. 173. (The italicized text is in English in the original.)

French literature and the Holocaust

Jeffrey Mehlman

One's initial uneasiness in pairing the categories of French literature and the Holocaust relates to the fact that an exaggerated appreciation of the affinities between them, the spurious notion that the Holocaust may always already have been contaminated by fiction, is a principal plank of Holocaust denial, one that has enjoyed a measure of notoriety in France and in particular on the French far left.[1] That notion was sufficiently current in the France of the 1980s for the eminent Hellenist and public intellectual Pierre Vidal-Naquet to feel obliged to address it, while refusing to dignify it with a refutation, in a somewhat disheveled volume, *Assassins of Memory*, in 1987, and for the philosopher Jean-François Lyotard to deal with it as the prime illustration of the kind of language game he analyzed under the rubric of *Le Différend*.[2] Finally, the "negationist" fever, although sporadically fueled by rising anti-Zionism in Europe, subsided in the wake of Alain Finkielkraut's demonstration of just what a godsend the thesis denying the gas chambers was for a far left eager to efface the differences between fascism and any other mode of capitalism.[3] If there were no gas chambers, the argument went, there could be no basis for the left to side with anti-fascist liberalism against a fascism in no *essential* way different from it. *Exit* the phenomenon of Holocaust denial as a movement with any claim to plausibility.[4]

There are further complicating considerations. For it would not be an exaggeration to claim that even as the Holocaust was ceasing to be regarded in various quarters as always already "literary" or fictive, French literature, in its highest precincts, began to view itself as a kind of Holocaust memorial project. The key text here is *Chateaubriand: Poésie et terreur*, a mammoth volume by France's preeminent literary historian, Marc Fumaroli.[5] It argues that French literature per se was constituted by Chateaubriand, in the first half of the nineteenth century, as a national project whose aim was to memorialize the mass killing known as the Terror. From Chateaubriand's *Mémoires d'outre-tombe* on through Proust and beyond, French literature would be fueled by nostalgia for the "sweet liberty" that had been definitively lost amidst the massacres of 1792–1793. And just as a doomed Walter Benjamin, brandishing a theologically inflected version of Marx, would serve as an icon of literature's essential link with the Holocaust, so would Fumaroli, brandishing his Tocqueville, promote Chateaubriand to iconic status as exemplary victim in his relation to the Terror. For nothing of his work could be grasped, according to the critic, "if one had forgotten that he had survived a holocaust."[6]

Fumaroli, heir to Roland Barthes at the pinnacle of French literary speculation, makes the parallel more explicit still: "The shock was as violent, in its way, as the fright experienced by the Jewish aristocracy of the mind . . . once it came to understand the fate which governments of the nations whose philosophical, historical, literary, and scientific intelligence had become its own source of pride were reserving for it."[7] That link between an anti-Semitic Holocaust and an anti-aristocratic Terror, curiously enough, surfaces as the key heuristic motif or metaphor in the section on anti-Semitism in Hannah Arendt's classic *The Origins of Totalitarianism.* (Her analysis, moreover, proceeds by way of a consideration of the quintessential French novelist, Proust.) "According to Tocqueville," Arendt writes, "the French people hated aristocrats about to lose their power more than it had ever hated them before, precisely because their rapid loss of real power was not accompanied by any considerable decline in their fortunes." The statement is immediately followed by a parallel: "Antisemitism reached its climax [i.e. the Nazi genocide] when Jews had similarly lost their public functions and their influence [classically, those of the court Jew], and were left with nothing but their wealth."[8] My point is not the validity of Arendt's argument, but the insistence of a constellation that brings French literature, the Reign of Terror, and the Nazi Holocaust into proximity.

Or perhaps it might be possible to circumscribe the relation between French literature and the Holocaust – or to expand its strangeness – still further. On November 29, 1942, Antoine de Saint-Exupéry, the most celebrated French author to seek refuge in wartime New York, published an "Open Letter to Frenchmen Everywhere." His purpose was to call on the French diaspora to put aside its quarrels and join common combat to liberate France. What is most striking are the terms of his description of the French situation. The French, he claimed, were not defeated combatants, but rather "hostages" who, given the crushing disparity in arms in comparison with the Germans, never had a chance. By the time the letter was published, with the Germans having occupied the entirety of French territory, the only metaphor that occurs to Saint-Exupéry as adequate for the French situation is *night*: "France is nothing but a silence; she is lost somewhere in the night with all lights out, like a ship." More striking still, the night that has befallen France is associated with a specific numerical figure: "The rot of German prison camps yields only corpses. My country was thus threatened, purely and simply, with the utter extermination, under legal and administrative pretense, of 6,000,000 men. France was armed only with sticks to resist this slave hunt."[9] With the utter passivity of the hostage situation, the ensuing dehumanization, the reference to "extermination" (and not "concentration") camps, and, most strikingly, the invocation of what would eventually be the canonical figure of 6 million deaths, French literature, in the person of Saint-Exupéry, appears to be feeling its way toward the rhetoric of the Holocaust. But it is being applied to the French rather than to the Jews. As though the tension between the Holocaust and (French) literature with which we began had reached the point of seeing the former being obliterated by the latter.

A second case of virtual obliteration: Shortly after the war, in a Resistance anthology titled *La Patrie se fait tous les jours*, Jean Paulhan, a leader of the Resistance among French writers, and Dominique Aury published a poem by Louis Aragon, an exemplary Resistance poet, titled "Auschwitz."[10] It was, in fact, the conclusion of *Le Musée Grévin*, the long polemical poem published by Aragon under the pseudonym François la Colère in 1943. Here is a characteristic fragment of Aragon's "Auschwitz":

> Ce sont ici des Olympiques de souffrance
> Où l'épouvante bat la mort à tous les coups
> Et nous avons notre équipe de France
> Et nous avons ici cent femmes de chez nous.
> (These are the Olympics of suffering
> In which fear beats out death at every turn
> And we have our French team
> And we have here a hundred women from back home.)

This is an Auschwitz not for Jews but for (French) women, and the poem, which may have been inspired by the "female convoy" of January 24, 1943, is addressed to them in the very Christian mode of a collective "Hail Mary": "Je vous salue Marie" modulates to the plural "Je vous salue Maries de France" and finally to "Je vous salue ma France" – with not a mention of Jews. Moreover, the notion that fear beats out death in the Olympics of suffering, that the principal thing that we have to fear is fear itself, makes of this Auschwitz anything but the locus of irrevocable and unfathomable evil with which it has since become associated. It is as though Aragon, in his poem "Auschwitz," had invented Holocaust denial . . . before the Holocaust was even consummated.

The disparity between Aragon's "Auschwitz" and the Auschwitz that has seared its way into our postwar imagination is, in fact, visible on the streets of Paris. On the one hand, at the tip of the Ile de la Cité is to be found a Mémorial des martyrs de la Déportation. Originally conceived in 1953 and inaugurated in 1962, it bears inscriptions from such French authors as Saint-Exupéry, Sartre, Aragon, and Eluard. Indeed, surveying the monument, one might suspect that Hitler's principal targets were existentialists and surrealists. Today that monument is scarcely visited. Cross the bridge, however, and one will find a thriving museum, the Mémorial de la Shoah, launched by President Jacques Chirac in 2005.[11] The Resistance hero has given way to the Holocaust victim as principal focus of commemoration. More specifically, between the inaugurations of the two memorial sites a sea change had taken place at about the time that de Gaulle left power in 1969. The turning point of the French experience of World War II was determined to have been not November 1942, when Philippe Pétain, head of the puppet state in Vichy, neglecting to make his way to newly liberated French territory in Algeria, stood accused of intelligence with the enemy, but rather the summer of the same year, when the Vichy Secretary-General of the Police, René Bousquet, having negotiated an agreement with the Gestapo that would allow the French police relative autonomy in rounding up Jews for deportation, stood accused of crimes against humanity.

Having made our way through the various obstacles that impede a consideration of the relation between French literature and the Holocaust, let us turn now to one of the inaugural texts of what one hesitates to call the tradition, Elie Wiesel's *La Nuit* (*Night*).[12] An initial objection may be posed: why should a memoir about the excruciating ordeal of a Hungarian Jew, written in Yiddish, first published (in that language) in Buenos Aires, and only subsequently translated – and abridged – into French, be in any way considered a part of French literature?[13] The answer is best approached by way of the preface to the French edition written by the novelist François Mauriac. It was Mauriac, awarded the Nobel Prize in Literature for 1952, who would dub Wiesel's treatment of his ordeal "different, distinct, unique."[14] But for all Wiesel's putative uniqueness, Mauriac was able to come up with a term of comparison: "Lazarus risen from the dead" (p. ix). The Catholic novelist, that is, offered up the Jewish memoirist as a miracle performed by Christ. By the end of Mauriac's preface, he finds himself speaking directly of Christ: "Did I speak of that other Jew, his brother, who may have resembled him – the Crucified, whose Cross has conquered the world? Did I confirm that the stumbling block to his faith was the cornerstone of mine?" (p. x).

The Wiesel of *Night* may have been imaginable to Mauriac as a Christian to the extent that he seemed to be abjuring the God of Abraham, Isaac, and Jacob. "I was the accuser, and God the accused," Wiesel writes (p. x). But simultaneously the author of *Night* seems to be appealing to a more radical renunciation. Observing the slow death of a child by hanging, he observes: "My eyes were open and I was alone – terribly alone in a world without God and without man ... I stood amid that praying congregation, observing it like a stranger" (p. x). The "stranger" renouncing God Himself in a fit of rage is a borrowing from *L'Etranger*, the classic existentialist novella by Albert Camus, who would himself win the Nobel Prize in Literature in 1957. And even the metaphysical title *La Nuit*, plainly a departure from the recriminating title – *Und die velt hat geschvign* (And the world remained silent) – of the original Yiddish version, seems a stylistic borrowing from the author of *La Chute* (even as it echoes a metaphor used by Saint-Exupéry in his open letter in the *New York Times* cited above).

Perched as it was, when it originally appeared in French in 1958, between the preface by the French Nobel laureate of 1952 and its inspiration in the nihilism of the French Nobel laureate of 1957, that is, between two poles of French literature at the time, *Night*, even as it recorded the destruction of European Jewry, was a bold gesture of assimilation into the international eminence of French literature. No doubt the breadth of its eventual success, above and beyond its considerable merits, owes something to French literature's residual ability to make good on its universalizing claims. There remain, of course, the twin accusations of fabulation and sentimentality. Readers comparing the Yiddish and French versions of the book have uncovered a variety of discrepancies (concerning, for instance, the age of the "boy" being hanged), from which they have been inclined to derive excessive conclusions. As for the accusations of sentimentality (concerning, for instance, Juliek playing his violin on his death march), one need but recall Proust's Duchesse de Guermantes and her egregious preference of Esterhazy's "style" to the "idiotic, heavy-handed" letters Dreyfus was writing from Devil's Island to recognize in them traces of France's hoary tradition of aesthetic anti-Semitism.[15]

If the success of *Night* was not immediate, such was not the case for André Schwarz-Bart's novel, published in 1959, *Le Dernier des justes* (*The Last of the Just*).[16] The book is rooted in the tradition of the Lamed-vovniks, the thirty-six just men on whose existence the persistence of the world depends. The author modifies the legend, which has the thirty-six coexisting in every generation, unaware of each other and even of their own special status, and deals with the transmission of the "just man" or *tzadik*'s special grace within a single long-suffering family – from Rabbi Yom Tov Lévy in twelfth-century York to Ernie Lévy, who disappears in the Holocaust.

The novel's success was profound and immediate, and soon the Goncourt Academy found itself awarding Schwarz-Bart its coveted prize in advance of the date stipulated in its own bylaws lest another literary jury, awarding the Femina Prize, crown him first. The book is a kind of Jewish counterpart to Victor Hugo's epic *Légende des siècles*. According to the author, it was an effort to impart a measure of dignity to a history of Jewish suffering whose heirs remained painfully unaware of it. Yet almost as captivating as the book itself is the fate it appears to have visited on its author.[17] Simultaneous with its immense success, which had one critic, Pierre de Boisdeffre, calling it the most distinguished French novel since Camus' *The Plague* (and Marc Chagall offering to supply illustrations), accusations of plagiarism, ignorance of Jewish tradition, and ineptitude began to surface in the French press, and these were generally attributed to a number of Jewish writers said to be envious of Schwarz-Bart's success and egged on by their publisher, Calmann-Lévy. The first great novelistic success of Holocaust literature, that is, had issued in an *affaire*, in the French mode, of a distinctly anti-Semitic flavor. The more benign view of the hostility provoked by Schwarz-Bart in a number of Jewish quarters is that it was triggered by what was perceived to be the author's lachrymose and even Christ-like view of Jewish history, a protracted justification for the redemptive role of Jewish suffering. Whatever the basis for the campaign against *Le Dernier des justes*, its effect on its melancholic author was catastrophic. By February 1960, he had left Paris and its literary circles definitively; by 1962, he had destroyed his manuscripts. His literary focus shifted to the Antilles, although when he died in 2006, he left behind a futurist fantasy rooted in the Holocaust and titled *Etoile du matin* (*Morning Star*).[18]

* * *

There has been, since 1969, a "Vichy syndrome" in France, a will to wallow in the remembrance of France's real or alleged complicity with the Nazi genocide, that is more or less contemporary with and every bit as insistent as the United States' "Vietnam syndrome," which appears to have inspired the coinage.[19] One of the more interesting anticipations of that Vichy syndrome is a protracted episode that may be encapsulated as follows: between 1945, when Theodor Adorno suggested that he understood the Marquis de Sade because he was a German who had lived under Nazism, and 1975, when Pier Paolo Pasolini, through his film *Salò*, seemed to be saying that he understood Sade because he had been an Italian who had lived under fascism, three generations of French intellectuals appear to have made it their intellectual mission to de-Nazify the Marquis de Sade.[20] Those thirty years were the period in which a virtual cult of Sade as exemplary literary radical held sway in France.

The novelist and critic Maurice Blanchot, perhaps the central figure in the postwar Sade cult, is particularly worthy of attention. "The originality of Sade," he wrote, "seems to us to lie in his extremely firm claim to ground the sovereignty of man in a transcendental power of negation, a power that in no way depends on the objects he destroys, since, in order to destroy them, he does not even presuppose their prior existence . . . having always and already, in advance, considered them to be null."[21] Such then are the "gigantic murders," the "immense hecatomb" that have Blanchot's Sade afloat between Hegel, the West's principal philosopher of negation, and the murderous Terror of the Revolution, but also in surprising proximity to the excesses of the fascist era that had just ended in Europe.

And then, within Blanchot's text, there is an implosion. The "right to death" endorsed by Blanchot in the exemplary case of Sade, gives way to an "impossibility of dying," an endlessness of dying, "the curse of renascence" that seems to be an erosion of that very "right."[22] We have left Sade for Kafka and Kabbala and are plainly among the victims. Sade and the charms of "transcendental negation" give way to an almost unthinkable "negative transcendence." And that reversal effects a farewell to fascism, an identification with the victims, that would also herald a certain French postmodernity.

The full measure of Blanchot's trajectory, however, needs be expanded. For before World War II, he had been a journalist affiliated with efforts to forge a full-blown French fascism.[23] In his "Le terrorisme comme méthode de salut publique" (1936), he had called for acts of terrorism against Jews and communists.[24] Since he had been inclined to fascism out of a French nationalism that was fundamentally anti-Hitlerian, it was in the order of things that he would break with his right-wing allegiance of the 1930s once the impending war seemed inevitable.[25] (Anti-Semitism, after all, was the ideological specialty of France's national enemy; to do anything other than put it behind one might entail major difficulties once the war had begun.) Still, immediately after the war, as if to rehearse the traumatic ethical possibilities he had narrowly avoided, we find him extolling the murderous Sade who had identified so perfectly with the Terror of the Revolution, a posture that seemed to be inseparable from its own unraveling in a still deeper identification with the most abject victims of the war – that is, the Jews. Eventually he would return to politics during the failed insurrection of May 1968, writing tracts in favor of a movement whose most striking slogan was taken to be: "We are all German Jews (*Nous sommes tous des Juifs allemands*)."[26] By 1983, in the context of an evocation of May 1968, Blanchot would evoke Judaism and what he calls a "communism without heritage" as exemplary social impulses.[27] From the Jews and communists to be shot (1936), by way of an affirmation of Sade and the Terror (1948), to Judaism and a skewed version of communism as exemplary political inspirations (1983), he had done a complete reversal. The resulting disorientation, it may be speculated, would fuel the postmodern fragilities of Blanchot and a number of those inspired by them.

As for the postwar French Sade cult more generally, was it not an effort to stake a French claim to what all were beginning to sense was *the* event of the twentieth century? Already before the war, the French were claiming that fascism had had its earliest European incarnation in the emphatically Gallic fusion of left-wing anarcho-syndicalism and right-wing monarchist nationalism that fueled the Cercle Proudhon of 1913, but failed to survive World War I.[28] Was not the Sade cult of the French intelligentsia of 1947 an effort to antedate the French origins of fascism even further, even as that linkage was simultaneously denied? French collaboration in the Holocaust, that is, may have been more a function of France's will to autonomy during the war than of its anti-Semitism. Might not the Sade cult, then, in all of its figural murderousness, have been an effort to relive actively, if only in fantasy, the French experience during a period of relative passivity of being reduced to merely *pretending* to be in charge?

* * *

The year 1968, which saw a generation claim its identity in pretending to be "German Jews," was also the year of publication of one of the inaugurally symptomatic novels of the "Vichy syndrome," Patrick Modiano's *La Place de l'étoile*.[29] The title derives from a Jewish tale that has a German officer approaching a young Jew on a Paris street in June 1942 and asking for the location of the Place de l'Etoile – literally the "place of the star," but also the name of the intersection (since renamed the Place Charles de Gaulle) at whose center lies the Arch of Triumph. The Jew, in response, points to the left side of his chest, where he has been instructed to sew his yellow star. There is thus a confusion between the radiating center of French culture and the drama of Jewish exclusion. And that confusion provides the key to Modiano's novel, which pretends to follow one

Raphael Schlemilovitch, at once a literary-minded French Jew and a Nazi collaborator, as he makes his way through Modiano's carnivalesque phantasmagoria of a novel.

The novel is profligate, even reckless, in its allusiveness, both to French literature and to the history of France during the "dark years." It is as though the author sought to expose the reader to a hallucinatory congruence between the two series. It was one thing, that is, for Marcel Proust, half-Jew and self-proclaimed "first of the Dreyfusards," to declare that the royalist and anti-Semitic newspaper *L'Action française* was the sole newspaper to which he subscribed and that he did so for stylistic reasons (the paper being edited by the virtuoso *prosateur* Léon Daudet), and even though the content made him sick to his stomach.[30] But it was an altogether different thing for Schlemilovitch manically to offer his services, under the *nom de guerre* "Marcel Proust," to the French Gestapo of the rue Lauriston. Whereas Proust seemed to raise the question of whether the cult of French style was a balm for Jewish suffering or its cause, Modiano appeared to be saying that it did not make much difference. The key move was to plunge allusively into the cultural density of both realms, to savor the torture of their imagined equivalence (i.e. the two senses of the book's title), and to invoke the postwar birth of the author as an alibi that allowed him to get away with doing so.

The Holocaust made an oblique appearance at the center of what many have considered *the* French literary achievement of the 1970s, the series of works appearing under the pseudonym "Emile Ajar." Consider the most successful novel of the series, a work that attains a kind of zero degree of political correctness, *La Vie devant soi* (*The Life Before Us*).[31] It is the love story of an Arab orphan, Momo, and Madame Rosa, a former prostitute and inmate of Auschwitz, a Jew who has made it her clandestine business, in old age, to take care of the children of prostitutes in her apartment in the rundown Belleville section of Paris. The novel's pathos comes in large measure from Madame Rosa's confusion, in her advancing senility, between the Nazis, who had threatened her life during her youth, and the welfare-medical establishment of contemporary France, which seems intent on using inhuman means to extend a life she no longer thinks worth living. But the book's piquancy is entirely a function of Momo's narrative voice. For he is condemned to recount what he would never think of calling his love for the decrepit Jewess in the only idiom at his disposal: the street clichés of prostitution and anti-Semitism.

It was not until the suicide of the author of *La Vie devant soi*, in 1980, that "Emile Ajar" was revealed to be the pseudonym of the veteran French novelist and ex-Resistance aviator Romain Gary, and an understanding of

Gary-Ajar's accomplishment, which was major, is necessary to an appreciation of *La Vie devant soi* itself. "Gary," we learn from his memoir *La Promesse de l'aube*, was itself a pseudonym of one "Roman Kacew," the Lithuanian-born son of a wildly Francophilic single mother, who nursed the insane dream, first in Vilnius, then in Warsaw, that her son was destined to be a great Frenchman. Eventually she made her way to Nice, where she settled and inspired her Lithuanian outcast of a son, not without a few crucial deceptions, to turn himself into the much admired French novelist Romain Gary, the "happy end" of his mother's life (her death, which in fact occurred early in the war, having been kept secret from him). "Romain Gary," that is, East European Jew become toast of the existentialist generation at the end of the war, offers an interesting parallel to the Elie Wiesel who entered French literature perched between Camus and Mauriac not that much later. It is in this context that the transition from "Gary" to "Ajar" is illuminating. For the first Ajar work, *Gros-Câlin*, recounts the adventures of a lost soul of a statistician and his two obsessions, his pet python and his barely articulated love for a black co-worker, one Mademoiselle Dreyfus, in his office. By novel's end, the statistician comes across his adored would-be mistress in a brothel he frequents, and he ends up metamorphosing psychotically into his pet. With its insistence on his alienation from French society (iconically adrip with Beaujolais), the novel, one is tempted to say, appears to enact an unraveling of the mother's prime accomplishment. "Romain Gary," Frenchman par excellence, his mother's imaginary "happy end" or phallus, becomes undone in a quasi-Kafkan fable by "Emile Ajar": he – it? – bespeaks the humiliations of life as a pseudo-Frenchman (or bogus human) and slithers off into clandestinity.

The alienated statistician-become-python of *Gros-Câlin*, in his estrangement from French values, would turn into the alienated Arab orphan of *La Vie devant soi*, even as the formidable mother of *La Promesse de l'aube* would turn into Madame Rosa, Auschwitz survivor and dying matriarch of her clandestine orphanage. "Ajar," that is, in his alienation from French values, figured the return of the East European child (Roman Kacew) whom it was "Romain Gary"'s mission, in the name of *francité*, to repress. Whereupon the final novel in the Ajar series, *L'Angoisse du roi Salomon*, takes up the Holocaust theme one last time, but in order to bid it farewell. The novel's subject is the successful effort of the young narrator to reunite, in old age, two lovers whom life had conspired to separate: he, Salomon Rubenstein, the retired "pants king," who had foregone a visa to Portugal at the beginning of the war so he could stay in hiding in Paris and be with her, Cora, a would-be *chanteuse* who fell in love with a French Gestapo agent as soon as the Occupation began and proceeded to pretend Salomon did not exist. When the war is over, it is left to Salomon to testify at her trial for collaborationism that it was indeed Cora's silence that saved his life. When the two are finally reunited (through the efforts of the young narrator), it is on one stipulation: no mention must be made between them of their wartime misadventure. An amnesty, in the wake of the Holocaust, was hammered out, and a year later Kacew *alias* Gary *alias* Ajar committed suicide.

* * *

The year of Gary/Ajar's *La Vie devant soi*, 1975, was also the year of publication of an indirect treatment of the Nazi genocide by France's most deadly serious literary gamesman, Georges Perec. The book was titled *W ou le souvenir d'enfance* and it was composed, in all its mystifying complexity, in tandem with his psychoanalysis (conducted by J.-B. Pontalis).[32] It consists of two discrete texts that end up as oblique commentaries on each other. One is the elaboration of a fantasy entertained by the author since childhood of W, an island republic off the coast of Latin America that is governed by the Olympic ideal of competitive sport. The other is the disjointed and fragmentary memoir of the author's childhood, a time of misery dominated by the death of his father in combat toward the beginning of World War II and the deportation of his mother in 1943 to Auschwitz, from which she never returned. Now whereas one might have suspected that the grandiose fantasy of Olympic sport was conceived as an imaginary consolation or redemption for the dishevelment and sorrow of a chaotic childhood, the world of that fantasy soon reveals a sinister underside evocative of the totalitarian camps of World War II: selection, exacerbated competition, ritual elimination, punishment for the defeated, severe rationing of food . . . The consolatory fiction, that is, becomes a glorified version of the very hell from which redemption had been sought.

Perec, a Jew who was baptized as a child during the war and who never quite knew what to make of his Jewishness (other than not to deny it), derived his inspiration for *W* from two political prisoners of the Nazi camps who were not Jews: Robert Antelme, whose *L'Espèce humaine* (1947) was described by Perec as "one of the finest books to the glory of mankind," and David Rousset, from whose *L'Univers concentrationnaire* (1945) Perec drew the statement that "the structure of punishment camps . . . is determined by two fundamental policies: no work but 'sport' and derisory feeding . . ."[33] There is nonetheless an enigmatic Jewish motif in *W*. The earliest childhood memory retained by the author in the autobiographical section of the book is of his being congratulated by his ecstatic relatives for identifying a Hebrew letter in a Yiddish newspaper. Before long, however, we are told by the narrator that the letter was misidentified, and it has taken the wit of a number of literary scholars to determine (or speculate) that the Hebrew letter is part of a screen memory masking a recollection of the letter M (an inversion of W), the title of Fritz Lang's 1931 film of a psychotic child-murderer, which ends with the words: "Mothers, take better care of your children."[34]

* * *

Of all the encounters between French literature and the Holocaust, the most wrenching may be that of Irène Némirovsky, the accomplished Russian-born Jewish novelist who converted to Catholicism in February 1939. Her final unfinished work, *Suite française*, a chronicle of the defeat of 1940 as refracted through the personal lives of the French, was published posthumously in 2004 and immediately became an international sensation.[35] On the one hand, we find virtually no reference to the plight of the Jews in a novel written, in hiding, during the war; on the other, the novel was published along with an appendix detailing the pitiful attempts of her husband to save the life of the author, who was carted off to the French camp of Pithiviers on July 16, 1942, deported to Poland in Convoy 6 the following day, and murdered on August 17, 1942, in Auschwitz, after being treated for a severe bout of typhus.[36] (Michel Epstein, her husband, ignorant of these developments, wrote to Pétain, requesting permission to replace his wife, whose health was fragile, in her labor team. He was deported via the French camp at Drancy and immediately gassed upon arrival at Auschwitz, November 6, 1942.)

If the persecution of the Jews, in sum, is nowhere present in *Suite française*, except as the reason for its incompletion, it is the very substance of the epistolary appendix accompanying the published text. Before turning to that appendix, however, an additional complication needs be confronted. For the irony of Némirovsky's prose, throughout her career, was never more corrosive than in her evocation of her Jewish characters. It begins with her first novel, *David Golder* (1929), a mesmerizing tale of the rise and fall of a crude and rapacious Jewish magnate, his unfaithful wife, and his frivolous and ungrateful daughter. For its "purity" of prose, the book immediately earned the praise of Robert Brasillach, rabid anti-Semite and sole literary figure to be executed during the postwar liberation.[37] All in all, it has been suggested, Némirovsky experienced a kind of "fascinated horror" in the face of what she called "Jewish insolence."[38]

There has been a debate concerning a putative "anti-Semitism" of French literature's prototypal victim of the Holocaust. She herself denied that *David Golder* targeted the Jews. In 1935, she remarked: "It is absolutely certain that had there been a Hitler at the time, I would definitely have softened *David Golder*, and I would not have written it in the same way."[39] To which she tellingly added: "And yet I would have been wrong, it would have been a weakness unworthy of a real writer." It seems clear that under Hitler, anti-Semitism had come to be something murderous, mendacious, and contemptuous of Jews. Némirovsky was intent on preserving the contempt while stripping it of the murderousness and the mendacity. For which she paid a high price.

This is painfully plain in the epistolary appendix to *Suite française*. In an effort to locate and free his wife, who had just been taken to the French camp in Pithiviers, Michel Epstein tried to convince Otto Abetz, the German ambassador to Paris, that on the Jewish question, Némirovsky did not pose an insuperable problem: "although she is of Jewish racial origin, she speaks of the Jews [in her books] without the slightest tenderness."[40] In Epstein's exchanges with representatives of Némirovsky's publisher, Albin Michel, two potential defenders, neither of them in any way efficacious, are referred to in code. "Ami" was the designation for Jacques Benoît-Méchin, whose principal effort at the time was to convince the Germans, as roving ambassador for Vichy, that the proper French role in the war was to actively collaborate in combat on the side of the Germans.[41] (Hitler, who distrusted the French, was not convinced.) "Mme Paul," on the other hand, was the Romanian Princess Soutzo, wife of the writer Paul Morand, who served as Vichy's ambassador to Bucharest.[42] Revelations of anti-Semitic touches in Paul Morand's writings are regularly explained by way of the "profound anti-Semitism" of his wife. Neither "Mme Paul" nor "friend" Benoît-Méchin, both of whom enjoyed a lasting intimacy with Proust, it may be noted, appear to have been ideal choices for saving Némirovsky's life.

* * *

The French literary sensation of 2006, winner of the Prix Goncourt and the Grand Prix du Roman de l'Académie française, was an ambitious fictional effort by the American writer Jonathan Littell to view the genocide of the Jews from the point of view of an unapologetic German officer and participant prepared to argue that he was in no essential way different from the "human brothers," his readers, whom he addresses in the first words of his 894-page novel. The book was titled *Les Bienveillantes* (*The Kindly Ones*), a rendering of the title of the third part of the Aeschylean *Oresteia, The Eumenides*, and it thus demanded reading on at least two levels.[43] On the one hand, the author had done an impressive amount of research, allowing his protagonist, Maximilien Aue, to be so assiduously present at every turn of the genocide – from *Einsatzgruppen* to gas chambers and beyond – as to have been described by one critic, in a reference to Woody Allen's protagonist, as the Zelig of the Holocaust.[44] (Claude Lanzmann, moreover, whose film, *Shoah*, was described by the author as one of his inspirations, characteristically opined, after some initial grousing, that Littell's scholarship was such that only two individuals were fully equipped to understand his novel: the doyen of Holocaust historians, Raul Hilberg, and Lanzmann himself.)[45] On the other hand, the novel maps the myth of Orestes – an incestuous, homosexual, matricidal Orestes – onto the historical matter, and opinions have been sharply divided as to whether that mapping is successful. Daniel Mendelsohn has suggested that the point of juncture is to be found in the protagonist's perusal during the war of Blanchot's critique of Sartre's wartime dramatization of the Orestes myth, *Les Mouches*.[46] The upshot (according to Mendelsohn): a return to the postwar Sade cult whose emergence and subsequent waning, under the aegis of Blanchot, we have commented on earlier. What seemed to go unmentioned was the fact that France's leading literary awards were going to an American, whose prose, from the stylistic point of view, rarely rose above the pedestrian. Might French literature be turning into a franchise of American culture?

* * *

It has been our position from the beginning of these pages that the encounter between French literature and the Holocaust was fraught with dangers. Within the space opened up by those (frequently unexpected) perils, the series of differently angled evocations offered has been designed with an eye to transmitting a sense of how quirky the articulation of the two realms might be. If one were to choose a vector organizing these readings, it might be in terms of the arc sketched by the three Goncourt Prizewinners we have encountered. *Le Dernier des justes* (1959), from the period of France's honeymoon period with Israel, and *La Vie devant soi* (1975), from the heyday of France's "Vichy syndrome," are both rooted in the experience of victims of the Holocaust: Ernie Lévy, Madame Rosa, and so on. *Les Bienveillantes*, on the other hand, shifts its focus to one of the perpetrators:

Maximilien Aue. It is as though French literature, whose imperative since Baudelaire has been to relieve tedium (rather than to promote justice), were on the brink of declaring the Holocaust one more *topos* approaching exhaustion.

And if the evolution of the *topos* has been such that only an empathy with the anti-Semite can save it from exhaustion (or piety), as already on occasion appears to be the case, then the dangers anticipated in the confrontation between French literature and the Holocaust will have been realized.[47]

Notes

1. It may be noted that Robert Faurisson, the patron saint of Holocaust denial in France, was a professor of French literature in Lyon, who had come to prominence initially not for questioning the existence of the gas chambers – in an article in *Le Monde* in 1979 – but for a denial of the transgressive greatness of the nineteenth-century poet Lautréamont years before. See J. Mehlman, Foreword to Pierre Vidal-Naquet, *Assassins of Memory* (New York: Columbia University Press, 1992), p. xx.

2. See Vidal-Naquet, *Assassins*, and Jean-François Lyotard, *Le Différend* (Paris: Minuit, 1983), p. 16.

3. Alain Finkielkraut, *L'Avenir d'une négation: Réflexion sur la question du génocide* (Paris: Seuil, 1983), pp. 15–58.

4. See, however, for what comes close to being a transcendental variant of "negationism," Giorgio Agamben's promotion of the *Muselmann*, the camp zombie, to the combined status of "complete witness" and least trustworthy – because of his depletion – of speakers. "Let us, indeed, posit Auschwitz, that to which it is not possible to bear witness; and let us also posit the *Muselmann* as the absolute impossibility of bearing witness . . ." Agamben, *Remnants of Auschwitz: The Witness and the Archive*, trans. Daniel Heller-Roazen (New York: Zone Books, 2008), p. 164.

5. *Chateaubriand: Poésie et terreur* (Paris: Bernard de Fallois, 2003).

6. Ibid., p. 144.

7. Ibid., p. 16.

8. Hannah Arendt, "Antisemitism," Part I of *The Origins of Totalitarianism* (New York: Harcout Brace, 1951), p. 4.

9. See A. de Saint-Exupéry, *Ecrits de guerre, 1939–1944* (Paris: Gallimard, 1982), pp. 210–16, from which the reference to "6,000,000" threatened with "extermination" has been cut.

10. *La Patrie se fait tous les jours* (Paris: Minuit, 1947), pp. 375–78. The poem is discussed at greater length in J. Mehlman, "The Tiger Leaps: Louis Aragon, Gustave Cohen, and the Poetry of Resistance," in Christopher Benfey and Karen Remmler (eds.), *Artists, Intellectuals and World War II: The Pontigny Encounters at Mount Holyoke College, 1942–1944* (Amherst: University of Massachusetts Press, 2006), pp. 162–72.

11. See Régis Debray, *Le Moment fraternité* (Paris: Gallimard, 2009), pp. 65–66.

12. Elie Wiesel, *Night*, trans. Stella Rodway (New York: Hill and Wang, 1960).

13. On the publishing history of *Night*, see Naomi Seidman, "Elie Wiesel and the Scandal of Jewish Rage," *Jewish Social Studies: History, Culture and Society* 3/1 (December 1996): 1–19.

14. Wiesel, *Night*, p. viii. Subsequent page references are given in the text.

15. Marcel Proust, *The Guermantes Way*, trans. M. Traharne (New York: Penguin Classics, 2005), p. 233.

16. André Schwarz-Bart, *Le Dernier des justes* (Paris: Seuil, 1959).

17. Francine Kaufmann, "Les enjeux de la polémique autour du best-seller français de la littérature de la Shoah," *Revue d'Histoire de la Shoah* 176 (September–December 2002): 68–96.

18. André Schwarz-Bart, *Etoile du matin* (Paris: Seuil, 2009).

19. Henry Rousso, *The Vichy Syndrome*, trans. A. Goldhammer (Cambridge, MA: Harvard University Press, 1994).

20. For a full treatment of the subject, see Eric Marty, *Pourquoi le XXme siècle a-t-il pris Sade au sérieux?* (Paris: Seuil, 2011).

21. Maurice Blanchot, *Lautréamont et Sade* (Paris: Minuit, 1949), p. 36.

22. Blanchot, "La littérature et le droit à la mort," in *La Part du feu* (Paris: Gallimard, 1949), p. 339.

23. See Zeev Sternhell, *Ni droite ni gauche: L'idéologie fasciste en France* (Paris: Seuil, 1983), p. 241.

24. Maurice Blanchot, "Le terrorisme comme méthode de salut publique," *Combat* 1/7 (July 1936).

25. See J. Mehlman, "Iphigénie 38: Deconstruction, History, and the Case of *L'arrêt de mort*," in *Genealogies of the Text: Literature, Psychoanalysis, and Politics in Modern France* (Cambridge University Press, 1995), pp. 82–96.

26. Ibid., pp. 94–95. The identification with "German Jews" was manifestly with Daniel Cohn-Bendit, the *gauchiste* leader of May 1968, but the Holocaust reference was implicit.

27. M. Blanchot, *La Communauté inavouable* (Paris: Minuit, 1983).

28. See J. Mehlman, "Blanchot at Combat: Literature and Terror," in *Legacies of Anti-Semitism in France* (Minneapolis: University of Minnesota Press, 1983).

29. Patrick Modiano, *La Place de l'etoile* (Paris: Gallimard, 1968).

30. Marcel Proust, *Contre Sainte-Beuve* (Paris: Gallimard, 1954), pp. 439–40.

31. Emile Ajar (Romain Gary), *La Vie devant soi* (Paris: Mercure de France, 1975).

32. For Perec's psychoanalysis and its relation to *W*, see David Bellos, *Georges Perec: A Life in Words* (Boston: David Godine, 1993).

33. Ibid., pp. 277 and 551.

34. Ibid., p. 555.

35. Irène Némirovsky, *Suite française* (Paris: Denoël, 2004).

36. See Myrian Anissimov, Preface to *Suite française*, p. 22.

37. Ibid., p. 11.

38. Ibid., p. 14.

39. Quoted in the *New York Times*, April 25, 2010.

40. Némirovsky, *Suite française*, "Annexe," p. 421.
41. Ibid., p. 49. On Benoît-Méchin's role during the war, see Robert O. Paxton, *Vichy France: Old Guard and New Order, 1940–1944* (New York: Norton, 1972), pp. 387–90.
42. Némirovsky, *Suite française*, p. 427.
43. Jonathan Littell, *Les Bienveillantes* (Paris: Gallimard, 2006).
44. Samuel Moyn, "A Nazi Zelig: Jonathan Littell's the Kindly Ones," *The Nation*, March 4, 2009.
45. Benjamin Pollak, "*The Kindly Ones* in America" (interview with Charlotte Mandell), JBooks: www.jbooks.com/interviews/index/IP_Pollak_Mandell.htm.
46. Daniel Mendelsohn, "Transgression," *The New York Review of Books*, March 20, 2009.
47. Marc-Edouard Nabe's self-published (but well-received) novel, *L'Enculé* (an obscenity loosely translated as *Screwed*) is a case in point. The book is about Dominique Strauss-Kahn and is anti-Semitic. But it is not directed against Strauss-Kahn, with whose nihilism Nabe identifies, but against his wife, Anne Sinclair, whose obsession with the Holocaust is said to have driven Strauss-Kahn himself to anti-Semitism. In *Le Point* ("La Fortune de Nabe," October 21, 2011), a popular weekly, Patrick Besson praises Nabe's novel as "the most pertinent and jovial synthesis of all that could be read, seen, and heard of last summer's DSK affair."

PART III

Other approaches

CHAPTER 12

Oral memoir and the Shoah

Alessandro Portelli

Time is running out

Recording the voices and filming the faces of Holocaust survivors has been perceived as necessary in order to establish this memory as the metonymy of the history of our time and to anticipate the risk of its extinction. "At least 100,000 survivor accounts have been collected since 1944 in many languages, contexts, and formats,"[1] with most of them ending up in major or minor archives in dozens of countries. No scholar can even think of mastering them all.

In this chapter, I will try to outline a few questions of method, based primarily on interviews I have listened to or recorded myself, focusing on the Italian examples with which I am most familiar. One thing that makes oral history different is that the historian does not simply "collect" the stories, but also contributes to their creation and is inevitably involved in the result. *Shoah* narratives especially challenge the interviewer to cultivate a form of listening that combines personal empathy with historical objectivity, thus making such empathy an essential part of critical understanding.

Testimony and narrative

The word "testimony" covers a range of connotations, including legal, religious, didactic, and personal. Strictly speaking, testimony means a public narrative about events that the narrator has witnessed or participated in. In the case of the *Shoah*, testimony has been drawn on primarily in the judicial realm and as a rebuttal to the perverse denial that the Holocaust ever took place.

This is why Annette Wieviorka opens what she calls "the era of the witness" with the testimony of survivors at the trial of Adolf Eichmann in the early 1960s. While the Nuremberg trials held in the aftermath of World War II were based on archival documents, and witnesses were used mainly to confirm the documents, the prosecution in the Eichmann trial chose oral courtroom testimony to convey a broader perspective on the events. The witnesses' bodies, voices, and language established the terms for the reconstruction of the meaning and impact of the murderous events in question, in a way much more far-reaching, however, than the specific case under examination. Beyond the testimony's content, the expressive force of the witnesses' gaze and body performed, in the highest sense of the word, a theatrical function.

In addition to playing the role of corroborating a truth, testimony also bears a *spiritual* connotation. Beyond the legal and the historical, testimony also calls upon the deep identity of the witnesses and their relationship with the sacred and the social. The Latin words at the root of testimony include *superstes*, survivor. Filip Müller, a member of the Sonderkommando at Auschwitz, recalls that, as he watched the victims being herded into the crematorium, he too entered the gas chamber resolved to die. But some of the women about to be killed recognized him and told him: "Your death won't give us back our lives. That's no way. You must get out of here alive, you must bear witness to our suffering, and to the injustice done to us."[2]

Some narrators describe testimony as a *mitzvah*, a sacred obligation. "I only am escaped alone *to tell thee*," says the book of Job; and Shlomo Venezia confirms: "I am now in life in order to tell what has occurred." And Settimia Spizzichino: "I made a solemn promise to my fifty women comrades [who were killed in the camp]: I kept saying, Lord, save me, save me, because I must go back and tell about it."[3] As Primo Levi wrote: "The need to narrate, to 'tell it,' goes back to the very time of captivity; sometimes, it is almost a vow, a promise that believers give to God and secularists to themselves. The hope of survival coincides, ultimately, with the obsessive hope of making others know."[4]

Testimony in the spiritual sense was for some survivors a continuation of a resistance to death that began inside the camp. But it also was a form of thanksgiving for the circumstances that allowed them to survive while others were lost, even a form of atonement for having survived. The personal urge to speak became a moral and social responsibility.

Hence, testimony as *teaching*: a narrative intended to generate a change in the narratee. The survivor's account is a lesson and a warning, especially when addressed to younger generations that might not know or know only vaguely. The Shoah Foundation affirms that "eyewitness accounts could have a profound effect on education, and the survivors could become teachers of humanity for generations to come."[5] Often, testimony takes place in a classroom. For instance, Nedo Fiano in a school in Florence:

Take warning now: I am going to tell you about hell.
I am not joking. This occasion has been very painful for me, as is always the case when I face a generation that came after that hell.
This is not a lesson, but *the* lesson. Not because I'm the one that gives it, but because it comes from very far. There is no other like it.[6]

Survivors have accompanied students on visits to the camps, such as those organized by the city of Rome to Auschwitz since 2004. They met with students and teachers before the journey, and testified standing in the places most representative of their own experience: Shlomo Venezia by the ruins of the gas chambers, Enzo Camerino at the Judenrampe, Piero Terracina by the train tracks, Andra and Tatiana Bucci in the children's barracks where they were held at the age of four and six.

The impact of the testimony is thus reinforced by space. In the video interviews conducted in the camps by the Milan Jewish Documentation Center, narrative and space support and validate each other: what I am telling you is real, because real are the ruins from which I speak. Much of the power of Claude Lanzmann's *Shoah* lies in this imaginative relation between narrative and place.

Finally, testimony is an intensely *personal* act. At this level, the word "testimony" becomes entirely inadequate. Testimony in legal and strictly historical terms is about an outer-oriented truth, about something narrators have seen but of which they may or may not be a part. Christopher Browning writes about the judge who dismissed survivor witnesses claiming that acceptable testimony must be given by an "'indifferent, attentive, intelligent observer' who observed events in a 'disinterested' and 'distanced' way."[7] But oral narratives are always more inner-oriented, always about both the facts and their meaning, and the narrators themselves.[8]

As long as we care about only tangible "facts," the narrator's personality may even be perceived as a source of interference, a distortion of some objective truth out there. In this way, however, we forget that all these stories are in some ineradicable manner different and unique, because different and unique are the tellers, and because the story is always about their unique individuality. The Rashomon-effect of sometimes contradictory and conflicting narratives about the same event is a confirmation of their intensely and deeply personal nature. Oral memoir recognizes narrators not as "bearers" of memory but rather as "authors" who must be recognized, whenever possible, with their names and identities. Hence, much of the best work on survivor interviews adopts approaches derived from literature, narratology, and psychology – disciplines which lend themselves to the subjective dimension of the account.

Another implication of testimony is that it exists somewhere *before* the act of testifying, to be "released" by the narrator and "collected" by the historian. However, all oral narrative is a dialogue with a specific "audience," in search of attention, belief, and resonance. I am thinking of Shlomo Venezia, a Sonderkommando survivor, on the landing of a hotel in Krakow, surrounded by young people crouching for hours on the floor to listen to him: "I don't expect that all who hear will believe; but those who believe, please tell others." Alberto Sed explains:

> We say that it takes a deportee to understand a deportee. Other people don't understand, they think we're crazy. For instance . . ., he was the first who returned to Italy. He started telling his family what had happened, of the ovens and all, and no one believed him. They even had him examined! Yet, how could they believe all that? Then of course the rest of us returned and by then they realized that it was all true, but at first they thought that he was crazy.[9]

One function of narrative is that of (re)establishing contact with others. Narrative, however, can also be a self-referential act: the attempt to give shape and form to the turmoil of memory, to separate the speakable from the unspeakable, to elaborate mourning, to reconstruct a form of self-representation. The accent shifts again: from outer-oriented (teaching the truth to others) to inner-oriented (reconstructing one's sense of oneself).

On returning from his first visit to Auschwitz after sixty years, Sami Modiano told the students: "The agony now is over. I have done my duty."[10] Whether testimony also has a therapeutic effect remains to be verified in each individual case. But the moment a person rises to speak may mark a turning point in one's inner search – if nothing else because, if speaking is felt to be a duty, the act of testifying offers at least the sense of a duty done.

Contexts

Anna Bravo and Daniele Jallà write: "Though they differ in form, courtroom testimony and spontaneous narrative are both acts of piety toward the dead whose memory they wish to retrieve, and of denunciation against perpetrators who manage to become invisible, against abettors and indifferent bystanders, against the world that was so slow to believe and to act, and still doubts them."[11] The distinction between "testimony" and "narrative," then, is based on the form and contexts of the performance: the oral memoir interview is a result of the dialogic encounter of speaker and interviewer; courtroom testimony is an essentially asymmetrical form in which the initiative remains in the hands of the interrogator.

Of course, in practice it is impossible to completely repress the witnesses' impulse of self-representation and to completely separate what the witnesses have seen from their story or from their past and present pain. Sometimes – as in the case of the Eichmann trial – the prosecutor's strategy may rely precisely on those specific aspects of the witness. Yet even then the witness's personal account was still subject to the prosecutor's construction of narrative space and meaning.

Personal or didactic testimony is more monologic than a courtroom question-and-answer format. The physical presence of hearers who, by paying attention, showing understanding, or evincing emotion, directly or indirectly affect the narrative performance is still crucial. But once attention is assured, the speaker is in control: the story is ultimately an answer to questions the speaker asks of him- or herself. This is why Bravo and Jallà may write of a "spontaneous" narrative: speakers claim control, resisting inclusion in someone else's narrative or interpretation. "I was there," states Jean Améry: no listener, he insists, is entitled to impose an interpretation on the tale of those who saw it first-hand.

In February 2006, Piero Terracina spoke to the students of the Lucrezio Caro high school in Rome. A teacher in that school had had her students read a book of Hitler's monologues (prefaced by a notorious Fascist extremist), claiming that in this way she was putting them in touch with the historical source. When it was suggested that her students meet Piero Terracina, she replied that she wanted them to know the facts, not the emotions – once again, identifying orality with emotion and writing with rationality, as if Hitler's monologues (originally oral anyway) were not a hodgepodge of crude emotions; as if the narratives of the survivors were not rooted in the first-hand knowledge of facts; and as if the correct "scientific" attitude consisted in rooting out the knowledge generated by deeply felt personal relationships with the historical material.

Piero Terracina delivered an hour-long monologue, beginning with a painstaking exposition of historical facts about Italy's 1938 race laws, followed by an account of his own experience in the framework of collective social history. No one spoke after him, no questions were asked: the power of this testimonial narrative seemed to lie in its rounded self-sufficiency. Information was at no time separate from feeling; indeed, emotion aided historical understanding, while historical knowledge generated emotions and feelings.

Speakers thus constantly oscillate between personal narrative that is the life of the discourse, and testimony in which they attempt to validate their narrative by indicating the sources of information. Comments such as "'I saw it with these eyes, I heard of it, I learned it later, I read it . . .'" or "This is how it was, I'm not exaggerating . . . it seems to, I don't remember well . . . from my point of view, as far as I know . . ." are not incidental remarks, but traces of how events and images stand in memory. Yet I would insist that even these apparently merely factual controls also bear an emotional meaning. To say that one has lived through certain events in the first person is an invitation to the listeners (or readers) to imagine themselves in the place and time of the story and, as far as possible, share it. "I was like you," Nedo Fiano told the students, "exactly like you, I smiled as you do, I thought and I laughed at the most terrible things, because a smile is the gift of your age."

Oral histories and dialogue

Amos Luzzatto, former president of Italy's Jewish communities, writes: "I think we should distinguish the act of *listening* to the survivors from the act of *interrogating* them."[12] This distinction helps us distinguish between *testimony* and *oral sources*.

Of course, in practice the distinction can be uncertain: interrogation is implicit in listening, even when the story is ostensibly a monologue. Oral history, however, is predicated on the historian's active role in what becomes less a "spontaneous" narrative than the result of a collaboration or confrontation. Oral sources always have at least two "authors" – the narrator and the person whose questions (indeed, whose mere willing presence) open the space and create the time for the account to be given, and who intervenes dialogically (if only through body language) in the course of its unfolding. Here – when it intersects with research – is when memory is no longer a self-referential entity but rather becomes a *source* for the making of history.

Of course, some dialogue is always implicit in any oral narrative, including courtroom or classroom testimony; yet even in the most dialogic interviews it is frequently difficult for an interviewer to overcome awe and fear of intrusiveness. As Wieviorka says, often the historian as interrogator and listener is affected by the pain that comes through the tale of a survivor who may be the last in a chain of remembered dead.

The interviewer's silence may be due to the wish to avoid interfering with the (supposed) authenticity and spontaneity of the testimony: many interviews in the Yale Fortunoff Archive display a strategy of non-intervention meant to encourage the free flow of memory, a strategy more akin to a psychoanalyst's silence than the historian's interrogation. Yet even the interviewer's silence takes place in a space and format structured by them.

Indeed, the interpretive framework is implicit in the staging of the interview, such as a preference for video or audio interviews, or in the choice of location in which the interview is to take place. As a case in point, Alan Rosen notes that "Holocaust testimony has become synonymous with video testimony." In support of this development, Geoffrey Hartman insists that audio "disembodies" the narrator's voice.[13] Actually, so does video: all forms of representation are based on the absence of the body. Indeed, video is a *representation* of the body, while audio is a *reproduction* of the voice. Audio includes the interviewer's presence (as opposed to "talking-head" video interviews), and does not try to pretend that we are dealing with "the real thing." Video does preserve body language and spatial context, and lends itself better to communication and teaching. One wishes, however, for less impressionistic ways of reading visual hints, and for more creative use of the camera. Location, too, must play its part. The dark background in the Fortunoff interviews suggests a psychoanalytic approach in which survivors have suffered an immutable trauma that isolates them from all others. In contrast, the domestic setting of the Shoah Foundation interviews assumes a belief in human resilience and implies that, though the trauma may not be fully overcome, the interviewees have nonetheless managed to make acceptable lives for themselves.

The historian may know that the narrator is departing from the factual truth of historic events, but is powerless to intervene because he feels morally unable to "spoil" the narrators' memories and beliefs. "Indeed," Browning writes, "to intrude upon the survivors' memories with such a banal or mundane concern [such as "factual accuracy"] is deemed irrelevant and inappropriate, or even insensitive and disrespectful"[14] – and even bordering on negationism. Often, the respect for the "authenticity" of the speaker's feelings stands in the way of the critical attitude that is essential to historical, narratological, and linguistic interpretation.

Yet interviewers' silences may not depend entirely on moral scruples but also on their own awareness that they do *not* possess all the necessary information: the interview takes place precisely because the narrator knows things that the historian doesn't. *Shoah* survivors force historians into being not only passive "listeners" but also active "hearers" who must suspend their sense of what is normal and expected, and accept a voice coming both from a distant past *and* from the immediate present. What is at play is the narrator's subjectivity, and the historian's as well.

The first time I met Settimia Spizzichino, an iconic *Shoah* survivor and narrator, her moral authority, my ignorance, and her long-honed narrative skills were such that I could do little more than just listen. The same was the case with my first interview with Piero Terracina: that recording is one of the two in my collection in which my voice goes unheard for a whole side of the tape. This does not imply that I was not involved in the exchange: besides non-verbal forms of expression, my silence itself communicated the story's impact on me. While empathy and emotion prevailed, that the interview with Spizzichino deserved the name of historical research was confirmed when I went back to the recordings for critical listening and analysis. Indeed, my critical listening of the recording allowed me to recognize narrative strategies, gaps and silences that I was later able to discuss with Settimia and Piero. The meaning of these strategies, moreover, I might not have understood without the empathic experience to begin with.

Amos Luzzatto adds that "interrogation is a difficult task, which not all know how to perform. One cannot ask everything, indiscriminately. One must have an idea of what, in the witness's experience, is relevant to our contemporary context . . . and which are the points we wish to clarify on the basis of this testimony."[15] The interview, then, is a meeting of two agendas (the interviewer's and the narrator's) with a story – plus the new agenda that arises from the encounter and that changes the initial framework of both scholar and survivor.

An interview is not a crossfire of questions and answers ("we must be wary of inquest-like interrogations that can be answered with a 'yes' or 'no,'" Luzzatto warns). It is rather an "experiment in equality," the opening of a narrative space in which the interviewer negotiates what the narrators wish (or are able) to tell, whether asked about it or not.

As we have seen, narrative has both a communicative and a personal function: certain things cannot be told and others *must* be told. In an interview about growing up in Rome's Pitigliani Jewish orphanage, Alberto Sed, an Auschwitz survivor, introduced an apparently unrelated digression:

> My wife and I went to Israel, where most [of my friends] live. Later, she told me she didn't know whether she was happier for seeing Israel or for meeting my friends. I had been in the concentration camp, and everybody knew, and when I went to Israel we all would get together, in Tel Aviv, in Nathania . . .

The interviewer tries to bring him back to the interview's topic: "Let's go back for a moment . . ." Yet, the digression turns out to be important precisely in order to understand Sed's orphanage experience:

Often my wife wonders, "How come everybody complains about the orphanage and my husband speaks so well of it?" But it's normal. Most children, once they left it went home, to their family. Or to Israel. I, instead, went to the concentration camp, and I saw the difference between that and the orphanage. No wonder I speak well of it.[16]

At this point the interviewer understands that Sed cannot speak of his life without measuring all his experiences on the basis of Auschwitz. So she asks him whether the education he received in the orphanage helped him there. Sed answers that the physical education he was given at the orphanage did ("I was in good shape, thanks to the institution"), but then goes on to other episodes that have no relationship to the Pitigliani orphanage – and the interviewer is wise enough not to interrupt him. Sed had earned the narrative space to tell stories that simply had to be told, no matter what the interview was supposed to be about.

I had a sense of the difference between *listening to* and *interrogating* when I investigated an incident that narrators often skipped: the two nights that the group of Jews who were raided by the Nazis on October 16, 1943, and who were shortly after deported, spent in Rome's Army College. Settimia Spizzichino, for instance, did not mention it in her first interview with me; she proceeded directly from a description of the raid to "I, my mother and [my sister] Giuditta were taken to Auschwitz."[17]

Like most transitional times and places (the Regina Coeli jail, the Fossoli transit camp, the Risiera transit and concentration camp in Trieste), these two nights in Rome's Army College fall through the cracks of the story, dwarfed by what came after – and by the fact that interviewers who did not know about them or did not see their importance failed to ask about them.[18] When I interviewed Settimia again, I did it also to "interrogate" her about these two nights. Another survivor's story, that of Lello Di Segni, also tells of having gone straight from the raid to the train:

DI SEGNI ... they loaded us on a cattle car, they did. Wagons – I mean: cattle cars. Which they never opened. I mean, we would relieve ourselves inside. We had my grandmother with us who was ill, and she had to do everything in there. We made do. And, as I remember, I was sixteen, now I'm seventy-two, you can figure.

PORTELLI Back when you were in the Army College, what did you think would happen?

DI SEGNI We didn't think – I'll explain it later, because – we didn't think any of all this.

The Army College episode, which took place less than half a mile from the Vatican, is but a footnote in history. It is, however, important methodologically. In the first place, the episode reveals the narrators' sense of time. Most of the interviewees believe it lasted longer than it actually did: Enzo Camerino remembers "three days"; Lello Di Segni says it was "more or less I guess a couple of weeks; ten to fifteen days for sure, I think." Then, the episode also raises the question of the relationship between the deportees, the city, and its institutions – including the Vatican.[19] Claudio Fano, a former president of Rome's Jewish community, noted that "the Vatican is a short walk away" from the Army College, "and the Pope had a car and he had fuel. All he had to do was send some cardinal or bishop, even his secretary." But nobody showed up.[20]

The short interlude spent at the Army College may be a minor detail to the survivors, but the city of Rome and the Catholic Church would do well to consider their role in this small piece of the *Shoah* at their threshold.

Interrogating the testimony

That the historian's dialogic interrogation is the substance of oral memoir does not mean that one cannot also treat other forms of testimony as historical sources. However, while in an interview the historian contributes to the formation of the narrative, monologic testimony and archival sources (whether of written or oral origin) are documents that can be *interrogated* only metaphorically – that is, *interpreted* critically.

Wieviorka mentions historians' concerns about the reliability of oral sources. Another distinguished historian, Marc Bloch, insists that there is no such thing as a good witness, or a completely reliable testimony.[21] Actually, the opposite is true: there is no such thing as a useless witness or a narrative that is not brimming with historically significant information – even more so when they depart from strictly factual accuracy. "Errors," *once recognized as such*, may be the sites of imagination, desire, implicit and subconscious creativity. In oral memoir – which is also history of memory and subjectivity – this truth ultimately counts as much as conventional factual reliability.

Most of the information couched in memory narratives is actually accurate and verifiable, which means, however, that it is also available elsewhere. Alberto Maruffi, a survivor of Mauthausen, says: "I never spoke of these things. Then I read them in a book, *Il tunnel*, and then I said: well, now I can talk about it, too, and they will believe me."[22] Fortunately, Maruffi's narrative and the book that ought to validate it are not the same: if nothing else, because Maruffi is not in the book. The contribution of oral sources lies in the uniqueness of voice, subjectivity, point of view, and narrative strategies. Saul Friedlander suggests replacing the binary opposition of history versus memory with a continuum hinging on historical consciousness, in which history and memory "are joined whenever there is a serious effort to understand, explain and represent the past that impacts the way we shape the present."[23]

While insisting on the reliability of oral testimony, literary and oral memoir scholar Lawrence Langer notes that Dr. Josef Mengele "seems from these testimonies to have single-handedly selected a million Jews for the gas chambers."[24] Historians may recognize in this often imaginary detail[25] frequent motifs that recur in oral history narratives: some narrators actually believe that the officer who presided over the selections was the infamous Dr. Mengele; others aim, consciously or not, to enhance the importance of their story by connecting it with recognized history, or to help listeners by placing it in a context with which they may be less unfamiliar. Sometimes, it may be an example of simply calling *every* Nazi medical officer by the name "Mengele." In any case, the factual error contains another kind of truth, one that concerns the narrators' relationship to the meaning of the experience.

Interrogation, then, consists in listening for the lower frequencies, the implicit, the unsaid. At the Shoah Foundation I was shown, as an example of their (admirable) system of cataloging and access to sources, a clip in which a Hungarian survivor described his arrival at Birkenau. He told how the prisoners were unloaded from the trains, the confrontation with the SS, the breakup of families, and then said: "And you know what came after." Actually, we do not know, unless those who lived it tell us. And even then, we don't really *know*. His way of telling us is another rhetorical figure: reticence, litotes. It tells us that what we know is that such an experience is unknowable and unspeakable.

Unspeakability is ingrained in many *Shoah* narratives. Piero Terracina recollected his father's last words, as they stood against the wall in the Regina Coeli jail before deportation: "Anything may happen, so I only have one thing to tell you: never lose your dignity." A long, unbearable pause followed, which I naïvely tried to fill.

PORTELLI This was the most important teaching he could give.
TERRACINA Yes.
PORTELLI Because, together with your life, that was what they were trying to take from you.

Another long silence. Then, with effort, Terracina went forward: "Well – let's continue. And unfortunately that – saving our dignity as human beings, that was not possible, after all." The reticence on how and why dignity was lost is more eloquent than any detailed account.[26]

The narratives of the *Shoah* are surrounded and crossed by silences. A distinction is, however, in order: by "silence" we mean both something not told, and a break in the telling. While the former applies to written *and* to oral accounts, the latter relates only to oral performance, when speech ceases and an unbearable time of emptiness begins (hence my effort to bridge with an inane comment the heavy silence in the interview with Piero Terracina).

In both written and oral testimony, silence as omission and reticence is often motivated, as Piero Terracina puts it, by a sense of "decency" about one's body and feelings (especially in a face-to-face interview situation). Oral silence, however, is more often caused by the difficulty of speaking of experiences that are beyond the possibilities and boundaries of narrative and language. "There and then, there began the . . . the unspeakability," says Andra Bucci, deported at age six.[27] The very word "unspeakability" seems unspeakable as she hesitates before uttering it. All narrators seem to linger in search for the least inadequate words: "When we began to come into contact with so many . . . so many corpses . . . it was a shock . . . it's impossible to explain what it was like," said Shlomo Venezia, a Sonderkommando survivor. And then: "One thousand and fifty people went directly . . ." – and, like the Hungarian deportee, he left the sentence unfinished. No matter how many times he tells his story, Terracina struggles against the limits of language as if it were the first: "The chaos was something . . . something unspeakable . . . it's hard to tell what used to go on in this place"; "something that to call it horrible is by no means . . . by no means adequate, this is not the word that can describe what actually happened."

The *Shoah* was also a linguistic experience. This is how Raimondo Vazon put it: "We walk into a room, they give us orders, I don't understand a thing and neither do the others. Inhuman shouts: they didn't speak, they screamed. It was shouts, knocks, whippings . . . everything *schnell*, quick, quick."[28] As they get off the train, Andra and Tatiana Bucci meet the violence of a shouted alien language: "All these voices, everybody shouting, giving orders in a language unknown to me and the people were shouting, screaming."

The abolition of language was an attempt to turn human beings into "pieces" or brutes. Angelo Travaglia recalls:

> Only once did I speak to an SS, because the SS did not speak to us, they always spoke through the kapos, through the criminals, because we were *Untermenschen*, subhuman. To them, it would have been like talking to a rat.[29]

Ithzak Dugin, a member of the Sonderkommando, describes the perpetrators' linguistic strategies: "The Germans forbade us to use the words 'corpse' or 'victim.' The dead were blocks of wood, shit, of absolutely no importance. Anyone who uttered the words 'corpse' or 'victim' was beaten. The Germans made us refer to the bodies as *Figuren*, that is, as puppets, or dolls, or as *Schmattes*, meaning 'rags.'"[30] Prisoners slide from their own language to a foreign tongue, and to the non-language of the stick and the whip: "We understood," said Otello Vecchio, "we didn't need interpreters. The interpreter was the stick."[31]

"No book and no orator will ever be able to say that cold is cold, that hunger is hunger," recounts Alberto Mongarli, a survivor of Flossenbürg. Enzo Trabucchi, a survivor of Dachau: "The problem there was hunger and thirst, the lack of everything, the cold ... it's a language, this, that all understand." Piero Terracina: "No use to speak of the hunger, of the cold; to tell of these things is all but useless. Who can remember the hunger? This morning I had a good breakfast, and to speak of hunger ... one ought to experience it. What I can say is this: the hunger of one who has gone one, two, three days without food, is completely different, because our hunger was a hunger without hope."[32]

Re-membering the fragments

Shoah narratives are bound to be fragments. Too many elements interfere with the possibility of closure and positive ending. As Nedo Fiano says, from the extermination camp "you don't come out either dead or alive." Hedda K. explains: "This experience – you can live with it, it's like constant pain: you never forget, you never get rid of it, but you learn to live with it. And that sets you apart from other people."[33]

These narratives are fragmented by the lack of an adequate tongue, by the effort of wresting the words out of silence, by the failure of others to listen and understand. Most survivors never had an open narrative space in which to unfold their tale: often, the stories were told in anecdotal form, in sudden surges of memory, in digressive family conversations, to listeners who didn't always listen or believe. Nella Baroncini, a political prisoner in Ravensbrück, explained:

> When I get started, I speak hurriedly, I can't stop, and while I speak I have visions, all that I'm speaking of is in front of my eyes; and at the end, I realize that what I was able to communicate is but little. So I try to speak as rarely as possible, I only speak when I'm asked, when I'm dragged into it.[34]

The dissonance between the past apocalypse and "normal" present makes any adequate representation impossible. The most unbridgeable gap is inside the narrators themselves, between the witness's "I was there, I saw it" and the narrator's "I am here, I can't believe what I saw": "I was fourteen and what I went through is coming back to my mind and I can't believe it myself" (Enzo Camerino); "I'm telling you a story, as if it had happened to someone else, not to me" (Shlomo Venezia); "Sometimes, when I happen to be speaking about it, suddenly I wonder: 'Am I really talking about myself?' The words sound false and I am moved to stop" (Nella Baroncini).[35]

Narratives are often fragmented because they are about experiences in which the narrator was radically void of agency: "you're not going to 'nowhere'. . . they're *taking you* to 'nowhere'" (Zoltan G.); "it seems to me that my life was always decided by other people, while I was in railroad cars" (Peter C.). People who were treated as pieces to be transported can hardly produce tales according to the Western narrative tradition based on the individuals' mastery of their fate: "My fate push me, you know, I not help myself" [sic] (Eva K.).[36]

The name is the symbol of this loss of agency. Many linger on the trauma of having their name replaced by a number in a foreign tongue that could be formulated in so many hard-to-remember ways: "I wasn't me anymore; I was fifty-eight thousand and . . . six hundred eighty-one, and my cousin was eighty-two" (Paolo Baima).[37] Andra and Tatiana Bucci recall that their mother "would tell us, wisely, to remember our names. She kept saying: your name is Andra and your name is Tatiana Bucci."

Yet, many survivor stories are about taking another name: "Your name is now Gabriel Blomberg. No longer Gunther Ritter, but Gabriel Blomberg."[38] In hiding, Jewish-sounding names are dangerous markers of identity: Ester must remember that her name is Giovanna, Giulia Spizzichino learns that her new name is Urbani. In hiding, the subject is fragmented between her visible and invisible parts, as in a play of masks. Ester Fano, a child refugee in a Catholic convent under a false name, recalls that *playing* at theater "was a metaphoric liberation from the reality we were living: you could have a situation in which fiction was fiction, play was play, and it made you feel better."[39] After liberation, Gunther Ritter/Gabriel Blomberg became an actor.

Thus, narratives oscillate between loss and reassertion of identity, between moments in which the narrator disappears in the crowd of the deported, and the point at which the first person reemerges. Iterative passages and impersonal or plural pronouns are interrupted by eruptions into the first person. Giuseppe Di Porto shifts from the iterative to the singular, from the impersonal "one" to the personal "I," from repetitive "those days" to "one Sunday": "*One would* steal, because of hunger, *one would do* anything, out of hunger. In *those days* one ration of bread meant life. And *one Sunday* when there was no work, as *I* was walking out on my own, I *run* into this guy." There follows a long story in which Di Porto promises "the guy" to get him a spoon in exchange for a ration of bread. He finds a spoon without having to pay for it and gives it to him, but in the end doesn't have the heart to ask for the bread. The first-person singular outlines a small story of resistance to dehumanization, whereas the iterative impersonal third person distances the narrator from behavior in which he was no longer "himself."

Next to the room where I interviewed Giuseppe Di Porto sat his wife, also a survivor, who had always refused to speak.

GIUSEPPE DI PORTO My wife's story ... I suffered much, all deportees suffered ... but I think my wife's suffering was exceptional. In those days my wife was a child, she was fifteen, fourteen and a half, and only God knows how she survived ... only God knows, because ... we have never yet discussed her deportation.

PORTELLI You don't talk about it even between you two?

DI PORTO No, no, no ... I only have some vague information that she had to let me have in order to get her papers, but I only learned about my wife indirectly, from two other women survivors. I never asked her for more information, because I felt like I was violating ... my wife's privacy. I never asked, I never wanted to know.

Stories

The contrast between the willingness to speak and the defense of silence, even by a husband and wife, evokes the ultimate quality of oral sources: they are all different from one another, deeply personal, impossible to gather under a unifying interpretive framework. This may help explain why, in the literature on the *Shoah*, we find a wealth of testimony and narratives, but no real *oral history* – that is, almost no attempt to create out of the multitude of stories a comprehensive picture, a mosaic, a design beyond mere montage of quotes.[40] Not only were the experiences different, but so were the survivors' later life trajectories. Oral sources are *about* the past but *of* the present; we are inevitably faced with a mutable range of possible relationships between the narrated and the narrating self. Much of the power of Lanzmann's *Shoah* lies in the character of narrative time: events are chronological, but memory is simultaneous, containing all the remembered events in the time of remembering. Hence, Lanzmann tells the story in the "present tense": in

Treblinka and Chelmno, the gap between the obliterated traces of what was done there versus the vivid traces in survivors' memories, is a metaphor for the distance between memory and event, for the presence of memory in our own time, and for the need for imagination as we attempt, and fail, to bridge the gap.

Rather than a unified collective memory, oral memoir outlines a horizon of possibilities, manifold accounts of the multivariate things possible in the past that can be remembered and told in the present. An oral history of the *Shoah* would have to be a history of how survivors have remembered it over the years, of how memories became different as they were created and re-created. It would be a huge task, if nothing else because of the abundance of sources. But it would help us think of the *Shoah* both as *one* tragedy and as *millions* of crimes committed against whole peoples and against single individuals who today, by remembering and telling – as they did then by surviving – defend, reaffirm, and explore their fragile identities.

Notes

1. Henry Greenspan, "Survivors' Accounts," in Peter Hayes and John K. Roth (eds.), *The Oxford Handbook of Holocaust Studies* (New York: Oxford University Press, 2011), p. 414.
2. Claude Lanzmann, *Shoah* (New York: Da Capo Press, 1995), p. 165.
3. Shlomo Venezia, to students at Birkenau, 10.20.2004; Settimia Spizzichino, Rome, 11.22.1997.
4. Primo Levi, Introduction to Anna Bravo and Daniele Jallà (eds.), *La vita offesa: Storia e memoria dei lager nazisti nei racconti di duecento sopravvissuti* (Milan: Angeli, 1986), pp. 8–9.
5. www.businesswire.com/news/home/20110308006631/en/Steven-Spielberg-USC-Shoah-Foundation-Institute-Honor; www.usc.edu/schools/college/vhi/.
6. *Voci della Shoah: Testimonianze per non dimenticare* (Firenze: La Nuova Italia, 1995).
7. Christopher Browning, *Remembering Survival: Inside a Nazi Slave Labor Camp* (New York: Norton, 2010), p. 2.
8. Alan Rosen, *The Wonder of Their Voices: The 1946 Holocaust Interviews of David Boder* (New York: Oxford University Press, 2010), pp. 16–20.
9. Alberto Sed, interviewed by Grazia di Veroli, Rome, 6.26.2001.
10. Sami Modiano, b. 1930, Birkenau, 10.9.2005.
11. Bravo and Jallà (eds.), *La vita offesa*, p. 27.
12. Amos Luzzatto, Afterword to Annette Wieviorka, *Auschwitz spiegato a mia figlia* (Torino: Einaudi 1999), p. 74.
13. Rosen, *The Wonder of Their Voices*, pp. 149, 151.
14. Browning, *Remembering Survival*, p. 7.
15. Luzzatto, Afterword, p. 74.

16. Alberto Sed, b. 1928, deported from Rome on 3.21.1944; interviewed by Grazia Di Veroli, 6.26.2001.

17. Cesare De Simone, *Roma città prigioniera* (Milano: Mursia, 1994), p. 34; interview with Settimia Spizzichino, 11.22.1997. Renzo De Felice's standard *Storia degli ebrei italiani sotto il fascismo* (Turin: Einaudi, 1961), pp. 469–70, also ignores the episode. An informal survey carried out in 1999–2000 confirmed that most people believe that the Jews were taken directly from the ghetto to the trains.

18. Settimia Spizzichino mentions the Army College in her memoir, *Gli anni rubati: Le memorie di Settimia Spizzichino, reduce dai Lager di Auschwitz e Bergen-Belsen*, written with Ida Di Nepi Olper (Comune di Cava de Tirreni, 1996), pp. 22–24.

19. Lello Di Segni, b. 1926, Rome, 12.30.1999; Enzo Camerino, b. 1928, Birkenau, 10.11.2005.

20. Claudio Fano, b. 1935, Rome, 12.16.1997. See my "Non s'è presentato nessuno: i due giorni dei deportati ebrei romani al Collegio Militare di piazza Della Rovere," in Luigi Fiorani and Adriano Prosperi (eds.), *Roma, Città del Papa – Storia d'Italia Annali 16* (Torino: Einaudi, 2000), pp. 583–603; Arminio Wachsberger, *L'interprete*, ed. Chiara Wachsberger and Silia Wachsberger (Milan: Proedi, 2010).

21. Marc Bloch, *La guerra e le false notizie* (Roma: Donzelli 1994), p. 80.

22. Alberto Maruffi, in Bravo and Jallà (eds.), *La vita offesa*, p. 171. The book to which he refers is André Lacaze's *Il tunnel* (Milano: Rizzoli, 1980).

23. Saul Friedlander, *Memory, History and the Extermination of the Jews of Europe* (Bloomington: Indiana University Press, 1993), p. viii.

24. Lawrence Langer, Foreword to Joshua M. Greene and Shiva Kumar (eds.), *Witness: Voices from the Holocaust* (New York: Free Press, 2000), p. xvii.

25. Often, not always: Settimia Spizzichino was actually subjected to Dr. Mengele's experiments.

26. Piero Terracina, b. 1928, deported from Rome to Auschwitz on 4.7.1944; interviewed 2.8.1998.

27. Andra and Tatiana Bucci, b. 1939 and 1937, deported from Fiume on 3.28.1944; interviewed 12.12.2004

28. Bravo and Jallà (eds.), *La vita offesa*, p. 46.

29. Ibid., p. 155.

30. Lanzmann, *Shoah*, p. 9.

31. Bravo and Jallà (eds.), *La vita offesa*, p. 186.

32. Ibid., pp. 59, 185; Terracina, testimony at Auschwitz, 10.20.2004.

33. Hedda K., in Lawrence L. Langer, *Holocaust Testimonies: The Ruins of Memory* (New Haven, CT: Yale University Press, 2001), p. 35.

34. Nella Baroncini, b. 1925, in Lidia Beccaria Rolfi and Anna Maria Bruzzone, *Le donne di Ravensbrück: Testimonianze di deportate politiche italiane* (Torino: Einaudi, 2003), p. 279.

35. Ibid., p. 280.

36. Zoltan G., Peter C., Eva K., in Langer, *Holocaust Testimonies*, pp. 47, 173, 158.

37. Bravo and Jallà (eds.), *La vita offesa*, p. 147.
38. Kenneth Jacobson, *Embattled Selves: An Investigation into the Nature of Identity Through Oral Histories of Holocaust Survivors* (New York: The Atlantic Monthly Press, 1994), p. 73.
39. Alessandro Portelli, *The Order Has Been Carried Out: History, Memory, and Meaning of a Nazi Massacre in Rome* (New York: Palgrave, 2003), p. 87.
40. Marcello Pezzetti, *Il libro della Shoah italiana* (Turin: Einaudi, 2009).

CHAPTER 13

Songs of the Holocaust

Shirli Gilbert

The songs that were created by Nazism's victims are some of the most valuable contemporary oral and written texts to have been produced during the Holocaust. Numbering in the thousands, they chronicle the experiences and responses of diverse individuals and groups across the European continent. Jews, political prisoners, Roma and Sinti, Soviet prisoners of war, Jehovah's Witnesses, and countless others used song as a means through which to document, interpret, and respond to what was happening to them, from the earliest concentration camps established in 1933 through to the liberation in 1945 and beyond.

As a major body of texts originating from the time, songs stand alongside the diaries, ghetto chronicles, poems, and other literary creations that were preserved. In this sense, they belong firmly within the canon of Holocaust literature, although their close relationship with non-musical texts is often overlooked. The reason for this is probably that songs, unlike other literary forms, were seldom published or even written down at the time. For the most part, they were preserved as oral texts, not only by their creators but more frequently by others who heard and remembered them; indeed, in many cases we do not know who originally wrote them. Rather than being buried in the ground or safely hidden away, they were preserved precisely because they were sung: in other words, their survival depended on active oral transmission among individuals and groups. This fact in turn allows us cautiously to infer that the songs that survived did so because they resonated in some way with those who sang them. In a world where newspapers, radios, and other forms of communication had almost or entirely ceased functioning, songs became an informal space where information and experiences could be shared. They acknowledged wishes, fears, and uncertainties in the public realm; as they circulated, people identified with them, modified them, rejected them, or perhaps did not engage with them at all. The access they offer is of course not direct or uncomplicated: the process through which songs were created and circulated was informal and unregulated, and it would be impossible to extract from them a representative collective narrative. Nonetheless, they offer significant insight into the ideas and perspectives with which victims identified, and the concerns that preoccupied them.

This chapter offers an overview of this rich body of compositions, identifying some of the songs' key functions and themes. Given the sheer number of camps and ghettos that existed across occupied Europe over a twelve-year period, it would be impossible to provide a comprehensive account. Instead, the chapter presents a few detailed examples from some of the better-known ghettos and camps, focusing primarily on Jewish victims in keeping with the volume as a whole. Its emphasis is on the music created and performed on an informal basis among the mass of "ordinary" prisoners rather than on formal or professional music-making. There is also a brief discussion of songs that circulated among other victim groups in the camps. For those interested in pursuing the subject further, details of additional sources are provided in the Guide to further reading.

Of the many musical activities that took place under Nazi internment, the most popular and widespread was singing. This is unsurprising, since singing was accessible to everyone (including those with no musical training), did not require special preparation or instruments, and could take place practically anywhere. It was also an easy medium for connecting with past traditions, experiences, and communities, and it was by and large practiced as a communal rather than an individual activity. Nazism's victims sang in many different contexts and for many different reasons: to chronicle what they were witnessing, to find comfort, to raise morale, to oppose the regime, or simply to find temporary distraction and entertainment.

In the Eastern European ghettos, Jewish communities organized a wide array of musical activities, including choirs, orchestras, music schools, and theaters, many of which built on the vibrant cultural life of the interwar years. Inmates also developed a rich culture of informal music-making, particularly singing, in youth clubs, private homes, workplaces, and on the streets. To a large extent they drew on familiar songs from the prewar period, but many new songs were also written reflecting on contemporary events. Often these consisted simply of new lyrics set to existing melodies, a longstanding tradition in Yiddish song and a widespread practice under Nazi internment. Songs of hunger and oppression (an integral part of the Jewish experience prior to World War II) were particularly adaptable, but even songs from "normal" life – lullabies, love songs, and songs about children – acquired radically new associations and provided revealing commentary about the new reality.

The song "Papirosn" (Cigarettes) was written by Herman Yablokoff in the 1920s, and quickly established itself as one of the most popular Yiddish theater songs. It described the misery of an orphan peddling his wares on the streets, struggling to sustain himself alone at a time of enormous deprivation; the context was probably the period around World War I. The song retained its popularity among ghetto Jews, and was used as the basis for several new songs, including one about a starving orphan from the Warsaw ghetto titled "Di broyt farkoyferin" (The bread seller); another from Lodz titled "Nishtu kayn przydziel" (There are no more coupons), which lamented the lack of food in the ghetto; and one from Vilna titled "S'iz geven a zumertog" (It was a summer's day).

The latter was written by eighteen-year-old Rikle Glezer in the summer of 1941, shortly after the Nazi invasion of the Soviet Union. The advancing forces wasted no time in implementing the mass slaughter of Vilna Jewry: on July 4, barely two weeks after the invasion, mobile killing units began rounding up Jews and shooting them into mass graves at Ponar, a forest and popular recreation area just south of the city. By the time the Vilna ghetto was set up in September 1941, approximately twenty thousand Jews had already been killed; thousands more were shot in subsequent months. By the end of December 1941, the Vilna Jewish community had been reduced to a third of its original size.

Left reeling from the carnage it had witnessed, the traumatized community turned to one of its richest and most trusted resources as a way both of counteracting shock and of reestablishing the footholds of its existence. With astonishing rapidity, the ghetto was able to revive some of its most cherished cultural institutions, and within a few weeks had already launched several new ones. Glezer's song is a vivid illustration of how ghetto inmates sought to draw on familiar cultural frameworks to make the new reality more assimilable. Using the popular melody of "Papirosn," the song painfully chronicled the events that the community had witnessed:

> It was a summer's day,
> Sunny and lovely as always,
> And nature then
> Had so much charm,
> Birds sang,
> Hopped around cheerfully,
> We were ordered to go into the ghetto.
>
> Oh, just imagine what happened to us!
> We understood: everything was lost.
> Of no use were our pleas

That someone should save us –
We still left our home.

The road stretched far.
It was difficult to walk.
I think that, looking at us,
A stone would have wept.
Old people and children went
Like cattle to be sacrificed,
Human blood flowed in the street.

Now we are all caged in,
Tortured, deceived by life.
Some without fathers, without mothers,
Seldom are they together.
The enemy has achieved his great goal.

There were too many of us –
The master ordered
That Jews from the area be brought
And shot at Ponar.
Houses became empty,
But graves therefore filled up.
The enemy has achieved his great goal.

At Ponar one can now see on the roads
Things, rain-soaked hats,
These things belonged to the victims,
To the holy souls,
The earth has covered them forever.

And now it's sunny and lovely once again,
Everything around smells wonderful,
And we are tortured
And all suffer silently.
Cut off from the world,
Blocked by high walls,
A ray of hope barely awakens.[1]

Glezer's descriptions were explicit: Jews being herded into the ghetto, their futile pleas for help, mass murder at Ponar. She also left no doubt as to the emotional state in which this had left the Vilna Jews. Helpless and alone, severed from their homes and families, they could not even protect the most vulnerable among them from being sacrificed on the streets "like cattle." But in bearing witness to the devastation of her community, Glezer also drew on familiar and comforting language and imagery. First, she constructed her song as the lament not of an individual but of a community.

With Hebrew-derived words such as "akeyde" and "korbones" – both meaning "sacrifice(s)" and bearing distinctly biblical associations – she also brought the narrative of suffering into an explicitly Jewish context. Writers during this period frequently turned to earlier episodes in the long history of Jewish suffering, from the Bible to the tsarist pogroms, in order to provide a common framework within which people could try to absorb what was happening. This kind of language provided consolation not only because it gave some meaning to the events within the context of Jewish history, but also because it brought with it an affirmation, however faint, that despite its tragic history the Jewish nation had always managed to sustain its existence. "S'iz geven a zumertog" was very popular in the ghetto, a fact that becomes clear from its frequent mention in postwar testimonies. Using a familiar melody, Glezer was able to set in stark relief "what happened to us" while also reaffirming a sense of communal identity, placing the understanding of these new events within the context of what had come before. Many ghetto songs assumed a similar documentary function, echoing myriad other efforts taking place at the time to chronicle what was happening. Melodies functioned as a particularly useful mnemonic device for recording information that could not be written down.

Not all ghetto songs were as bleak as "S'iz geven a zumertog," nor were they always focused on documenting the grim reality that was unfolding. In ghetto theaters, musical variety shows were staged, showcasing talented young performers and presenting inmates with encouraging and uplifting songs. In some ghettos, theaters met with concerted opposition: in Vilna, most famously, members of the socialist *Bund* charged that "One does not stage theater in a cemetery" (Oyf a besalmen makht men nisht teater). By and large, however, audiences welcomed these performances as an opportunity to go out, find comfort in the company of friends, and forget temporarily the reality that surrounded them. Songs such as "Mir shpannen tsum bessern morgn" (We are striding toward a better tomorrow) and "Mir lebn eybik" (We live forever), written for a 1943 Vilna theater revue, expressed hope for a better future and asserted the tenacity and strength of the Jewish people. A similarly confident and forward-looking view was offered in the song "Es shlogt di sho" (The hour strikes):

> The hour strikes,
> We are here,
> We look into the distance.
> The sky becomes blue again,
> New times are coming.
> And though it is pitch dark now,

> We wait patiently,
> The day will come, the hour strikes –
> Then he who is guilty will fall.[2]

The song's lyricist, Kasriel Broydo, was one of the most important writers producing revues in the Vilna ghetto, and many of his texts similarly encouraged ghetto inmates to adopt an attitude of confidence and strength in the face of adversity. To be sure, ghetto songs also confronted the fears and difficulties of daily life, and many were intended simply as distracting entertainment. It is interesting to note, however, that as life in the ghetto grew increasingly fraught, the revues often became more encouraging and optimistic: as conditions worsened, the need for hope and solace unsurprisingly grew stronger.

While some ghetto songs, like "Es shlogt di sho" and "S'iz geven a zumertog," openly or obliquely mentioned the Nazi enemy, many were also focused on internal Jewish community concerns. In Lodz, the popular street troubadour Yankele Herszkowicz earned a living for several months performing his hit song "Rumkowski Chaim," a sarcastic praise song for the head of the ghetto's Jewish Council of Elders which mocked Rumkowski's heartless attitude toward his fellow ghetto inmates. In Warsaw, a popular song titled "Moes, moes" (Money, money) similarly criticized abuse of power by ghetto leaders and parodied the enormous social inequalities that were felt in the ghetto:

> Money, money, money is the first thing.
> If you have no money, woe to you,
> Give away your ration-card and say good day.
> Money, money, money is the best thing.
>
> Money, money, money is the best thing,
> The Jewish Council takes taxes from us
> Yet it feeds us bread with saccharin. –
> Money, money, money is the best thing.
>
> Money, money, money is the best thing,
> All trades have had it these days,
> Only bakers ride on horses. –
> Money, money, money is the best thing.
>
> Money, money, money is the best thing,
> At home I ate oranges,
> Today I am eaten by lice and bed bugs.
> Money, money, money is the best thing.
>
> Money, money, money is the best thing,
> The Jewish policeman is just a scoundrel,
> Puts you on the train and sends you away to a camp.
> Money, money, money is the best thing.

Money, money
Money is a good thing.
If you have no money,
I have a plan for you:
Give away your ration-card
And crawl into Pinkert's little box . . .
Money, money
Money is a fine thing.[3]

Several variants of "Moes, moes" were collected after the war, suggesting that it circulated widely. Set to a prewar American jazz hit, the song was a biting satire of corruption and moral decline, focusing its criticism on the ill-treatment of the ghetto masses at the hands of the powerful and wealthy elite. The Jewish Council could impose taxes and provide nothing in return; the Jewish police protected their positions by deporting members of their own community to the camps. Those who were left could hope for little more than to "crawl into Pinkert's little box," Pinkert being the head of the ghetto's burial society. Songs such as this offer a glimpse into the complicated social landscape of the Eastern European ghettos, which housed hundreds of thousands of individuals with diverse religious, political, and class identities. The disparities that characterized Warsaw ghetto society, as reflected in "Moes, moes," were a source of anger and despair for many, and similar sentiments were voiced in other ghettos as well. In addition to these songs' function as a form of entertainment at the time, they are thus also a valuable source for historians seeking to understand the internal world of inmate communities and their multifaceted responses to the Nazi onslaught.

Most of the songs we have encountered thus far remain largely unfamiliar to contemporary audiences. By contrast, there is a small subset of Holocaust songs that still appear regularly in the public realm, particularly at commemoration ceremonies. Some of the most prominent among these are the songs that were produced by resistance groups.

The Vilna ghetto offers an especially rich case study for understanding the relationship between music and resistance among Jewish victims. One of the most significant forces in the ghetto was the United Partisans' Organization (Fareynigte partizaner organizatsye, FPO), an underground group active in armed resistance primarily in the forests surrounding Vilna in cooperation with the Soviet partisan movement. Made up of young men and women mostly in their twenties, the FPO was also a significant source of cultural activity; its members included prominent writers like Abraham Sutzkever, Shmerke Katsherginski, Abba Kovner, and Hirsh Glik. Songs were seen as an effective way of promoting the partisans' cause, encouraging active resistance, and rousing a spirit of defiance and communal strength. Many of the songs that became associated with the movement engaged with a common set of themes: the bravery of the partisans, the strength and endurance of the Jewish nation, and the desire for revenge.

Probably the best known of the ghetto songs is Hirsh Glik's "Zog nit keynmol az du geyst dem letstn veg" (Never say that you are walking the final road). Based on a stirring Soviet march melody, the song expressed a rebellious and optimistic sentiment:

> Never say that you are walking the final road,
> Though leaden skies obscure blue days;
> The hour we have been longing for will still come,
> Our steps will drum – we are here!
>
> From green palm-land to distant land of snow,
> We arrive with our pain, with our sorrow,
> And where a spurt of our blood has fallen,
> There will sprout our strength, our courage.
>
> The morning sun will tinge our today with gold,
> And yesterday will vanish with the enemy,
> But if the sun and the dawn are delayed –
> Like a watchword this song will go from generation to generation.
>
> This song is written with blood and not with lead,
> It's not a song about a bird that is free
> A people, between falling walls,
> Sang this song with pistols in their hands.
>
> So never say that you are walking the final road
> Though leaden skies obscure blue days.
> The hour we have been longing for will still come –
> Our steps will drum – we are here![4]

"Zog nit keynmol" was created shortly after news of the Warsaw Ghetto Uprising was received in Vilna in the spring of 1943. The image of Jewish fighters boldly attacking the enemy greatly encouraged the partisans, and Glik, who was barely in his twenties at the time, infused his text with an inspiring and defiant spirit. It is no coincidence that he drew on a Soviet melody for his base: many of the partisan-writers were drawn more to the martial rhythms and heroic character of popular Soviet songs than they were to those of the Yiddish folksong and theater tradition. Glik's song was quickly adopted as the official hymn of the FPO, and its immense and enduring popularity is clear from the fact that by the war's end it had spread to hundreds of ghettos, camps, and resistance groups across occupied Europe. Today, it still features prominently in Holocaust commemoration ceremonies across the world.

Interestingly, Glik's song was not so much a battle cry as a powerful affirmation of Jewish endurance. In asserting resolutely that "we are here" – a pervasive phrase in the literature of that period – Glik was referring not only to the partisans but also to the collective Jewish people, who had wandered "from green palm-land to distant land of snow," arriving each time only with "pain" and "sorrow" to shed their blood once again. As we have seen, invoking the long history of Jewish suffering was common to many other contemporary texts, and was a way of situating the present struggle in the context of a long and proud history. It was also a powerful means of creating unity and a feeling of collective strength in the fight against Nazism.

Other partisan songs similarly stressed the idea of Jewish endurance, repeating the affirmation "we are here" to emphasize that Jews refused to submit anonymously to their fates. Shmerke Katsherginski, a renowned Vilna poet and partisan, wrote "Partizaner marsh" (Partisan march) when large numbers of fighters were departing to the forests in August 1943:

> – Hey F. P. O!
> – We are here!
> Boldly and with courage into battle.
> Today partisans
> are going to beat the enemy,
> In the struggle for workers' power.[5]

The spirit of the partisans was also evident in the activities of the Vilna youth club, a vibrant social and educational center for teenagers in the ghetto. On December 11, 1942, the fifteen-year-old inmate Yitskhok Rudashevski wrote in his diary:

> Until late into the night we sang with the adults songs which tell about youthfulness and hope . . . Today we have demonstrated that even within the three small streets we can maintain our youthful zeal. We have proved that from the ghetto there will not emerge a youth broken in spirit; from the ghetto there will emerge a strong youth which is hardy and cheerful.[6]

Members of the partisans were actively involved with the youth club, providing support and intellectual guidance, and generally imbuing the children with a mood of hope and encouragement. Katsherginski's song "Yugnt him" (Youth hymn) was dedicated to the club and performed at its

official meetings. Set to an upbeat melody that mirrored the spirit of the
partisan songs, its first verse reads as follows:

> Our song is full of sadness, –
> Bold is our cheerful step,
> Although the enemy stands guard at the gate, –
> Young people storm in song:
>> Young are all, all, all who want to be,
>> Years have no meaning,
>> Old people can, can, can also be children
>> Of a new and free age.[7]

Katsherginski encouraged his young charges to be "bold" and "cheerful,"
and to derive strength from the group; similar words and sentiments
encouraged his fellow fighters. The song also urged young people to take
courage from the fact that anyone who so chose could participate in the
"new and free age." There is no mention of fighting or weapons in the song,
but the youth clubs did in fact become important sites of underground
activity in the latter part of the ghetto's existence.

Thus far we have explored songs created by Jewish victims in the ghettos
and in partisan resistance. The possibilities for musical activity in the camps
were markedly different. In the ghettos, Jews were allowed to manage many
aspects of their daily lives and communal affairs, and although ultimately
they were at the mercy of the Nazi authorities, on the everyday level they
were able to carve out a semblance of autonomy and self-sufficiency. In the
camps, by contrast, Nazi control was pervasive and brutal. Jews fell at the
very bottom of the Nazi racial hierarchy and thus suffered especially harsh
treatment; as a result, unsurprisingly, far fewer songs survive from the camps
to give insight into their experiences.

Among the few Jewish camp songs that were preserved, one of the most
intriguing is the chillingly named "Jüdischer Todessang" (Jewish death
song) created in the Sachsenhausen concentration camp. The writer was a
Polish-born inmate named Rosebery d'Arguto (aka Martin Rosenberg), a
respected musician and political activist who had made a name for himself
conducting workers' choirs in interwar Berlin. D'Arguto was deported to
Sachsenhausen shortly after the outbreak of war in September 1939 and was
imprisoned in the cordoned-off section of the camp known euphemistically
as the *Sonderlager* (special camp), which was reserved for Jews. Here,
inmates were subject to even harsher labor and more brutal punishments
than in the main camp; the opportunities for voluntary activities of any kind
were thus severely limited. Despite the circumstances, d'Arguto had within

a few months of his incarceration established a small choir of between twenty and thirty members. According to witness testimonies, he worked tirelessly with his singers during free time: he was obsessed with his work not only from an artistic point of view, but because he saw the choir as a vehicle for conveying urgent political imperatives and expressing opposition to the regime.

Information about the choir's activities is scant, since most of those who came into contact with it did not survive. Of the handful of songs it sang, perhaps the most important to have been preserved was the "Jüdischer Todessang," which was based on the Yiddish folksong "Tsen brider" (Ten brothers). The original song recounted the fates of ten brothers, traders in cargo and flax, who die one by one until only one is left; in keeping with the tragicomic spirit of Yiddish song, the refrain playfully reads: "Oy, Shmerl with the fiddle, Tevye with the bass, Play a little song for me in the middle of the street!"[8] Quoted here is the song's German camp adaptation:

> We were ten brothers, we traded in wine
> One died – we were left nine.
> Oy-oy! Oy-oy!
> Yidl [little Jew] with the fiddle, Moyshe with the bass,
> Sing a little song for me, we have to go into the gas!
> I am the only brother left; with whom shall I now cry?
> The others have been murdered! Think of all nine!
> Oy-oy! Oy-oy!
> Yidl with the fiddle, Moyshe with the bass,
> Hear my last little song; I also have to go into the gas!
> We were ten brothers
> We never hurt anyone.[9]

According to inmate Aleksander Kulisiewicz, who was a close friend of d'Arguto's in Sachsenhausen and was himself an accomplished musician, the choir found out in late 1942 that a transport would soon be taking Jewish prisoners to Auschwitz-Birkenau or Majdanek. In the three weeks before it was due to depart, d'Arguto wrote the new song, shortening "Tsen Brider" from ten stanzas to two, modifying the words, and translating it into German so that a larger number of prisoners would be able to understand it. This applied not only to German Jews in the *Sonderlager*, but perhaps more importantly to non-Jewish prisoners in the main camp. The German version played sardonically on the word "Gas," which translates in Yiddish not as "gas" but as "street." In the new version, the Jewish minstrels no longer sang for the brothers "in the middle of the street," but because they were now being forced "to go to the gas," a phrase emphasized in the new musical setting.

In basing his new text on a well-known Yiddish folksong, d'Arguto was perpetuating a longstanding tradition, as we have already seen. What is particularly interesting is that the experience of the camp led someone like d'Arguto – a non-practicing Jew who had gone so far as to de-Judaize his name – to write an explicitly Jewish lament. That d'Arguto and his fellow inmates found meaning in singing about the communal Jewish fate suggests that, as in the ghettos, Jews found meaning in forging links with their past, and situating their experiences within a Jewish historical trajectory. This phenomenon is all the more striking here because German Jews, who made up the bulk of Sachsenhausen's Jewish population, were historically more assimilated than their Polish and Lithuanian counterparts in the ghettos.

In addition to Jews, the Nazi camps were home to hundreds of thousands of prisoners of diverse nationalities, religions, and political affiliations. Many songs survive to attest to the experiences of distinct groups including Jehovah's Witnesses, Roma, and Sinti, as well as German, Polish, Soviet, Czech, and countless other inmates. As in the ghettos, one of the most popular activities among camp prisoners was informal singing, usually among small groups of friends or within a barracks. Music was used to strengthen group identity, raise morale, provide comfort, and express opposition to the regime. It also afforded prisoners temporary diversion from camp existence, and helped them to reconnect with their prewar lives and reassert their agency and identity in the face of the camp's dehumanizing onslaught. As Kulisiewicz put it, "In the camps we could not use our fists to express our fury against our oppressors, so we lashed out at them with curses and disdain . . . we took heart from the poetry and song that welled up from the depths of our ever-burning hearts and always-empty stomachs."[10]

One of the earliest and best-known camp songs was the "Moorsoldatenlied" (Moor soldiers' song), composed in Börgermoor in 1933 by Johannes Esser, Wolfgang Langhoff, and Rudi Goguel and subsequently popularized in many other camps. The song "Fest steht" (Stand fast), composed by Erich Frost in 1942, was sung by Jehovah's Witnesses and became one of their most popular hymns after the war. Many camps produced their own "anthems," often on the order of camp authorities or through specially convened competitions, such as the "Buchenwaldlied" (Buchenwald song) created by Fritz Löhner-Beda and Hermann Leopoldi in 1938. Others, like the "Dachaulied" (Dachau song) by Herbert Zipper and Jura Soyfer (1938), were created on the initiative of the prisoners and only later became unofficial anthems. While most songwriters from the camps remain unknown, a few creative individuals stand out for their prolific compositions, among them Ludmila Peškařová in Ravensbrück, Józef Kropiński in Auschwitz and Buchenwald, and Kulisiewicz in Sachsenhausen.

An overview of music during the Holocaust would not be complete without mention of Theresienstadt (Terezín in Czech), a garrison town located outside Prague that became a "model" or "show" camp under the Nazis. Partly in order to serve propagandistic aims, the Nazi authorities tolerated and later encouraged an unparalleled range of musical activities including operas, chamber and orchestral concerts, choirs, cabarets, jazz bands, and solo recitals. Much new music was also composed in Theresienstadt by several serious composers who had already been active in the prewar years. Research and recordings have to a large extent focused on the composers from Theresienstadt and their works, in part because of a bias toward art music; rather less research has been done on popular songs of the kind discussed in this chapter. Despite the prominence of Theresienstadt's cultural life, it should be stressed that it was, like other Nazi ghettos, a place of hunger, disease, and unremitting suffering, and most musicians were not spared the fate of the majority of inmates: deportation to Auschwitz.

Research on the subject of songs during the Holocaust is still developing, and source material is plentiful. A number of important collection projects were carried out in the postwar years, including by the Tsentrale historishe komisye (Central Historical Commission) in Munich, by the psychologist David Boder in Central and Western Europe, by Shmerke Katsherginski largely in Poland, and by the Polish-American immigrant Ben Stonehill in Manhattan. They contain hundreds of Yiddish songs from the Holocaust period, most of which are scarcely known. While documentation initiatives after the war tended to focus on testimonies, many also consistently demonstrated interest in songs, stories, jokes, and other cultural remnants of the communities that had been destroyed; in most cases, including those mentioned above, these sources were conceived as integral to the larger mission of preservation rather than as items of interest on their own terms. Another significant song collection is that of Kulisiewicz, who was interned in Sachsenhausen from 1940 to 1945; in addition to his own compositions, Kulisiewicz collected hundreds of songs, poems, and testimonies from other inmates, primarily Polish, during the 1950s and 1960s. Substantial additional material relating to songs from the ghettos and camps is held at archives in Germany, Poland, Israel, the United States, and elsewhere, much of which remains unexplored. In addition, substantial material has already been published.

Songs from the Nazi ghettos and camps have much to tell us about the diversity of inmates' experiences. While it could not be claimed that they offer an inclusive or representative account, they are nonetheless valuable literary documents from the time that are often missed by scholars focused on written rather than oral artifacts. Although oral transmission results in a text that is perhaps less stable or defined than one that has been written down, the inherently participatory nature of songs means that they are also able to offer significant insight into aspects of life under Nazism that non-musical texts cannot. As a contemporary source, they convey to us not the retrospective understanding of individuals who survived, as do, for instance, postwar testimonies, but the uncertain and constantly shifting perspectives of prisoners facing new daily realities over an extended time period. As a public medium, orally conveyed and preserved, they are a unique legacy of the time, revealing fragments of shared ideas and interpretation from communities that otherwise left few traces.

Notes

1. Shirli Gilbert, *Music in the Holocaust: Confronting Life in the Nazi Ghettos and Camps* (Oxford University Press, 2005), pp. 63–66.
2. Ibid., p. 86.
3. Ibid., pp. 21–22.
4. Ibid., pp. 70–71.
5. Ibid., pp. 73–74.
6. Yitskhok Rudashevski, *The Diary of the Vilna Ghetto, June 1941-April 1943* (Acco, Israel: Ghetto Fighters' House, 1973), pp. 104–105.
7. Gilbert, *Music in the Holocaust*, pp. 77–78.
8. Eleanor Mlotek and Joseph Mlotek, eds., *Pearls of Yiddish Song: Favorite Folk, Art and Theater Songs* (New York: The Education Department of the Workmen's Circle), pp. 121–23.
9. Gilbert, *Music in the Holocaust*, pp. 137–39.
10. Aleksander Kulisiewicz, "Polish Camp Songs, 1939–1945," *Modern Language Studies* 16 (1986): 3–9, here 4.

CHAPTER 14

Sephardic literary responses to the Holocaust

Judith Roumani

Sephardim in the Holocaust

In 1993, Esther Benbassa and Aron Rodrigue observed, "As for the fate of the Sephardim [mostly Balkan and North African Jews of medieval Iberian descent] . . . they remain to this day on the margins of the history of the Holocaust."[1] Holocaust historiography has advanced since then to recognize and commemorate the estimated 160,000 European (Balkan) Sephardic victims of the Nazis. Though this number pales in comparison with the millions of Ashkenazi victims, it is approximately 80 percent of the 200,000 Sephardic Jews residing in Europe in 1933 (these figures do not include Italy, France, and other countries where it was difficult to distinguish between Ashkenazim and Sephardim during this period). For example, 90 percent of the 56,000 Jews in Greece perished, with almost total devastation of the communities in Rhodes, Corfu, Crete, and Salonika. With these losses, Sephardic culture lost its major European centers along with their Judeo-Spanish or Ladino heritage.

In North Africa, Sephardim suffered at the hands of the Italian Fascists (Libya) and French Vichy regimes (Tunisia, Algeria, Morocco). German occupation afflicted Tunisian Jewry by means of internment, forced labor, starvation, and disease; in addition, Jewish slave-laborers were forced to dig trenches for the Germans under Allied bombing. Algeria's anti-Semitic laws depriving Jews of their civil status, livelihood, and assets were even harsher than in Vichy France. In Libya, all foreign Jews were deported and Libyan Jews were interned in concentration camps in the desert, where over five hundred died.

These collective and personal traumas have given rise to a Holocaust literature among Sephardic prose writers and poets whose literary responses addressed intimate tragedies involving their relatives as well as the overwhelming catastrophe of European and North African Jewry.

Sephardic poetry of the Holocaust

Sephardic poetry of the *Shoah* is expressed in at least three languages (French, Judeo-Arabic, and Ladino) and varies greatly in form. It can also be divided between poetry of the North African communities where the Holocaust was experienced in attenuated forms, and poetry from European communities that directly suffered atrocities.

French

Among the North African communities, French had largely taken over as the natural means of expression, due to colonization and the influence of the ubiquitous Alliance Israélite Universelle schools over the previous century. From Isaac Knafo of Morocco and his early satirical *Hitlériques* (1938), to Ryvel of Tunisia and his Baudelairian *Le Nebel du galouth* (1946), to Jacques Taraboulos of Egypt (1949), traditional French poetic forms prevailed in the early years. In Ryvel's thirty-eight-page collection, we see a progression from more elaborate poems with biblical imagery to simpler poems of emotion. For example, "Mères martyres" (Martyr mothers) decries the conversions by priests of Jewish children saved from the Holocaust, whose mothers had thought that sacrificing their own lives would save their children's. Ryvel did not resort to his customary naturalistic melodrama found in his prose, but rather used an almost restrained style:

> Vous êtes, Allemands, musiciens adroits! . . .
> Vous avez fait chanter – vivants claviers – les corps
> Par vous promis a la torture avant la mort.
> (Germans, what deft musicians you are! . . .
> You made the bodies – living keyboards – sing
> Bodies promised to torture before death.)[2]

Images of flowers pervade Ryvel's poems: in Hitler's garden grows an "infernal flower" nourished on human flesh, while elsewhere the beauty of the innocent rose is ignored in a time of mourning. His "Dayenou" (Enough!) reflects a tradition of lament for Jewish suffering, in an ironic reversal of the Passover song celebrating miracles.

Marcel Chalom of Turkey created the free sonnet-like form of "Arbre généalogique" ("Genealogical Tree," 1949). His poem is memorable in its defiant sense of hope among the survivors: "Your mother died in a crematory oven / [. . .] But you, their last bastion, / You are their resurrection."[3]

Judeo-Arabic

A few Tunisian Jews were moved to write *kinot* (lamentations) about the *Shoah*, continuing a tradition of Judeo-Arabic poetry on current events. These poems may also be related to Sephardic Hebrew *kinot* recited on Tisha b'Av, mourning the major catastrophes of Jewish history, such as a *kina* for "Gerush Sefarad," the forced exile from medieval Spain. These Tunisian *kinot* on the *Shoah* were published anonymously in the southern town of Sousse in 1946. Shortly thereafter, events related to independence roiled the communities of North Africa, and Judeo-Arabic largely ceased to be used as a means of publication.

Ladino/Judeo-Spanish

The most moving Sephardic poetry of the Holocaust is in the vernacular language of the Sephardic European communities, Ladino/Judeo-Spanish. Since so many of the Sephardim who spoke the language perished, the language itself became endangered. The voices of the dead echo through this poetry more than almost any other language. A poem in Ladino is thus a double memorial, commemorating both the victims and Judeo-Spanish culture itself. Poetry and song were always crucial elements in Balkan Sephardic culture, and Bouena Sarfatty (a defiant poet-partisan), began composing under the first Nazi blows, even as starvation and confinement in a ghetto prior to deportation afflicted the Salonikan community. Employing the traditional genre of satirical rhyming *komplas* or *koplas* (couplets), she composed a song about Hitler as Pharaoh, and a parody of the biblical Book of Esther, which tells of a holocaust averted. A *kompla* about Passover in the ghetto on the eve of deportation goes: "Elijah began to sing, everyone began to cry; the *kantigas* continued by cursing Hitler . . ."[4] Indeed, she specialized in cataloging curses (collecting some four hundred), invoking humor, and weaving in proverbs. Alone among Sephardic women, she composed a long epic poem of *komplas* describing the destruction of the Jewish community of Salonika. Such compositions are the modern expression of a venerable narrative tradition going back to Iberia.

The Greek Jewish women in Auschwitz continued composing songs (based on folksongs) and formed the Koro Saloniko there. A Ladino-language plaque finally installed at Auschwitz in 2003 was inaugurated at a ceremony including performance of their songs. From Macedonian Greece comes the *Agada de los Partizanes*. This is one of the most important of a genre of *agadot de gera*, satirical, humorous *hagadot* composed from the later nineteenth century, which had already been flourishing during the several Balkan wars of the early twentieth century. This *Agada*, composed in 1944 by Salom Sani Altarac, exists in an audiotape and one manuscript. It details the partisans' wanderings under incredibly harsh conditions from one village to another, always hungry, in winter always cold, their dearest wish being to be rescued by the Allies. "This year here, Next year we'll drink raki," or ". . . Next year we'll be in Sarajevo."[5] These variations on the traditional Passover storytelling rite combine Hebrew, Ladino, and Serbo-Croatian, in an attempt to lighten the partisans' spirits.

Traditional rhyming quatrains are a preferred form for several Ladino-language poets. The *koplas, romances* (ballads) or *endechas* (laments) brought from Iberia provided the form for narrative poetry over four-and-a-half centuries. Thus Yehuda Haim Perahia, writing in hiding between 1941 and 1945, uses traditional verse forms to express his pain as he gradually learns of the fate of those deported in the nineteen transits from Salonika to Auschwitz. His mounting despair is reflected in such titles as "El primer grito en la angustia" (The first cry in anguish, March 17, 1943); "El Segoundo grito en la angustia" (The second cry in anguish, March 30, 1943); and "El terzo grito en la angustia en Salonique" (The third cry in anguish in Salonika, May 16, 1943). The classic rhythms beat out his pain and prayers, which included a questioning of God without losing his faith in Him. Two other fairly early poets are Itzhak Ben-Rubi and Chelomo Reuven, writing in traditional Ladino poetry in 1950s and 1960s Israel, where sometimes their poems were performed on the Ladino radio program. Thus, Sephardic Holocaust poetry maintained its links to Hispanic oral poetry and ballad.

Though greatly reduced in numbers, a new generation of Ladino speakers began a minor renaissance in Ladino poetry of the Holocaust in the late 1970s. Some of these recent poets, David Haim (1981), Avner Peretz (1986), and Moshe Ha-Elion (2000), who write mostly in Israel, and Flory Jagoda, who writes in the United States (*Arvoliko*, 2006), continue to return to the traditional verse forms of Ladino poetry. A few have taken a different direction. Living in France, Clarisse Nicoïdski published her free verse collection, *Lus ojus, las manus, la boca* (*Eyes, Hands, Mouth*) in 1978 in Bosnian Ladino with English translation. This was considered a literary event, both because of her highly creative poems, and because earlier Ladino postwar poets were practically unknown in Europe and English-speaking countries. She was also hailed at the time as the last of the Judeo-Spanish poets, which has turned out not to be the case. If anything, she was an innovator, turning her back on traditional verse forms, setting a trend of experimental poetry, and inspiring others, such as Juan Gelman of Argentina. Nicoïdski's poetry does not refer to the Holocaust explicitly. But as the various parts of her body attempt to speak to each other in the language of the dead, one cannot help but think this is a response to the Holocaust. Nicoïdski as a child spent several years in hiding with her family from the Nazis in Lyon, where she learned the Sephardic language. Though the poems are addressed to her dead mother, there are echoes of what the Lyon experience must have been. Her mouth either spews fire like a scream, or slams shut like a door on a street where blood is being shed, reminding us of Picasso's *Guernica* or the poetry of García Lorca. As devastating as the death of a loved one is the death of a language when the mouth falls silent.

Those who were close to horrors beyond the limit-experience, as Gary Mole has termed it, have gone far in turning extreme grief into poetry or song. Wartime and postwar Sephardic poets have channeled extreme emotions through conventional verse forms in French or Ladino. The rhythms of traditional poetry, like those of *Echa* and *kinot*, are a means for communicating the unsayable which nevertheless had to be said. Just as in mourning we turn to tradition and ritual, Sephardic poetry has generally stayed close to its origins in folksong and in meters that hark back to medieval Spanish narrative epics. Thus, a lack of poetic innovation (except among younger poets such as Clarisse Nicoïdski and Evelyne Kadouche) cannot be counted a negative when the cadences of Ladino, commemorating the Holocaust dead, receive new life in the poetry of Sephardim.

Memoirs, autobiographies, interviews

Sephardic memoirists may or may not be aware of a long prose tradition of Sephardic historiography detailing series of catastrophes: Yosef ha-Kohen (1496–1578), born four years after his parents were expelled from Spain, wrote his *Emeq ha-baka* (Vale of tears) in 1560; it was translated into Ladino and published as *El vaye de los yoros* in Salonika in 1935, just a few short years before the greatest catastrophe was unleashed.

One of the earliest Holocaust memoirs is an account from Nazi-occupied Tunisia by Paul Ghez, *Six mois sous la botte* (Six months under the boot). Written in 1943 and 1944, and published in 1946, the memoir is in the form of a diary of events as they unfolded. Ghez was one of the leaders of the Jewish community who was charged with delivering to the Nazis what they demanded. Though the Nazis did not have the time or resources to begin implementing the Final Solution in Tunisia, and their presence in the country was to counteract the Allied advances from Morocco and Algeria to the west and Libya to the east, they had an immediate need for slave-laborers to dig defensive trenches across Tunisia. Ghez's task was to organize in a few days' time Jewish men aged 18–45 into a labor force of more than a thousand strong, providing them with food, medical care, and transportation to the front, all at the Jewish community's expense.

That he managed to placate the Nazis while conserving Jewish lives was certainly praiseworthy. However, meeting the Nazis' demands obviously set him up for criticism. There was little support for the Jews either from Muslims (with occasional exceptions) or from the Tunisian-based French. Within the Jewish community, there were accusations that sons of the wealthy received medical exemptions from forced labor and were sent home as "sick" or "injured" in inordinate numbers. There were even minor riots outside community offices in Tunis.

Ghez's memoir tells his side of the story. He writes that, after the Nazis had taken a hundred hostages to be killed if the laborers were not provided, "There was no more thinking to be done. We had to get organized, take care of our young people, limit the suffering, and avoid a pogrom. I was involved in a violent battle in which the existence of the Jewish population was at stake."[6] Aided by the fortunate fact that six months later the Nazis were defeated and fled the country, the leaders of the community were successful in this battle.

Matilda Koen Sarano's Ladino *kuentos* straddle an intermediate genre between memoir and storytelling, recounting the period when her family was in hiding in Italy. Some tales are told by her father and some she tells herself about her early childhood. The subject is the family's experience eluding the Nazis, but the form is that of the traditional *kuentos* or *konsejas*, short pithy stories often with a moral, evincing traditional wisdom.

Regarding the Balkans, the Sephardic heartland, where the outcome was infinitely more tragic, there are many published memoirs, and probably many more unpublished ones. They recount the terrible events that befell those Sephardic communities where the Nazis did have time to carry out their evil intention, and reading them dispels any impression that Sephardim were somehow exempt from destruction. Erica Kounio Amariglio's *From Thessaloniki to Auschwitz and Back*, written in Greek in 1945 and published in 2000 in her daughter's translation, begins by narrating an idyllic traditional childhood growing up by the Mediterranean, which stands in utter contrast with what came after. Later, following deportation to and imprisonment in Auschwitz, one is able to sense the continued solidarity of her extended family as cousins endeavor to search out cousins in the morass of the camp and ascertain if they are still alive. Those already in the know simply point to the chimneys and the rising smoke. She describes the job that helped her survive as that of a "book-keeper of death."

Ya'acov Handeli's *A Greek Jew from Salonica Remembers* was originally published in Hebrew under the title *From the White Tower to the Gates of Auschwitz* (1992). Handeli's narrative is preceded by a preface by Elie Wiesel, who says they had undoubtedly met "there" and highlights the other inmates' impressions of the Salonikan Jews: that they were kinder and had more group cohesion than the Ashkenazim. These qualities, it has been argued elsewhere, led to slightly higher survival rates among the Sephardic inmates at Auschwitz. Handeli talks about those heroes who preferred to be shot rather than perform certain tasks. He is matter-of-fact, avoids philosophizing, and only wonders why he, who was no better than the others, survived.

Around the same time Rebecca Camhi Fromer interviewed Daniel Bennahmias for her book of his memoirs, *The Holocaust Odyssey of Daniel Bennahmias, Sonderkommando* (1993). In restrained tones, the memoir chronicles the experiences of cruelty, loss of family, degradation, the ultimate horror of the Sonderkommando's work in the gas chambers and crematoria, the struggle for survival, and the death march. A bitter awakening comes early when Bennahmias explains that he had been brought up in a culture of mutual respect and, still under the illusion that these values would govern any civilized people, approaches a Nazi soldier, china cup in hand, to ask for a drink of water for his mother. Many illusions and inhibitions were shattered during the long boxcar ride to Auschwitz.

Most of these memoirs were originally written in Greek, a few in Ladino, Hebrew, or Italian (some with English translation). The memoirists are more concerned with witnessing to as wide a public as possible (including a non-Jewish public) than in conveying emotion, aestheticizing experience, or safeguarding a cultural patrimony. Unfinished and unpublished memoirs (such as those of Yomtov Yacoel of Salonika, betrayed when in hiding and sent to Auschwitz) can elucidate previously obscure aspects. Of course the question of authorship is a moot point in the interview-based texts: interviewers may subtly edit the text or channel the conversation. Though the memoirs follow a similar shape, dictated by events, only Koen-Sarano deliberately orders her less searing Holocaust memoirs into art.

However, interviewers also play an important role in eliciting previously unknown historical facts. For example, in the Italian concentration camp at Giado (Libya) two thousand Jews were incarcerated, of whom over five hundred died of starvation and typhus. Italian colonial archives suppressed this fact, though interviewers in the 1960s learned it from survivors in Israel, and reports by the liberators were recently published. Though memories may be fading, a few new stories from the camps have likewise emerged recently through sensitive interviewing of previously reluctant survivors.

Fiction

Sephardic novels of the Holocaust belong to various languages and national traditions. The early writers of the 1930s to 1960s began writing on the sharp edge of the Holocaust, had lived through it in one way or another, and combined autobiography with psychological realism. They engaged the Holocaust passionately, vividly, and profoundly. In contrast, the writers after the 1960s were minimally involved in the remnants of Sephardic life and culture. Thus after the first generation, despite the Sephardim having overcome certain hurdles of reticence, the importance of the *Shoah* has diminished, the pain and the passion have receded, and the Holocaust has become less an aspect of identity and more a part of history.

Even before the war, a few Sephardim began to address the plight of Jews in countries terrorized by the Nazis. Albert Cohen, born in 1895 in Greece (Italian-influenced Corfu), moved at a young age to Marseille and produced masterful French novels lovingly satirizing the colorful Sephardic characters of his childhood. His early novels, such as *Solal* (1930), show the tragic effects of anti-Semitism before the Holocaust. Cohen moved to Switzerland and became an official of the United Nations, in 1946 drafting the agreement of the committee on refugees to issue a travel document for stateless persons. He claimed that this was "my best book." His most impressive novel, *Belle du Seigneur*, published only after his retirement from the United Nations in 1968, shows the utter incompatibility of these naïve, gentle, ridiculous characters with the savage world of European sophistication and anti-Semitism on the eve of the Holocaust.

Born in Bulgaria and educated in Austria, Elias Canetti wrote in German. Indeed, he is likely best known for his novel, *Die Blendung* (in English *Auto-da-Fé*), a biting satirical portrait of proto-fascists in Austria actually published in 1935, and then banned in Hitler's Germany. But Canetti's later autobiographical writings deal with his Sephardic childhood in Bulgaria (with some words in Ladino), his subsequent moves to Austria and other countries, and finally his refugee life in London. In the 1950s Canetti wrote a series of plays depicting dystopias where power is wielded by authorities who inflict death for minor infractions. Though his entire oeuvre could be seen as engaged with the Holocaust, he did not actually use the word. His major philosophical essay, *Crowds and Power* (1960), encapsulates the view that in fascist states power is wielded by those who deploy violence.

Veza Canetti, his wife of similar background, also authored a trenchant early response to Nazi terror. Her novel, *The Tortoises* (1939, published 1999, three decades after her death), provides incisive psychological portraits of would-be Holocaust refugees who maintain their optimism even though they are losing their chance to escape. Their own attempts at storytelling, moreover, recounting brushes with ostensibly benign authorities, is pitifully inadequate to help them deal with Nazi reality. Through grammatical inconsistencies, Veza has a way of subtly indicating the lapses of characters' reasoning in desperate circumstances. Like Elias's memoirs, Veza's imaginative fiction stays close to autobiography.

If the Canettis' prewar writing centered on the fate of German Jews, and that of Albert Cohen on the Jews of Corfu, Albert Memmi committed himself soon after the war to portray the specific anguish suffered by North Africa's Jews. Each writer, however, used his or her specific community to exemplify what Memmi called "the Jewish fate." His own semi-autobiographical *La Statue de sel* (*The Pillar of Salt*) (1953) recounts the vicissitudes of a young Tunisian Jew caught in the Nazi occupation. Though he grew up in Tunisia, Memmi moved after independence to France, where his previous experiences with the anti-Semitism of the Nazis and of the Free French army in Algeria (he had tried to enlist but they did not want Jews) intersected with his readings of Jean-Paul Sartre on anti-Semitism and, likely, Albert Cohen's prewar novels. *The Pillar of Salt* strives to be totally honest about Memmi's experiences, torn between the Arab, the Jewish, and the French cultures he experienced in Tunisia. It is a novel of personal anguish, of psychological catharsis, of exorcism; it shocked many by its realism and marked the beginning of modern novel writing in the new nations of North Africa. Known as a theorist of decolonization and an opponent of racism, Memmi has been a strong Zionist, impelled by his experiences of North African and European anti-Semitism.

The Holocaust's pernicious destruction knew few boundaries. As Giorgio Bassani showed, even Italy's wealthy Sephardic aristocracy could not escape unscathed. Bassani also began writing before the Holocaust, his first book being published under a pseudonym in 1940. An Italian novelist whose community of Ferrara was decimated by the Nazis, he also happened to portray the small minority of Sephardim in Ferrara. The Ferraran Jewish community boasts antecedents in the Abravanels of Spain and the Mendes-Nasis from Portugal. Bassani's *The Garden of the Finzi-Continis* chronicles a small Sephardic aristocracy, immured from reality and living behind the walls of their garden. Eventually the whole family is deported, leaving the unnamed first-person narrator with memories of an ambiguous love affair. Bassani is usually thought of as a purely Italian Jewish writer, but the subtle cultural differences of his Sephardim (from Italian Jews, from Ashkenazim, and between themselves) are an essential element in his story. Like the Canettis, Cohen, and Memmi, all grounded in psychological realism, Bassani's fictional Ferrara is strongly autobiographical.

Cultivating a lyrical, oblique approach to the Holocaust, the Egyptian-born Edmond Jabès weaves alienation into the heart of his communicative act. Such an approach came only at a high price. Jabès was pressured to leave his native Egypt by anti-Jewish agitation following the 1956 Suez crisis, when Egyptian Jews were forced out by expropriation of their businesses, freezing of their bank accounts, imprisonment as so-called Zionist spies, and physical threats by the secret police. Most had to leave with nothing. Jabès came to France, whose culture he had always admired. Soon after arriving in Paris, he experienced a sort of revelation: that he was nowhere at home. This sense of alienation coupled with the trauma of exile from Egypt developed into his vocation as a novelist of the Holocaust.

His multi-volume work, *The Book of Questions* (1963–1973), traces the doomed relationship of lovers, Sarah and Yukel, survivors from extermination camps: though they came out alive, she has gone mad and he contemplates suicide. The situation is commented on by a sort of Greek chorus of ancient and modern rabbis and their students. The questions hardly ever have answers, but rather evoke further questions which in themselves do not have answers. The rabbis continue this age-old Jewish conversation in the face of the repeated catastrophes that have befallen Jews over the centuries. With no hope of an earthly residence, the true home of the Jew is in the book, and the Jew's natural mode of being (for Jabès) is alienation and exile. Jabès was a precursor of the second generation of Sephardic writers of the Holocaust, those too young to have experienced it, but old enough to assimilate the trauma.

Lyricism continued to receive expression in the novels of North African Sephardim. A decade after Jabès, Algerian-born Albert Bensoussan's *Frimaldjézar* (1976) gives a lyrical child's-eye view of traditional Jewish life in a quiet coastal town, where during the Vichy period Jews from Europe took refuge. These Jews hid in the small towns and villages, bringing with them from one continent to another rumors of boxcars and crematoria.

For a new generation of Sephardic writers, the Holocaust became mainly a plot element in historical novels. Tunisian/French Nine Moati's *La Passagère sans étoile* (Passenger without a star, 1989) tells of an assimilated Frenchwoman of Livornese/Tunisian origin who escapes from the Nazis via a circuitous route, eventually returning to Paris only to witness her mother's arrest. She then joins the resistance and participates in the rescue of Jewish children. The novel has a cinematic quality, with much action and changes of scene, the heroine through a series of coincidences managing to witness many major events of the war. Moati has her heroine meet (and of course admire) the characters from the film *Casablanca*, while she figures in a novel by a famous English novelist. These fictional ploys undermine the apparent factualness of this historical novel and serve to distance the Holocaust.

In contrast to Moati's heroic and romantic characters, the French writer Patrick Modiano (of Italian-Greek origin on his father's side) has written a historical trilogy of novels (1968, 1969, and 1972) parodying anti-Semitic stereotypes while portraying Jewish collaborators. Modiano is a transitional writer – initially he would not even admit that he was born in 1945 (claiming instead that he was born in 1947), a strategy taken perhaps in order to distance himself from the war and the painful knowledge that his father had been a Jewish collaborator. He has, however, not avoided the issue, having in addition to his novels written the script for the Louis Malle film about a collaborator, *Lacombe Lucien* (1974). He also has a later novel, *Rue des boutiques obscures* (1978) (*Missing Person*, 2004), about a detective who, having lost his memory, discovers he is a Greek Jew from Salonika. This novel, too, shows a kind of distancing from the Holocaust, which has receded into history and thereby become a rich source for new plots in fiction.

Writing in English and using a form of stream of consciousness, Stanley Sultan's 1977 novel, *Rabbi*, portrays a growing awareness of the Holocaust's significance among Sephardim, specifically within the close-knit Syrian community of Brooklyn. Awareness of the Holocaust in the 1950s is part of this community's gradual opening to modernity, a double-edged development which also entails the danger of losing its young people (though even today this is a remarkably cohesive community). The rabbi of the title is the aging, ailing patriarch who must assimilate knowledge of the *Shoah* as another test of his faith. Nevertheless, he is uncompromising in his belief that catastrophes are brought on the Jewish people because God loves them more than others and thus holds them to a higher standard.

Israeli Sephardic novelist A. B. Yehoshua's *Mar Mani* (Mr. Mani) (1990) portrays a Sephardic family with a streak of eccentricity (actually, slight madness) through several generations. However, the encounter with the Mani family is almost always indirect, through the recounting of their exploits by an outsider. One central account is set in wartime Crete under the Nazi occupation. The Jews of Crete have been rounded up and shipped off to Auschwitz (historically, their ship was sunk along the way and there were no survivors). One local Jew, the tour guide Efrayim Mani, had temporarily managed to hide out, and the exchange in this case takes place between a Nazi officer who had conversed with him and the Nazi's grandmother who is briefly visiting Crete. We thus see the Sephardim and the tragedy of Crete through the prism of a completely alien civilization.

A Proustian labyrinth of Egyptian memories, Andre Aciman's *Out of Egypt* (1994), "remembers" a generation before his own birth, imagining how his parents had come together in then-cosmopolitan Alexandria, how his two grandmothers could have met each other, and, more generally, how the relationships unfolded between Ladino-speaking Turkish Jews with a French veneer and the "Arab Jews" who had originated from Syria rather than from Turkey. During the war years, the families lived in growing anxiety over the Axis forces closing in on Egypt. The large extended family clustered together in the grandmother's apartment for weeks, glued to the radio and feeding each other's fears. The one Ashkenazi among them describes them as "pathologically Sephardi."

The danger passed and they returned to their normal lives. But something changed in the atmosphere of Egypt, and only ten years later they suffered treatment almost as bad, losing their jobs, assets, and freedom, until they have to flee. The night before they leave, Aciman (now a teenager) describes a sort of parody of the traditional Passover Seder, where they are grief-stricken at having to leave Egypt, even though they are bound for Italy and France. Thus, for Aciman the war years evoke warm family solidarity rather than danger, and leaving Egypt means that this family cohesion will come to an end for ever, as individuals and couples go their own ways. Aciman is thus another consummate writer of the many exiles of the Sephardim; in this case the Holocaust years are softened by distance and nostalgia for a traditional way of life. Not really grasping the import of what they were going through, fear and fantasy merge with history to produce an oblique backward glimpse of the Holocaust.

Two recent Sephardic writers take steps toward bringing back a more direct approach to the Holocaust. Gini Alhadeff's *The Sun at Midday* (1997), an English-language memoir by an author born in Alexandria in the same year as Aciman, seems to drink from the same Alexandrian Sephardic sources. Yet the content and results are different. Alhadeff's parents had the entire family converted to Catholicism and she did not know she had Jewish roots until the age of twenty. Thereafter she has been assiduously in search of identity: a search that must incorporate the specter of Auschwitz as chronicled in her uncle's newly discovered memoir. The identity she fixes on entails total self-determination – she does not want to identify as Jewish just because Hitler would have considered her so. From a different vantage point, Moris Farhi's tale of growing up in multiethnic 1940s Istanbul also brings the Holocaust into the limelight. *Young Turk* (2005) portrays the arrival of German-Jewish academic refugees who enriched Turkish universities, the onerous head tax placed on the Turkish Jews, and a daring attempt to rescue Salonikan relatives in "Robbie: A Tale of Two Cities," a story reminiscent of boys' adventure fiction gone tragically wrong. Though the Holocaust is viewed as one historical tragedy among several, Farhi shows how multiethnic Turks remain inconsolable after the Holocaust death of a Jewish boy who was part of the fabric and the future of Turkey. For Alhadeff and Farhi, then, the Holocaust becomes almost central, with the pain of the survivor newly reinvoked, undiminished.

Notes

1. Esther Benbassa and Aron Rodrigue, *The Jews of the Balkans* (Oxford: Blackwell, 1995), p. 196.
2. "Symphonie allemande," in Ryvel (Raphaël Lévy), *Le Nebel du galouth* (The Lyre of the Galut) (Tunis: La Cité des Livres, 1946), p. 19; trans. Gary Mole in "The Representation of the Holocaust in French-Language Jewish Poetry," *Covenant* 2/1 (May 2008/Nissan 5768): http://covenant.idc.ac.il/en/vol2/issue2/the-representation-of-the-holocaust.html.
3. Isaac Jack Lévy, ed. and trans., *And the World Stood Silent: Sephardic Poetry of the Holocaust* (Urbana: University. of Illinois Press, 1989), pp. 74–75.
4. Judith Cohen, "Selanikli Humour in Montreal: The Repertoire of Bouena Sarfatty Garfinkle," in Rena Molho, H. Pomeroy, and E. Romero (eds.), *Judeo-Espaniol: Satirical Texts in Judeo-Spanish by and about the Jews in Thessaloniki* (Salonika: Ets Ahaim Foundation, 2011), p. 224.
5. Eliezer Papo, "Tzhok karnevali ke-derech hitmodedut im traumot ve-ke emtzai le-havnayat ha-zikaron ha-kvutzati" (Parody as a way of managing trauma and as a means for handling collective memory), in David Bunis (ed.), *Languages and Literatures of Sephardic and Oriental Jews* (Jerusalem: Misgav Yerushalayim, 2009), p. 201.
6. Paul Ghez, *Six mois sous la botte* (Paris: Manuscrit, 2009), p. 65. My translation.

CHAPTER 15

Anthologizing the Holocaust

Alan Rosen

Holocaust anthologies, notes one editor, are something of a contradiction in terms. Since the root meaning of anthology "is a collection of flowers, a thing of joy and beauty," such a collection could only be titled "flowers of evil" – with a nod toward Baudelaire's very different collection of poems by this name.[1]

Most editors have not explicitly pointed to the etymological tension. But the problem of classifying what a Holocaust anthology is, or should be, may find expression in the practical exigencies of the library catalog. The United States Library of Congress, for example, doesn't use the heading "literary anthologies" at all, preferring "literary collections." The Yad Vashem library, which relies on a different cataloging system, forgoes "literary collections," grouping all collections, literary and otherwise, simply under "anthologies." These rubrics are harbingers of blurred lines and hybrid assortments: Holocaust literature anthologies vary considerably, most often also contain non-literary writings, and resist uniform classification – which can make locating them a challenge.

Indeed, from the word go such anthologies have not been purely belletristic, but rather have included a range of responses and materials. To be sure, they have dutifully drawn from poems and stories, excerpted novels and dramas, and featured autobiographical memoirs, letters, and diaries. But they have also enfolded court testimony and depositions, historical essays, reportage, and even perpetrator decrees and commands. This interweaving of historical record with literary views derives not from a postmodern reflex that wishes to show their similarly constructed status. It rather points to the heavy burden of history that informs anything to do with the Holocaust. Holocaust-related anthologies are of course not the only ones to include "documents" of this kind. But in order to tether the license of literature to the sobriety of history, it happens in this case more often than most.

Interweaving the two domains has gone the other way as well. While literature anthologies have mostly not been pure, general anthologies have imported literature, sometimes explicitly under that rubric, other times under a different (less objectionable?) one, such as "chronicles," or "witness," or "experience."

As with victim responses in general, anthologies of Holocaust literature came on the scene early rather than, as has often been presumed, only belatedly. Anthologies of primary sources of Holocaust literature – or at least primary sources of literature for those compelled to endure the Holocaust – emerged even as the war continued to rage.

Such anthologies, including a 1940 Warsaw collection entitled, *Suffering and Heroism in the Jewish Past in Light of the Present*, had a clear purpose: to link the fate of wartime Jewry to the fate of persecuted Jews throughout history and to inspire similar resolution. *Z otchłani* (From the abyss), published in Poland in Polish clandestinely in the spring of 1944 and featuring contributions from Jewish and non-Jewish poets, hoped to galvanize resistance. And even in the distant United States, as early as 1941 twelve accounts of flight from Europe were published as *We Escaped*, a volume presumably aiming to cultivate the United States' stubborn sympathy for other imperiled refugees still in search of asylum from Nazi persecution.

Postwar anthologies had a different audience and different purpose. But they often continued to yoke the bitter fate of European Jewry with Jewry at large or to convey, from multiple vantage points, the full extent of what happened and what was lost. These anthologies often bear the stamp of a certain movement or group, who sought to weave a tapestry of writings together (or assemble a bouquet of flowers of evil) in order to establish or enlarge a literary canon of Holocaust writings, frequently with an eye to supporting or countering a particular historical interpretation. The process has moved horizontally as well as vertically. Various countries and languages (as some essays in this volume have noted) have been more or less dedicated to the enterprise of anthologizing Holocaust literature: efforts in Hebrew and Yiddish, for example, have been persistent; in Polish, German, and French seemingly more sporadic; and in Chinese (despite China's growing interest in Jewish history and the Holocaust) still in the formative stage. While this chapter will focus on English-language collections, I will nevertheless attend to the way these anthologies draw on other languages for their translated content as well as how they view the languages of the Holocaust as a subject of contention in its own right.

One of the earliest English-language postwar anthologies, *The Jewish Frontier Anthology* (1945), placed a dozen Holocaust writings under the unsensational heading of "Europe," this section following "Zionism," "America," and "Palestine." It tellingly interspersed accounts of the

Holocaust period, such as "The Flag on the Ghetto Wall," by Marie Syrkin (author of the soon-to-be published *Blessed Is the Match*), with several historically earlier poems of Chaim Bialik, suggesting that each should be seen in the light of the other. Most striking is the manner in which the heading of "Europe" contains (both holds and limits) the Holocaust entries. Europe was the continent that had suffered the onslaught (the North African Jews who perished in wartime persecution would generally not enter the ledger until years later); the other continents were at a remove. Geography was truly destiny.

Embedding Holocaust literature within a broader sweep of Jewish life and culture continued as one anthological option. Indeed, ten years later the *"Jewish Life" Anthology, 1946–1956* took a similar tack. One of four major sections, the nine selections of Holocaust literature goes under the exhorting title: "Never to Forgive, Never to Forget," a phrase said by the anthology's editor to have been the message of the Warsaw ghetto fighters. The focus has become sharper, so that the section contains only writing from or on the Holocaust era. Beginning with Hirsh Glik's wartime Yiddish poem qua song, "Zog Nisht Keynmol" ("Never Say" – also known as the "Partisan's Hymn") the section – true to the hybrid form – mixes poetry, story, diary, and essay, drawing on both wartime and postwar writings. A decade after the end of the war, Holocaust literature thus earned a significant place in the repertoire of the Jewish literary anthology, installing it as a necessary canon of writing for an audience concerned about postwar Jewish life in general.

Yet a different trend in Holocaust literature anthologies emerged parallel to these. Still in the late 1940s appeared an English-language anthology singly devoted to the Holocaust. Leo Schwarz's *The Root and the Bough: The Epic of an Enduring People* (1949) strives to show the "epic," that is, the history-making, character of the events. It does this, nonetheless, through assembling some thirty short contributions, ranging in length from three to thirty pages (the longest being that of Vilna poet and partisan Abraham Sutzkever). The collection is divided into three sections: "The Fire's Center," "Flame of the Spirit," and "The Undying Spark," with the first section subdivided into "The Epic of the Warsaw Ghetto" and "In the White Russian Forests." The "fire" motif linking the sections seems to proceed in reverse order (fire, flame, spark), suggesting through its diminished substance the quenching, but not extinguishing, of "the Enduring People." Though the collection included no other writer of Sutzkever's stature, it gave an early airing to several whose names would become associated with chronicling the Holocaust: Bernard Goldstein, Marek Edelman, Yankel Wiernik, and Leon Weliczker (Wells).

The volume's editor, Leo Schwarz, who helped administer aid to displaced persons in the postwar years, views the purpose of the collection as "plumb[ing] the sources of endurance that seemed to govern the lives of the remarkable survivors of that tornado of wrath."[2] These sources in turn reveal "hidden resources": "the stories of these survivors are a clue to the ultimate hidden resources in humankind" (p. xi). In the final analysis, they – the "still small voices" – offer "not only a condemnation of tyranny but above all constitute a grand testament to human valor and endurance" (p. xv). This is an early statement of a recurring conviction in the anthologies that come after: that despite the grim episodes that necessarily dominate the literature, Holocaust chronicles reveal human strengths that would under normal circumstances have remained untested or unnoticed.

At this early postwar date – 1949 – conceiving such a collection was meant to encourage written recollection, a process similar to other testimonial efforts that have moved victims to render written and oral accounts. Two other assumptions are worth noting. First, though Schwarz acknowledges some wartime writing, he highlights what he believes was the "unprecedented" wartime silence. Indeed, to his mind, this wartime silence contrasts with the postwar vitality of which the anthology itself bears witness. Second, he presents a strikingly broad vision of what constitutes "literature" of the Holocaust, including "a stout prayer book written by hand from memory by a religious soul who believed that his people's destruction was at hand" (p. xiii). In Schwarz's view, tradition continued to assert itself even while confronting the worst – and that that scribe's act of fidelity is also to be considered Holocaust literature.

Polish-Jewish author Adolph Rudnicki's (né Aron Hirszhorn) anthology, *Lest We Forget* (1955), takes a radically different approach. The slim yet searing volume mixes perspective and genre, combining summaries of perpetrator trials with excerpts from victim diaries and memoirs, stories, and poems. Contributions by Poles and Jews alternate throughout the collection, with prescient accommodation made for a single poignant memoir excerpt from a Gypsy, Stefke. The volume opens with a story of arrest, brutal interrogation, and foiled escape. But it moves quickly to accounts of Auschwitz and Treblinka, a different order of terror on Polish soil. And while the chapter's descriptions of the sites of torture and murder are graphic and relentless, the editor intersperses a rhythm of reflection: "The Nazis," writes Julian Pryzbos, in a haunting meditation, "wanted to rob the death of the Jews of even the sense, of even the name of death. When shall we comprehend, when shall we be able to bear that moral horror?"[3]

Lacking a table of contents and forgoing titles for most entries, *Lest We Forget* comes across as a raw collection of assembled documents. But the variety shows a caring literary hand at work, dedicated to an overarching moral goal. "I am deeply convinced," writes Rudnicki in the introduction, of the importance "of reading and popularizing books that reveal the bare truth about death camps, not," he polemically adds, "avoiding these books as some would like to." Most intriguing is his call for a public forum: these books should be "read aloud in the big stadiums of large cities, before big audiences listening in solemn silence." In a closing assessment, he notes that the books (or the entries in the anthology) "that tell of inhuman tortures" are not subject to usual literary standards, but rather are meant "to arouse with compelling force, a hatred for cruelties, for wars, for fascism" (p. 12). The raison d'être of Holocaust writing is pointedly the cultivation of a "hatred" for the crimes it recounts.

Anthologies of the 1960s were shaped by watershed developments in historical writing. Systematic review of German documents had led to a more accurate assessment of how the perpetrators carried out the destruction of most of European Jewry. But this advance also brought with it a distortion of the Jewish response, either minimizing it or accusing the Jews of complicity. In the polemic that followed (and, to some degree, continues), anthologies weighed in, attempting to restore a proper sense of proportion. One of these emerged in translation from Israel: *The Massacre of European Jewry: An Anthology* (1963). Organized in three sections, "Background," "Massacre," and "Resistance," this history-based compendium sprinkled excerpts from diaries and memoirs, letters, and poems in order to highlight the victim's response and responsiveness. Certain names had already become de rigueur in the list of contributors: Emanuel Ringelblum, chronicler of the Warsaw ghetto and overseer of the Oyneg Shabes archival project; and, once again, Hirsh Glik, whose "Song of the Jewish Partisans" (presented in English and Hebrew translations as well as the Yiddish original) concludes the volume's chapters. A "short extract" from Yitzhak Katzenelson's "The Song of the Slaughtered Jewish People," a (truly) epic poem written in the wake of the destruction of the Warsaw ghetto by one of its leading wartime bards, holds a central position. So while the anthology's explicit agenda is to rescue Jewish honor through chronicling multiple forms of armed resistance, it also deploys literature to reclaim the victim's story.

Jacob Glatstein's *Anthology of Holocaust Literature* (*AHL*, 1968) continued through a multifaceted approach the polemic against the defamation of Jewish wartime honor. By highlighting Yiddish, the Jewish language par excellence of Eastern European victims, the anthology insisted on relaying the victim's point of view. The dedication to this enterprise is signaled in the first reading, a chapter from Elie Wiesel's 1956 memoir, translated not from the better-known French adaptation, *La Nuit*, but rather in this case from the Yiddish original, *And the World Remained Silent*.

In close to four hundred pages, *AHL* groups the writings into six sections: (1) "Occupations, Actions, Selections"; (2) "Life in the Ghettos"; (3) "Children"; (4) "Concentration and Death Camps"; (5) "Resistance"; and (6) "The Non-Jews." Chronology is important only as regards the movement from ghettos (section 2) to camps (section 4); otherwise topical and thematic headings lead the way. In addition to Wiesel, authors include many of Eastern Europe's finest wartime Yiddish-language chroniclers: Emanuel Ringelblum, Mordechai Gerbirtig, Shmerke Katsherginski, Rachmil Bryks, Bernard Goldstein, Isaiah Spiegel, Peretz Opoczynski, Rachel Auerbach, and Hirsh Glik. This emphasis on Yiddish does not mean that Western European Jewry is overlooked, as excerpts from the writings of Anne Frank, Primo Levi, and Arnost Lustig eloquently demonstrate. Generically diverse, the chapters are drawn from diaries, letters, memoirs, stories, novels, reportage, poems, songs, and, in a few cases, scholarly overviews (by Philip Friedman, Abraham Foxman, and Donald Lowrie).

Though it didn't mention the "villifiers" by name, *AHL*'s introduction addressed the need for a polemical anthology: the skewed assessment of the victim arises because the enemy's "reports do not disclose [the Jew's heroism]; they either pass it by or falsify it. What there is of this [information of Jewish response] is mainly Yiddish and partly in Hebrew, and the accusers who would sully the memory of the Six Million, rely chiefly upon non-Jewish sources and have apparently little knowledge, if any, of Yiddish and Hebrew."[4] Knowledge of languages and access to sources is the root cause. To fill this gap, *AHL* translates most of its chapters from these generally inaccessible languages; lack of knowledge will no longer be an excuse. To right the balance, *AHL* includes no perpetrator writing, court depositions, or documents whatsoever.

This assemblage of victim writings in the victim's languages tries to go a step further, claiming for these writings a sacred status. It aims to compile a "modern sacred book to be preserved for our children and their children and all the subsequent generations, a book commemorating forever the Six Million, as an enduring temple for their spirit."[5] The goal is to produce a new Book of Lamentations, the name given to the biblical book said to have been written by the prophet Jeremiah to commemorate the destruction of the ancient Temple in Jerusalem. For the secular editors, literary response is the proper (and sacred) way to commemorate – and that commemoration is what one hopes to achieve.

Lucy Dawidowicz's *A Holocaust Reader* (1975), a companion to her treatise *The War Against the Jews* (1975), carried forward this polemic in a more complicated fashion. Her *Reader* is clearly not, in any strict sense of the term, a literary anthology. But it nonetheless would be hollowed out if the literary contributions – diaries, songs, letters, and reportage, by Peretz Opoczynski, Josef Zelkowicz, Janusz Korczak, and Zelig Kalmanovitsh – were expunged. Dawidowicz's introduction, moreover, challenges a presumption that documents from the hands of the perpetrators are more authoritative (because they were ostensibly less constructed) than the ghetto reportage from that of the victims. And in keeping with this judgment, Dawidowicz devotes nearly two-thirds of the volume (the second part, referred to as "The Holocaust," in contrast to the first part, entitled "The Final Solution") to a full range of victim writing – the authority of which stands on its own.

David Roskies' *The Literature of Destruction: Jewish Responses to Catastrophe* (*LOD*, 1989) builds on two trajectories of the Holocaust anthology. Like Glatstein, he highlights the centrality of Jewish languages, the active role of an anthology in fashioning a tradition, and the sacredness of the enterprise and the literature assembled. And like the earlier efforts of the *Jewish Frontier* and *Jewish Life*, the *LOD* situates the Holocaust in the broader realm of Jewish history and experience; the chapters on the Holocaust thus constitute only a part of the overall readings. The organization thus conveys a resolute message: as unprecedented as the Holocaust's destruction may have been, it continues to be embedded within the larger fabric of Jewish experience.

But these similarities should not obscure *LOD*'s novelty. Beginning with the Bible and proceeding chronologically, Roskies anthologizes a history of Jewish responses to catastrophe, at the end of which surfaces the Holocaust. Twenty sections cull a hundred readings, the round figure of one hundred likely indicating that only such wide scope and historical breadth can reach a sense of completeness. Four of the sections bring ancient texts, three medieval and early modern, and the bulk lay out modern responses. The section headings mark historical periods or evoke key themes, and include "Hurban/The First Destruction," "Rabbinic Theology in Midrash," "The Spanish Exile," "Oracles of Kishinev, 1903," and "Between the [World] Wars: Prophecy and Profanation."

The Holocaust receives a weighty five sections, far more than any other single event. But there is a catch: the multitude of Holocaust responses – twenty-two from the period of the war, four in its aftermath, a number of them familiar but most previously unanthologized – cannot be fathomed without the historical and textual backdrop. Indeed, many of the writers took for granted such a foreground of response; in some cases, it was explicitly articulated. The assembled readings are meant to incarnate Roskies' thesis set forth discursively a few years before in his interpretive study, *Against the Apocalypse: Responses to Catastrophe in Modern Jewish Culture* (1984). Both volumes have in mind to open up a compressed, involuted history of the Holocaust. The latter cannot stand on its own. It rather comprises another link in the chain of Jewish responses to catastrophe.

In its focus on Yiddish, *LOD* takes Glatstein's mission, set forth in *AHL* twenty years earlier, a step further. Except for Władysław Szlengel's Warsaw ghetto Polish-language poems, *LOD*'s other Holocaust-era poems, stories, songs, and reportage were crafted in Yiddish. Narrowing the linguistic focus serves as a means to several ends, showing above all the remarkable wartime creativity in the ghettos. Schwarz's claim in *The Root and the Bough* of "unprecedented wartime silence" has here gone by the wayside. Thus four of *LOD*'s five Holocaust sections were written during the war, and almost all of those were composed in the ghettos on Polish soil. Once again, geography was destiny. Finally, almost all of the authors (seventeen of twenty-one) did not survive the war. It was thus not the survivors who established the terms of Holocaust victim writing but rather the wartime writers who set the terms for the survivors themselves. Roskies sacrifices breadth in time and space in order to demonstrate that victim response came during the war years and was not in the least belated. Just as Schwarz was convinced that reading such chronicles are a "clue to the ultimate hidden resources in humankind," Roskies believes in the sacredness of this literature "because in the reading of it, one discovers the ultimate value of life."[6]

If an appreciation for life's ultimate value and the sacredness that attends it has guided most Holocaust anthologies, others have veered from this course. In *Art from the Ashes: A Holocaust Anthology* (1995), Lawrence Langer's stated aim is to "give the readers a chance to encounter the variety and complexity" of both fact and fiction. Hence the sequence of sections moves from the "literal to the literary": (1) memoir and essay, called "The Way It Was"; (2) journal and diaries; (3) prose fiction; (4) one work of drama; and, finally, (5) poetry. In contrast to the general anthological premise that Holocaust literature reveals some fundamental element of being human, Langer presumes that there was no meaning to be found in these events – which accounts for the absence of Anne Frank from the roster of authors, and likewise the absence of any religious writing or writing that dramatizes the predicament of religious Jews.

Langer wishes to avoid excerpts – seemingly because they will violate the integrity of the literary work – but includes them for journals and diaries. This preference for presenting the complete work gives the collection a strikingly finished look – a far cry from the appearance of a raw assemblage of documents that one found in Rudnicki's early collection. The entries are drawn from a wide variety of original languages: German, Polish, Yiddish, French, Italian. Yet Langer does not comment on the diversity or, in contrast to Glatstein, Roskies, and others, on the special role of Yiddish. All languages are seemingly equal in their relation to the Holocaust. This practical rather than reflective approach to the languages of the Holocaust may be why one does not find writings from Yiddish or Hebrew represented in the first section, "The Way It Was." *Art from the Ashes* thus introduced a new direction in Holocaust literature anthologies, elevating aesthetic standards while eliminating the idiom of commemoration, downplaying the polemical emphasis on Yiddish and Hebrew sources, and inverting the belief in Holocaust literature's task of uncovering life's ultimate value.

Not only general anthologies have endeavored to make primary sources of Holocaust writing available to learned and popular audiences. By narrowing the compass, thematic and generic collections have aimed to include more rigorously or intensively what the general version cannot. Thematic anthologies include those devoted to children, to women, or to resistance; generic anthologies usually feature a single kind of writing: poetry, drama, story, memoir, or diary.

Postwar collections of children's testimony appeared as early as 1947, the first, *One of a City and Two of a Family*, in Hebrew, the second, *Children Accuse*, in Polish. Both highlighted the simplicity of the reports in contrast to the overwhelming ordeal the young authors had suffered. These accounts issued from children who had gratefully survived the devastation; the majority of Europe's Jewish children, more than 80 percent, did not. One of the most celebrated anthologies of children's writing, *I Never Saw Another Butterfly* (1963), shifted the accent. It featured poems and drawings of children rendered in the concentration camp Terezin, most of whom were deported to their death in Auschwitz. "The heaviest wheel rolls across our foreheads / To bury itself deep somewhere inside our memories," observes one of the children, Miff, writing in 1944.[7]

The twin poles of wondrous simplicity and crushing loss continued to guide such anthologies four decades on. The gathering of children's

Holocaust diaries in *Salvaged Pages: Young Writers' Diaries of the Holocaust* (2002) shows how extensive and varied were those who, like Anne Frank, kept a day-to-day wartime chronicle (Anne Frank's diary has circulated so widely that the editor felt no need to include it). Drawing on Yiddish, Hebrew, and a plethora of European languages, the fourteen children's chronicles written by nine boys and seven girls (with two cases of authors doubling up) represent a broad spectrum of young Jewish chroniclers, where the day-to-day ordeals described by Torah-observant Jews alternate with those of assimilated Jews, with most of the chroniclers falling somewhere in between. Moshe Flinker, who hid with his parents and six siblings in Brussels until betrayed just before Passover in 1944, wrote in Hebrew about the family's ordeal, his unease of passing as a non-Jew, and his life of prayer and study. Otto Wolf, for his part, describes in Czech the family's hiding in the Moravian forest, focusing on the routine details of a displaced life. When he was captured a few weeks before the war's end, his sister took over in his stead.

Like children, the fate of women in the Holocaust received attention from early on, and anthologies on the Holocaust regularly included women's contributions. But unlike children, collections devoted singly to women's Holocaust experience and expression appeared only later. *Different Voices: Women and the Holocaust* (1993) draws on the earlier, frames it in terms of 1990s gender studies, and uses literature as a point of entry and reflection. The volume does not intend to collect in order to survey what has been written, but rather endeavors to bring story, poem, drama, and letters by and about women to tease out the nature of the "different voice." Divided into three sections, the first ("Voices of Experience") and last ("Voices of Reflection") highlight literary contributions, including those by Ida Fink and Charlotte Delbo. The introduction movingly chronicles the life and writing of German-Jewish author Gertrud Kolmar, who perished in Auschwitz in 1943. In contrast to *Salvaged Pages*'s wartime focus on children's diaries, however, all but one of the book's chapters has its origins in the postwar period.

Kin to Schwarz's "stout prayer book written by hand from memory," postwar writing of a very specific kind is also the province of *The Forgotten Memoirs*, featuring fifteen accounts by distinguished rabbis who survived the war. This volume, too, aims to give a forum to "different voices" that, for reasons of language, culture, and idiom, have not generally had an airing in discussions of the Holocaust. Written almost exclusively in Hebrew and steeped in reference and allusion to the Torah and its commentaries, the accounts were by and large penned in the first decades after the war. But

since most rabbinic survivors refrained from publishing a Holocaust memoir per se, preferring to publish their chronicles as prefaces or afterwords to
traditional volumes of Torah study, the accounts are largely unknown.
Hence the title, *The Forgotten Memoirs*.

In many respects, these bitter chronicles echo those generally found in
anthologies. They, too, relay the incremental destruction of community,
home, possessions, and family, the tortures inflicted and suffered, and the
challenge of survival amidst increasing privation and perilous deportation.
Rhetorically, they, too, emphasize the overwhelming difficulty of describing
what happened. "I have written down," writes Rabbi Moshe Rothenberg,
"only a fraction of my experiences – if I recorded them all, I would never
finish."[8] And some invoke the unique suffering that they faced. Rabbi
Yaakov Avigdor, for instance, refers to "the horrific events, unprecedented
not only in the Jewish annals of martyrdom, but the history of humanity as
a whole" (p. 44).

Less familiar, however, is the regular refrain of miracles, thanksgiving,
and allusion to traditional Torah texts. "I hereby prepare myself," writes
Rabbi Yitzchak Yaakov Weiss, "to extol my Creator with blessings of
thanksgiving to the Awesome One, for His kindness in aiding me to
complete this book, and for the miracles He performed on our behalf"
(p. 536). Or Rabbi Yechiel Yaakov Weinberg, who feels called to speak of
gratitude: "In this preface to my book, I lift my hands heavenward in
thanksgiving to God, Who in His compassion and mercy brought me out
of Germany, that bloodsoaked land" (p. 438). Or Rabbi Moshe Nosson
Notta Lemberger, who views writing about his experience as an obligation:
"It is certainly our duty to retell and remember forever what the Amalekites,
the evil ones of the foreign nations, did to us in every generation" (p. 197).
The invocation of a sacred duty to remember and transmit what was
endured thus follows the same path as editors Schwarz, Glatstein, and
Roskies – all of whom claimed a sacred status for the anthology each had
assembled (Langer's anthology, eschewing a vocabulary of the sacred, is
strangely idiosyncratic in this regard). This compilation takes such a charge
another step by culling its contributions from volumes more likely to be
found in synagogues than in university libraries.

Single theme or genre Holocaust literature anthologies have thus endeavored to compensate for what has been previously overlooked and undervalued. Occasionally, collections have tried to break new ground by
combining one or another. *Truth and Lamentation: Stories and Poems on the
Holocaust* (1993) tries to fuse theme and genre, and, in addition, to combine
two genres linked by the criterion of (relative) brevity. The themes translate

into a melding of factual description ("Truth") and emotional response ("Lamentation"); the twin themes draw on examples from both genres.

The editors cast their net widely, drawing from prewar, wartime, and postwar writings in a number of languages. The first section, "Transmitting Truth," contains twelve stories and forty-eight poems; the second section, "Lamentation," eight stories and forty-two poems. Strikingly, although it weaves in late-twentieth-century American responses, the collection makes a dedicated effort to include (at times even to feature) wartime writing, including Lodz ghetto poet Simcha Bunim Shayevitsh and his Warsaw-based counterpart Yitzhak Katzenelson. In this vein, a story by Lodz ghetto writer Josef Zelkowicz leads off the anthology as a whole.

But the wartime writing isn't always recognizable as such, since it gets mixed in with prewar and postwar alike. The reader is left to sort out what came when. This can have the effect of missing the driving force of the poem or story. Although Jacob Glatstein's poem "Good Night, World" was penned before the war, in spring 1938, it comes late in the entries (p. 484), making it difficult to appreciate the shock and prescience of Glatstein's decision to "go back into the ghetto" wearing "My fiery, yellow patch" – long before patches and ghettos had been forced upon any of Europe's Jews.[9]

The wartime focus becomes much sharper in a recent online anthology, *Poetry in Hell*, edited by Sarah Traister Moscovitz. Almost all of the 148 items (poetry, with a few prose additions) were collected in the Oyneg Shabes archives, assembled in Warsaw from 1939 to 1943 under the direction of historian Emanuel Ringelblum, and later buried in three caches, two of which were found after the war. Many of the poems were written during the war, some others were written before but evidently circulated in the ghetto. For the most part, we are reading what was stowed away, intimately revealing how under conditions of immense privation life (and poetry) was negotiated. So Zusman Segalovitch can continue to see signs of great-ness in the everyday:

> And still it is beautiful as a miracle,
> This rosy twig of lilac . . .
> Even in our days
> of evil, terror and dread.[10]

Or the strategies of coping articulated by Miriam Ulinover:

> Whom should I call to come quick to help,
> when I am not feeling well.
> There is no wire
> in the walls for telegraph.

> But I know now whom I should call
> when pain takes me where I am,
> to great God above,
> From my heart, I'll send a telegram.[11]

Yiddish-language facsimiles of each deposited item intensify the sense of eavesdropping on ghetto life. In presentation and focus, this anthology goes furthest in cleaving to its origins and context.

Yet two factors complicate entry to this localized anthology. First, the editor distributes the poems under five thematic headings (nature, home, ghetto, death, and tradition). We read this excavated collection only through categories externally imposed rather than, say, through some attempt at chronological headings. The first point leads to the second. Prewar and wartime poems are listed seamlessly together under these thematic headings, giving the impression that all hail from similar circumstances. So while the reader is able to read with the eyes of the ghetto reader, we are unable to know what truly came from the ghetto and what did not. To be sure, including earlier poems may demonstrate the hard-earned continuity with the past that existed in the ghetto, despite being sealed off from the world. Yet, in the end, both anthologies – *Truth and Lamentation* as well as *Poetry in Hell* – blur contextual boundaries even as they broaden and intensify the inventory of shorter writing.

The short, the condensed, the lyrical: to anthologize what can fit draws attention to Holocaust writing too big to find a place in even the most copious collection. Chava Rosenfarb's *The Tree of Life*; André Schwarz-Bart's *The Last of the Just*; Günter Grass's *The Tin Drum* – all are more or less massive novels, crucial to any library of Holocaust writing. Yet only a fraction can find its way into an anthology. But the same limitations hold true for many essential diaries, logbooks, memoirs. We settle for extracts at best. Yet the restriction may have its benefit, shortening the time spent immersed in the grueling confrontation with Holocaust chronicles, in any format. For most students, only so much time can one endure (and should be made to endure) reading about losses heaped upon losses. By and large, however, anthologies include more than exclude, translating and publishing dozens of writings that otherwise would not see the light of day.

At bottom, the Holocaust anthology aims for a prismatic effect, creating the impression that a library of catastrophe can be contained in a single book. In fashioning such a volume – a bouquet of evil-drenched flowers – most editors view the anthologizing task of assembling and excerpting as itself a sacred act, serving to commemorate the Holocaust's victims even as it establishes a canon of tormented, if essential, texts.

Notes

1. Israel Knox, Introduction to Jacob Glatstein, Israel Knox, and Samuel Margoshes (eds.), *Anthology of Holocaust Literature* (New York: Atheneum, 1980), p. xiii.
2. Leo W. Schwarz, *The Root and the Bough: The Epic of an Enduring People* (New York: Rinehart and Company, 1949), p. xi. The page numbers of subsequent citations from this volume are given in the text.
3. Adolph Rudnicki, ed., *Lest We Forget* (Warsaw: Polonia, 1955), pp. 129–30.
4. Knox, Introduction to *AHL*, p. xx.
5. Ibid., p. xiv.
6. David Roskies, ed., *The Literature of Destruction: Jewish Responses to Catastrophe* (Philadelphia: Jewish Publication Society of America, 1989), p. 10.
7. *I Never Saw Another Butterfly: Children's Drawings and Poems from Terezin Concentration Camp, 1942–1944* (New York: Schocken Books, 1964; exp. 2nd edn. 1993), p. 17.
8. Esther Farbstein, ed., *The Forgotten Memoirs* (Brooklyn: Shaar, 2011), p. 388. The page numbers of subsequent citations are given in the text.
9. Milton Teichman and Sharon Leder, eds., *Truth and Lamentation: Stories and Poems on the Holocaust* (Urbana: University of Illinois Press, 1993), p. 484.
10. Zusman Segalovitch, "Like a Miracle," in Sarah Traister Moscovitz (ed. and trans.), *Poetry in Hell: Yiddish Poetry from the Ringelblum Archives*: http://poetryinhell.org/index-by-authors/segalovitch-zusman/like-a-miracle/.
11. Miriam Ulinover, "Girl All Alone," in Moscovitz (ed. and trans.), *Poetry in Hell*: http://poetryinhell.org/ghetto-hunger-struggle-2/miriam-ulinover-girl-all-alone/.

CHAPTER 16

The historian's anvil, the novelist's crucible

Eric J. Sundquist

"The concentration camp is imaginable only and exclusively as literature, never as reality," Imre Kertész has written, "least of all, when we have directly experienced it."[1] Kertész's heterodox assessment of the relationship between historical fact and artistic representation underpins *Fatelessness* (1975), a novel based on his experience as a teenage prisoner in Auschwitz and Buchenwald, but narrated in a voice whose thoroughgoing naïveté imbues familiar scenes with a bewildering sense of wonder. In his strict allegiance to the powers of the imagination, Kertész sought to combat two totalitarian regimes, Nazism and postwar Soviet communism, that had stripped him of control over his own fate. The "fragile gift" of his life having been "expropriated by alien forces, and circumscribed, marked up, branded," as he put it in his Nobel Prize Address, Kertész had to take it back "from 'History,' this dreadful Moloch, because it was mine and mine alone."[2]

Kertész's provocative argument suggests the degree to which all of us today gain access to the *Shoah* through multiple forms of evidence, including contested modes of narrative reconstruction that are inherently "imaginative" – sometimes dangerously so. We need only bear in mind the cautionary tale of Binjamin Wilkomirski's infamous memoir, *Fragments* (1995), which elicited moving corroboration from survivors, who acclaimed its acute reflection of their own experiences before it was proved to be pure fiction. Yet in revealing that the emotional authority of survivor testimony may be "autonomous from history," as Michael Bernard-Donals puts it,[3] Wilkomirski's hoax also paradoxically demonstrated literature's power to illuminate the Holocaust by, in effect, ventriloquizing the voice of history.

The extraordinary outpouring of testimonial witness and historical scholarship over the past sixty years has been accompanied by depictions in many media, all of which make up the network of ideas and images that constitute popular understanding of the Holocaust. Because the historian facing a human catastrophe so painful can act at best as "a pathologist, hardly a physician," Yosef Yerushalmi somberly concluded in 1982, contemporary understanding of the Holocaust was being shaped "not at the historian's anvil, but in the novelist's crucible."[4] Yerushalmi meant to distinguish the writing of Jewish history as a professional practice from the mélange of facts, half-truths, and myths that produce collective memory. In borrowing his formulation for my title, I do not mean to set aside the claims of history but rather, embracing his admonition, to explore the ways in which Holocaust fiction both depends intrinsically on factual allegiance and pushes the boundaries of fact so as to confront us with dimensions of human experience that elude documentary or analytic interpretation.

The strategies available in fiction have proved as various as they are numerous. By fabricating a narrative from raw documents not yet translated or published, the novelist may credibly anticipate the work of later historians, as did John Hersey, whose novel of the Warsaw Ghetto Uprising, *The Wall* (1950), required him, as he said, to "invent a memory."[5] By choosing a strategy of displacement, the novelist may approach the Holocaust through its antecedents, as did Bernard Malamud in *The Fixer* (1966), which dramatized Jewish resistance to state-sponsored anti-Semitism through a fictionalization of the Mendel Beilis blood libel trial in 1911 Kiev and thus rehearsed issues of persecution and resistance at a historical remove potentially less painful. By erasing facts the reader is expected to know, the novelist may convey the shocking incomprehensibility of the Holocaust as it unfolded. Such is the case in Aharon Appelfeld's *Badenheim 1939* (1978), which details the delusions of a group of Jews in an Austrian resort who fail to interpret correctly the signs of German menace when they are required to register for "emigration" to Poland with the local "Sanitation Department," complete with its own travel agency and colorful brochures, until suddenly they are whisked into filthy freight cars bound for a death camp. Readers familiar with the Nazi occupation of Austria, as Appelfeld pointed out, would "fill in what was missing."[6]

The history that is missing may, in fact, be found in the writer's own work. Readers coming to "Alice's Leg" in Charlotte Delbo's memoir *None of Us Will Return* (1965), for example, encounter an eerie vignette about an Auschwitz prisoner whose artificial leg serves symbolically to entangle the dehumanization of the victim with the trauma of Delbo and others who witness her death:

> It is a haystack of carefully piled corpses, as with a real haystack under the moon light and snow, at night. But we look at them without fear. We know that here one is on the borderline of the bearable and we struggle against letting go.

>   Lying in the snow, Alice's leg is alive and sentient. It must have detached
>   itself from the dead Alice.
>   We kept on going there to see if it was still there, and each time it was
>   intolerable. Alice abandoned, dying in the snow . . . Alice dying alone, not
>   calling anyone.[7]

In *Convoy to Auschwitz* (1965), Delbo's collective biography of 230 French
women with whom she was transported to Auschwitz, we find that Alice
Viterbo was an Italian singer born in Alexandria, Egypt, who had performed
at the Paris Opera before losing her leg in an automobile accident. Forced to
run a gauntlet of armed guards on February 10, 1943, perhaps in revenge for
the German army's defeat at Stalingrad, Alice

>   made a superhuman effort to run . . . dragged along by Hélène Solomon. But
>   she fell and was pulled out of the ranks and thrown into Block 25 [the prison
>   block]. She lasted longer than anyone else. For days we saw her at the
>   window, upright and lucid . . . Alice Viterbo must have died on February
>   25 or 26, 1943. Her artificial leg lay in the snow for a long time.[8]

Distilled from the stark data of Alice Viterbo's life and death in *Convoy to
Auschwitz*, the deranged yet lyrical voice of "Alice's Leg" makes visceral the
emotional anguish absent from the biography.

A similar, but more complicated, instance of the tension between the
aesthetic and the historical appears in Cynthia Ozick's short story "The
Shawl" (1980) and its companion piece "Rosa" (1983), which were published
together as *The Shawl* in 1989. The initial story, rendered in overwrought
poetic diction that flies straight in the face of any prohibitions about artistic
representations of the Holocaust, is ethereal. Its three characters, a mother
(Rosa), her fifteen-month-old daughter (Magda), and her fourteen-year-old
niece (Stella), are named, but the story otherwise offers us no facts about
their earlier lives, the camp in which they are imprisoned, how they got
there, or the date of the story's simple action. Bereft of the swaddling shawl
that has hidden her, Magda is discovered by a camp guard and thrown into
an electrified fence: "like a butterfly touching a silver vine . . . her pencil legs
and balloonish belly and zigzag arms splashed against the fence."[9]

Such elaborate metaphors, with which the story is saturated, appear
meant to strip the action of historical specificity, while presenting the reader
with an interpretive enigma in which horror and art are fiercely entwined.
And yet "Rosa" forces a return to the historical, not only in its setting in
1977 Miami but also by providing clues to what is missing in the first story.
On the basis of the second story, we are able to reconstruct a family, Rosa
and Stella being its only survivors, that once consisted of Rosa's

cosmopolitan Warsaw parents; her older brother, his wife, and their daughter (Stella); her two younger brothers; Magda; Andrzej, the Polish gentile
who may be Madga's father (unless Magda, as Stella alleges, is the offspring
of a Nazi); and Andrzej's parents (a gentile father and a mother who is a
Jewish convert to Christianity, thus making Magda a racial Jew according to
the Nuremberg Laws). We can calculate birthdates for Rosa (1919) and
Stella (1928), and narrow the date of Magda's birth to mid-1941 to early
1942, depending on when and to what camp we believe the women were
transported from the Warsaw ghetto – if earlier, then probably to Treblinka,
where it is doubtful they would have survived as depicted in "The Shawl,"
or to Majdanek, the story's most likely setting.

The Shawl does not give us enough information to settle these matters
beyond doubt; indeed, its very resistance to such analysis is part of its
intrigue and strategy. Yet Ozick issues a challenge, on the basis of the
facts she does give us, to locate the action in history and to measure the
opening story's hyper-aestheticization against her own ambivalence about
writing Holocaust fiction. "I am not in favor of making fiction of the data,
or of mythologizing or poeticizing it," Ozick told participants in a 1987
conference on writing and the Holocaust, yet "I constantly violate this
tenet; my brother's blood cries out from the ground, and I am drawn and
driven."[10]

On that same occasion Leslie Epstein defended his controversial novel
King of the Jews (1979), which refashioned the life of Chaim Rumkowski,
leader of the Lodz ghetto and a figure of moral compromise studied to great
effect by Primo Levi and others, in the character of Isaiah Trumpelman.
While taking Rumkowski's penchant for pompous theatrical rule to farcical
extremes, Epstein's novel hews rather closely to historical events. But it does
so by freely transferring to Lodz actions that took place in other ghettos,
including Warsaw and Vilna, as well as borrowing the deliberations of other
Jewish Councils and the words of other Jewish elders. Epstein spelled out
his strategy in later remarks. The goal of history, he said, is

> the determination of facts ... The recombining and splitting and turning
> upside down and inside out of events, so that ... a river from Warsaw should
> run through Lodz, that horses which froze in Finland should have their
> manes crystallized in Poland, and that babies whose birth was outlawed in
> Vilna should nonetheless howl in the [Lodz ghetto]: all this of course is
> anathema to the historian. So, too, is the exercise of humor and irony and
> personality and point of view, as well as fits of anger, disgust, giving way to
> despair, to manic laughter, or to an overarching sense of wryness – even
> though, oddly, every single one of these qualities shines through the work of

those historians, the archivists of Lodz, the [Emanuel] Ringelblum group in
Warsaw, who had to work in secret and in danger and on the spot.[11]

In the spirit of the ghetto historians and diarists who viewed Rumkowski
with a mixture of admiration, amusement, and contempt, *King of the Jews*
takes up many aspects of his role in the ghetto, subjecting all of it to antic
satire. Before considering further the novelist's obligation to history, we
should take note of one of Eptstein's most significant alterations in the
documentary record.

On December 16, 1941, less than two weeks after the first Jews from
outlying villages were killed at the Chelmno death camp, Rumkowski was
ordered by German authorities to select 20,000 Jews for "resettlement," a
number he managed to reduce to 10,000. The first transports of Jews from
Lodz – purportedly to work camps or farms but in reality to Chelmno –
took place on January 16, 1942, and continued throughout the year, with the
most horrendous events unfolding in September, when, suddenly, hospitals
were liquidated and orders issued for the roundup of everyone over the age
of sixty-five and under the age of ten. At what point Rumkowski realized
that the Jews of Lodz were being sent to their deaths cannot be clearly
determined; speculation has ranged from early spring through the summer
of 1942. In a chapter entitled "The Yellow Bus," however, Epstein alters
history to provide a surprisingly clear answer.

Determined to discover where those deported from the ghetto are going,
a young boy named Nisel Lipiczany, the novel's surviving narrator, follows
a rail spur to its destination – Chelmno. There, in mid-December 1941,
he witnesses the murder of Jews from Lodz, one trainload after another, in
a gas van:

> The day passed that way . . . Four different times the bus was washed out
> with barrels of water. Once, with Jews aboard, something went wrong with
> the engine. It ran for a bit, then sputtered and stopped. How quiet and
> peaceful the spot became! A Man of Valor . . . walked to the side of the coach.
> He placed his ear against it.
> "Just like in a synagogue," he said.[12]

The scene is harrowing, not least because of the macabre comment of the SS
officer, at first glance one more example of the novel's baroque comedy.
Epstein, however, did not invent the comment but borrowed it from the
historical record. Reflecting on his reading at the YIVO Institute for Jewish
Research, Epstein recalled an epiphany: "I dropped my eyes to the book. In
it a German officer was putting his ear to the side of a bus in which Jews
were being gassed. 'Just like in a synagogue,' he said; and that, word for

word, is how I recorded the line in my notebook and the novel to come."[13] And there, indeed, is the line in question, overheard by Nisel Lipiczany in *King of the Jews.*

For those acquainted with the facts of the Nazi extermination, however, the line is right but the context is wrong. Epstein took the line from Kurt Gerstein's famous deposition about the gassing of Jews at Belzec, which appeared in the English translation Epstein follows in Lucy Dawidowicz's *Holocaust Reader* (1976). In his position as chief disinfection officer in the Main Hygienic Office of the Waffen SS, Gerstein, along with Professor Wilhelm Pfannenstiel, went to Belzec in August 1942 charged with improving the disinfection of clothing taken from Jews and others killed at the facility, as well as consulting about upgrading the service of the gas chambers themselves. On one occasion, as hundreds of naked men, women, and children were herded into gas chambers, Gerstein watched the driver of the diesel truck whose exhaust supplied the gas struggle to start his engine: "My stop watch showed it all, 50 minutes, 70 minutes, and the diesel did not start! The people wait inside the gas chambers. In vain. They can be heard weeping, 'like in a synagogue,' says Professor Pfannenstiel, his eyes glued to the window in the wooden door . . . After two hours and 49 minutes – the stop watch recorded it all – the diesel started."[14]

Epstein's transformation of the gas van known with sardonic affection among locals as the "Ghetto Autobus"[15] into a yellow vehicle reminiscent of a school bus is a minor change; so, too, his reassignment of Pfannenstiel's comment, his borrowing from Gerstein's language when Nisel witnesses an emaciated Jewish prisoner cutting the hair from women's bodies for the Reich's industrial use, and his reference to "the roar of the grindstone,"[16] an allusion to Rumkowski's having received a letter from the ghetto administration requesting a bone grinder in July 1942 when it was determined that, with mass graves overflowing and corpses putrefying in the heat, it was necessary to burn the bodies and obliterate the bones.[17] Taken together, however, such changes belong to the chronological compression through which Epstein frames the issue of Rumkowski's complicity.

The Wannsee Conference, usually credited as the occasion on which plans for the Final Solution were set in place, occurred on January 20, 1942. It was originally scheduled for December 9, 1941, however, and was postponed only at the last minute, on December 8 – the day Chelmno became operational – in all likelihood because of Japan's attack on Pearl Harbor the day before and the entry of the United States into the war. Chelmno was perhaps foremost among those efforts that Reinhard Heydrich had in mind when he remarked at Wannsee that "even now practical experience is being gathered that is of major significance in view of the coming Final Solution."[18] Although gas vans were rendered obsolete by the completion of gas chambers at Belzec, Auschwitz-Birkenau, and other camps in 1942, Epstein's telescoping of events makes Nisel an eyewitness to the onset of the Final Solution as industrialized genocide and underscores the suicidal logic of self-destruction with which ghetto leaders such as Rumkowski were faced. When Nisel confronts Trumpelman with the truth about Chelmno at a Christmas Eve mass for Jewish converts, he replies, "What if it's true? What do you want the Elder to do? . . . It's better if they think they are going to a farm."[19]

Although historians today tend to be more sympathetic to Rumkowski's doomed attempt, through guile and imperious rule, to save a remnant of Lodz Jews by sacrificing others, Epstein is attuned to the less forgiving judgments of some of Rumkowski's contemporaries. A "man sick with megalomania" given to making "Führer-like" speeches, according to Dawid Sierakowiak,[20] Rumkowski came to be known, even in Warsaw, as "Chaim the Terrible."[21] Wishing "to play the role of the one who created Noah's ark . . . [and] to go down in history as the savior," concluded Oskar Rosenfeld, less harshly, Rumkowski made himself a slave of the Germans. "Will he be held responsible by somebody?" asked Rosenfeld in his journal. Or will history prove him to be "the true *shofet* [judge]?"[22]

Insofar as his comic rearrangement of various ghetto histories into a kind of novelistic jigsaw puzzle makes Trumpelman a composite character, moreover, Epstein also entered into one of the most inflamed arguments of his own day. In giving Trumpelman knowledge of the Final Solution before the gas chambers at Belzec and Auschwitz had been built, before the Wannsee Conference had taken place, and before any of the real Jews of Lodz had been murdered at Chelmno, Epstein created a representative ghetto leader who conformed to the charges leveled by Raul Hilberg and Hannah Arendt – in *The Destruction of the European Jews* (1961) and *Eichmann in Jerusalem* (1963), respectively – that ghetto leaders were themselves significantly responsible for the annihilation of their communities. Those charges were quickly contested, but subsequent debate about *alleged* Jewish passivity and complicity set the context in which Epstein's novel appeared and in which must be best judged.

* * *

His defense of the novelist's freedom notwithstanding, Epstein remarked while working on *King of the Jews* that "almost any eye-witness testimony of the Holocaust is more moving and more successful at creating a sense of what it must have been like in the ghettos and the camps than *almost* any fictional account of the same events."[23] More moving in some instances, perhaps, but not always, and by no means, as the case of Wilkomirski reminds us, more trustworthy. The problem is all the more delicate when testimony and fiction are closely interwoven, as in the depiction of his own concentration camp experience by Tadeusz Borowski, a non-Jewish Pole who was imprisoned at Auschwitz and served briefly in the camp's Sonderkommando, the squad that processed the dead and their belongings. In the stories later collected in *This Way to the Gas, Ladies and Gentlemen* (1959), some of which first appeared in *We Were at Auschwitz* (1946), a volume combining documentary sketches, written principally by his co-authors Janusz Nel Siedlecki and Krystyn Olszewski, with documentary fiction written principally by Borowski, he adopted the voice of a cynical narrator who alternately mocks Jewish victims and recoils in disgust at their suffering.

"Fact-haunted," Sidra Ezrahi has called Borowski's writing,[24] an apt description of stories in which factual history retains a ghostly presence – not overtly false but everywhere contorted by Borowski's ironic voice. An example that underscores the instability of eyewitness testimony, as well as the ease with which the writing of history may encroach upon fiction, can be found in Borowksi's contribution to the group of narratives that depict the death of Josef Schillinger, a *Rapportführer* (roll-call officer) at Auschwitz shot on October 23, 1943, by a woman who refused to go quietly to her death. The incident is widely documented – widely but by no means conclusively, and the diversity of the accounts, as well as the variety of irreconcilable details they feature, provides a case study of the hazardous terrain between historical fact and imaginative reconstruction.

In Borowski's "The Death of Schillinger," one of several fictional treatments of the incident, Schillinger is given to us as a brutal man who "liked to watch people being shoved into the gas chambers." Welcome news of his death circulates among the prisoners in conflicting accounts, but the narrator reports, "I myself was inclined to believe the Sonderkommando foreman," and it is in his voice that the story of Schillinger's death is told. Recalling the arrival of the first truckloads of prisoners from an August 1943 transport, the foreman dwells on the "hard work" and tact required of the Sonderkommando to instill faith among the prisoners in the "false bath-houses" they are about to enter, as well as their need to make the work "snappy" since Polish Jews are more likely than others to recognize the threat awaiting them. There is turmoil as the prisoners, men and women together, are commanded to undress and the SS have their weapons drawn. When Schillinger, "taking a fancy to a certain body," pulls the naked woman aside, as if for his sexual pleasure, she suddenly bends down, scoops up a handful of gravel, and throws it in his face. After he cries out in pain and drops his revolver, the woman grabs it and shoots him in the stomach. Although the SS scatter, the men of the Sonderkommando, practiced and obedient, proceed with their duty: "We drove them all right into the chamber with clubs, bolted the doors and called the S. S. to administer Cyclone B [gas]. After all, we've had time to acquire some experience." As they later carry the mortally wounded Schillinger to a car, he groans, "O God, my God, what have I done to deserve such suffering?"[25]

"What [a] strange irony of fate," the narrator replies, that Schillinger should fail to understand why he was attacked. As in all of Borowski's fiction, Schillinger's words, along with the mock professionalism of the Sonderkommando and the narrator's own satiric tone, are but one aspect of the story's multiple ironies. Because of the documentary detail his writing often displays, however, we might still be inclined to find Borowski's version reliable. And, in fact, Otto Friedrich, in his supposedly factual study *The Kingdom of Auschwitz* (1982), faithfully repeats Borowski's version, even including the beseeching comment attributed to Schillinger.[26]

But what, indeed, is the truth about Schillinger's death, and where does history end and fiction begin in our composition of that truth?

Borowski places the incident in August 1943, so as to link it to his other stories about the arrival of Jews from the ghettos of Sosnowiec and Bedzin, and he leaves the setting ambiguous. Men and women are undressing side by side, where normally they were separated, and they are in a location where the woman can pick up gravel, and Schillinger, after being shot, can be seen "clawing the dirt in pain." In "Revenge of a Dancer," one entry in her *Auschwitz: True Tales from a Grotesque Land* (1985), Sara Nomberg-Przytyk places the event in July 1944, perhaps to bring it into closer proximity with the revolt of the Auschwitz Sonderkommando that occurred in October 1944, and she presents it as a story heard from a young girl who survived a chaotic nighttime selection among five hundred women prisoners disembarking at the Auschwitz ramp. In Nomberg-Przytyk's version, neither a "true tale" nor pure fiction, the woman is identified as a dancer from Paris. Ordered by an unnamed SS officer to strip naked, the dancer refuses. When he comes closer, she grabs his pistol and shoots him, firing at other men as well but saving "the last bullet for herself." The Birkenau women listen to the girl's story of this heroic act "as if [they] were hearing the most beautiful music."[27]

In addition to specifying the October date on which Schillinger was actually killed, however, most testimonial accounts place the woman's rebellion not on the Auschwitz ramp where selections took place but in the undressing room outside the gas chamber of Crematorium II, where women had been separated from men, and converge around a few details in which we can have some confidence.

The prisoners were Warsaw Jews who, through an extortion plan hatched by the Gestapo, had been provided passports for Latin American countries on the pretext that they were to be exchanged for German prisoners. Taken first to Bergen-Belsen, they were eventually sent to Auschwitz – not a stop along their journey to Switzerland, as they had been led to believe, but rather their final destination. When the women were ordered to undress and their valuables seized, one woman managed to take Schillinger's pistol and shoot him, also wounding a fellow officer, Wilhelm Emmerich, who survived. Her act prompted other women to attack the SS with their bare hands. Some later accounts have claimed that the woman in question was Franceska Mann,[28] a well-known Warsaw dancer, while Ota Kraus and Erich Kulka, Polish political prisoners who provided one of the earliest descriptions of Auschwitz in *The Death Factory* (1946), identified her as a woman named Horowitz who, acting with a business magnate named Mazur, was a conduit for the false passports.[29]

As the renditions of Borowski and Nomberg-Przytyk suggest, the confrontation between the woman and Schillinger quickly acquired mythic status. "The incident passed on from mouth to mouth and embellished in various ways grew into a legend," Auschwitz survivor Wieslaw Kielar wrote some years later, prompting renewed hope among the prisoners and giving rise to "a spontaneous, although still weak, campaign of self-defense."[30] In separating fact from legend, we might assume that immediate eyewitnesses, here members of the Sonderkommando on duty at the time, would be the best place to turn. Yet these several accounts make clear that no witness, even an immediate eyewitness, knows the whole story.

Shlomo Dragon, standing only 5 meters away, as he recalled, got "a close-up view of what happened." What he remembered was an unusual transport of "very refined" people who wore fancy clothing, including fur coats and gold jewelry, and showed no signs of having endured life in a ghetto. When an elegantly dressed woman, later said to be an actress, refused to disrobe completely, Schillinger "pointed his handgun at her bra," whereupon she undid it, "waved it in his face, and hit him on the arm." When he dropped the gun, she picked it up and shot him. Because Schillinger had a reputation as "a terrible, horrific sadist," said Dragon, news of the incident spread quickly and provoked a "real celebration" in the barracks.[31]

Dragon looked back on the incident from a distance of nearly fifty years, as did Ya'akov Silberberg, who asserted that the woman, after shooting Schillinger, was "strangled . . . along with everyone else."[32] But in an April 1945 deposition, Stanislaw Jankowski testified that the prisoners said they had weapons and could thus join with the Sonderkommando in mounting a revolt, and that the woman grabbed a gun not from Schillinger but from another SS officer, Walter Quackernack. After she shot Schillinger, Silberberg recalled, "other women hurled themselves upon the SS men," who at length, and with the assistance of additional guards called to the scene, killed the majority of the transport with gunfire and hand grenades, and then gassed the remainder.[33] For Zalmen Gradowski, a member of the Sonderkommando who did not survive but left several testimonial manuscripts buried in the crematoria, the incident likewise stood out as one of the few examples of Jews refusing to go to their deaths "like sheep to slaughter." "A splendid young woman, a dancer from Warsaw," he wrote, "snatched a revolver from Quackernack and shot Schillinger," a deed that "bolstered the courage of the other brave women, who in turn slapped and threw vials and other such things into the faces of those vicious, uniformed beasts – the SS." Like Jankowski, Gradowski does not seem actually to have seen the event, only heard about it, but he recorded the woman's act as one "before which I bow my head in deep respect."[34]

Not surprisingly, the perspectives of later historians depend significantly on the testimonial accounts they follow. In his influential book *The Theory and Practice of Hell* (1946), Eugene Kogon followed Janda Weiss, a teenage prisoner from Brno who recounted the events for a postwar report compiled by the Psychological Warfare Division of the United States Army. "On one occasion," writes Kogon, "Roll Call Officer Schillinger" – Weiss calls him "that drunken pig" – "made an Italian dancer perform naked before the crematory. Taking advantage of a favorable moment, the woman approached him, seized his gun, and shot him down. In the ensuing struggle she herself was killed, at least escaping death by gas."[35] In his study of Jewish resistance, Reuben Ainsztein depended significantly on Kraus and Kulka but depicted a gunfight between prisoners and the SS before the prisoners were overpowered, an enlargement that allowed him to portray the event as "an attempt at armed revolt inside of one of the crematoria."[36] Martin Gilbert in turn drew on Ainsztein but added striking details taken from the account of Auschwitz escapee Jerzy Tabeau, whose testimony, called "The Polish Major's Report," first appeared in the War Refugee Board publication *German Extermination Camps: Auschwitz and Birkenau* (1944) and was introduced at the Nuremberg Trials a year later.

The woman's attack, said Tabeau, "gave the signal for the others to attack the executioners and their henchmen. One SS man had his nose torn off, another was scalped."[37]

An act of resistance so electrifying in its courage and satisfying in its vengeance was bound to prompt speculation and invention, not only in fiction writers but also in memoirists and historians. Drawing on Tabeau and others whose postwar reports were collected by the Auschwitz state museum, Danuta Czech presented a summary generally consistent with the known facts in her authoritative *Auschwitz Chronicle* (1990).[38] Yet in an appendix to *Death Dealer* (1992),[39] the memoirs of Auschwitz commandant Rudolph Höss, she offered a far more vivid account, one indebted, it seems, to Filip Müller, another member of the Sonderkommando whose testimony was recorded by Polish scholars immediately after the war but who did not publish his extended recollections, *Eyewitness Auschwitz*, until 1979.

Indeed, Müller surpasses Czech in his elaboration of setting, motive, and act. He spends a good deal of time, for example, on the deception intended to trick these particular prisoners upon arrival: the air is sprayed with a sweet fragrance, they are continually addressed as "Ladies and Gentlemen," and they are politely invited into the bathhouses for the "disinfection" said to be required for entry into Switzerland. More remarkable is Müller's dramatization of the woman's resistance, supposedly based on his presence in the room where the incident took place. When the women become suspicious, the guards resort to threats and blows to force them to undress while Schillinger and Quackernack strut back and forth:

> Suddenly they stopped in their tracks, attracted by a strikingly handsome woman with blue-black hair who was taking off her right shoe. The woman, as soon as she noticed that the two men were ogling her, launched into what appeared to be a titillating and seductive strip-tease act. She lifted her skirt to allow a glimpse of thigh and suspender. Slowly she undid her stocking and pealed it off her foot ... The two SS men were fascinated by her performance and paid no attention to anyone else ... their whips dangling from their wrists, and their eyes firmly glued on the woman ... She had taken off her blouse and was standing in front of her lecherous audience in her brassiere. Then she steadied herself against a concrete pillar with her left arm and bent down, slightly lifting her foot, in order to take off her shoe. What happened next took place with lightning speed: quick as a flash she grabbed her shoe and slammed its heel violently against Quackernack's forehead. He winced with pain and covered his face with both hands. At this moment the young woman flung herself at him and made a quick grab for his pistol. Then there was a shot. Schillinger cried out and fell to the ground.

As in Czech's account, the woman disappears into the tumult; the SS men escape; the lights are put out and the doors bolted; the men of the Sonderkommando are called out; and machine guns are brought in to slaughter those left in the changing room.[40]

What is the status of such testimony?

In his foreword to the English translation of Müller's book, the historian Yehuda Bauer writes: "There is no embellishment, no deviation. This is not a work of art. It is a testimony."[41] Like a number of commentators, Müller emphasizes the woman's calculation and her incitement of rebellion among her comrades, but in extrapolating from Schillinger's lechery to her deliberate use of sexuality to seduce and kill him, he does something more. He writes a kind of fiction – lucid, detailed, and startling. It is an open question whether Müller's account is more accurate than those of other witnesses. In its delineation of consciousness and its narrative coherence, however, its closest analog appears in Arnost Lustig's novel *A Prayer for Katerina Horovitzova* (1973). In Lustig's version, which provides a fully worked out back story of the extortion plot in which the prisoners were caught, Katerina employs her seductive charms, first refusing to undress and then removing her clothes "with a slow deliberateness that grew out of something inside her" before suddenly ripping off her bra and striking the entranced Schillinger between the eyes with its hooks:

> He was momentarily blinded by surprise as well as by pain. Hundreds of thousands of people had already passed through this dressing room, as docile as sheep, and nothing like this had ever happened before . . . Eyes blinded by stinging tears, he could feel Katerina Horovitzova yanking the pistol out of his holster. It felt as though it were happening far away. He groped for the gun but it was gone and she shot him in the stomach.

At the same time, however, Lustig blunts the heroism of Katerina's action by telling us that the fire that flashed from the muzzle of the pistol was "only a tiny flicker in comparison to all those belching chimneys and, unlike them, it soon went out."[42]

In the aftermath, Katerina's body is put on display as an object lesson for the SS. Whereas Müller says this took place in the dissecting room, Lustig appears to return us to the reverential sentiments of Zalmen Gradowski by placing it in the warehouse where hair "cut from the heads of dead women when they came out of the gas chambers" is dried – and where Katerina is prayed over by Rabbi Dajem, a member of the Sonderkommando. Although Dajem's prayer is sincere and moving – "May your name be blessed, even before God's own name," he intones – Lustig requires that we judge it against the horror of his role. Dajem himself is not killed because "once, when he had begun to sing in the transport group which was going to the gas chambers," he had been picked out and assigned "to sing to the dead women's hair until it was dry and ready to be shipped off to Germany, where it would be used for making nets and mattresses and cloth."[43] Like Müller, Lustig gives the dancer's story a complexity and psychological nuance more in keeping with her legend than the few certain facts of her life and death can convey, but in his insistence that we measure it against the Nazi operation of industrialized murder he also reminds us that the historical record of the Third Reich is replete with facts that rival our powers of invention.

The case of Schillinger and the dancer is unusual in that its wide documentation, in several genres, still leaves so many questions unanswered. For that reason, however, it is a fascinating example of literature's ability to provide what Lillian Kremer has called "witness through the imagination."[44] In determining what the dancer's act of resistance tells us about the Holocaust, we cannot rely solely on an inspiring testimony or a commanding work of fiction, but neither must we settle for the few verifiable details that may be gathered from the conflicting accounts provided by those who witnessed or heard about the death of Schillinger at the time. Although Holocaust fiction has an obligation to bear in mind the history it purports to represent, the living texture of events, not least those terrifying and seemingly beyond our understanding, must sometimes be imagined.

Notes

1. Imre Kertész, "Who Owns Auschwitz?" trans. John MacKay, *Yale Journal of Criticism* 14 (2001): 268.
2. Imre Kertész, "Heureka!" Nobel Prize Lecture (2002): www.nobelprize.org/ nobel_prizes/literature/laureates/2002/kertesz-lecture-e.html, accessed November 7, 2011.
3. Michael Bernard-Donals, "Beyond the Question of Authenticity: Witness and Testimony in the *Fragments* Controversy," in Michael Bernard-Donals and Richard Glejzer (eds.), *Witnessing the Disaster: Essays on Representation and the Holocaust* (Madison: University of Wisconsin Press, 2003), p. 198.
4. Yosef Hayim Yerushalmi, *Zakhor: Jewish History and Jewish Memory* (1982; repr. Seattle: University of Washington Press, 1996), pp. 94, 98.
5. John Hersey, *To Invent a Memory* (Baltimore Hebrew University, 1990).
6. Aharon Appelfeld, "Interview with Philip Roth," in Philip Roth, *Shop Talk: A Writer and His Colleagues and Their Work* (Boston: Houghton Mifflin, 2001), p. 25.
7. Charlotte Delbo, *None of Us Will Return* (1965), in *Auschwitz and After*, trans. Rosette C. Lamont (New Haven, CT: Yale University Press, 1995), p. 41.

8. Charlotte Delbo, *Convoy to Auschwitz: Women of the French Resistance* (1965), trans. Carol Cosman (Boston: Northeastern University Press, 1997), p. 215.

9. Cynthia Ozick, *The Shawl* (1989; repr. New York: Vintage, 1990), p. 10.

10. Cynthia Ozick, "Roundtable Discussion," in Berel Lang (ed.), *Writing and the Holocaust* (New York: Holmes and Meier, 1988), p. 284.

11. Leslie Epstein, "Writing about the Holocaust," in Lang (ed.), *Writing and the Holocaust*, p. 264.

12. Leslie Epstein, *King of the Jews* (1976; repr. New York: W. W. Norton, 1993), p. 232.

13. Leslie Epstein, "Round Up the Usual Suspects," *New York Times*, October 10, 1982, BR28.

14. Kurt Gerstein, "Deathwatch at Belzec: Kurt Gerstein's Deposition," trans. Rose Feitelson, in Lucy Dawidowicz (ed.), *A Holocaust Reader* (West Orange, NJ: Behrman House, 1976), p. 108.

15. Gerald Reitlinger, *The Final Solution: The Attempt to Exterminate the Jews of Europe, 1939–1945* (1953; repr. New York: A. S. Barnes, 1961), p. 139.

16. Epstein, *King of the Jews*, p. 235.

17. Raul Hilberg, *The Destruction of the European Jews*, 3rd edn., 3 vols. (New Haven, CT: Yale University Press, 2003), vol. III, p. 1043.

18. Reinhard Heydrich, quoted in Lucy Dawidowicz, *The War Against the Jews, 1933–1945* (1975; repr. New York: Bantam, 1986), p. 136.

19. Epstein, *King of the Jews*, p. 241.

20. Dawid Sierakowiak, *The Diary of Dawid Sierakowiak: Five Notebooks from the Lodz Ghetto*, ed. Alan Adelson, trans. Kamil Turowski (New York: Oxford University Press, 1996), pp. 153, 124.

21. Adam Czerniakow, *The Warsaw Diary of Adam Czerniakow*, ed. Raul Hilberg, Stanislaw Staron, and Josef Kermisz, trans. Stanislaw Staron et al. (Chicago: Ivan R. Dee, 1979), p. 191.

22. Oskar Rosenfeld, *In the Beginning Was the Ghetto: Notebooks from Lodz*, ed. Hanna Loewy, trans. Brigitte M. Goldstein (Evanston, IL: Northwestern University Press, 2002), p. 109.

23. Epstein, "Writing about the Holocaust," p. 261, referring to his earlier essay "The Reality of Evil," *Partisan Review* 43 (1976): 639–40.

24. Sidra DeKoven Ezrahi, *By Words Alone: The Holocaust in Literature* (University of Chicago Press, 1980), p. 49.

25. Tadeusz Borowski, *This Way to the Gas, Ladies and Gentlemen* (1959), trans. Barbara Vedder (1967; repr. New York: Penguin 1976), pp. 143–46.

26. Otto Friedrich, *The Kingdom of Auschwitz* (1982; repr. New York: Harper Perennial, 1994), pp. 27–28.

27. Sara Nomberg-Przytyk, *Auschwitz: True Tales from a Grotesque Land*, trans. Roslyn Hirsch, ed. Eli Pfefferkorn and David H. Hirsch (Chapel Hill: University of North Carolina Press, 1985), pp. 107–109.

28. Kirsty Chatwood, "Schillinger and the Dancer: Representing Agency and Sexual Violence in Holocaust Testimonies," in Sonja M. Hedgepeth and

Rochelle G. Saidel (eds.), *Sexual Violence Against Jewish Women During the Holocaust* (Waltham: Brandeis University Press, 2010), p. 63.

29. Ota Kraus and Erich Kulka, *The Death Factory: Document on Auschwitz* (1946), trans. Stephen Jolly (Oxford: Pergamon Press, 1966), p. 155.

30. Wieslaw Kielar, *Anus Mundi: 1,500 Days in Auschwitz/Birkenau* (1972), trans. Susanne Flatauer (New York: Times Books, 1980), pp. 178–79.

31. Abraham and Shlomo Dragon, "Together – in Despair and Hope," in Gideon Greif, *We Wept Without Tears: Testimonies of the Jewish Sonderkommando from Auschwitz* (German edn. 1995; New Haven, CT: Yale University Press, 2005), pp. 161–63.

32. Ya'akov Silberberg, "One Day in the Crematorium Felt Like a Year," in Greif, *We Wept Without Tears*, p. 325.

33. Stanislaw Jankowski, "Deposition" (1945), in Jadwiga Bezwinska (ed.), *Amidst a Nightmare of Crime: Manuscripts of Members of the Sonderkommando*, trans. Krystyna Michalik (Oswiecim: Publications of State Museum at Oswiecim, 1973), pp. 55–56.

34. Zalmen Gradowski, "The Czech Transport: A Chronicle of the Auschwitz Sonderkommando," in David G. Roskies (ed.), *The Literature of Destruction: Jewish Responses to Catastrophe* (New York: The Jewish Publication Society, 1988), p. 549.

35. Janda Weiss, "Experiences of a Fifteen-Year-Old in Birkenau," in *The Buchenwald Report* (1945), trans. David A. Hackett (Boulder, CO: Westview Press, 1995), p. 350; Eugene Kogon, *The Theory and Practice of Hell*, trans. Heinz Norden (1950; repr. New York: Berkley Books, 1980), p. 240.

36. Reuben Ainsztein, *Jewish Resistance in Nazi-Occupied Eastern Europe* (London: Paul Elek, 1974), pp. 795–96.

37. "Transport (The Polish Major's Report)," in *German Extermination Camps: Auschwitz and Birkenau* (Washington, DC: War Refugee Board, 1944), p. 14; Martin Gilbert, *The Holocaust: A History of the Jews of Europe During the Second World War* (New York: Holt, Rinehart and Winston, 1985), p. 621.

38. Danuta Czech, *Auschwitz Chronicle, 1939–1945: From the Archives of the Auschwitz Memorial and the German Federal Archives*, trans. anon. (1990; repr. New York: Owl Books, 1997), p. 513.

39. Danuta Czech, "Appendix II: Chronology of the Important Events at Auschwitz-Birkenau," in Rudolph Höss, *Death Dealer: the Memoirs of the SS Kommandant at Auschwitz*, ed. Steven Paskuly and trans. Andrew Pollinger (1992; repr. New York: Da Capo, 1996), pp. 355–56.

40. Filip Müller, *Eyewitness Auschwitz* (1979), trans. Suzanne Flatauer (Chicago: Ivan R. Dee, 1999), pp. 87–89.

41. Yehuda Bauer, Foreword to Müller, *Eyewitness Auschwitz*, p. ix.

42. Arnost Lustig, *A Prayer for Katerina Horovitzova* (1973), trans. Jeanne Nemcova (London: Quartet Books, 1990), p. 152.

43. Ibid., pp. 161, 164.

44. S. Lillian Kremer, *Witness Through the Imagination: Jewish American Fiction* (Detroit: Wayne State University Press, 1989).

Guide to further reading

Primary sources are generally listed in chronological order; secondary sources are listed in alphabetical order. The chronological sequence of primary texts reinforces the chronological overview set forth in most of the chapters. This approach enables readers to quickly see that Holocaust literature did not begin in the 1960s, which continues to be a widely held mistaken assumption. To be sure, the volume's chapters offer a corrective, showing that literary response emerged during the war and in the early years following its end. The chronological listing of primary texts underscores this crucial point and relays it visually in a way that the chapters cannot.

INTRODUCTION
Primary sources

Huberband, Rabbi Shimon. *Kiddush Hashem: Jewish Religious and Cultural Life in Poland During the Holocaust*, trans. David E. Fishman, ed. Jeffrey S. Gurock and Robert S. Hirt. Hoboken, NJ: Ktav; New York: Yeshiva University Press, 1987.

Wasserman, Rabbi Elchonon. "Tractate: The Onset of the Messiah." In Steven Katz, Shlomo Biderman, and Gershon Greenberg (eds.), *Wrestling with God: Jewish Theological Responses During and After the Holocaust*. New York: Oxford University Press, 2007, pp. 29–38.

Ehrenreich, Rabbi Shlomo Zalman. "What I Preached on [the Festival of] Simhat Torah 4 October, 1942." In Steven Katz, Shlomo Biderman, and Gershon Greenberg (eds.), *Wrestling with God: Jewish Theological Responses During and After the Holocaust*. New York: Oxford University Press, 2007, pp. 61–72.

Rabinowitz, Rabbi Baruch. "Miracle by Miracle." In Esther Farbstein (ed.), *The Forgotten Memoirs*. Brooklyn: Shaar, 2011, pp. 317–43.

Zapruder, Alexandra, ed. *Salvaged Pages: Young Writers' Diaries of the Holocaust*. New Haven, CT: Yale University Press, 2002.

Minco, Margo, *Bitter Herbs: A Little Chronicle* [1957], trans. Roy Edwards. London: Penguin, 1991.

Kiš, Danilo. *Hourglass* [1972], trans. Ralph Mannheim. New York: Farrar, Straus and Giroux, 1990.

    Homo Poeticus: Essays and Interviews, ed. Susan Sontag. New York: Farrar, Straus and Giroux, 1995.

Semprun, Jorge. *The Long Voyage* [1963], trans. Richard Seaver. New York: Grove, 1964.

    What a Beautiful Sunday! [1980], trans. Alan Sheridan. San Diego: Harcourt Brace Jovanovich, 1982.

    Literature or Life [1994], trans. Linda Coverdale. New York: Viking, 1997.

Wiesel, Elie. *Night* [1956]. New York: Hill and Wang, 1960.

    The Gates of the Forest [1964], trans. Francis Freneye. New York: Holt, Rinehart, and Winston, 1966.

    Legends of Our Time [1966], trans. New York: Holt, Rinehart, and Winston, 1968.

    A Jew Today [1977], trans. Marion Wiesel. New York: Random House, 1978.

    The Fifth Son [1983], trans. Marion Wiesel. New York: Summit, 1985.

    All Rivers Run to the Sea: Memoirs [1994]. New York: Knopf, 1995.

    The Sonderberg Case [2008], trans. Catherine Temerson. New York: Knopf, 2010.

Secondary sources

Felstiner, John. *Paul Celan: Poet, Survivor, Jew.* New Haven, CT: Yale University Press, 1995.

Friedländer, Saul. *The Years of Extermination: Nazi Germany and the Jews, 1939–1945.* New York: HarperCollins, 2007.

1 WARTIME VICTIM WRITING IN EASTERN EUROPE

Primary sources

Adler, Stanisław. *In the Warsaw Ghetto 1949–1943: An Account of a Witness*, trans. Sara Chmielewska Philip. Jerusalem: Yad Vashem, 1982.

Auerbach, Rachel. "Yizkor, 1943," trans. Leonard Wolf. In David G. Roskies (ed.), *The Literature of Destruction: Jewish Responses to Catastrophe.* Philadelphia: Jewish Publication Society of America, 1989, pp. 459–64.

Davidson Draenger, Gusta. *Justyna's Narrative*, ed. and intro. Eli Pfefferkorn and David H. Hirsch, trans. Roslyn Hirsch and David H. Hirsch. Amherst: University of Massachusetts Press, 1996.

Draenger, Shimshon. *Hechalutz Halochem: bit'on hano'ar hayehudi hahalutsi bemahteret Krakov, ogust-oktober 1943*, ed. Michal Uffenheimer and Tsvi Oren, trans. Tsvi Arad. 2nd rev. edn. Israel: Beit Lohamei Hageta'ot, 2006.

Goldin, Leyb. "Chronicle of a Single Day," trans. Elinor Robinson. In Roskies (ed.), *Literature of Destruction*, pp. 424–34.

Gradowski, Zalmen. "Fartseykhenungen." In Ber Mark (ed.), *Megeles Oysvits*. Tel-Aviv: Yisroel-bukh, 1977, pp. 288–346.

In harts fun genem: a dokument fun oyshvitser zonder-komando, 1944. Prefaces by David Sfard and Yehoshue Wygodski, ed. Chaim Wolnerman. Jerusalem: Chaim Wolnerman, 1977.

"Writings." In *The Scrolls of Auschwitz*, trans. Sharon Neemani. Adapted from the original Yiddish text. Tel Aviv: Am Oved, 1985, pp. 173–205.

"The Czech Transport: A Chronicle of the Auschwitz Sonderkommando," trans. Robert Wolf. In Roskies (ed.), *Literature of Destruction*, pp. 548–64.

Kalmanovitsh, Zelig. "Three Sermons," trans. Shlomo Noble. In Roskies (ed.), *Literature of Destruction*, pp. 509–13.

Kaplan, Chaim A. *Scroll of Agony: The Warsaw Diary of Chaim A. Kaplan*, ed. and trans. Abraham I. Katsh. 2nd rev. edn. New York: Colliers, 1973.

Katzenelson, Yitzhak. *Vittel Diary [22.5.43–16.9.43]*, trans. Myer Cohen. Israel: Ghetto Fighters' House, 1964.

Yidishe geto-ksovim Varshe 1940–1943, ed. Yechiel Szeintuch. Tel Aviv: Beit Lohamei Hageta'ot and Hakibbutz Hameuchad, 1984.

Lewin, Abraham. *A Cup of Tears: A Diary of the Warsaw Ghetto*, ed. and intro. Antony Polonsky, trans. Christopher Hutton. Oxford and New York: Basil Blackwell in association with the Institute for Polish-Jewish Studies, Oxford, 1988.

Opoczynski, Peretz. "The Jewish Letter Carrier," trans. E. Chase. In Jacob Glatstein, Israel Knox, and Samuel Margoshes (eds.), *Anthology of Holocaust Literature*. Philadelphia: Jewish Publication Society of America, 1969, pp. 57–70.

"Smuggling in the Warsaw Ghetto," trans. Adah B. Fogel. In Lucy S. Dawidowicz (ed.), *A Holocaust Reader*. New York: Behrman House, 1976, pp. 197–207.

"House No. 21," trans. Robert Wolf. In Roskies (ed.), *Literature of Destruction*, pp. 408–24.

Peretz, I. L. "Three Gifts." In Ruth R. Wisse (ed. and intro.), *The I. L. Peretz Reader*. 2nd rev. edn. New Haven, CT: Yale University Press, 2002, pp. 222–30.

Perle, Yehoshue. "Khurbn Varshe." In Leyb Olicki (ed.), *Tsvishn lebn un toyt*. Warsaw: Yidish bukh, 1955, pp. 100–41.

"4580," trans. Elinor Robinson. In Roskies (ed.), *Literature of Destruction*, pp. 450–54.

Ringelblum, Emanuel. "Oyneg Shabbes," trans. Elinor Robinson. In Roskies (ed.), *Literature of Destruction*, pp. 386–98.

Polish-Jewish Relations During the Second World War. Foreword by Yehuda Bauer, ed. Joseph Kermish and Shmuel Krakowski, trans. Dafna Allon, Danuta Dabrowska, and Dana Keren. Evanston, IL: Northwestern University Press, 1992.

Rosenfeld, Oskar. *In the Beginning Was the Ghetto*, ed. and intro. Hanno Loewy, trans. Brigitte M. Goldstein. Evanston, IL: Northwestern University Press, 2002.

Rudashevski, Yitskhok. *Diary of the Vilna Ghetto June 1941–April 1943*, ed. and trans. Percy Matenko. Tel Aviv: Ghetto Fighters' House and Hakibbutz Hameuchad, 1973.

Shayevitsh, Simkhe-Bunem. "Lekh-lekho," trans. Leah Robinson. In Roskies (ed.), *Literature of Destruction*, pp. 520–30.

Sutzkever, Abraham. *Lider fun yam hamoves: fun vilner geto, vald, un vander*. Tel Aviv and New York: Remembrance Award Library, 1968.

"No Sad Songs Please," trans. C. K. Williams. In Roskies (ed.), *Literature of Destruction*, pp. 500–501.

"Song for the Last," trans. C. K. Williams. In Roskies (ed.), *Literature of Destruction*, pp. 97–99.

"Teacher Mira." In *A. Sutzkever: Selected Poetry and Prose*, intro. Benjamin Harshav, trans. Barbara and Benjamin Harshav. Berkeley: University of California Press, 1991, pp. 160–62.

Szlengel, Władysław. "Things," trans. John R. Carpenter. *Chicago Review* 52 (Autumn 2006): 283–86.

Tenenbaum-Tamaroff, Mordecai. *Dapim min hadelekah pirke yoman, mikhtavim ureshimot*, ed. Bronka Klibanski and Zvi Szner. 2nd rev. edn. Yad Vashem: Beit Lohamei Hagetta'ot and Hakibbutz Hameuchad, 1987.

Wygodski, Yehoshua [Stanysław]. "A vort fun a gevezenem osir in Oyshvits." In Zelman Gradowski, *In harts fun genem: a dokument fun oyshvitser zonderkomando, 1944*, ed. Chaim Wolnerman. Preface by David Sfard. Jerusalem: Chaim Wolnerman, 1977, pp. 9–15.

Zelkowicz, Josef. "Twenty-Five Live Chickens and One Dead Document," trans. Joachim Neugroschel. In Alan Adelson and Robert Lapides (eds.), *Lodz Ghetto: Inside a Community under Siege*. New York: Viking, 1989, pp. 62–67.

Secondary sources

Cohen, Nathan. "Diaries of the Sonderkommando." In Yisrael Gutman and Michael Berenbaum (eds.), *Anatomy of the Auschwitz Death Camp*. Bloomington: Indiana University Press, 1994, pp. 522–34.

Engel, David. "'Will They Dare?': Perceptions of Threat in Diaries from the Warsaw Ghetto." In Robert Moses Shapiro (ed.), *Holocaust Chronicles: Individualizing the Holocaust Through Diaries and Other Contemporaneous Personal Accounts*. Intro. Ruth R. Wisse. Hoboken, NJ: Ktav, 1999, pp. 71–82.

Garbarini, Alexandra. *Numbered Days: Diaries and the Holocaust*. New Haven, CT and London: Yale University Press, 2006.

Kassow, Samuel David. *Who Will Write Our History? Emanuel Ringelblum, the Warsaw Ghetto, and the Oyneg Shabes Archive*. Bloomington: Indiana University Press, 2007.

Miron, Dan. *The Image of the Shtetl and Other Studies of Modern Jewish Literary Imagination*. Syracuse University Press, 2000.

Polonsky, Antony. Introduction to Abraham Lewin, *A Cup of Tears: A Diary of the Warsaw Ghetto*, ed. Antony Polonsky, trans. Christopher Hutton. Oxford and New York: Basil Blackwell in association with the Institute for Polish-Jewish Studies, Oxford, 1988, pp. 1–54.

Roskies, David G. *The Jewish Search for a Usable Past*. Bloomington: Indiana University Press, 1999.

2 WARTIME VICTIM WRITING IN WESTERN EUROPE

Primary sources

Berr, Hélène. *The Journal of Hélène Berr*, trans. David Bellos. New York: Weinstein Books, 2008.

Feiner, Hertha. *Before Deportation: Letters from a Mother to Her Daughters, January 1939–December 1942*, ed. Karl Heins Jahke, trans. Margot Bettaure Dembo. Evanston, IL: Northwestern University Press, 1999.

Flinker, Moshe. *Young Moshe's Diary: The Spiritual Torment of a Jewish Boy in Nazi Europe*, intro. Shaul Esh and Geoffrey Wigoder. Jerusalem: Yad Vashem, 1971.

Frank, Anne. *The Diary of a Young Girl*, trans. B. M. Mooyart-Doubleday. New York: Modern Library, 1952.

  The Diary of Anne Frank: Revised Critical Edition, trans. Arnold J. Pomerans, B. M. Mooyart-Doubleday, and Susan Massotty. New York: Doubleday, 2003.

Herzberg, Abel J. *Between Two Streams: A Diary from Bergen-Belsen*, trans. Jack Santcross. London: I. B. Tauris, 1997.

Hillesum, Etty. *Etty: The Letters and Diaries of Etty Hillesum, 1941–1943*, trans. Arnold J. Pomerans. Grand Rapids, MI: Eerdmans, 2002.

Kessel, Joseph. *Army of Shadows*, trans. Haakon Chevalier. London: Cresset Press, 1944.

Klemperer, Victor. *I Will Bear Witness: A Diary of the Nazi Years, 1933–1941*, trans. Martin Chalmers. New York: Random House, 1998.

  I Will Bear Witness: A Diary of the Nazi Years, 1942–1945, trans. Martin Chalmers. New York: Random House, 1999.

Kolmar, Gertrude. *A Jewish Mother from Berlin* and *Susanna*, trans. Brigitte M. Goldstein. New York: Holmes and Meier, 1997.

  My Gaze Is Turned Inward: Letters, 1934–1943, ed. Johanna Woltmann, trans. Brigitte M. Goldstein. Evanston, IL: Northwestern University Press, 2004.

Lévinas, Emmanuel. *Existence and Existents*, trans. Alphonso Lingis. The Hague: Martinus Nijhoff, 1978.

Mechanicus, Philip. *Year of Fear: A Jewish Prisoner Waits for Auschwitz*, trans. Irene S. Gibbons. New York: Hawthorne, 1964.

Némirovsky, Irène. *Suite française*, trans. Sandra Smith. New York: Alfred A. Knopf, 2006.

Wessels, Benjamin Leo. *Ben's Story: Holocaust Letters with Selections from the Dutch Underground Press*, ed. Kees W. Bolle. Carbondale: Southern Illinois University Press, 2001.

Secondary sources

Patterson, David. *Along the Edge of Annihilation: The Collapse and Recovery of Life in the Holocaust Diary*. Seattle: University of Washington Press, 1999.

Patterson, David, Alan L. Berger, and Sarita Cargas, eds. *Encyclopedia of Holocaust Literature*. Westport, CT: Oryx Press, 2002.

Prose, Francine. *Anne Frank: The Book, the Life, the Afterlife*. New York: HarperCollins, 2009.

Riggs, Thomas, ed. *Reference Guide to Holocaust Literature*. Farmington Hills, MI: St. James Press, 2002.

Rosenfeld, Alvin. "Popularization and Memory: The Case of Anne Frank." In Peter Hayes (ed.), *Lessons and Legacies: The Meaning of the Holocaust in a Changing World*. Evanston, IL: Northwestern University Press, 1991, pp. 243–37.

Syrkin, Marie. "Holocaust Literature I: Diaries." In Byron L. Sherwin and Susan G. Ament (eds.), *Encountering the Holocaust: An Interdisciplinary Survey*. Chicago: Impact Press, 1979, pp. 226–43.

Weiss, Jonathan. *Irène Némirovsky: Her Life and Works*. Stanford University Press, 2006.

Weiss, Renata Laqueur. *Writing in Defiance: Concentration Camp Diaries in Dutch, French and German*. Ann Arbor, MI: University Microfilms, 1971.

3 THE HOLOCAUST AND ITALIAN LITERATURE

Primary sources

Malaparte, Curzio. *Kaputt* [1944]. New York: New York Review of Books, 2005.

Debenedetti, Giacomo. *October 16, 1943; Eight Jews* [1945]. Notre Dame: University of Notre Dame Press, 2001.

Saba, Umberto. *The Stories and Recollections of Umberto Saba* [1946]. New York: Sheep Meadow Press, 1993.

De Benedetti, Leonardo and Primo Levi. *Auschwitz Report* [1946]. New York: Verso, 2006.

Levi, Primo. *If This Is a Man* [1947]. New York: Orion, 1959.

Millu, Liana. *Smoke over Birkenau* [1947]. Philadelphia: Jewish Publication Society of America, 1991.

Bassani, Giorgio. *Five Stories of Ferrara* [1956]. New York: Harcourt Brace Jovanovich, 1971.

The Garden of the Finzi-Continis [1962]. London: Quartet, 1978.

Ginzburg, Natalia. *Family Sayings* [1963]. New York: Arcade, 1987.

Morante, Elsa. *History* [1974]. New York: Knopf, 1977.

Levi, Primo. *Shema* [1974]. London: Menard Press, 1976.

Levi, Primo. *Moments of Reprieve* [1981]. New York: Summit, 1986.

Pressburger, Giorgio and Nicola Pressburger. *Homage to the Eighth District* [1986]. London: Readers International, 1990.

Levi, Primo. *The Drowned and the Saved* [1986]. New York: Summit, 1988.

Dan Segre, Vittorio. *Memoirs of a Fortunate Jew* [1987]. University of Chicago Press, 2008.

Tedeschi, Giuliana. *There Is a Place on Earth* [1988]. New York: Pantheon Books, 1992.

Maurensig, Paolo. *The Lüneberg Variation* [1993]. New York: Farrar, Straus and Giroux, 1997.

Loy, Rosetta. *First Words* [1997]. New York: Metropolitan, 2000.

Maurensig, Paolo. *Canone inverso* [1997]. New York: Holt, 1998.

Sonnino, Piera. *This Has Happened* [2004]. New York: Palgrave Macmillan, 2006.

Secondary sources

Gordon, Robert S. C., ed. *Cambridge Companion to Primo Levi*. Cambridge University Press, 2005.

  The Holocaust in Italian Culture, 1944–2010. Stanford University Press, 2012.

Levi, Primo. *The Voice of Memory Interviews 1961–1987*. New York: New Press, 2001.

Sodi, Risa. *Narrative and Imperative: The First Fifty Years of Italian Holocaust Writing 1944–1994*. New York: Peter Lang, 2007.

Steinberg, Jonathan. *All or Nothing: The Axis and the Holocaust 1941–43*. London: Routledge, 1990.

Stille, Alexander. *Benevolence and Betrayal: Five Italian Jewish Families under Fascism*. New York: Summit Books, 1991.

Zimmerman, Joshua, ed. *Jews in Italy under Fascist and Nazi Rule, 1922–1945*. Cambridge University Press, 2005.

Zuccotti, Susan. *The Italians and the Holocaust: Persecution, Rescue and Survival*. London: Basic Books, 1987.

4 GERMAN LITERATURE AND THE HOLOCAUST

Primary sources

Seghers, Anna. *Das siebte Kreuz* (The Seventh Cross). Mexico City: El Libro Libre, 1942.

  Der Ausflug der toten Mädchen (The Outing of the Dead Girls). Mexico City: El Libro Libre, 1943.

Frankl, Viktor. *Trotzdem ja zum Leben sagen* (Man's Search for Meaning). Vienna: Deuticke, 1946.

Mann, Thomas. *Doktor Faustus* (Doctor Faustus). Frankfurt am Main: S. Fischer Verlag, 1947.

Sachs, Nelly. "Schornsteine" ("O the Chimneys"). In *In den Wohnungen des Todes*. Berlin: Aufbau Verlag, 1947.

Celan, Paul. "Todesfuge" ("Deathfugue"). In *Der Sand aus den Urnen*. Vienna: Agathon, 1948.

Weil, Grete. *Ans Ende der Welt* (At the World's End). Berlin: Volk und Welt, 1949.

Böll, Heinrich. *Wo warst du, Adam?* (Where Were You, Adam?). Opladen: Middelhauve, 1951.

Adler, H. G. *Theresienstadt.* Tübingen: Mohr, 1955.

Andersch, Alfred. *Sansibar oder der letzte Grund* (Flight to Afar). Olten and Freiburg: Walter-Verlag, 1957.

Apitz, Bruno. *Nackt unter Wölfen* (Naked among Wolves). Halle: Mitteldeutscher Verlag, 1958.

Adler, H. G. *Die Reise* (The Journey). Bonn: Verlag Bibliotheca Christina, 1962.

Hochhuth, Rolf. *Der Stellvertreter* (The Deputy). Hamburg: Rowohlt Verlag, 1963.

Hilsenrath, Edgar. *Nacht* (Night). Munich: Kindler Verlag, 1964.

Weiss, Peter. *Die Ermittlung* (The Investigation). Frankfurt am Main: Suhrkamp, 1965.

Améry, Jean. *Jenseits von Schuld und Sühne.* Munich: Szczesny, 1966.

Becker, Jurek. *Jakob der Lügner* (Jacob the Liar). Berlin: Aufbau Verlag, 1969.

Wander, Franz. *Der siebente Brunnen* (The Seventh Well). Berlin: Aufbau Verlag, 1971.

Klüger, Ruth. *weiter leben* (Still Alive). Göttingen: Wallstein, 1992.

Sebald, W. G. *Die Ausgewanderten* (The Emigrants). Frankfurt am Main: Eichborn Verlag, 1992.

Klemperer, Victor. *Tagebücher 1933–1945* (I Will Bear Witness: A Diary of the Nazi Years). Berlin: Aufbau Verlag, 1995.

Schlink, Bernhard. *Der Vorleser* (The Reader). Zurich: Diogenes, 1995.

Sebald, W. G. *Austerlitz.* Munich: Hanser Verlag, 2001.

Rotenberg, Stella. *Shards.* Edinburgh: Centre for the History of Ideas in Scotland, 2003.

Secondary sources

Arnold, Heinz-Ludwig, ed. *Literatur und Holocaust.* Munich: text + kritik, 1999.

Bos, Pascale R. *German-Jewish Literature in the Wake of the Holocaust: Grete Weil, Ruth Klüger, and the Politics of Address.* New York: Palgrave Macmillan, 2005.

Braese, Stephan, Holger Gehle, and Doron Kiesel, eds. *Deutsche Nachkriegsliteratur und der Holocaust.* Frankfurt am Main: Campus Verlag, 1998.

Cernyak-Spatz, Susan E. *German Holocaust Literature.* New York, Bern, Frankfurt am Main, and Paris: Peter Lang, 1985.

Gilman, Sander L. *Inscribing the Other.* Lincoln: University of Nebraska Press, 1991.

Herzog, Todd. *Rebirth of a Culture: Jewish Identity and Jewish Writing in Germany and Austria Today.* New York and Oxford: Berghahn Books, 2008.

Kiedaisch, Petra, ed. *Lyrik nach Auschwitz? Adorno und die Dichter.* Stuttgart: Reclam, 1993.

Köppen, Manuel and Klaus R. Scherpe, eds. *Bilder des Holocaust. Literatur-Film-Bildende Kunst.* Cologne: Böhlau, 1997.

Lorenz, Dagmar C. G. *Verfolgung bis zum Massenmord: Holocaust-Diskurse in deutscher Sprache aus der Sicht der Verfolgten.* New York: Lang, 1992.

McGlothlin, Erin. *Second-Generation Holocaust Literature: Legacies of Survival and Perpetration*. Rochester, NY: Camden House, 2006.

Reiter, Andrea. *"Auf daß sie entsteigen der Dunkelheit": Die literarische Bewältigung von KZ-Erfahrung*. Vienna: Löcker, 1995.

Narrating the Holocaust. London: Continuum, 2005.

Rosenfeld, Alvin. *A Double Dying: Reflections on Holocaust Literature*. Bloomington: Indiana University Press, 1980.

Schlant, Ernestine. *The Language of Silence: West German Literature and the Holocaust*. New York, Routledge, 1999.

Schmitz, Helmut. *On Their Own Terms: The Legacy of National Socialism in Post-1990 German Fiction*. Birmingham University Press, 2004.

5 HEBREW LITERATURE OF THE HOLOCAUST
Primary sources

Agnon, S. Y. *A Guest for the Night* [Hebrew, 1939]. New York: Schocken Books, 1968.

Ka-Tzetnik. *Salamandra*. Tel Aviv: Dvir, 1946.

Greenberg, Uri Tzvi. *Streets of the River*. Jerusalem: Schocken Books, 1950.

Ka-Tzetnik. *House of Dolls* [Hebrew, 1953]. New York: Simon and Schuster, 1955.

Goldberg, Leah. "Lady of the Castle" [Hebrew, 1955], trans. T. Carmi. In Michael Taub (ed.), *Israeli Holocaust Drama*. New York: Syracuse University Press, 1996, pp. 21–78.

Ka-Tzetnik. *Piepel: Kronikah shel Mishpahat Yehudi ba-Meah ha-Esrim*. Tel Aviv: Am-ha-Sefer, 1961.

Tomer, Ben Zion. *Children of the Shadows* [Hebrew, 1962], trans. Hillel Halkin. In Taub (ed.), *Israeli Holocaust Drama*, pp. 127–85.

Amichai, Yehuda. *Not of This Time, Not of This Place* [Hebrew, 1963], trans. Shlomo Katz. New York: Harper and Row, 1968.

Gouri, Haim. *The Chocolate Deal* [Hebrew, 1965]. New York: Holt, 1968.

Bartov, Hanokh. *The Brigade* [Hebrew, 1965]. New York: Holt, 1968.

Kaniuk, Yoram. *Adam Resurrected* [Hebrew, 1969]. New York: Harper, 1978.

Kovner, Abba. *Selected Poems of Abba Kovner*, ed. Stephen Spender. Harmondsworth: Penguin, 1971.

Ka-Tzetnik. *Shaon*. Yerushalayim: Mosad Bialik, 1972.

Ka-Tzetnik. *ha-'Imut: Robed Sheni*. [Israel]: A. Levin Ephstin-Modan, 1975.

Appelfeld, Aharon. *The Age of Wonders* [Hebrew, 1978]. Boston: Godine, 1981.

Badenheim 1939 [Hebrew, 1979]. Boston: Godine, 1980.

Pagis, Dan. *Points of Departure*. Philadelphia: Jewish Publication Society of America, 1981.

Sobol, Joshua. *Ghetto* [Hebrew, 1983]. Tel Aviv: Institute for the Translation of Hebrew, 1986.

Appelfeld, Aharon. *Tzili: The Story of a Life*. New York: E. P. Dutton, 1983.

Lerner, Motti. "Kastner" [Hebrew, 1985], trans. Imre Goldstein. In Taub (ed.), *Israeli Holocaust Drama*, pp. 186–267.

Grossman, David. *See Under: Love* [Hebrew, 1986]. New York: Farrar, Straus and Giroux, 1989.

Semel, Nava. *Kova Zkhukhit.* Tel Aviv: Sifriyat Poalim, 1986.

Liebricht, Savyon. *Apples from the Desert* [Hebrew, 1987]. New York: Feminist Press, 1998.

Peleg, Dorit. *Unah: Roman.* Tel Aviv: ha-Kibutz ha-Meuhad, 1988.

Levi, Itamar. *Agadat ha-Agamim ha-Atsuvim.* Jerusalem: Keter, 1989.

Pagis, Dan. *Variable Directions.* San Francisco: North Point Press, 1989.

Hareven, Shulamit. *Twilight and Other Stories.* San Francisco: Mercury House, 1992.

Taub, Michael, ed. *Israeli Holocaust Drama.* Syracuse University Press, 1996.

Pagis, Dan. *Selected Poetry of Dan Pagis.* Berkeley: University of California Press, 1996.

Bukhan, Yaakov. *Yeled Shakuf.* Tel Aviv: Zemorah Bitan, 1998.

Gutfreund, Amir. *Our Holocaust* [Hebrew, 2000]. New Milford: Toby, 2006.

Semel, Nava. *And the Rat Laughed* [Hebrew, 2001]. Melbourne: Hybrid, 2008.

Someck, Ronny. *The Fire Stays in Red: Poems by Ronny Someck,* trans. Moshe Dor and Barbara Goldberg. Madison: University of Wisconsin, 2002.

Rivka Miriam. *These Mountains: Selected Poems of Rivka Miriam,* trans. Linda Zisquit. New Milford: Toby Press, 2009.

Secondary sources

Abramson, Glenda. *Drama and Ideology in Modern Israel.* Cambridge University Press, 1998.

Alexander, Edward. *The Resonance of Dust: Essays on Holocaust Literature and Jewish Fate.* Columbus: Ohio State University Press, 1979.

Alter, Robert. "The Israeli Scene: Confronting the Holocaust." In *After the Tradition: Essays on Modern Jewish Writing.* New York: Dutton, 1969.

Arendt, Hannah. *Eichmann in Jerusalem: A Report on the Banality of Evil.* New York: Viking Press, 1963.

Bartov, Omer. "Kitsch and Sadism in Ka-Tzetnik's Other Planet: Israeli Youth Imagine the Holocaust." *Jewish Social Studies* 3/2 (1997).

Budick, Emily Miller. *Aharon Appelfeld's Fiction: Acknowledging the Holocaust.* Bloomington: Indiana University Press, 2005.

Domb, Risa. *New Women's Writing from Israel.* Portland, OR: Valentine Mitchell, 1996.

Friedlander, Saul, ed. *Probing the Limits of Representation: Nazism and the "Final Solution."* Cambridge, MA: Harvard University Press, 1992.

Fuchs, Esther. *Women and the Holocaust: Narrative and Representation.* Lanham, MD: University Press of America, 1999.

Glasner-Heled, Galia. "Reader, Writer and Holocaust Literature: The Case of Ka-Tzetnik." *Israel Studies* 12/3 (2007): 109–33.

Hirsch, Marianne and Irene Kacandes, eds. *Teaching the Representation of the Holocaust.* New York: Modern Language Association, 2004.

Mazor, Yair. *Israeli Poetry of the Holocaust.* Madison, NJ: Farleigh Dickinson University Press, 2008

Mintz, Alan. *Hurban: Responses to Catastrophe in Hebrew Literature.* New York: Columbia, 1984.

Pelli, Moshe. *The Shadow of Death: Letters in Flames.* Lanham, MD: University Press of America, 2008.

Porat, Dina. *The Fall of a Sparrow: The Life and Times of Abba Kovner*, trans. and ed. Elizabeth Yuval. Stanford University Press, 2010.

Roskies, David. *The Literature of Destruction: Jewish Responses to Catastrophe.* Philadelphia: Jewish Publication Society of America, 1988.

Segev, Tom. *The Seventh Million: The Israelis and the Holocaust*, trans. Haim Watzmann. New York: Hill and Wang, 1993.

Sicher, Efraim, ed. *Breaking Crystal: Writing and Memory after Auschwitz.* Urbana: University of Illinois, 1998.

"The Return of the Past: The Intergenerational Transmission of Holocaust Memory in Israeli Fiction." *Shofar* **19**/2 (Winter 2001): 26–52.

Weingrad, Michael. *American Hebrew Literature: Writing Jewish National Identity in the United States.* Syracuse University Press, 2011.

Yablonka, Hanna. *The State of Israel vs. Adolf Eichmann.* New York: Schocken Books, 2004.

Yudkin, Leon. *Hebrew Literature in the Wake of the Holocaust.* Rutherford: Farleigh Dickinson University Press, 1993.

Yuter, Alan J. *The Holocaust in Hebrew Literature: From Genocide to Rebirth.* Port Washington: Associated Faculty Press, 1983.

Zerubavel, Yael. *Recovered Roots: Collective Memory and the Making of Israeli National Tradition.* University of Chicago Press, 1995.

6 THE HOLOCAUST AND POSTWAR YIDDISH LITERATURE

Primary sources

Leivick, H. *In treblinke bin ikh nit geven: Lider un poemes* (In Treblinka I Was Not: Poems). New York: CYCO Farlag, 1945.

Sutzkever, Abraham. *Vilner geto, 1941–1944* (Vilna Ghetto, 1941–1944). Paris: Farband fun di vilner in frankraykh, 1946.

Kolitz, Zvi. *Yosl Rakover Talks to God* [1946]. Afterword by Emanuel Levinas and Leon Wieseltier. New York: Pantheon Books, 1999.

Heschel, Abraham Joshua. *The Earth Is the Lord's: The Inner World of the Jew in East Europe* [1946]. New York: H. Schuman, 1950.

Strigler, Mordechai. *Maydanek.* Dos poylishe yidntum 20. Buenos Aires: Tsentral-Farband fun poylishe yidn in Argentine, 1947.

Auerbach, Rachel. "In the Fields of Treblinka" [1947]. In Alexander Donat (ed.), *Death Camp Treblinka: A Documentary.* New York: Holocaust Library, 1979, pp. 19–73.

Zeitlin, Aaron. *Gezamlte lider* (Collected Poems), 2 vols. New York: Matones, 1947.

Bergelson, Dovid. *Naye dertseylungen* (New Stories). Moscow: Emes, 1948.

Turkov, Jonas. *Azoy iz es geven: khurbn varshe* (That's How It Was: The Destruction of Warsaw). Dos poylishe yidntum 27. Buenos Aires: Tsentral-Farband fun poylishe yidn in Argentine, 1948.

Strigler, Mordechai. *In di fabrikn fun toyt* (In the Factories of Death). Dos poylishe yidntum 32. Buenos Aires: Tsentral-Farband fun poylishe yidn in Argentine, 1948.

Niger, Shmuel, ed. *Kidush hashem* (The Sanctification of the Name). New York: CYCO Farlag, 1948.

Rosenfarb, Chava. *Geto un andere lider: Oykh fragmentn fun tog-bukh* (Ghetto and Other Poems: Also Diary Fragments). Montreal: H. Hershman, 1948.

Rochman, Leib. *The Pit and the Trap: A Chronicle of Survival* [1949]. New York: Holocaust Library.

Turkov, Jonas. *In kamf farn lebn* (In Struggle for Life). Dos poylishe yidntum 53. Buenos Aires: Tsentral-Farband fun poylishe yidn in Argentine, 1949.

Strigler, Mordechai. *Verk "C."* Dos poylishe yidntum, 64–65. Buenos Aires: Tsentral-Farband fun poylishe yidn in Argentine, 1950.

Elberg, Yehuda. *Unter kuperne himln* (Under Copper Skies). Dos poylishe yidntum 73. Buenos Aires: Tsentral-Farband fun poylishe yidn in Argentine, 1951.

Strigler, Mordechai. *Goyroles* (Destinies). Dos poylishe yidntum, 85–86. Buenos Aires: Tsentral-Farband fun poylishe yidn in Argentine, 1952.

Shpiegl, Isaiah. *Ghetto Kingdom: Tales of the Lodz Ghetto* [1952]. Evanston, IL: Northwestern University Press, 1998.

Bryks, Rakhmiel. *Kiddush hashem* [1952]. New York: Behrman House, 1977.

Turkov, Jonas. *Farloshene shtern* (Extinguished Stars). Dos poylishe yidntum, 95–96. Buenos Aires: Tsentral-Farband fun poylishe yidn in Argentine, 1953.

Sutzkever, Abraham. *Griner akvarium: dertseylungen* [1953] (Green Aquarium: Stories). Jerusalem: Hebrew University, 1975.

Grade, Chaim. "My Struggle with Hersh Rasseyner." In Irving Howe and Eliezer Greenberg (eds.), *A Treasury of Yiddish Stories*. New York: Viking Press, 1954, pp. 579–606.

Ka-Tzetnik. *House of Dolls*. New York: Simon and Schuster, 1955.

Mark, Bernard, ed. *Tvishn lebn un toyt* (Between Life and Death). Warsaw: Yidish-bukh, 1955.

Grade, Chaim. *My Mother's Sabbath Days: A Memoir* [1955]. Northvale, NJ: Aronson, 1997.

Wiesel, Eliezer. *Un di velt hot geshvign* (And the World Was Silent). Dos poylishe yidntum 117. Buenos Aires: Tsentral-Farband fun poylishe yidn in Argentine, 1956.

Singer, Isaac Bashevis. *Shadows on the Hudson* [Serialized in *Forverts*, 1957–1958]. New York: Farrar, Straus and Giroux, 1998.

Turkov, Jonas. *Nokh der bafrayung: zikhroynes* (After the Liberation: Memoirs). Dos poylishe yidntum 145. Buenos Aires: Tsentral-Farband fun poylishe yidn in Argentine, 1959.

Molodowsky, Kadya. *Paper Bridges: Selected Poems of Kadya Molodowsky* [1962]. Detroit: Wayne State University Press, 1999.

Man, Mendel. *At the Gates of Moscow: A Novel.* New York: St. Martin's Press, 1963.

Zeitlin, Aaron. *Poems of The Holocaust and Poems of Faith* [1967], ed. and trans. Morris M. Faierstein. New York: iUniverse, 2007.

A. Sutzkever: Selected Poetry and Prose [1967]. Berkeley: University of Californa Press, 1991.

Rochman, Leib. *Mit blinde shrit iber der erd* (With Blind Steps over the Earth). Tel Aviv: Menorah, 1968.

Singer, Isaac Bashevis. *Enemies: A Love Story.* New York: Farrar, Straus and Giroux, 1972.

Auerbach, Rachel. *Varshever tshvoes* (Warsaw Testimonies). Tel Aviv: Yisroel-bukh, 1974.

Rochman, Leib. *Der mabl: dertseylungen* (The Flood: Stories). Jerusalem, 1979.

Sutzkever, Abraham. *Di ershte nakht in geto* (The First Night in the Ghetto). Tel Aviv: Farlag Di goldene Keyt, 1979.

Grade, Chaim. *Fun unter der erd* (From the Underground) [Serialized in *Forverts*, 1983].

Schekhtman, Eli. *Erev: roman* (Evening: Novel), 7 vols. Tel Aviv: Yisroel Bukh, 1983.

Sutzkever, Abraham. *Di nevue fun shvartsaplen: dertseylungen* (The Prophecy of the Pupils: Stories). Jerusalem: Hebrew University, 1989.

Glatshteyn, Yankev. *I Keep Recalling: The Holocaust Poems of Jacob Glatstein.* Hoboken, NJ: Ktav, 1993.

Rosenfarb, Chava. *Survivors: Seven Short Stories.* Toronto: Comorant Books, 2004.

Rosenfarb, Chava. *The Tree of Life.* Madison: University of Wisconsin Press, 2004.

Singer, Isaac Bashevis. *Collected Stories*, 3 vols., ed. Ilan Stavans. New York: Library of America, 2004.

Secondary sources

Aleksiun, Natalia, Gaby Finder, Anthony Polonsky, and Jan Schwarz, eds. "Memorializing the Holocaust." *POLIN 20: Studies in Polish Jewry* (2007).

Chaver, Yael. *What Must Be Forgotten: The Survival of Yiddish in Zionist Palestine.* Syracuse University Press, 2004.

Diner, Hasia. *We Remember with Reverence and Love: American Jews and the Myth of Silence after the Holocaust, 1945–1962.* New York University Press, 2009.

Estraykh, Gennady. *Yiddish in the Cold War.* London: Legenda, 2008.

Horowitz, Rosemary, ed. *Memorial Books of Eastern European Jewry: Essays on the History and Meanings of Yizker Volumes.* Jefferson, NC: McFarland Press, 2011.

Mintz, Alan. *Popular Culture and the Shaping of Holocaust Memory in America.* Seattle: University of Washington Press, 2001.

Norich, Anita. *Discovering Exile: Yiddish and Jewish American Culture During the Holocaust.* Stanford University Press, 2007.

Roskies, David. "Dividing the Ruins: Communal Memory in Yiddish and Hebrew." In David Cesarani and Eric J. Sundquist (eds.), *After the*

Holocaust: Challenging the Myth of Silence. London and New York: Routledge, 2012, pp. 67–82.

Schulman, Elias. *The Holocaust in Yiddish Literature*. New York: Workman's Circle, 1983.

Schwarz, Jan. *Survivors and Exiles: Yiddish Culture after the Holocaust*. Detroit: Wayne State University Press, forthcoming.

Shandler, Jeffrey. *Adventures in Yiddishland: Postvernacular Language and Culture*. Berkeley: University of California Press, 2006.

7 THE HOLOCAUST IN RUSSIAN LITERATURE

Primary sources

Selvinsky, Ilya. "Ya eto videl!" (I Saw This!). *Bol'shevik*. January 23, 1942; repr. *Krasnaia zvezda*, February 27, 1942: 3.

Grossman, Vasily. "Ukraine Without Jews" [1943], trans. Polly Zacadivker. *Jewish Quarterly* 217 (2011): 12–18.

"The Old Teacher" [1943]. In *The Road: Stories, Journalism, and Essays*, trans. Robert and Elizabeth Chandler with Olga Mukovnikova. New York: New York Review of Books, 2010, pp. 84–115.

Der Nister. *Korbones* (Victims). Moscow: Emes, 1943.

Grossman, Vasily. "The Hell of Treblinka" [1944]. In *The Road*, pp. 116–62.

Ehrenburg, Ilya. "Babi yar." *Novyi mir* (January 1945): 16.

Ehrenburg, Ilya and Vasily Grossman, eds. *The Complete Black Book of Russian Jewry* [1945], trans. and ed. David Patterson. New Brunswick, NJ: Transaction Publishers, 2002.

Ozerov, Lev. "Babi yar." *Oktiabr'* 3–4 (1946): 160–63; repr. in Ozerov's *Liven'*. Moscow: Molodaia gvardiia, 1947, pp. 25–32.

Ehrenburg, Ilya. *The Storm: A Novel* [1947], trans. Eric Hartley and Tatiana Shebunina. New York: Hutchinson International Authors, 1949.

Smoliar, Girsh. *Mstiteli getto* (Ghetto Avengers). Moscow: Emes, 1947.

Markish, Peretz. *Milkhome* (War) [1947]. Moscow: Emes, 1948.

Partizanskaia Druzhba: Vospominania of boevykh delakh partizan-evreev, uchastnikov Velikoi Otechestvennoi voiny (Partisan Friendship: Reminiscences on Wartime Deeds of Jewish Partisans of the Great Patriotic War). Moscow: Emes, 1948.

Meras, Icchokas. *Geltonas Lopas* (The Yellow Patch). Vilnius: Vaga, 1960.

Evtushenko, Evgeny. "Babi yar." *Literaturnaia gazeta* 4 (September 19, 1961): 4.

Rolnikaitė, Maria. *I Have to Tell You* [Yiddish, 1963]. *Ya dolzhna rasskazat' vam*. Moscow: Politizdat, 1965.

Meras, Icchokas. *Žemė visada gyva* (The Earth is Always Alive). Vilnius: Vaga, 1963. *Stalemate* [1963], trans. Jonas Zdanys. New York: Other Press, 2005.

Evtushenko, Evgeny. "Bratskaia GES." *Yunost'* 4 (1965).

Voznesensky, Andrei. "Zov Ozera" (The Call of the Lake). In *Den' poezii – 1966*. Moscow: Sovetskii pisatel', 1966, pp. 57–61.

Meras, Icchokas. *Ant ko laikosi pasaulis* (What the World Rests On: A Novel). Vilnius: Vaga, 1965.

Kuznetsov, Anatoly. *Babi Yar: A Documentary in the Form of a Novel* [1966], trans. David Floyd. New York: Farrar, Straus and Giroux, 1970.

Konstantinovsky, Ilya. *Srok davnosti* (The Statute of Limitations). Moscow: Sovetskii pisatel', 1966.

Markish, Peretz. *Trot fun doyres* (Footsteps of Generations). Moscow: Sovetskii pisatel', 1966.

Binkienė, Sofija, ed. *Ir be Ginklo Kariai* (Unarmed Warriors). Vilnius: Mintis, 1967.

Der Nister. *Regrowth: Seven Tales of Jewish Life Before, During, and After Nazi Occupation* [1969], trans. Eric Butler. Evanston, IL: Northwestern University Press, 2011.

Rybakov, Anatoly. *Heavy Sand* [1978], trans. Harold Shukman. New York: Viking, 1981.

Borshchagovsky, Aleksandr. *Damskii portnoi* (The Ladies' Tailor) [1980], a play.

Voznesensky, Andrei. "Rov" (The Ditch). *Yunost'* 7 (1986): 6–15.

Grossman, Vasily. *Life and Fate* [Russian, 1988], trans. Robert Chandler. New York: Harper and Row, 1986.

Slutsky, Boris. *Zapiski o voine* (Notes about the War), ed. Pyotr Gorelik. St. Petersburg: Logos, 2000.

Secondary sources

Altshuler, Mordechai. "The Unique Features of the Holocaust in the Soviet Union." In Yaacov Ro'i (ed.), *Jews and Jewish Life in Russia and the Soviet Union*. London: Frank Cass, 1995, pp. 171–88.

Bocharov, A. G. *Vasilii Grossman: Zhizn', tvorchestvo, sud'ba*. Moscow: Sovetskii pisatel', 1990.

Clowes, Edith. "Constructing the Memory of the Holocaust: The Ambiguous Treatment of Babii Yar in Soviet Literature." *Partial Answers* 3/2 (2005): 153–82.

Dobroszycki, Lucjan and Jeffrey S. Gurock, eds. *The Holocaust in the Soviet Union: Studies and Sources on the Destruction of the Jews in the Nazi-Occupied Territories of the USSR, 1941–1945*. Armonk, NY: M. E. Sharpe, 1993.

Garrard, John. "The Nazi Holocaust in the Soviet Union: Interpreting Newly Opened Russian Archives." *East European Jewish Affairs* 25/2 (1995): 3–40.

Garrard, John and Carol Garrard. *The Bones of Berdichev: The Life and Fate of Vasily Grossman*. New York: Free Press, 1996.

Gitelman, Zvi, ed. *Bitter Legacy: Confronting the Holocaust in the USSR*. Bloomington: Indiana University Press, 1997.

Hirszowicz, Lukasz. "The Holocaust in the Soviet Mirror." In Dobroszycki and Gurock (eds.), *Holocaust in the Soviet Union*, pp. 29–59.

Kandel, Felix. *Kniga vremion i sobytii*, vols. IV–VI. Jerusalem: Gesharim / Moscow: Mosty kul'tury, 2004.

Kovriguina, A. and A. Epelboin. *Littérature des ravins*. Paris: Robert Laffont, 2013.

Murav, Harriet. "Violating the Canon: Reading Der Nister with Vasilii Grossman." *Slavic Review* 66/3 (2007): 642–61.

Redlich, Shimon. *War, Holocaust, and Stalinism: A Documented Study of the Jewish Anti-Fascist Committee in the USSR*. Luxembourg: Harwood Academic Publishers, 1995.

Rosenshield, Gary. "Socialist Realism and the Holocaust: Jewish Life and Death in Anatoly Rybakov's *Heavy Sand*." *PMLA* 111/2 (1996): 240–55.

Rubenstein, Joshua. *Tangled Loyalties: The Life, and Times of Ilya Ehrenburg*. New York: Basic Books, 1996.

Rubenstein, Joshua and Vladimir P. Naumov, eds. *Stalin's Secret Pogrom*. New Haven, CT: Yale University Press, 2001.

Sheldon, Richard. "The Transformations of Babi Yar." In Terry L. Thompson and Richard Sheldon (eds.), *Soviet Society and Culture: Essays in Honor of Vera S. Dunham*. Boulder, CO: Westview, 1988, pp. 124–61.

Shrayer, Maxim D., ed. *An Anthology of Jewish-Russian Literature: Two Centuries of Dual Identity in Prose and Poetry*, 2 vols. Armonk, NY: M. E. Sharpe, 2007.

Toker, Leona. "Anatolii Kuznetsov." In *Holocaust Novelists: Dictionary of Literary Biography*, vol. 299, ed. Efraim Sicher. Detroit: Bruccoli, Clark, Layman (Gale), 2004, pp. 195–200.

8 THE HOLOCAUST IN ENGLISH-LANGUAGE LITERATURES

Primary sources

Klein, A. M. *The Hitleriad*. New York: New Directions, 1944.

Bellow, Saul. *The Victim*. New York: Vanguard, 1947.

Hersey, John. *The Wall*. New York: Alfred A. Knopf, 1950.

Klein, A. M. *The Second Scroll*. New York, Alfred A. Knopf, 1951.

Karmel, Ilona. *Stephania*. Boston: Houghton Mifflin, 1953.

Richler, Mordecai. *The Acrobats*. London: A. Deutsch, 1954.

Malamud, Bernard. "Lady of the Lake." In *The Magic Barrel*. New York: Random House, 1958.

Raphael, Frederic. *The Limits of Love*. London: Cassell, 1960.

Kreisel, Henry. *The Rich Man*. Toronto: McClelland and Stewart, 1961.

Silken, Jon. "The Coldness." In *The Re-Ordering of the Stones*. London: Chatto & Windus, 1961.

Uris, Leon. *Mila 18*. Garden City, NY: Doubleday, 1961.

Wallant, Edward Lewis. *The Pawnbroker*. New York: Harcourt Brace Jovanovich, 1961.

Malamud, Bernard. "The German Refugee." In *Idiots First*. New York: Dell Publishing Co., 1963.

Cohen, Leonard. *Flowers for Hitler*. Toronto: McClelland and Stewart, 1964.

Segal, Lore. *Other People's Houses*. New York: Harcourt, Brace & World, 1964.

Miller, Arthur. *Incident at Vichy*. New York: Viking, 1965.

Jacobson, Dan. *The Beginners*. New York: The Macmillan Company, 1966.

Ozick, Cynthia. *Trust.* New York: The New American Library, 1966.
Elman, Richard. *The 28th Day of Elul.* New York: Charles Scribner's Sons, 1967.
Potok, Chaim. *The Chosen.* New York: Simon and Schuster, 1967.
Elman, Richard. *Lilo's Diary.* New York: Charles Scribner's Sons, 1968.
Richler, Mordecai. *Cocksure.* London: Weidenfeld and Nicolson, 1968.
Elman, Richard. *The Reckoning: The Daily Ledgers of Newman Yagodah Advokat and Factor.* New York: Charles Scribner's Sons, 1969.
Karmel, Ilona. *An Estate of Memory.* Boston: Houghton Mifflin, 1969.
Rosen, Norma. *Touching Evil.* New York: Harcourt, Brace & World, 1969.
Bellow, Saul. *Mr. Sammler's Planet.* New York: Viking, 1970.
Ettinger, Elżbieta. *Kindergarten.* Boston: Houghton Mifflin, 1970.
Kreisel, Henry. *The Betrayal.* Toronto: McClelland and Stewart, 1971.
Layton, Irving. *The Collected Poems of Irving Layton.* Toronto: McClelland and Stewart, 1971.
Ozick, Cynthia. "The Suitcase." In *The Pagan Rabbi and Other Stories.* New York: Alfred A. Knopf, 1971.
Richler, Mordecai. *St. Urbain's Horseman* London: Weidenfeld and Nicolson, 1971.
Cohen, Arthur. *In the Days of Simon Stern.* New York: Random House, 1972.
Schaeffer, Susan Fromberg. *Anya.* New York: Macmillan, 1974.
Silken, Jon. "The People." In *The Principle of Water.* Cheadle, Cheshire: Carcanet/ New York: Wild & Wooley, 1974.
Reznikoff, Charles. *Holocaust.* Santa Rosa, CA: Black Sparrow Books, 1975.
Ozick, Cynthia. "Bloodshed." In *Bloodshed and Three Novellas.* New York: Alfred A. Knopf, 1976.
Raphael, Frederic. *The Glittering Prizes.* Harmondsworth: Penguin, 1976.
Heyen, William. *The Swastika Poems.* New York: Vanguard, 1977.
Barnes, Peter. *Auschwitz.* Second play in *Laughter!* London: Heinemann, 1978.
Epstein, Helen. *Children of the Holocaust.* New York: C. P. Putnam, 1979.
Epstein, Leslie. *King of the Jews.* New York: Avon Books, 1979.
Roth, Philip. *The Ghost Writer.* New York: Farrar, Straus and Giroux, 1979.
Styron, William. *Sophie's Choice.* New York: Random House, 1979.
Steiner, George. *Anno Domini.* London: Faber and Faber, 1980
Thomas, D. M. *The White Hotel.* Harmondsworth: Penguin, 1981.
Lieberman, Harold and Edith. "Throne of Straw." In Robert Skloot (ed.), *The Theater of the Holocaust.* Madison: University of Wisconsin Press, 1982.
Steiner, George. *The Portage to San Cristobal of A. H.* New York: Simon and Schuster, 1982.
Ozick, Cynthia. *The Cannibal Galaxy.* New York: Alfred A. Knopf, 1983.
Friedman, Thomas. *Damaged Goods.* Sag Harbor, NY: Permanent Press, 1984.
Heyen, William. *Erika, Poems of the Holocaust.* New York: Vanguard, 1984. 2nd rev. edn. St. Louis: Time Being Books, 2007.
Gershon, Karen. *Bread of Exile.* London: V. Gollancz, 1985.
Keneally, Thomas. *Schindler's List* [first published, *Schindler's Ark*, 1982]. London: Sceptre, 1986.

Spiegelman, Art. *Maus: A Survivor's Tale: My Father Bleeds History.* New York: Pantheon, 1986

Whitman, Ruth. *The Testing of Hanna Senesh.* Detroit: Wayne State University Press, 1986.

Kramer, Lotte. "At Dover Harbor." In *The Shoemaker's Wife and Other Poems.* Sutton: Hippopotamus Press, 1987.

Ozick, Cynthia. *The Messiah of Stockholm.* New York: Alfred A. Knopf, 1987.

Piercy, Marge. *Gone to Soldiers.* New York: Summit Books, 1987.

Brookner, Anita. *Latecomers.* London: Jonathan Cape, 1988.

Nissenson, Hugh. "The Pit." In *The Elephant and My Jewish Problem: Selected Stories and Journals, 1957–1987.* New York: Harper and Row, 1988.

Ozick, Cynthia. *The Shawl.* New York: Alfred A. Knopf, 1989.

Rothenberg, Jerome. *Khurbn and Other Poems.* New York: New Directions, 1989.

Klepfisz, Irena. *A Few Words in the Mother Tongue: Poems Selected and New (1971– 1990).* Portland, OR: Eight Mountain Press, 1990.

Miller, Arthur. *Playing for Time.* London: N. Hern, 1990.

Raphael, Lev. *Dancing on Tisha B'Av.* New York: St. Martin's Press, 1990.

Amis, Martin. *Time's Arrow.* Harmondsworth: Penguin, 1991.

Begley, Louis. *Wartime Lies.* London: Picado, 1991.

Rich, Adrienne. *An Atlas of the Difficult World: Poems 1988–1991.* New York: Norton, 1991.

Spiegelman, Art. *Maus II, A Survivor's Tale: And Here My Troubles Began.* New York: Pantheon, 1991.

Bukiet, Melvin Jules. *Stories of an Imaginary Childhood.* Evanston, IL: Northwestern University Press, 1992.

Harris, Robert. *Fatherland.* New York: Random House, 1992.

Goldstein, Rebecca. "The Legacy of Rachel Kadish." In *Strange Attractors.* New York: Viking, 1993.

Potok, Chaim. *Het Kanaal* (The Canal). Netherlands: BZZTôH, 1993.

Steinfeld, J. J. *Dancing at the Club Holocaust: Stories New and Selected.* Charlottetown, Prince Edward Island: Ragwood Press, 1993.

Gershon, Karen. *A Lesser Child: An Autobiography.* London: Dufour, 1994.

Kramer, Lotte. "Cocoon." In *Earthquake and Other Poems.* Ware, UK: Rockingham Press, 1994.

Miller, Arthur. *Broken Glass.* New York: Penguin, 1994.

Bukiet, Melvin Jules. *While the Messiah Tarries.* New York: Harcourt, Brace, 1995.

Hamburger, Michael. *Collected Poems 1941–1994.* London: Anvil Press, 1995.

Samuels, Diane. *Kindertransport.* New York: Plume, 1995.

Bukiet, Melvin Jules. *After.* New York: St. Martin's Press, 1996.

Karpf, Anne. *The War After: Living with the Holocaust.* London: Heinemann, 1996.

Michaels, Anne. *Fugitive Pieces.* London: Bloomsbury, 1996.

Pinter, Harold. *Ashes to Ashes.* London and Boston: Faber and Faber, 1996.

Rosenbaum, Thane. *Elijah Visible: Stories.* New York: St. Martin's Press, 1996.

Prose, Francine. "Guided Tours of Hell." In *Guided Tours of Hell: Novellas.* New York: Henry Holt and Co., 1997.

Skibell, Joseph. *A Blessing on the Moon*. Chapel Hill, NC: Algonquin Books, 1997.
Stollman, Aryeh Lev. *The Far Euphrates*. New York: Riverhead Books, 1997.
Rosenbaum, Thane. *Second Hand Smoke: A Novel*. New York: St. Martin's Press, 1999.
Chabon, Michael. *The Amazing Adventures of Kavalier and Clay*. New York: Random House, 2000.
Foer, Jonathan Safran. *Everything Is Illuminated*. New York: Houghton Mifflin Company, 2002.
Rosenbaum, Thane. *The Golems of Gotham: A Novel*. New York: HarperCollins, 2002.
Krauss, Nicole. *The History of Love*. New York: W. W. Norton, 2005.
Fishman, Charlese, ed. *Blood to Remember: American Poets on the Holocaust*. 2nd rev. edn. St. Louis: Time Being Books, 2007.
Jacobson, Howard. *Kalooki Nights*. New York: Simon and Schuster, 2007.
Reich, Tova. *My Holocaust*. New York: HarperCollins, 2007.
Krauss, Nicole. *Great House*. New York: W. W. Norton, 2010.

Secondary sources

Alexander, Edward. *The Resonance of Dust: Essays on Holocaust Literature and Jewish Fate*. Columbus: Ohio State University Press, 1979.
Alter, Robert. "Confronting the Holocaust." In *After the Tradition*. New York: E. P. Dutton & Co., 1969, pp. 163–80.
  Defenses of the Imagination: Jewish Writers and Modern Historical Crisis. Philadelphia: Jewish Publication Society of America, 1977.
Berger, Alan L. *Crisis and Covenant: The Holocaust in American Jewish Fiction*. State University of New York Press, 1985.
  Children of Job: American Second-Generation Witnesses to the Holocaust. Albany: State University of New York Press, 1997.
Bilik, Dorothy Seidman. *Immigrant Survivors: Post-Holocaust Consciousness in Recent Jewish American Literature*. Middletown, CT: Wesleyan University Press, 1981.
Brauner, David. *Post-War Jewish Fiction: Ambivalence, Self-Explanation and Transatlantic Connections*. Hampshire: Palgrave, 2001.
Brenner, Rachel Feldhay. "A. M. Klein and Mordecai Richler: Canadian Responses to the Holocaust." *Journal of Canadian Studies* 24/2 (1989): 65–77.
Budick, Emily Miller. "Acknowledging the Holocaust in Contemporary American Fiction and Criticism." In Efraim Sicher (ed.), *Breaking Crystal: Writing and Memory after Auschwitz*. Chicago: University of Illinois Press, 1998, pp. 160–69.
Burstein, Janet Handler. *Telling the Little Secrets: American Jewish Writing since the 1980s*. Madison: University of Wisconsin Press, 2006.
Flanzbaum, Hilene, ed. *The Americanization of the Holocaust*. Baltimore: The Johns Hopkins University Press, 1999.
Foley, Barbara. "Fact, Fiction, Fascism: Testimony and Mimesis in Holocaust Narratives." *Comparative Literature* 34/4 (1982): 330–60.

Greenstein, Michael. *Third Solitudes: Tradition and Discontinuity in Canadian-Jewish Literature*. Kingston and Montreal: McGill-Queen's University Press, 1989.

Hart, Alexander. "Writing and the Diaspora: A Bibliography and Critical Commentary on post-Shoah English Language Jewish Fiction in Australia, South Africa and Canada." Ph.D. diss. University of British Columbia, December 1996.

Hirsch, Marianne. *Family Frames: Photography, Narrative, and Postmemory*. Cambridge, MA: Harvard University Press, 1997.

Kremer, S. Lillian. *Witness Through the Imagination: Jewish American Holocaust Literature*. Detroit: Wayne State University Press, 1989.

Women's Holocaust Writing: Memory and Imagination. Lincoln and London: University of Nebraska Press, 1999.

Langer, Lawrence. *Admitting the Holocaust: Collected Essays*. Oxford and New York: Oxford University Press, 1995.

Mintz, Alan. *Popular Culture and the Shaping of Holocaust Memory in America*. Seattle: University of Washington Press, 2001.

Parmet, Harriet L. *The Terror of Our Days: Four American Poets Respond to the Holocaust*. Bethlehem: Lehigh University Press, 2001.

Rosen, Norma. *Accidents of Influence: Writing as a Woman and a Jew in America*. State University of New York Press, 1992.

Rosenfeld, Alvin. "The Holocaust in American Popular Culture." *Midstream* **29**/6 (1983): 53–59.

Imagining Hitler. Bloomington: Indiana University Press, 1985.

Sicher, Efraim. *Beyond Marginality: Anglo-Jewish Literature after the Holocaust*. New York: State University of New York Press, 1985.

"Writing After: Literary and Moral Reflections of the Holocaust." *Holocaust Studies Annual* (1991): 147–68.

Vice, Sue. *Holocaust Fiction*. New York: Routledge, 2000.

9 POLISH LITERATURE ON THE HOLOCAUST

Primary sources

Milosz, Czeslaw. "Campo dei Fiori" and "A Poor Christian Looks at the Ghetto" [1943]. In Antony Polonsky (ed.), *'My Brother's Keeper?' Recent Polish Debates on the Holocaust*. New York: Routledge, 1990, pp. 49–50, 51.

Tuwim, Julian. *We, Polish Jews... / Anu, Yehude Polin ... / Mir, Poylishe Yidn ...* [1944], ed. Chone Shmeruk. Jerusalem: Magnes Press, 1984.

Nalkowska, Zofia. *Medallions* [1946], trans. and intro. Diana Kuprel. Evanston, IL: Northwestern University Press, 2000.

Szpilman, Władysław. *The Pianist: The Extraordinary True Story of One Man's Survival in Warsaw 1939–45* [1946], trans. Anthea Bell. London: Victor Gollancz, 1999.

Rudnicki, Adolf. *Ascent to Heaven* [1946], trans. H. C. Stevens. New York: Roy Publishers, 1951.

Borowski, Tadeusz. *This Way for the Gas, Ladies and Gentlemen* [1946/1948], selected and trans. Barbara Vedder. New York: Penguin, 1976.

Rubinowicz, Dawid. *The Diary of Dawid Rubinowicz* [1960], trans. Derek Bowman. Edmonds, WA: Creative Option Publishers, 1982.

Sierakowiak, Dawid. *The Diary of David Sierakowiak: Five Notebooks from the Lodz Ghetto* [1960], ed. and intro. Alan Adelson, trans. Kamil Turowski. New York: Oxford University Press, 1996.

Grynberg, Henryk. *The Jewish War* [1965], trans. Celina Wieniewska, and Richard Lourie. Evanston, IL: Northwestern University Press 2001.

Wojdowski, Bogdan. *Bread for the Departed* [1971], trans. Madeline G. Levine. Evanston, IL: Northwestern University Press, 1997.

Krall, Hanna. *Shielding the Flame: An Intimate Conversation with Dr. Marek Edelman, the Last Surviving Leader of the Warsaw Ghetto Uprising* [1977], trans. Joanna Stasinska and Lawrence Wechsler. New York: Henry Holt and Co., 1986.

Ficowski, Jerzy. *Odczytanie popiołów/A Reading of Ashes* [1979], bilingual edn., trans. Keith Bosley. Warsaw: Browarna 1993.

Benski, Stanisław. *Missing Pieces: Stories* [1982], trans. Walter Arndt. San Diego: Harcourt Brace Jovanovich, 1990.

Czerniakow, Adam. *Warsaw Diary of Adam Czerniakow: Prelude to Doom* [1979/1983], ed. Raul Hilberg, Staislaw Staron, and Josef Kermisz; trans. Stanislaw Staron and the staff of Yad Vashem. New York: Stein and Day, 1979.

Krall, Hanna. *The Subtenant: To Outwit God* [1985], trans. Jaroslaw Anders. Evanston, IL: Northwestern University Press, 1992.

Szczypiorski, Andrzej. *The Beautiful Mrs. Seidenman* [1986], trans. Klara Glowczewska. New York: Grove Weidenfeld, 1989.

Bauman, Janina. *Winter in the Morning: A Young Girl's Life in the Warsaw Ghetto and Beyond, 1939–1945*. London: Virago, 1986.

Huelle, Paweł. *Who Was David Weiser?* [1987], trans. Michael Kandel. San Diego: Harcourt Brace, 1994.

Szewc, Piotr. *Annihilation: A Novel* [1987], trans. Ewa Hryniewicz-Yarbrough. Normal, IL: Dalkey Archive Press, 1993.

Fink, Ida. *A Scrap of Time and Other Stories*, trans. Madeline G. Levine and Francine Prose. New York: Pantheon Books, 1987.

Rymkiewicz, Jarosław Marek. *Final Station: Umschlagplatz* [1988], trans. Nina Taylor. New York: Farrar, Straus and Giroux, 1994.

Fink, Ida. *The Journey* [1990], trans. Joanne Wechsler and Francine Prose. New York: Farrar, Straus and Giroux, 1992.

Krall, Hanna. *The Woman from Hamburg and Other True Stories* [1993–2001], trans. Madeline G. Levine. New York: Other Press 2005.

Grynberg, Henryk. *Children of Zion* [1994], trans. Jacqueline Mitchell. Afterword by Israel Gutman. Evanston, IL: Northwestern University Press, 1997.

Fink, Ida. *Traces: Stories* [1996], trans. Philip Boehm and Francine Prose. New York: Metropolitan Books, 1997.

Dichter, Wilhelm. *God's Horse* [1996] *and The Atheists' School* [1999], trans. Madeline G. Levine. Evanston, IL: Northwestern University Press, 2012.

Grynberg, Henryk. *Drohobycz, Drohobycz and Other Stories: True Tales from the Holocaust and Life After* [1997], trans. Alicia Nitecki. New York: Penguin, 2002.

Głowiński, Michał. *The Black Seasons* [1998], trans. Marci Shore. Evanston, IL: Northwestern University Press, 2005.

Ligocka, Roma. *The Girl in the Red Coat* [2001], trans. Margot Bettauer Dembo. London: Sceptre 2002.

Polonsky, Antony and Monika Adamczyk-Garbowska, eds. *Contemporary Jewish Writing in Poland: An Anthology*. Lincoln and London: University of Nebraska Press, 2001.

Secondary sources

Adamczyk-Garbowska, Monika. "A New Generation of Voices in Polish Holocaust Literature." *Prooftexts: A Journal of Jewish Literary History* 3 (1989): 273–87.

Grynberg, Henryk. "The Holocaust in Polish Literature." *Notre Dame English Journal: A Journal of Religion and Literature* 2 (1979): 115–40.

The Holocaust as a Literary Experience. Occasional Paper (Monna and Otto Weinmann Lecture Series, May 12, 2004). Washington, DC: United States Holocaust Memorial Museum, Center for Advanced Holocaust Studies, 2004.

Levine, Madeline G. "Polish Literature and the Holocaust." *Holocaust Studies Annual* 3 (1985): 189–202.

10 HUNGARIAN HOLOCAUST LITERATURE

Primary sources

Szép, Ernő. *The Smell of Humans: A Memoir of the Holocaust in Hungary* [1945], trans. John Bátki. Budapest: Central European University Press, 1994.

Zsolt, Béla. *Nine Suitcases* [1946], trans. Ladislaus Löb. London: Pimlico, 2005.

Zsolt, Ágnes. *Éva lányom* [1948]. Budapest: Új Idők Irodalmi Intézet. In English: Jerusalem: Yad Vashem, 1988.

Mándy, Iván. "One Touch" [1957]. http://olddarkfriendsmatter.blogspot.co.il/2010/12/one-touch.html.

Kertész, Imre. *Fatelessness* [1975], trans. Tim Wilkinson. New York: Vintage, 2004.

Fiasco [1988], trans. Tim Wilkinson. Brooklyn: Melville House Publishing, 2011.

Kaddish for an Unborn Child [1990], trans. Tim Wilkinson. New York: Vintage, 2004.

Országh-Land, Thomas, trans. *Miklós Radnóti: 33 Poems*. Budapest: Maecenas, 1992.

Ozsváth, Zsuzsanna and Frederick Turner, trans. *Foamy Sky: The Major Poems of Miklós Radnóti*. Princeton University Press, 1992.

Nádas, Péter. *The End of a Family Story* [1993], trans. Imre Goldstein. New York: Farrar, Straus and Giroux, 1998.

Vámos, Miklós. *The Book of the Fathers* [2000], trans. Peter Sherwood. London: Abacus, 2006.

Kertész, Imre. *Liquidation* [2003], trans. Tim Wilkinson. New York: Alfred
A. Knopf, 2004.

Secondary sources

Braham, Randolph L. *The Politics of Genocide: The Holocaust in Hungary.* New
York: Columbia University Press, 1994.
Forgács, Éva and Susan Rubin Suleiman, eds. *Contemporary Jewish Writing in
Hungary: An Anthology.* Lincoln: University of Nebraska Press, 2003.
Horváth, Rita, "A Changing Genre: Jewish Hungarian Family Novels after the
Shoah." *Yad Vashem Studies* 32 (2004): 209–26. Repr. in Randolph L. Braham
(ed.), *The Treatment of the Holocaust in Hungary and Romania During
the Post-Communist Era.* New York: Columbia University Press, 2004,
pp. 201–15.
Molnár, Judit, ed. *The Holocaust in Hungary: A European Perspective.* Budapest:
Balassi Kiadó, 2005.
Ozsváth, Zsuzsanna. *In the Footsteps of Orpheus: The Life and Times of Miklós
Radnóti.* Bloomington and Indianapolis: Indiana University Press, 2000.
"Trauma and Distortion: Holocaust Fiction and the Ban on Jewish Memory
in Hungary." In Randolph L. Braham and Brewster S. Chamberlin (eds.),
The Holocaust in Hungary: Sixty Years Later. The Rosenthal Institute for
Holocaust Studies, Graduate Center of the City University of New York/
Social Science Monographs in association with the United States Holocaust
Memorial Museum, 2006, pp. 337–48.
Sanders, Ivan. "Jewish Literary Renaissance in Post-Communist Hungary." In
Braham and Chamberlin (eds.), *The Holocaust in Hungary*, pp. 365–76.
Szegedy-Maszák, Mihály. "National and International Implications in Radnóti's
Poetry." *Hungarian Studies* 1 (1996): 13–28.
Vasvári, Louise O. and Steven Tötösy de Zepetnek. *Imre Kertész and Holocaust
Literature.* West Lafayette, IN: Purdue University Press, 2005.

11 FRENCH LITERATURE AND THE HOLOCAUST

Primary sources

Proust, Marcel. *Contre Sainte-Beuve.* Paris: Gallimard, 1954.
The Guermantes Way, trans. M. Traharne. New York: Penguin Classics, 2005.
Antoine de Saint-Exupéry. "Open Letter to Frenchmen Everywhere." *The New
York Times,* November 29, 1942.
Aragon, Louis. "Auschwitz." In Jean Paulhan and Dominique Aury, *La Patrie se
fait tous les jours.* Paris: Minuit, 1947, pp. 375–78.
Wiesel, Elie. *La Nuit.* Preface by François Mauriac. Paris: Minuit, 1958.
Schwarz-Bart, André. *Le Dernier des justes.* Paris: Seuil, 1959.
Blanchot, Maurice. *Lautréamont et Sade.* Paris: Minuit, 1949.
Modiano, Patrick. *La Place de l'étoile.* Paris: Gallimard, 1968.

Romain Gary (Emile Ajar). *La Vie devant soi.* Paris: Mercure de France, 1975.

Perec, Georges. *W ou le souvenir d'enfance.* Paris: Denoël, 1975.

Nemirovsky, Irène. *Suite française.* Paris: Denoêl, 2004.

Littell, Jonathan. *Les Bienveillantes.* Paris: Gallimard, 2006.

Secondary sources

Agamben, Giorgio. *Remnants of Auschwitz: The Witness and the Archive,* trans. Daniel Heller-Roazen. New York: Zone Books, 2008.

Bellos, David. *Georges Perec: A Life in Words.* Boston: David Godine, 1993.

Benfey, Christopher and Karen Remmler. *Artists, Intellectuals and World War II: The Pontigny Encounters at Mount Holyoke College, 1942–1944.* Amherst: University of Massachusetts Press, 2006.

Debray, Régis. *Le Moment fraternité.* Paris: Gallimard, 2009.

Finkielkraut, Alain. *The Future of a Negation: Reflections on the Question of Genocide.* Lincoln: University of Nebraska Press, 1998.

Kaufmann, Francine. "Les enjeux de la polémique autour du best-seller français de la littérature de la Shoah." *Revue d'Histoire de la Shoah* **176** (September–December 2002): 68–96.

Lyotard, Jean-François. *The Differend: Phrases in Dispute,* trans. Georges Van Den Abbeele. Minneapolis: University of Minnesota Press, 1988.

Marty, Eric. *Pourquoi le XXme siècle a-t-il pris Sade au sérieux?* Paris: Seuil, 2011.

Mehlman, Jeffrey. "Iphigénie 38: Deconstruction, History, and the Case of *L'arrêt de mort.*" In *Genealogies of the Text: Literature, Psychoanalysis, and Politics in Modern France.* Cambridge University Press, 1995, pp. 82–96.

Paxton, Robert O. *Vichy France: Old Guard and New Order, 1940–1944.* New York: Norton, 1972.

Rousso, Henry. *The Vichy Syndrome,* trans. A. Goldhammer. Cambridge, MA: Harvard University Press, 1994.

Seidman, Naomi. "Elie Wiesel and the Scandal of Jewish Rage." *Jewish Social Studies* **3**/1 (Fall 1996): 1–19.

Sternhell, Zeev. *Ni droite ni gauche: L'idéologie fasciste en France* (Paris: Seuil, 1983).

Vidal-Naquet, Pierre. *Assassins of Memory: Essays on the Denial of the Holocaust,* trans. Jeffrey Mehlman. New York: Columbia University Press, 1992.

12 ORAL MEMOIR AND THE *SHOAH*

Primary sources

Boder, David, *I Did Not Interview the Dead.* Urbana: University of Illinois Press, 1949.

Topical Autobiographies of Displaced Persons, 16 vols. Chicago and Los Angeles: self-published, 1950–1957.

Rothchild, Sylvia, ed. *Voices from the Holocaust.* New York: New American Library, 1981.

Eliach, Yaffa. *Hasidic Tales of the Holocaust.* New York: Oxford University Press, 1982.

Bravo, Anna and Daniele Jallà, eds. *La vita offesa: Storia e memoria dei lager nazisti nei racconti di duecento sopravvissuti.* Milan: Franco Angeli, 1986.

For repertories of audiovisual archives on the *Shoah,* see:

"Holocaust: Archives," *History in Focus* (Summer 2004). Institute of Historical Research, University of London, www.history.ac.uk/ihr/Focus/Holocaust/archives.html.

"Oral History": United States Holocaust Memorial Museum, www.ushmm.org/research/collections/oralhistory.

"Voices of the Holocaust": Galvin Library, Illinois Institute of Technology, http://voices.iit.edu.

Secondary sources

Chevrie, Marc and Hervé Le Roux. "Site and Speech: An Interview with Claude Lanzmann about *Shoah.*" In Stuart Liebman (ed.), *Claude Lanzmann's Shoah: Key Essays.* New York: Oxford University Press, 2007, pp. 37–49.

Cohen, Boaz. "Rachel Auerbach, Yad Vashem, and Holocaust Memory." *Polin* (2007): 197–221.

Douglas, Lawrence. *The Memory of Judgment: Making Law and History in the Trials of the Holocaust.* New Haven, CT: Yale University Press, 2005.

Greenspan, Henry. *On Listening to Holocaust Survivors.* St. Paul, MN: Paragon House, 2011.

Haidu, Peter. "The Dialectics of Unspeakability." In Saul Friedlander (ed.), *Probing the Limits of Representation: Nazism and the "Final Solution."* Cambridge, MA: Harvard University Press, 1992, pp. 277–99.

Hartman, Geoffrey. "Preserving the Personal Story: The Role of Video Documentation." In Marcia Littell, Richard Libowitz, and E. B. Rosen (eds.), *The Holocaust Forty Years After.* Lewiston, ME: Edwin Melton, 1989, pp. 53–60.

"The Ethics of Witness: An Interview with Geoffrey Hartman." In Rebecca Comay (ed.), *Lost in the Archives.* Cambridge, MA: Alphabet City, 2002, pp. 492–509.

Helmreich, William. *Against All Odds: Holocaust Survivors and the Successful Lives They Made in America.* New York: Simon and Schuster, 1992.

Jockush, Laura. *Collect and Record! Jewish Holocaust Documentation in Early Postwar Europe.* New York: Oxford, 2012.

Klee, Ernest, Willi Dressen, and Volker Riess. *"The Good Old Days": The Holocaust as Seen by Its Perpetrators and Bystanders.* New York: Free Press, 1991.

Langer, Lawrence L. *Holocaust Testimonies: The Ruins of Memory.* New Haven, CT: Yale University Press, 2001.

Lipstadt, Deborah. *The Eichmann Trial.* New York: Nextbook-Schocken, 2011.

Portelli, Alessandro. *The Battle of Valle Giulia: Oral History and the Art of Dialogue.* Madison: University of Wisconsin Press, 1997.

The Order Has Been Carried Out: History, Memory, and Meaning of a Nazi Massacre in Rome. New York: Palgrave, 2003.

Reich, Walter. "Unwelcome Narratives: Listening to Suppressed Themes in American Holocaust Testimony." *Poetics Today* 27 (2006): 463–72.

Ringelheim, Joan. "Intervention." *Du Temoignage audiovisuel/From the audiovisual testimony.* Brussels: La Fondation Auschwitz, 1996.

Rosen, Alan. *The Wonder of Their Voices: The 1946 Holocaust Interviews of David Boder.* New York: Oxford University Press, 2010.

13 SONGS OF THE HOLOCAUST
Primary sources

Feder, Samy. *Zamlung Fun Katset Un Geto Lider.* Bergen-Belsen: Central Jewish Committee in Bergen-Belsen, 1946.

Katsherginski, Shmerke. *Dos Gezang Fun Vilner Ghetto.* Paris: Committee of Jews of Vilna in France, 1947.

Katsherginski, Shmerke and H. Leivick, eds. *Lider fun di Getos un Lagern.* New York: Alveltlekher Yidisher Kultur-Kongres, 1948.

Pups, Ruta, and Bernard Mark. *Dos Lid Fun Geto: Zomlung.* Warsaw: Yidish-Bukh, 1962.

Lammel, Inge and Günter Hofmeyer, eds. *Lieder aus den Faschistischen Konzentrationslagern.* Leipzig: Friedrich Hofmeister, 1962.

Linde, Carsten, ed. *KZ-Lieder: Eine Auswahl aus dem Repertoire des Polnischen Sängers Alex Kulisiewicz.* Sievershütten: Wendepunkt, 1972.

Kalisch, Shoshana and Barbara Meister. *Yes, We Sang! Songs of the Ghettos and Concentration Camps.* New York: Harper and Row, 1985.

Morsch, Günter, ed. *Sachsenhausen-Liederbuch: Originalwiedergabe Eines Illegalen Häftlingsliederbuches Aus Dem Konzentrationslager Sachsenhausen.* Berlin: Hentrich, 1995.

Silverman, Jerry. *The Undying Flame: Ballads and Songs of the Holocaust.* Syracuse University Press, 2002

Online sources

"Music and the Holocaust." World ORT, http://holocaustmusic.ort.org/.

"Music of the Holocaust: Highlights from the Collection of the United States Holocaust Memorial Museum." www.ushmm.org/museum/exhibit/online/music/.

Secondary sources

Adler, Eliyana R. "No Raisins, No Almonds: Singing as Spiritual Resistance to the Holocaust." *Shofar: An Interdisciplinary Journal of Jewish Studies* 24 (2006): 50–66.

Bloch, David. "'No One Can Rob us of our Dreams': Solo Songs from Terezin." *Israel Studies in Musicology* 5 (1990): 69–80.

"Terezin, Music in." In *The Blackwell Companion to Jewish Culture*. Oxford: Blackwell Reference, 1989.

Brauer, Juliane. *Musik im Konzentrationslager Sachsenhausen*. Berlin: Metropol Verlag, 2008.

Fackler, Guido, ed. *"Des Lagers Stimme" – Music im KZ: Alltag und Häftlingskultur in den Konzentrationslagern 1933 bis 1936*. Bremen: Temmen, 2000.

Aleksander Kulisiewicz, Musik aus der Hölle. Würzburg: Königshausen & Neumann, 2007.

Flam, Gila. *Singing for Survival: Songs of the Lodz Ghetto*. Urbana and Chicago: University of Illinois Press, 1992.

Gilbert, Shirli. *Music in the Holocaust: Confronting Life in the Nazi Ghettos and Camps*. Oxford Historical Monographs. Oxford University Press, 2005.

"Buried Monuments: Yiddish Songs and Holocaust Memory." *History Workshop Journal* **66** (2008): 107–28.

"Music in the Nazi Ghettos and Camps." In Jonathan C. Friedman (ed.), *The Routledge History of the Holocaust*. London: Routledge, 2011, pp. 436–51.

Hoch, Moshe. *Kolot mitokh hakhoshekh* (Voices from the Darkness). Jerusalem: Yad Vashem, 2002.

Karas, Joža. *Music in Terezín 1941–1945*. 2nd edn. Hillsdale, NY: Pendragon Press, 2008.

Knapp, Gabriel. *Frauenstimmen: Musikerinnen erinnern an Ravensbrueck*. Berlin: Metropol-Verlag, 2003.

Kulisiewicz, Aleksander. "Polish Camp Songs, 1939–1945," trans. Roslyn Hirsch, *Modern Language Studies* **16** (1986): 3–9.

Kuna, Milan. *Musik an der Grenze des Lebens: Musikerinnen und Musiker aus Böhmischen Ländern in Nationalsozialistischen Konzentrationslagern und Gefängnissen*. Frankfurt/M: Zweitausendeins, 1993.

Roskies, David. *Against the Apocalypse: Responses to Catastrophe in Modern Jewish Culture*. Cambridge, MA: Harvard University Press, 1984.

Roskies, David, ed. *The Literature of Destruction*. Philadelphia: Jewish Publication Society of America, 1989.

Rubin, Ruth. *Voices of a People: The Story of Yiddish Folksong*. Philadelphia: Jewish Publication Society of America, 1979.

14 SEPHARDIC LITERARY RESPONSES TO THE HOLOCAUST

Primary sources

Where an English translation exists this is the edition given. Otherwise, titles are in the original language.

Canetti, Elias. *Auto-da-fé* [1935], trans. C. V. Wedgwood. New York: Farrar Straus, 1984.

Knafo, Isaac. "Les Hitlériques: Pamphlets de Isaac D. Knafo," 1939, www.melca .info/pamplets.html.

Ghez, Paul. *Six mois sous la botte* [1943]. Paris: Manuscrit, 2009.

Kounio Amariglio, Erika. *From Thessaloniki to Auschwitz and Back: Memoirs of a Survivor from Thessaloniki* [1945], trans. Theresa Sundt Amariglio. Portland, OR: Vallentine Mitchell, 2000.

Ryvel (Raphaël Lévy). *Le Nebel du Galouth* (The Lyre of Exile). Tunis: La Cité des Livres, 1946.

Ben-Rubi, Yitzhak. *El Sekreto del mudo*. Tel Aviv: Lidor, 1953.

Memmi, Albert. *The Pillar of Salt* [1953], trans. Edouard Roditi. Boston: Beacon, 1992.

Bassani, Giorgio. *The Garden of the Finzi-Continis* [1962], trans. Jamie McKendrick. London: Penguin, 2007.

Jabès, Edmond. *The Book of Questions* [1963–1965], trans. Rosemarie Waldrop. Middletown: Wesleyan, 1976–1977.

Cohen, Albert. *Belle du Seigneur* [1968], trans. David Coward. London: Viking, 1995.

Bensoussan, Albert. *Frimaldjézar*. Paris: Calmann-Lévy, 1976.

Sultan, Stanley. *Rabbi*. Whately, MA: ANCP, 1977.

Modiano, Patrick. *Missing Person* [1978], trans Daniel Weissbort. Boston: Godine, 2005.

Lévy, Isaac Jack. *And the World Stood Silent: Sephardic Poetry of the Holocaust*. Urbana: University of Illinois Press, 1989.

Moati, Nine. *La Passagère sans étoile*. Paris: Seuil, 1989.

Yehoshua, A. B. *Mr. Mani* [1990], trans. Hillel Halkin. New York: Doubleday, 1992.

Handeli, Ya'acov. *A Greek Jew from Salonica Remembers* [1992]. Intro. Elie Wiesel, trans. Martin Kett. Jerusalem: Roses Printing, n.d.

Camhi Fromer, Rebecca. *The Holocaust Odyssey of Daniel Bennahmias, Sonderkommando*. Intro. Steven Fromer. Tuscaloosa: University of Alabama Press, 1993.

Aciman, Andre. *Out of Egypt*. New York: Picador, 1994.

Alhadeff, Gini. *The Sun at Midday*. New York: Pantheon, 1997.

Samokovlija, Isak. *Tales of Old Sarajevo*, ed. Zdenko Lešić, trans. Celia Hawkesworth and Christina Pribićević-Zorić. Intro. Ivo Andrić. London: Vallentine Mitchell, 1997.

Canetti, Veza. *The Tortoises* [1999], trans. Ian Mitchell. New York: New Directions, 2001.

Farhi, Moris. *Young Turk*. New York: Arcade, 2005.

Jagoda, Flory. *Arvoliko* (Little Tree). Audio CD, Empowered Women International, 2006.

Koen Sarano, Matilda. *Por el plaser de contar: Kuentos de mi vida* (The Pleasure of Storytelling: Tales of My Life). Jerusalem: Nur Afakot. 2006.

Refael, Shmuel. *Un Grito en el silencio: La poesía sobre el Holocausto en lengua sefardí: Estudio y antolojía* (A Cry in the Silence: Holocaust Poetry in the Sephardic Language). Barcelona: Tirocinio, 2008.

Secondary sources

Balbuena, Monique. "*Dibaxu*: A Comparative Analysis of Clarisse Nicoïdski's and Juan Gelman's Bilingual Poetry." *Romance Studies* 27/4 (November 2009): 283–97.

Bortnick, Rachel Amado. "Shoa deskonosida" (The Unknown Shoah). *El Amaneser* (April 2007). www.ladinokomunita/files/Shoa/

Bowman, Steven B. *The Agony of Greek Jews, 1940–1945*. Stanford University Press, 2009.

Cohen, Judith. "Selanikli Humour in Montreal: The Repertoire of Bouena Sarfatty Garfinkle." In Rena Molho, Hilary Pomeroy, and Elena Romero (eds.), *Judeo-Espaniol: Satirical Texts in Judeo-Spanish by and about the Jews in Thessaloniki*. Salonika: Ets Ahaim Foundation, 2011, pp. 220–42.

Horn, Bernard. "The Shoah, the Akeda, and the Conversations in A. B. Yehoshua's *Mr. Mani*." *Symposium: A Quarterly Journal in Modern Literatures* 53/3 (1999): 136–50.

Israël-Pelletier, Aimée. "Edmond Jabès, Jacques Hassoun, and Melancholy: The Second Exodus in the Shadow of the Holocaust." *MLN* 123 (2008): 797–818.

Levine Melammed, Renee. "Ladino-Speaking Women of the 20th Century." In Mary G. Berg and Lanin A. Gyurko (eds.), *Studies in Honor of Denah Lida*. Potomac: Scripta Humanistica, 2005, pp. 391–402.

Matza, Diane. *Sephardic American Voices*. Hanover: Brandeis University Press, 1997.

Mole, Gary. "The Representation of the Holocaust in French-Language Jewish Poetry." *Covenant* 2/1 (May 2008). www.covenant.idc.ac.il

Papo, Eliezer. "Tzhok karnevali ke-derech hitmodedut im traumot ve-ke emtzai le-havnayat ha-zikaron ha-kvutzati" (Parody as a Way of Managing Trauma and as a Means for Handling Collective Memory). In David Bunis (ed.), *Languages and Literatures of Sephardic and Oriental Jews*. Jerusalem: Misgav Yerushalayim, 2009, pp. 142–216.

Serels, Mitchell and Solomon Gaon, eds. *Del Fuego: Sephardim and the Holocaust*. New York: Sepher-Hermon, 1995.

15 ANTHOLOGIZING THE HOLOCAUST

Primary sources

Gutkowski, Eliyohu and Yitzhak Zukerman, eds. "Suffering and Heroism in the Jewish Past in Light of the Present." *Warsaw*, 1940 (self-published mimeographed anthology).

Neilson, William Allan. *We Escaped: Twelve Personal Narratives of the Flight to America*. New York: Macmillan, 1941.

Sarnecki, Tadeusz, ed. *From the Abyss* [Polish]. Warsaw: Wydawnictwo Z. K. N., 1944.

The Jewish Frontier Anthology, 1934–1944. New York: Jewish Frontier Association, 1945.

Tenenbaum, Benjamin, ed. *One of a City and Two of a Family: A Selection from One Thousand Autobiographies of Jewish Children in Poland* [Hebrew]. Merhavyah: Sifriat Poalim, 1947.

Hochberg-Mariańska, Maria and Noe Grüss, eds. *Children Accuse* [Polish]. Cracow: Centralna Zydowska Komisja Historyczna w Polsce, 1947.

Schwarz, Leo, ed. *The Root and the Bough: The Epic of an Enduring People*. New York: Rinehart, 1949.

Rudnicki, Adoph, ed. *Lest We Forget*. Warsaw: Polonia, 1955.

Harap, Louis, ed. *The Jewish Life Anthology, 1946–1956*. New York: Jewish Life, 1956.

The Massacre of European Jewry: An Anthology. Kibbutz Merchavia, Israel: World Hashomer Hatzair, English Speaking Dept., 1963.

I Never Saw Another Butterfly: Children's Drawings and Poems from Theresienstadt Concentration Camp, 1942–1944. New York: McGraw-Hill, 1964.

Glatstein, Jacob, Israel Knox, and Samuel Margoshes, eds. *Anthology of Holocaust Literature*. Philadelphia: Jewish Publication Society of America, 1969.

Dawidowicz, Lucy, ed. *A Holocaust Reader*. New York: Behrman House, 1975.

Roskies, David, ed. *The Literature of Destruction: Jewish Responses to Catastrophe*. Philadelphia: Jewish Publication Society of America, 1989.

Rittner, Carol and John K. Roth. *Different Voices: Women and the Holocaust*. New York: Paragon House, 1993.

Teichman, Milton and Sharon Leder, eds. *Truth and Lamentation: Stories and Poems on the Holocaust*. Urbana: University of Illinois Press, 1994.

Langer, Lawrence. *Art from the Ashes: A Holocaust Anthology*. New York: Oxford University Press, 1995.

Zapruder, Alexandra. *Salvaged Pages: Young Writers' Diaries of the Holocaust*. New Haven, CT: Yale University Press, 2002.

Moscovitz, Sarah Traister, ed. and trans. *Poetry in Hell: Yiddish Poetry in the Ringelblum Archives*. www.poetryinhell.org/2010

Farbstein, Esther. *The Forgotten Memoirs*. Brooklyn: Shaar, 2011.

Secondary sources

Mintz, Alan. *Popular Culture and the Shaping of Holocaust Memory in America*. Seattle: University of Washington Press, 2001.

Roskies, David G. "Dividing the Ruins: Communal Memory in Yiddish and Hebrew." In David Cesarani and Eric J. Sundquist (eds.), *After the Holocaust: Challenging the Myth of Silence*. New York: Routledge, 2012, pp. 82–101.

"The Holocaust According to Its Anthologists." In Stern (ed.), *The Anthology in Jewish Literature*, pp. 335–50.

Stern, David, ed. *The Anthology in Jewish Literature*. New York: Oxford, 2004.

16 THE HISTORIAN'S ANVIL, THE NOVELIST'S CRUCIBLE

Primary sources

Sierakowiak, Dawid. *The Diary of Dawid Sierakowiak: Five Notebooks from the Lodz Ghetto*, ed. Alan Adelson, trans. Kamil Turowski. New York: Oxford University Press, 1996.

Rosenfeld, Oskar. *In the Beginning Was the Ghetto: Notebooks from Lodz*, ed. Hanna Loewy, trans. Brigitte M. Goldstein. Evanston, IL: Northwestern University Press, 2002.

Hersey, John. *The Wall*. New York: Alfred A. Knopf, 1950.

Borowski, Tadeusz. *This Way to the Gas, Ladies and Gentlemen* [1959], trans. Barbara Vedder. New York: Penguin, 1976.

Delbo, Charlotte. *Auschwitz and After* [1965], trans. Rosette C. Lamont. New Haven, CT: Yale University Press, 1995.

Delbo, Charlotte. *Convoy to Auschwitz: Women of the French Resistance* [1965], trans. Carol Cosman. Boston: Northeastern University Press, 1997.

Malamud, Bernard. *The Fixer* [1966]. New York: Penguin, 1967.

Lustig, Arnost. *A Prayer for Katerina Horovitzova* [1973], trans. Jeanne Nemcova. London: Quartet Books, 1990.

Appelfeld, Aharon. *Badenheim 1939* [1975], trans. Dalya Bilu. Boston: David R. Godine, 1980.

Epstein, Leslie. *King of the Jews* [1976]. New York: W. W. Norton, 1993.

Müller, Filip. *Eyewitness Auschwitz* [1979], trans. Suzanne Flatauer. Chicago: Ivan R. Dee, 1999.

Nomberg-Przytyk, Sara. *Auschwitz: True Tales from a Grotesque Land*, trans. Roslyn Hirsch, ed. Eli Pfefferkorn and David H. Hirsch. Chapel Hill: University of North Carolina Press, 1985.

Ozick, Cynthia. *The Shawl* [1989]. New York: Vintage, 1990.

Secondary sources

Bernstein, Michael André. *Foregone Conclusions: Against Apocalyptic History*. Berkeley: University of California Press, 1994.

Czech, Danuta. *Auschwitz Chronicle, 1939–1945: From the Archives of the Auschwitz Memorial and the German Federal Archives*, trans. anon. New York: Owl Books, 1997.

Dawidowicz, Lucy. *The War Against the Jews, 1933–1945* [1975]. New York: Bantam, 1986.

Ezrahi, Sidra DeKoven. *By Words Alone: The Holocaust in Literature*. University of Chicago Press, 1980.

Friedlander, Saul, ed. *Probing the Limits of Representation: Nazism and the "Final Solution."* Cambridge, MA: Harvard University Press, 1992.

Gerstein, Kurt. "Deathwatch at Belzec: Kurt Gerstein's Deposition," trans. Rose Feitelson. In Lucy Dawidowicz (ed.), *A Holocaust Reader*. West Orange, NJ: Behrman House, 1976, pp. 104–109.

Gilbert, Martin. *The Holocaust: A History of the Jews of Europe During the Second World War*. New York: Holt, Rinehart, and Winston, 1985.

Greif, Gideon. *We Wept Without Tears: Testimonies of the Jewish Sonderkommando from Auschwitz* [1995]. New Haven, CT: Yale University Press, 2005.

Hersey, John. "To Invent a Memory." Baltimore Hebrew University, 1990.

Kertész, Imre. "Who Owns Auschwitz?" Trans. John MacKay. *Yale Journal of Criticism* 14/1 (2001): 267–72.

Kogon, Eugene. *The Theory and Practice of Hell* [1950], trans. Heinz Norden. New York: Berkley Books, 1980.

Kremer, S. Lillian. *Witness Through the Imagination: Jewish American Fiction*. Detroit: Wayne State University Press, 1989.

LaCapra. Dominick. *Representing the Holocaust: History, Theory, Trauma*. Ithaca, NY: Cornell University Press, 1994.

Lang, Berel, ed. *Writing and the Holocaust*. New York: Holmes and Meier, 1988.

Marrus, Michael R. *The Holocaust in History*. New York: Penguin, 1987.

Montague, Patrick. *Chelmno and the Holocaust: The History of Hitler's First Death Camp*. Chapel Hill: University of North Carolina Press, 2012.

Ozick, Cynthia. "The Rights of History and the Rights of Imagination." *Commentary* 113 (March 1999): 22–27.

Rosenfeld, Alvin H. *The End of the Holocaust*. Bloomington: Indiana University Press, 2011.

Roskies, David G., ed. *The Literature of Destruction: Jewish Responses to Catastrophe*. Philadelphia: Jewish Publication Society of America, 1988.

Suleiman, Susan Rubin. "Do Facts Matter in Holocaust Memoirs? Wilkomirski/ Wiesel." In Steven Katz and Alan Rosen (eds.), *Obliged by Memory: Literature, Religion, Ethics*. Syracuse University Press, 2006, pp. 21–42.

Yerushalmi, Yosef Hayim. *Zakhor: Jewish History and Jewish Memory* [1982]. Seattle: University of Washington Press, 1996.

SELECTED CRITICAL STUDIES (IN CHRONOLOGICAL ORDER)

Steiner, George. *Language and Silence: Essays on Language, Literature, and the Inhuman*. New York: Atheneum, 1967.

Halperin, Irving. *Messengers from the Dead: Literature of the Holocaust*. Philadelphia: Westminster, 1970.

Langer, Lawrence. *The Holocaust and the Literary Imagination*. New Haven, CT: Yale University Press, 1975.

Des Pres, Terrence. *The Survivor: An Anatomy of Life in the Death Camps*. New York: Oxford University Press, 1976.

Ezrahi, Sidra Dekoven. *By Words Alone: The Holocaust in Literature.* University of Chicago Press, 1980.

Rosenfeld, Alvin. *A Double Dying: Reflections on Holocaust Literature.* Bloomington: Indiana University Press, 1980.

Mintz, Alan. *Hurban: Responses to Catastrophe in Hebrew Literature.* New York: Columbia University Press, 1984.

Roskies, David G. *Against the Apocalypse: Responses to Catastrophe in Modern Jewish Culture.* Cambridge, MA: Harvard University Press, 1984.

Lang, Berel, ed. *Writing and the Holocaust.* New York: Holmes and Meier, 1988.

Skloot, Robert. *The Darkness We Carry: The Drama of the Holocaust.* Madison: University of Wisconsin Press, 1988.

Young, James. *Writing and Rewriting the Holocaust.* Bloomington: Indiana University Press, 1988.

Aaron, Frieda. *Bearing the Unbearable: Yiddish and Polish Poetry in Ghettos and Concentration Camps.* Albany: State University of New York Press, 1990.

Felman, Shoshana and Dori Laub. *Testimony: Crises in Witnessing in Literature, Psychoanalysis, and History.* New York: Routledge, 1992.

Hartman, Geoffrey. *The Longest Shadow: In the Aftermath of the Holocaust.* Bloomington: Indiana University Press, 1996.

Horowitz, Sara. *Voicing the Void: Muteness and Memory in Holocaust Fiction.* Albany: State University of New York Press, 1997.

Gubar, Susan. *Poetry after Auschwitz: Remembering What One Never Knew.* Bloomington: Indiana University Press, 2003.

Kremer, S. Lillian, ed. *Holocaust Literature: An Encyclopedia of Writers and Their Work.* New York: Routledge, 2003.

Rosen, Alan. *Sounds of Defiance: The Holocaust, Multilingualism, and the Problem of English.* Lincoln: University of Nebraska Press, 2005.

Suleiman, Susan. *Crises of Memory and the Second World War.* Cambridge, MA: Harvard University Press, 2006.

Kassow, Samuel. *Who Will Write Our History? Emanuel Ringelblum, the Warsaw Ghetto, and the Oyneg Shabes Archive.* Bloomington: Indiana University Press, 2007.

Rothberg, Michael. *Multidimensional Memory: Remembering the Holocaust in the Age of Decolonization.* Stanford University Press, 2009.

Spargo, R. Clifton and Robert M. Ehrenreich, eds. *After Representation: The Holocaust, Literature, and Culture.* New Brunswick: Rutgers University Press, 2010.

Lothe, Jakob, Susan Rubin Suleiman, and James Phelan, eds. *After Testimony: The Ethics and Aesthetics of Holocaust Narrative for the Future.* Columbus: Ohio State University Press, 2012.

Roskies, David and Naomi Diamant. *Holocaust Literature: A History and Guide.* Waltham: Brandeis University Press, 2013.

Index

Aciman, Andre, 236
Adamczyk-Garbowska, Monika, 5
Adler, H. G., 28, 71, 74, 81, 82
Adler, Stanislaw, 28
Adorno, Theodore, 69, 70, 179
Affinati, Eraldo, 63, 64
Agamben, Giorgio, 63
Agnon, S. Y. (Shmuel Yosef), 86, 97, 99
Aichinger, Ilse, 73
Aini, Leah, 98
Ainsztein, Reuvan, 262
Akiva, Rabbi
  martyrdom of, 20
Alexandria, 236
Alhadeff, Gini, 236
Altarac, Salom Sani, 228
Altman, I., 129
American Hebrew poetry, 84
Amichai, Yehuda, 97
Amsterdam, 37, 40
analogy, 5, 16, 19, 26, 60.
  See also metaphor
  biblical, 15
  Szlengel's search for, 26
  used by ghetto chroniclers sardonically, 4, 17
Andersch, Alfred, 73, 79
Anielewicz, Mordechai, 96
Antelme, Robert, 184
Apitz, Bruno, 77
Appelfeld, Aharon, 7, 71, 92, 93, 94, 253
Aragon, Louis, 176, 177
archetypes, 19, 20
  the Holocaust as giving birth to new, 20
Arendt, Hannah, 75, 90, 131, 138, 145, 175, 258
Army College of Rome, 201
Artom, Emanuele, 58, 59
Auerbach, Rachel, 5, 7, 9, 24, 26–27, 80, 243
Aury, Dominique, 176
Auschwitz, vii, 6, 7, 29, 30, 35, 36, 37, 38, 40, 41, 42, 43, 46, 51, 52, 54, 56, 57, 61, 63, 64, 65, 69, 70, 71, 72, 74, 78, 79, 80, 89, 91, 109, 113, 121,

136, 137, 143, 144, 146, 147, 153, 154, 164, 165, 166, 167, 168, 176, 177, 182, 183, 184, 185, 188, 194, 195, 196, 200, 201, 209, 221, 223, 227, 228, 230, 231, 236, 237, 241, 246, 247, 252, 253, 254, 258, 259, 260, 261, 262, 263, 265, 266
Ausländer, Rose, 73
Avigdor, Rabbi Yaakov, 248

Babi Yar, 119, 120, 121, 122, 123, 124, 125, 126, 128
Bachmann, Ingeborg, 75
Baima, Paola, 206
Balkan Sephardic culture, 227
Barnes, Peter, 137
Barneveld (concentration camp), 39
Baron, Dvora, 86, 97
Baroncini, Nella, 205, 206
Bassani, Giorgio, 55, 56, 57, 58, 233
Bauer, Yehuda, 264
Becker, Jurek, 68, 69, 77
Beilis, Mendel
  blood libel against, 253
Belgium, 34, 41
Bellow, Saul, 111, 135, 140, 144
Belzec (death camp), 258
Benjamin, Walter, 175
Bennahmias, Daniel, 231
Ben-Rubi, Itzhak, 228
Benski, Stanisław, 157
Bensoussan, Albert, 234
Berdichev (city), 119
Berg, Mary, 157
Bergelson, David, 121
Bergen-Belsen (concentration camp), 6, 37, 38, 39, 40, 42, 113, 261
Berger, Alan and Naomi, 145
Bernard-Donals, Michael, 252
Bernshteyn, Mira
  courage of in Vilna ghetto, 20
Berr, Hélène, 41–42, 45
Bialik, Chaim Nachman, 23, 96, 127, 240

Biller, Maxim, 78, 79
Birkenau (concentration and death camp), 29,
    203, 258, 260, 262
Birstein, Yosl, 111
Bizzarri, Aldo, 54, 55
Blanchot, Maurice, 180
Bloch, Marc, 202
Blomberg, Gabriel, 206
Bobrowki, Johannes, 77
Boder, David, 223
Böll, Heinrich, 70
Bor (labor camp), 171
Borowski, Aleksandr, 259, 261
Borowski, Tadeusz, 153, 161
Borshchagovsky, Aleksandr, 128
Borwicz, Michal, 150, 153
Bosnian Ladino, 228
Bravo, Anna, 196
bridge generation (in Israel), 84–87
Broniewski, Władysław, 152, 153
Brookner, Anita, 142
Browning, Christopher, 195, 199
Broydo, Kasriel, 216
Bruck, Edith, 57, 60, 61, 62, 65
Bryks, Rachmiel, 243
Bucci, Andra and Tatiana, 195, 204, 206
Buchan, Yaakov, 98
Buchenwald (concentration camp), 6, 7, 57, 74,
    77, 135, 143, 144, 148, 222, 252
Buczkowski, Leopold, 154
Budapest, 89, 165, 166, 167, 168, 169, 171, 173
Budapest ghetto, 62
Bufalino, Gesualdo, 61, 62
Bukiet, Melvin, 143, 148

Camerino, Enzo, 195, 202, 206
Camhi Fromer, Rebecca, 231
Camus, Albert, 178
Canetti, Elias, 71, 232, 233
cattle-cars
    for deporting European Jews, 2, 24, 38, 42, 64,
        92, 142, 201, 213, 216, 231, 234
Celan, Paul, 7, 10, 68, 71, 95, 149
    repetition in the poetry of, 3
Céline, Louis-Ferdinand, 127
censorship, 5
    affect on Kuznetsov's *Babi Yar*, 124
    affect on postwar Holocaust literature, 120,
        124, 126
    and wartime letters, 35
    circumventing postwar Polish, 157
    in postwar Poland, 161
    intensification of in postwar Russia, 155
    relaxation of in 1980s Poland, 157
Central Historical Commission in Munich, 223

Chabon, Michael, 139
Chalom, Marcel, 226
Chateaubriand, 174
Chelmno (death camp), 208, 256, 257, 258
Children Accuse, 246
Chirac, Jacques, 177
Chopin, Frederick, 105
Cohen, Albert, 232, 233
Cohen, Arthur, 133, 144, 147, 148
Cohen, Leonard, 137, 146
collaboration, 44, 84, 88, 89, 90, 133, 181, 198
complicity. *See* collaboration
concentration camps, 2, 6, 7, 38, 39, 42, 68, 75,
    76, 80, 87, 88, 90, 92, 98, 108, 109, 113, 134,
    135, 137, 138, 140, 141, 142, 144, 145, 146, 164,
    167, 168, 200, 201, 211, 220, 225, 231, 246,
    252, 259
    anthems in, 222
    establishment of, 2
    See also under the names of individual camps
Corfu, 233
Crete, 236
Czech, Danuta, 263
Czerniaków, Adam, 157
Czernowitz (city), 10, 92

Dachau (concentration camp), 60, 205, 222
Dan Segre, Vittorio, 61
Dante, 59, 62, 97
d'Arguto, Rosebery (Martin Rosenberg), 220, 222
Dawidowicz, Lucy, 244, 257
de Saint-Exupéry, Antoine, 175
death camps, 2, 69, 74, 82, 89, 134, 136, 242 *See
    also* under the name of the individual camp
Debenedetti, Giacomo, 52, 53, 56, 60
Delbo, Charlotte, 7, 247, 253, 254
Der Emes (publisher), 120
Der Nister (Pincus Kahanovitch), 127
Di goldene keyt (journal), 111, 113. *See also*
    Sutzkever, Abraham
Di Porto, Giuseppe, 206, 207
Di Segni, Lello, 201, 202
diaries, 1, 33, 37, 39, 41, 42, 52, 109
    confessional, 27–29
Different Voices: Women and the Holocaust, 247
divine vengeance
    calls for by religious Jewish writers, 8
    synagogue plaques including a call for, 8
Dora Nordhausen (labor camp), 136
Dos poylishe yidntum (book series), 102, 103, 108,
    110, 115
Draenger, Shimshon and Gusta, 23
Dragon, Shlomo, 261
Drancy (transit camp), 41, 136, 185
Dresden (city), 69

Dreyfus, Albert, 123, 178, 183
Dugin, Ithzak, 205

Edel, Peter, 77
Edelman, Marek, 156
Ehrenburg, Ilya, 118, 119, 120, 121, 122, 123, 126
Ehrenreich, Rabbi Shlomo Zalmen, 8
Eichmann trial, 90, 91, 92, 112, 131, 137, 145, 193, 194, 197
Elberg, Yehuda, 112
Ember, Maria, 165
Emeq ha-baka (Vale of tears). *See* Yosef ha-Kohen
Emile Ajar. *See* Romain Gary
Enzensberger, Hans, 70
Epstein, Leslie, 133, 135, 148, 255–59
Esther, biblical book of
    parody on, 227
Ettinger, Elzbieta, 138
Evtushenko, Evgeny, 122, 123, 124
Existence and Existents. *See* Levinas, Emmanuel
exploitation of the Holocaust, 64
Ezrahi, Sidra, 151, 259

Fano, Claudio, 202, 206
Farhi, Morris, 237
Faurisson, Robert. *See* Holocaust denial
Feiner, Hertha, 36
Fenelon, Fania, 136
Ferrara, 233. *See also* Bassani, Giorgo
Feuchtwanger, Leon, 72
Fiano, Nedo, 194, 198, 205
Ficowski, Jerzy, 156
Fink, Ida, 160, 247
Finkielkraut, Alain, 174
Flinker, Moshe, 6, 9, 41, 45, 247
Flossenbürg (concentration camp), 205
Forgotten Memoirs, The, 247
Fosse Ardeatine massacre (in Rome), 59, 64
Fossoli (transit camp), 201
France, 34
Frank, Anne, 6, 37–38, 41, 45, 57, 68, 69, 80, 123, 126, 133, 146, 243, 246, 247
Frank, Otto, 53
Frankfurt (city)
    Lehrhaus, 106
Frankl, Victor, 71
Fried. Erich, 76
Friedlander, Saul, 3
Friedrich, Otto, 260
Frost, Eric, 222
Fumaroli, Marc, 174

Gary, Romain, 167, 182, 183
GDR (German Democtratic Repulbic), 73
Geiger, Arno, 78

Gelman, Juan, 229
Gerbirtig, Mordechai, 243
Gergely, Ágnes, 170
German
    as the language of the perpetrators, 69
German unification. *See also* Germany
Germany, 1, 2, 6, 19, 34, 37, 51, 68, 69, 70, 71, 73, 74, 75, 76, 79, 81, 82, 88, 97, 111, 122, 126, 132, 133, 137, 142, 159, 165, 168, 223, 232, 248, 265
Gershon, Karen, 131
Gerstein, Kurt, 257
ghetto poets
    approaches to martyrdom, 20
ghettos, 4, 15, 16, 17, 19, 21, 27, 29, 53, 68, 69, 108, 109, 110, 113, 115, 121, 124, 126, 132, 133, 134, 135, 136, 138, 139, 146, 148, 151, 152, 153, 154, 155, 156, 157, 158, 159, 160, 161, 165, 209, 211, 212, 213, 214, 215, 216, 217, 218, 219, 220, 222, 223, 224, 227, 242, 243, 244, 245, 249, 250, 255, 256, 257, 258, 259, 260, 261
    as a form of homelessness, 40
    as a social organism, 16
    couriers between, 22
    establishment of, 2
    final destruction of, 24
    postwar publication of writings from, 108
    reportage in, 16–19, 68
    smugglers in, 21
    the art of reading literature authored in, 4
    the special role of languages in, 9
Ghez, Paul, 229, 230
Gies, Miep, 37
Gilbert, Martin, 262
Gilbert, Shirli, 4
Ginzburg, Natalia, 59, 61
Glatstein, Jacob, 103, 110, 111, 242, 244, 248, 249
Glezer, Rikle, 213
Glik, Hersh, 217, 218, 219, 240, 242, 243
Głowiński, Michal, 159
Gödrös, Frigyes, 170
Goes, Albrecht, 73
Goethe, Johann Wolfgang von, 22, 74, 106
Goldberg, Leah, 87, 94
Goldin, Leyb, 19
Gordon, Robert, 7
Gouri, Haim, 91
Grade, Chaim, 103, 107, 108, 111, 112, 114, 115
Gradowski, Zalmen, 30, 262, 264
    as leader of the Sonderkommando revolt, 31
    listing perished family members, 29
    recruited for the Auschwitz Sonderkommando, 30
Grass, Günter, 60, 75, 76, 250
Great Deportation of Warsaw Jewry, 5, 9, 15, 24–27, 29, 155

Greenberg, Uri Tzvi, 85
Grossman, David, 98, 129, 148
Grossman, Mendel, 145
Grossman, Vasily, 7, 118, 120, 122, 125
Grynberg, Henryk, 150, 151, 155, 158, 161, 162
Gulag, 129
György, Péter, 166, 173
Gypsy. *See* Roma *and* Sinti

Ha-Elion, Moshe, 228
Hahn, Ulla, 78
Haim, David, 228
Hajnóczy, Péter, 172
Hamburger, Michael, 69, 71, 137
Handeli, Ya'acov, 231
Hareven, Shulamith, 97
Hartman, Geoffrey, 199
Hermlin, Stephan, 72
Hersey, John, 134, 253
Herszkowicz, Yankele, 216
Herzberg, Abel, 39
Heschel, Abraham Joshua, 105, 106, 107
Heyen, William, 136
Hilberg, Raul, 258
Hildesheimer, Wolfgang, 75
Hillesum, Etty, 38
Hilsenrath, Edgar, 68, 79
Hirszhorn, Aron, 241. *See* Rudnicki, Adolf
Hochhuth, Rolf, 74
Holocaust denial, 174, 177, 188
Holocaust literature
    as sacred, 243, 244, 245, 246
Horváth, Rita, 5
Howe, Irving, 111
Huberband, Rabbi Shimon, 8
Hungarian Fascist Arrow Cross, 166
Hungary, 7

I Never Saw Another Butterfly, 246
Israel
    politics of, 64
    Six Day War in, 59
Istanbul, 237

Jabès, Edmund, 234
Jacobson, Howard, 146
Jagoda, Flory, 228
Jallà, Daniele, 197
Janeczek, Helena, 63, 64
Jankowski, Stanislaw, 262
Jastrun, Mieczysław, 150
Jedwabne massacre, 160
Jehovah's Witnesses, 222
Jelinek, Elfriede, 80
Jerusalem's ancient Temples

and commemorating the Holocaust, 244
    the destruction of as the original *hurban*, 25
    witnessing the destruction of, 96
Jewish calendar, 15
    and Holocaust Remembrance Day, 88
Jewish Councils. *See* Judenrat
Jewish identity, 78, 142, 145, 148
    affirmation of, 145
    Imre Kertész's views on, 172
    in postwar Eastern Europe, 146
    in postwar Holocaust Hungary, 172
    in postwar Italy, 61
    of survivors' children, 142
    struggle with, 132
    the Holocaust's role in forming, 170
Jewish police, 88, 217
    Szlengel as former member of, 25
Job, biblical Book of, 194
Judenrat (Jewish council), 88, 89, 133, 134, 135, 216

Kacew, Roman, 183. *See also* Gary, Romain
Kadouche, Evelyn, 229
Kalmanovitsh, Zelig, 16, 244
Kaplan, Chaim, 1, 6, 15
kapos, 62, 88, 114, 204
Karmel, Ilona, 135, 137
Karpf, Anne, 148
Kastner, Rezso, 89
Katsherginski, Shmerke, 111, 112, 217, 219, 220, 223
Katzenelson, Yitzhak, 242
    arrival at the Vittel transit camp, 28
Ka-Tzetnik. *See* Yehiel Dinur
Keneally, Thomas, 136
Kerényi, Grácia, 167
Kertész, Imre, 7, 164, 165, 167, 172, 252
Kessel, Joseph, 44–45
Keszi, Imre, 168
khurbn, 104, 108, 109, 112
Kiddush Hashem, 20. *See also* martyrdom
Kielar, Wieslaw, 261
Kielce pogrom, 160
Kindertransport, 131
kinot (lamentations), 227
Kiš, Danilo, 7
Klein, A. M., 137, 148
Klemperer, Victor, 6, 34, 45, 69
Klüger, Ruth, 78
Klukowski, Zygmunt, 5
Koen Sarano, Mathilda, 230, 231
Koeppen, Wolfgang, 70
Kogon, Eugen, 74, 262
Kolitz, Zvi, 110
Kolmar, Gertrud, 35–36, 45, 72, 247
Kolomyia (town), 156
komplas (couplets), 227

Konstantinovsky, Ilya, 126, 127
Korczak, Janusz, 155, 244
Korn, Rochel, 112
Kornis, Mihály, 169
Kott, Jan, 150
Kounio Amariglio, Eric, 230
Kovner, Abba, 95, 96, 217
Krall, Hanna, 150, 151, 156, 157, 158, 161
Kramer, Lotte, 131, 132
Kraus, Ota, 261
Kremer, S. Lillian, 10, 265
Kristallnacht, 134
Kruk, Herman, 90
Kulisiewicz, Aleksander, 221, 222, 223
Kulka, Erich, 261
Kuznetsov, Anatoly, 124, 125, 126

Ladino, 9, 225, 226, 227, 228, 229, 230, 231, 232, 236
Lamentations, biblical Book of, 243
Langer, Lawrence, 203, 245, 246, 248
Langgässer, Elizabeth, 73
language
    as a means of escape, 9
    choice of chronicling in, 29
Lanzmann, Claude, 187, 195, 207, 208
Lasker-Schüler, Else, 73
Latvian, 120
Layton, Irving, 148
Leivick, H., 111
Lemberger, Rabbi Moshe Nosson Notta, 248
Lengyel, Péter, 170
letters, 33, 40
Lev, Mikhail, 128
Levi, Itamar, 98
Levi, Lia, 63
Levi, Primo, 6, 52, 54, 55, 56, 57, 58, 59, 60, 61, 62,
    63, 65, 66, 68, 69, 98, 149, 159, 194, 243, 255
Levinas, Emmanuel, 45–46
Levine, Madeline, 151
Lewin, Abraham, 6, 9, 27, 29
Leyeles, Aaron, 111
Lieberman, Harold and Edith, 135
Liebricht, Savyon, 98
Limentani, Giacoma, 58, 59
Lingua Tertii Imperii. *See* Klemperer, Victor
Lipkin, Semyon, 128
Lipski, Leo, 153
Lithuania, 130
    in Katzenelson's *Song of the Murdered Jewish
    People*, 10
    Kovner's appeal to the Jews of, 95
Lithuanian
    Holocaust writing in, 126
Lithuanians
    literary references to collaboration of, 120

Littell, Jonathan, 124, 186
Littner, Jacob, 70
Lodz, 9, 21, 113, 115, 135, 158, 213, 216, 249, 255, 256,
    258, 266
Lodz ghetto
    and Isaiah Spiegel, 109
    as compared to the fate of ancient
        Jerusalem, 18
    Jurek Becker's fictional treatment of, 77
    mass deportations in, 21
    Oskar Rosenfeld's chronicle of life in, 17
    search for analogies in Jewish history, 20
    Zelkowicz's writing in, 18
Loy, Rosetta, 56, 63, 64
Lustig, Arnost, 264
Luzzatto, Amos, 198, 200
Lyotard, Jean-François, 174

Magris, Claudio, 62
Majdanek (death camp), 54, 116, 123,
    221, 255
Makower, Henry, 157
Malamud, Bernard, 111, 148, 149, 253
Malaparte, Curzio, 52, 53
Malle, Louis, 235
Mándy, Ivan, 166
Manger, Itsik, 112, 113
Mann, Thomas, 62, 73, 74, 261
Máriássy, Felix, 167
Mark, Berl, 112
Markish, Peretz, 121, 127
Markov, Aleksei, 123
Marshak, Samuil, 123
Márton, László, 170
martyrdom
    GDR's focus on communist, 76
    identification with in Yiddish Holocaust
        literature, 102
    in Ilya Ehrenburg's *The Storm*, 121
    in Jon Silken's poetry, 133
    in Kuznetsov, 125
    in Shayevitsh, 21
    in Warsaw ghetto classroom study, 20
    of resistance fighters, 128
martyrology, 8, 248
    as defined by Yitzhak Katzenelson, 20
Maruffi, Alberto, 202
Masada
    armed ghetto resistance as emulating, 23
Matywiecki, Piotr, 160
Maurensig, Paolo, 63
Mauriac, François, 177
Mauthausen (concentration camp), 51,
    55, 202
Mayer, Gerda, 131

Mechanicus, Philip, 39
Meckel, Christoph, 76
Megged, Aharon, 89
Mehlman, Jeffrey, 5
Memmi, Albert, 233
Mémorial de la Shoah, 177
Mémorial des martyrs de la Déportation, 177
Menasse, Eva, 78
Meneghello, Luigi, 55, 56
Mengele, Dr. Josef, 203
Meras, Icchokas, 126
metaphor, 3, 5, 7, 58, 104, 141, 208, 254. *See also*
    analogy
metonymy, 23, 24, 25, 193
Michaels, Anne, 148
Mikhoels, Shlomo, 122
Milan Jewish Documentation Center, 195
Miller, Arthur, 134, 136, 167
Millu, Liana, 54, 55, 60, 61
Miłosz, Czeslaw, 150
Minco, Marga, 7
Minsk ghetto, 121
Minsk Mazowieck (town), 109
miracles
    alluded to in the memoir of Rabbi Yitzchak
        Yaakov Weiss, 248
    as described by religious Jewish authors, 8
    as enabling survival, 248
    at the center of Rabbi Baruch Rabinowitz's
        memoir, 7
    referred to in Zusman Segolovitch's poem, 249
Mirsky, Mikhl, 112
Moati, Nine, 235
Modiano, Patrick, 181, 182, 196, 235
Moldova, György, 166
Molodovsky, Kadya, 104, 110
Molotov–Ribbentrop Pact, 118
Mongarli, Alberto, 205
Morante, Elsa, 60
Moscovitz, Sarah Traister, 249
Moscow, 112, 121, 126, 127, 154
Mount Moriah
    Shayevitsh's allusion to, 22
Müller, Filip, 194, 263, 264
Munkacs (town), 7

Nádas, Péter, 170
Nałkowska, Zofia, 153, 159, 161
Némirovsky, Irene, 42–44, 45, 185, 186
Netherlands, 34, 37
New York (city), 60, 105, 108, 111, 141, 157, 175,
    178, 189
newspapers, 91, 110, 113, 122, 123, 127, 182,
    185, 211
Neyman, Yulia, 128

Nicoïdski, Clarisse, 228, 229
Niger, Shmuel, 109, 110
Nomberg-Przytyk, Sara, 260, 261
North Africa, 9, 225, 227, 233

Olszewski, Krystyn, 259
One of a City and Two of a Family, 246
Opoczynski, Peretz, 3, 16, 17, 243, 244
Örkény, István, 166
Oyneg Shabes
    anthology of writings from, 249
    Emanuel Ringelblum's direction of, 242
    in the aftermath of the Great Deportation of
        Warsaw Jewry, 24
    Rachel Auerbach dedication to, 24
    the role of, 249
Ozerov, Lev, 118, 119
Ozick, Cynthia, 111, 141, 144, 147, 254, 255

Pagis, Dan, 94, 95
Paris, 7, 42, 43, 71, 105, 107, 109, 112, 139, 157,
    161, 177, 179, 181, 182, 183, 186, 189, 234, 235,
    254, 260
Partisan march. *See* Katsherginsky, Shmerke
partisans, 54, 118, 121, 218, 219, 228, 240, 242
    in the Vilna ghetto, 22
Pasolini, Pier Paolo, 58, 59, 180
Passover, 41, 87, 88, 149, 226, 227, 228,
    236, 247
Patterson, David, 4
Paulhan, Jean, 176
Pawiak prison, 127
Pechersky, Aleksandr, 128
Peleg, Dorit, 98
Perahia, Yehuda Haim, 228
Perec, Georges, 184
perestroika, 118, 129
Peretz, Avner, 228
Peretz, I. L., 20
Perle, Yehoshua, 24, 25
perpetrators, 10, 69, 79, 81, 124, 147, 238, 243
    among the local population, 120
    and victim testimony, 196
    as authors of Holocaust literature, 72, 81
    as nurtured by German culture, 148
    assaulting language of, 204
    documents produced by, 244
    family of, 78
    focus on, 79, 187, 259–65
    in the writing of Holocaust history, 242
    individual portraits of, 79
    trials of, 108, 241. *See also* Eichmann trial
    use of euphemistic language by, 205
Pétain, Philippe, 177, 185
Pfeffer, Fritz, 37

Piazza, Bruno, 55, 56
Piercy, Marge, 133, 139
Pinter, Harold, 146
Pithiviers (transit camp), 42, 43, 185, 186
Plaszów (concentration camp), 136
Ponar, 213, 214
Portelli, Alessandro, 4, 56, 64
Potok, Chaim, 144
POWs (prisoners of war), 45, 211
Prague Spring, 124
Pressburger, Giorgio and Nicola, 61, 62
Prokow ghetto, 68
Pronicheva, Dina, 124
Prose, Francine, 146
Proust, Marcel, 174, 175, 178, 182, 186
Pryzbos, Julian, 241
Psalms, 10, 103

Quasimodo, Salvatore, 61

Rabinowitz, Rabbi Baruch, 7
radio, 68, 74, 133, 211, 228, 236
Radnóti, Miklós, 170, 171, 172
Radzyn
    Katzenelson's tribute to the Rebbe of, 20
Raphael, Frederick, 146
Raphael, Lev, 145
Ravensbrück (concentration camp), 7, 205, 223
Ravitsh, Melech, 110, 112
Reich, Tova, 146
Reiling, Netty. *See* Seghers, Anna
Reitlinger, Gerald, 56, 138
religious Jewish Holocaust writing, 7, 8, 247–48
Remarque, Erich Maria, 74
reparations, 88
resistance, 44
Reuven, Chelomo, 228
Reznikoff, Charles, 137
Rich, Adrienne, 146
Richler, Mordecai, 137
Richter, Hans-Werner, 73
Ringelblum, Emanuel, 4, 15, 16, 24, 31, 157, 242, 243, 256
    and the Oyneg Shabes archive, 108, 249
Risiera (transit and concentration camp), 201
Ritter, Gunther. *See* Blomberg, Gabriel
Rivka Miriam, 98
Rochman, Leib, 109, 111, 112
Rolnikaitė, Maria, 126
Roma and Sinti, 211, 222
Roman Catholic Church, 52, 64, 202
Romano, Sergio, 64
Rome, 18, 52, 53, 59, 60, 64, 65, 195, 197, 200, 201, 202, 208, 209
    deportations from site of medieval ghetto in, 52

Rosen, Norma, 145
Rosenbaum, Thane, 142, 143, 144, 149
Rosenberg, Martin, 220
Rosenfarb, Chava, 10, 102, 109, 112, 113, 114, 115, 250
Rosenfeld, Oskar, 17, 19, 258
Rosh Hashana, 15, 28
Roskies, David, 3, 4, 15, 244, 245, 246, 248
Rotenberg, Stella, 69
Roth, Philip, 146, 148
Rothenberg, Jerome, 146
Rothenberg, Rabbi Moshe, 8, 248
Roumani, Judith, 9
Rousset, David, 184
Różewicz, Tadeusz, 154
Rudashevski, Yitzhok, 20, 219
Rudnicki, Adolf, 150, 152, 159, 161, 241, 242
Rumkowski, Chaim, 113, 135, 216, 255, 256, 257, 258
Rwanda, 63, 75
Rybakov, Anatoly, 128
Rymkiewicz Jarosław Marek, 157, 159, 161
Ryvel (Raphaël Lévy), 226

Saba, Umberto, 52, 54
Sachs, Nelly, 70
Sachsenhausen (concentration camp), 220, 221, 222, 223
Salonika, 9, 225, 227, 228, 229, 231, 235, 237
Samizdat, 122
Samuels, Diane, 132
Sarajevo, 228
Sarfatty, Bouena, 227
Sartre, Jean-Paul, 233
Schaeffer, Susan Fromberg, 134
Schillinger, Josef, 259. *See also* perpetrators
Schindel, Robert, 80
Schindler, Oskar, 136
Schlink, Bernhard, 79
Schneider, Peter, 79
Schwarz, Leo, 240, 241, 245, 248
Schwarz-Bart, André, 1, 178, 250
Sebald, W. G., 80, 81
second-generation, 63, 157, 167, 169
Sed, Alberto, 196, 200, 201
Segal, Lore, 131
Segalovitch, Zusman, 249
Seghers, Anna, 72
Selvinsky, Igor, 118
Semel, Nava, 98
Semprun, Jorge, 7, 167
Senesh, Hannah, 89, 138

Şenocak, Zafer, 79
sermons
by Rabbi Shapiro in the Warsaw ghetto, 8
seventh million, 84, 87
Shaham, Natan, 89
Shapira, Rabbi Kalonymous Kalmen, 8
Shayevitsh, Simcha Bunem, 20, 21, 113, 249
Sheyres-ha-pleyte (saved remnant of survivors), 103
Shoah Foundation, 194, 199, 203
Sholem Aleichem, 17, 127
as inspiration for Opoczynski's ghetto writing, 17
Shostakovich, Dimitri, 123
shtetl (Eastern European Jewish town)
as a setting for Melvin Bukiet, 148
as a theme for Polish-Jewish writers, 152
as depicted by S. Y. Agnon, 86
in Opoczynski's writing, 17
Shtrigler, Mordechai, 109, 110, 111, 112
Siedlecki, Janusz Nel, 259
Sierakowiak, Dawid, 258
Silberberg, Ya'akov, 262
Silkin, Jon, 132
Simonov, Konstantin, 123
Singer, I. J., 115
Singer, Isaac Bashevis, 107, 108, 109, 110, 112, 114, 115, 116, 143, 155
Skibell, Joseph, 147
Slutsky, Boris, 128, 129
Smoliar, Hirsh, 121
Sobibor (death camp), 128
Sobol, Joshua, 90
Solzhenitsyn, Alexander, 122
Someck, Ronny, 98
Sonderkommando, 29, 31, 194, 196, 204, 205, 231, 259, 260, 261, 262, 263, 264
at Auschwitz-Birkenau, 30
songs, 219
"Papirosn" (Cigarettes), 213
as compared to ghetto reportage, 16
Sovetish Heymland, 112
Soviet Army, 118, 119, 129
Spiegel, Isaiah, 243
Spiegelman, Art, 142, 146, 147
Spiegelman, Vladek, 147
Spizzichino, Settimia, 194, 200, 201, 206, 209
star, 42
stars, 1, 3, 6, 10, 34, 134
starvation
in the Warsaw ghetto, 19
State of Israel, 84, 87, 88, 95, 97, 148
Steiner, George, 137
Steinfeld, J. J., 143
Stollman, Aryeh Lev, 145
Stryjkowski, Julian, 153, 154

Styron, William, 136
Suite française. See Némirovsky, Irene
Sultan, Stanley, 235
Sundquist, Eric, 4
survivor-writers
and suicide, 149
Sutzkever, Abraham, 4, 7, 10, 20, 21, 22, 23, 103, 105, 108, 109, 110, 111, 112, 115, 217, 240
Syrkin, Marie, 240
Szabó, István, 170
Szabolcsi, Bence, 168
Szálasi, Ferenc. *See* Hungarian Fascist Arrow Cross
Szántó, Erika, 168
Szép, Ernő, 166, 168, 173
Szlengel, Władysław, 25–26, 245

Taberner, Stuart, 10
Tamaro, Susanna, 63
Tamaroff, Mordechai, 23
Tanakh (Jewish scriptures)
as a source for Holocaust analogies, 19
Taraboulos, Jacques, 226
Tedeschi, Giuliana, 55, 61
Tel Aviv, 7, 87, 89, 96, 108, 112, 200
Terracina, Piero, 195, 197, 200, 203, 204, 205
testimonies
as collected by Kulisiewicz, 223
testimony, 7, 52, 56, 57, 63
against atrocities, 44
and "bearing witness", 147–49
and early postwar Hungarian literature, 166
and focus on the *shtetl*, 152
and Jewish family narratives, 61
and oral memoir, 193–96
and religious Jewish life, 144
and women's Holocaust writing, 61
as elevated by Hebrew, 29
as painful for the listener, 198
historical status of, 202
in the courtroom, 137, 196, 197
in early survivor-writing, 54
in Kuznetsov's *Babi Yar*, 124
in Ozick's "The Shawl," 141
in the writings of Edith Bruck, 65
the interviewer's silence during, 199
Primo Levi's innovative use of, 63
vicarious, 64
victim's diaries as, 33
wartime writing as, 33
"Testimony," a poem by Dan Pagis, 95
Theresienstadt (Terezin; ghetto and concentration camp), 246
Thomas, D. M., 124
Timm, Uwe, 78
Tocqueville, Alexis de, 175

Toker, Leona, 4
Tomer, Ben Zion, 89
Trabucchi, Enzo, 205
Travaglia, Angelo, 204
Treblinka (death camp), 9, 76, 119, 125, 155, 208, 241, 255
  as the final destination of Warsaw's deported Jews, 24
  Katzenelson's family deported to, 29
Truth and Lamentation: Stories and Poems on the Holocaust, 248
Tuwim, Julian, 152

Ukraine
  Holocaust memoirs produced in, 129
  mass shooting of Jews in, 2
  as the setting of Rybakov's *Heavy Sand*, 128
Ukrainian terror famine of 1929–1932, 120
Ukrainians
  in Ehrenberg's *The Storm*, 121
  literary references to collaboration of, 120
Ulinover. Miriam, 249
United Partisans' Organization, 217
United States Library of Congress classifications, 238
Uris, Leon, 134

Vámos, Miklós, 170
van Pels, Peter, 37
Vatican, 201
Vazon, Raimondo, 204
Vecchio, Otello, 205
Venezia, Shlomo, 194, 195, 196, 204, 206, 208
vengeance
  calls for by religious Jewish writers, 8. *See also* Divine vengeance
  in postwar Yiddish writing, 112
  in the writing of Melvin Bukiet, 143
  medieval forms of in relation to the Holocaust, 133
  the perpetrator's taking of, 15
Vertlib, Vladmir, 78, 79
Vesper, Bernhard, 76
Vichy, 134, 167, 177, 179, 181, 186, 187, 225, 234
Vichy syndrome, 179
Vidal-Naquet, Pierre, 174
Vienna, 71, 78, 165
Vilna, 20, 106, 107, 111, 114, 115, 134, 213, 214, 215, 216, 217, 218, 219, 240, 255
  as Jerusalem of Lithuania, 95
Vilna ghetto, 90, 95
  as shaping Sutzkever's Zionism, 105
  Kalmanovitsh as public intellectual and diarist in, 16
  Kovner's call to arms in, 95

  resistance in, 22
  schoolchildren's activism in, 17, 20
  Sobol's dramatization of events in, 90
  Sutzkever writing in, 4
  Sutzkever's commemoration of sabotage in, 21
  Sutzkever's memoir of, 7
Viterbo, Alice, 254
Voznesensky, Andrei, 123

Wallant, Edward Lewis, 140
Walser, Martin, 70
Wander, Fred, 77
Wannsee Conference, 257
Warsaw, 1, 5, 8, 9, 15, 16, 20, 23, 25, 26, 28, 30, 32, 85, 90, 105, 106, 109, 110, 112, 115, 127, 134, 138, 143, 150, 151, 152, 154, 155, 156, 157, 159, 160, 161, 183, 213, 216, 217, 218, 239, 240, 242, 245, 249, 253, 255, 258, 261, 262
Warsaw ghetto, 28, 72, 73, 96
  diaries written in, 15
  Goldin chronicling starvation in, 19
  in Opoczynski's writing, 3
  Israel's commemoration of the uprising in, 88
  Jewish letter carriers in, 16
  Malaparte's depiction of, 53
  Rabbi Shapiro's sermons in, 8
  resistance in, 22
  Ringelblum's leadership in, 4
  social services within, 24
  Szlengel's poetry in, 25
  underground publication in, 19
Wasserman, Rabbi Elchonon, 8
Weil, Grete, 72
Weinberg, Rabbi Yechiel Yaakov, 248
Weiss, Peter, 74, 75, 167
Weiss, Rabbi Yitzchak Yaakov, 248
Wessels, Benjamin, 40
Westerbork (transit camp), 37, 38, 39, 40, 146
Whitman, Ruth, 138
Wiechert, Ernst, 73, 74
Wiesel, Elie, 3, 5, 6, 10, 11, 45, 57, 68, 69, 143, 177, 178, 183, 231, 243
  on the pepetrator's language, 3
Wieviorka, Annette, 193, 198, 202
Wilkomirski, Binjamin, 252, 259
Wojdowski, Bogdan, 155, 159, 161
Wolf, Christa, 29, 76, 247
Wolf, Otto, 153
Wygodzki, Stanisław, 154

Yablokoff, Herman, 213
Yacoel, Yomtov, 231
Yad Vashem library classifications, 238

Yale Fortunoff Archive, 198
Yehiel Dinur, 90, 92
Yehoshua, A. B., 235
Yerushalmi, Yosef, 253
Yiddish
    Abraham Lewin switching to, 6, 9, 27
    Abraham Sutzkever and, 7, 10, 20
    Chava Rosenfarb's postwar view of, 10, 102,
        109, 112, 113
    Elie Wiesel's memoir in, 243
    Hersey in connection to, 134
    the history and features of, 8–9
    in postwar Poland Holocaust writing, 154
    Katzenelson in relation to, 9, 10, 19, 29
    postwar Holocaust literature in, 102–117

and postwar literary anthologies, 240, 242–43,
        245, 246, 247, 250
    and songs of the Holocaust, 212–220
    and Soviet Holocaust writing,
        119, 120, 121, 126, 127, 128
    the State of Israel and, 84
Yizker (memorial) books, 102, 103, 115
Yosef ha-Kohen, 229
Yugoslavia, 63

Zeitlin, Aaron, 104, 105, 106, 108,
        110, 115
Zelkowicz, Josef, 18, 244, 249
    comparing the fate of Lodz to Jerusalem, 18
Zsolt, Bela, 165, 166